Bibliography and Index of English Verse in Manuscript 1501–1558

Bibliography and Index of English Verse in Manuscript 1501–1558

William A. Ringler, Jr

Prepared and completed by
Michael Rudick and Susan J. Ringler

MANSELL

First published 1992 by
Mansell Publishing Limited, *A Cassell Imprint*
Villiers House, 41/47 Strand, London WC2N 5JE, England
387 Park Avenue South, New York, NY 10016-8810, USA

British Library Cataloguing-in-Publication Data

Ringler, William A.
Bibliography and Index of English Verse
in Manuscript, 1501–58
I. Title II. Rudick, Michael
III. Ringler, Susan J.
016.8212

ISBN 0-7201-2099-3

Library of Congress Cataloging-in-Publication Data

Ringler, William A., 1912–1987
Bibliography and index of English verse in manuscript, 1501–1558/
William A. Ringler, Jr.; prepared and completed by Michael Rudick
and Susan J. Ringler.
p. cm.
Companion to: Bibliography and index of English verse printed
1476–1558. 1988.
Includes indexes.
ISBN 0-7201-2099-3
1. English poetry—Early modern, 1500–1700—Manuscripts—Catalogs.
2. English poetry—Early modern, 1500–1700—Bibliography.
3. English poetry—Early modern, 1500–1700—Indexes.
4. Manuscripts, Renaissance—England—Catalogs. 5. Manuscripts,
English—Catalogs. I. Rudick, Michael, 1940– . II. Ringler,
Susan J., 1954– . III. Ringler, William A., 1912–1987 Bibliography and index
of English verse printed 1476–1558.
Z2014.P7R55 1992
[PR521]
016.821'208—dc20 92–18051
CIP

Typeset by Saxon Printing Ltd, Derby
Printed and bound in Great Britain by
Biddles Ltd, Guildford and King's Lynn

Contents

Preface

When William Ringler died on New Years Day, 1987, he had just completed and sent to press the typescript of his work on printed verse in the early Tudor period, published as *Bibliography and Index of English Verse Printed 1476–1558* (London: Mansell, 1988). The present volume is a companion to that, indexing the English verse preserved in manuscripts from 1501 through 1558. At his death, Professor Ringler had virtually finished his survey of manuscripts transcribed in that period, a task he began almost four decades ago, and had started to organize entries in a format comparable to that in the *Index* of printed verse. Our aim has been to produce the volume as he would have done, using his bibliographical principles (explained in the Introduction) and, as far as we can determine them, his most recent judgments on questions of the dating of documents, the authorship of poems, and like matters.

Our sources are the extensive papers related to the Index which Professor Ringler bequeathed to the Henry E. Huntington Library. These consist, first, of several thousand index cards on which he entered individual poems by their first lines (filed alphabetically) and the details of their transcriptions. We found the cards for poems transcribed in British Library manuscripts (representing over 50% of the verse preserved) entirely organized, and our task there was restricted to filling in whatever information was needed to complete each entry according to format specifications established in the *Index* of printed verse. Most of the remaining entries we have reconstructed from the second category of material left, Professor Ringler's working papers on the manuscripts he read. For many of these, he had analyzed the manuscripts and described their verse contents thoroughly; for others, he left only notes identifying the poems to be indexed, with their details to be filled in later. In those latter instances, we have supplied what was wanting from other sources (reprints, facsimiles, and occasional consultation of the primary documents). We can have some confidence that the index presented here is as complete as Professor Ringler expected it to be, since he had before his death drawn up summary sheets listing the pertinent manuscripts and the number of poems to be included from each. In all but a very few cases we have been able to achieve consonance between what we find in the working papers and what appears on the summary sheets. We have, of course, often enough needed to interpret the working notes and make our own decisions about what Professor Ringler's latest intentions were; in so doing, we have preferred to err on the side of inclusiveness.

The *Index* of printed verse was prepared entirely by hand, typewriter, and pocket calculator—in the words of one reviewer, "one of the last great bibliographical enterprises of the pre-computer age." This one was assisted by a computer; the individual poems were entered in a data base which alphabetized the entries, arranged the information for printing, compiled the indexes, and delivered the numerical data. A version of dBase 3+, it was initially programmed for us by Mr. Joseph Wortley with the assistance of funds provided by the California Institute of Technology and the Huntington Library. The computerized compilation of entries, numerical data, and indexes obviates certain kinds of errors and inconsistencies, but it is impossible that a work of this kind should be error-free; likewise, we do not expect that all the judgments made in it will be proof against dispute. We would appreciate corrections and alternative interpretations of the material, and such will be credited to their contributors in any subsequent editions or publications.

It was Professor Ringler's initial intention to include in the present volume a supplement indexing poems composed in the early Tudor period but preserved only in documents later than 1558. Time constraint has made it impossible to compile that index for this book. When published, Professor Steven May's index of Elizabethan verse will include a number of Tudor-composed poems extant in prints and manuscripts from 1559–1603, and we expect to publish a finding list for Tudor-composed verse printed in the seventeenth century and after from documents no longer extant.

Professor Ringler's obligations to persons and library staffs are recorded in his preface to the *Index* of printed verse. Further assistance came from two National Endowment for the Humanities grants awarded him in his lifetime. He would have added here further acknowledgments to the staffs of libraries holding the manuscripts used for this index and his personal thanks to individuals, including some of his former students, who contributed their help at different times over many years. Unfortunately, we cannot name them. Professor Rudick wishes to acknowledge a research leave granted by the University of Utah's College of Humanities. Our common debt is principally to the Huntington Library, to whose staff members in several departments we are grateful. We owe thanks to Professor Steven May who, along with the two of us, was instrumental in the initial sorting and organizing of the Ringler papers at the Huntington; to Professor Robert S. Kinsman for crucial assistance at certain points; finally and importantly, to Evelyn Ringler, for support, hospitality, and continued encouragement.

M. R.
Salt Lake City, Utah
S. J. R.
Menlo Park, California
April, 1992

Abbreviations and Short Citations

a. Ante, before.

allit. Alliterative verse.

Archiv. Archiv für das Studium der Neueren Sprachen.

BMP. British Manuscripts Project, American Council of Learned Societies (1941–45), cited by the index number under which the BMP microfilm reel is indicated.

BMQ. *British Museum Quarterly.*

BR. Carleton Brown and Rossell Hope Robbins, *Index of Middle English Verse* (1943); Robbins and John L. Cutler, *Supplement to the Index of Middle English Verse* (1965). Poems cited by their index numbers.

Brown, *Register.* Carleton Brown, *A Register of Middle English Religious and Didactic Verse*, 2 vols. (1916–20).

Brown XV. Carleton Brown (ed.), *Religious Lyrics of the XVth Century* (1939). Poems cited by their numbers.

burd. Burden (lines repeated after each stanza of a carol).

c. Circa, about.

Child, *Ballads.* F. J. Child, *The English and Scottish Popular Ballads*, 5 vols. (1860).

comp. Composed, date of composition.

Dyce, *Skelton. The Poetical Works of John Skelton*, ed. Alexander Dyce, 2 vols. (1843–44).

ed. Edition, editor.

EETS. Early English Text Society, Original Series, cited by volume, year and page number(s).

EETSes. Early English Text Society, Extra Series, cited by volume, year, and page number(s).

EHR. *English Historical Review.*

ELN. *English Language Notes.*

f., ff., fol(s). Folio(s).

Furnivall, *Ballads. Ballads from Manuscripts*, ed. Frederick J. Furnivall, Vol. 1, parts 1 and 2 (1868–72, rpt. 1968).

Greene. Richard Leighton Greene, *The Early English Carols* (1935; 2d ed. 1977). Poems cited by their numbers; poems with decimal numbers are those added in the second edition.

Hammond, *Chaucer–Surrey.* Eleanor Prescott Hammond (ed.), *English Verse between Chaucer and Surrey* (1927; rpt. 1969).

Hist. History, historical event.
HLQ. *Huntington Library Quarterly.*
Morfill, *Ballads. Ballads from Manuscripts*, ed. W. R. Morfill, Vol. 2, parts 1 and 2 (1873, rpt. 1968).
MLN. *Modern Language Notes.*
MLR. *Modern Language Review.*
mono. Monorhyme.
MP. *Modern Philology.*
MS(S). Manuscript(s).
MT. Monk's Tale stanza (ababbcbc).
Nar. Narrative.
NM. *Neuphilologische Mitteilungen.*
NQ. *Notes and Queries.*
PBSA. *Papers of the Bibliographical Society of America.*
Person, *ME Lyrics.* Henry Axel Person (ed.), *Cambridge Middle English Lyrics* (1953; 2d ed. 1963).
PQ. *Philological Quarterly.*
ptd. Printed.
REED. *Records of Early English Drama.*
ref. Refrain (verse repeated as the last line of each stanza in a poem).
Rel. Religion, religious.
Rel. Ant. Thomas Wright and J. O. Halliwell [-Phillipps], *Reliquiae Antiquae*, 2 vols. (1841–43, rpt. 1966), cited by volume and page number(s).
RES. *The Review of English Studies.*
Robbins, *Hist.* Rossell Hope Robbins (ed.), *Historical Poems of the XIVth and XVth Centuries* (1959), cited by poem numbers.
Robbins, *Sec.* Rossell Hope Robbins (ed.), *Secular Lyrics of the XIVth and XVth Centuries* (1952, 2d ed. 1955), cited by poem numbers.
RR. Rhyme royal stanza (ababbcc).
s. sh. Single sheet.
SB. *Studies in Bibliography.*
sig(s). Signature(s) (in early printed books).
SP. *Studies in Philology.*
STC. W. A. Jackson, F. S. Ferguson, & Katherine F. Pantzer, *A Short Title Catalogue of Books Printed in England, Scotland and Ireland ... 1475–1640*, 2d ed., 2 vols. (1976–86), cited by number.
STS. Scottish Text Society, cited by series, volume, and page numbers.
TM. Early Tudor manuscript transcription, poem numbers in this index.
TP. Early Tudor print, poem numbers in William A. Ringler, Jr, *Bibliography and Index of English Verse Printed 1476–1558* (1988).
tr. Translation, translator, translated by.
v., vv. Verse, verses.

Introduction

1. Scope

The Index and Bibliography aim to be as comprehensive a finding list as possible of all identifiable English verse—from major long poems occupying an entire manuscript down to occasional scraps and extracts jotted in margins and flyleaves of older books (manuscript and printed)—transcribed from 1501, the arbitrary cutoff date for Early Modern English as opposed to Middle English poetry, through 1558, the year of Queen Elizabeth I's accession. As such, it extends the scope of the Brown–Robbins–Cutler indexes of Middle English poetry in manuscript[1] through the early Tudor period, although, of necessity, the overlap with those volumes is considerable. Middle English poetry continued to be copied (and printed) extensively in the earlier 16th century. Brown and Robbins included a number of poems in their *Index* extant only in 16th-century manuscripts; indeed a number of these seem clearly to have been written after 1500. The Robbins–Cutler *Supplement* admittedly, and for stated reasons (see pp. xiv–xviii), extends its reach to early 16th-century poets such as Hawes, Skelton, and Dunbar, to the early Tudor songbooks, and to a good many anonymous compositions which appear in no documents before 1501. To underscore the continuity of much early Tudor poetry with that written in the 15th century is reasonable, particularly as all recognize the arbitrariness of 1500 as the dividing line. Likewise, the dating of manuscript entries, especially in books used and added to over many years, infrequently allows precision. Nevertheless, the present index should, as did its counterpart index of printed verse,[2] serve to make it possible in many more instances to discriminate 16th- from 15th-century poetry.

The first task in compiling this index was to identify as many manuscripts from the period as possible that contained English verse. William Ringler's procedure was to begin with modern notices, printings, and editions of manuscript verse, as well as bibliographical guides of various sorts.[3] He also studied descriptive catalogues of manuscripts in libraries large and small in order to identify and examine all manuscripts of English provenance which might carry poems that had escaped notice. Information on far the largest proportion of documents represented in this index comes from Ringler's examination of them. He was satisfied that he had found about as much as could be found, through 1988, from the British and Bodleian Libraries, the National Library of Scotland and Edinburgh University, and a number of smaller repositories in the United Kingdom, as well as the library of Trinity College, Dublin, and all the libraries in the United States known to hold 15th- and 16th-century manuscripts. These holdings amount to some 90 percent of the entries. Ringler's files and entries for the Cambridge University Library and the Cambridge colleges were less complete; entries for these sometimes come from secondary sources, as do entries for poems in a few other collections. It is probable that a concerted search in Cambridge manuscripts, particularly those in the colleges, will yield more entries, and it is of course inevitable that at least a few more manuscripts containing early Tudor verse will come to light in the future. The index as printed here, however, stands in a respectable state of completion: a large enough corpus of documents to give a confident representation of early Tudor poetry extant in manuscript.

The single qualification to this is the decision to include only verse whose transcription can be dated between the beginning of the century and 1558. This and the print index do not, then, record a complete corpus of early Tudor poetry, since many poems which originated within the chronological boundaries are known only from later documents, whether of Elizabethan date or from modern transcriptions of manuscripts no longer extant. A complete record of extant early Tudor poetry will have to await Professor May's publication of the Elizabethan segment of the index and a further finding list of poems (for the most part printed) in sources from the 17th through the 20th centuries.

2. *Organization*

The principles according to which entries are organized in this work conform, to the extent possible, to those used in the earlier index of printed verse (see Ringler, *Index*, pp. 1–5, 21–22). To identify what constitutes verse is sometimes difficult in an epoch when both language and literary norms were unsettled and there existed no authoritative literary establishment to judge what counted as poetry or poems. In general, rhyme is accepted as a conventional determinant, however shapeless the rhymed verses may be. Unrhymed but recognizably alliterative verse existed in the period, which also saw the invention of blank verse. These texts are, of course, included, but excluded are texts which may have seemed verse to previous scholars but appear to meet none of the norms—defined generously by induction—prevalent in the period.[4] The question of what constitutes a discrete poem, therefore entitled to an independent, numbered entry in the index, is complex enough in the realm of printed verse, while the conditions of manuscript circulation make it even more difficult, owing to the greater instability of texts in this form of preservation and transmission.[5] The text of a poem achieves a certain stability when printed, to the degree that later printings are based on it and are relatively invariant. In manuscript, a poem may assume various shapes in the course of its transmission, where collectors, irrespective of what they copied from, had their own ideas of what they wanted to preserve for themselves and felt no special obligation toward conformity with their exemplar or with some hypothetically authoritative text. Nevertheless, some of the print index's methods can be taken over here unproblematically. A text with a number of discrete units (e.g., TM 652, a set of verse recitations interspersed with prose narrative) is entered as one numbered poem since no unit of it is likely to be found or referred to apart from the whole. On the other hand, songs and lyrics within larger verse texts (e.g., TM 1318, from a play) are given separate numbered entries both because they are formally different from the text surrounding them and because their origin and authorship may be different from that of the surrounding text. Poems whose discrete units are or are likely to be found separately are given one number, and their units are cross-referenced without numbers by their first lines in the alphabetical sequence; examples are proverb collections (e.g., TM 219) and litanies (e.g., TM 467). In cases of wholesale manuscript transcription directly from printed works (e.g., *The Proverbs of Lydgate* in O: Arch. Selden B.10), the entries have been handled exactly as in the print index.

However, beyond such instances, the user of this index should be aware that its organization necessarily chooses for consistency's sake one path among alternatives, and that this path is not always clearly explicative of the status items of verse may be thought to have in the conditions of Tudor manuscript circulation. The simplest examples of problematic handling come from kinds of verse unique to manuscript circulation, such as ownership rhymes (TM 552, 1664, etc.). Here groups of variant texts can be subsumed under the single idea or conceit common to all, and given a single number, though the wordings of individual copies will differ substantially (in first lines, number of lines, etc.). Variance is to be expected because these traditional rhymes were conceived to be adaptable to and by the book owners who used them to mark their property; each owner may in some sense be named author of his or her rhyme, and we have sometimes numbered a version and credited its author, rather than making it a subentry, when the text displays some interesting enough variation from the norm. We use the same method for short, proverbial scraps (rarely more than a couplet). These transcriptions, too, show substantial variation in wording; their identity of sentiment (and of rhyme) allows them to be listed under one number. The problems extend to less trivial instances of poetry. There is in our period, for example, no complete transcript of Chaucer's *Troilus and Criseyde*, but a number of short extracts from it were copied into manuscripts, in all cases apparently from Thynne's edition of 1532 (TP 1702.5). Since the copyists had at hand a full, printed text, they were not furnishing themselves even a partial copy of Chaucer's poem so much as laying claim to

Chaucer's words for some purpose of their own, perhaps inferrable, perhaps not. It would be warranted to consider each of these extracts as having the status of an independent lyric because each was used as such, but we follow the method of the print index in entering them all under the first line of the *Troilus* (TM 1510) and giving their incipits without numbers where these fall alphabetically.[6] We use the same method to deal with discrete texts which are wholly or largely based on other, longer poems. An instance is the first manuscript cited under TM 429; this text contains enough quotation from Burgh's *Cato Major* to be considered an extract from that poem, and so is entered under its first line rather than being allowed a separate number. This method entails a certain bias in representation, as it shows more the early Tudor redactors' taste for older poetry and less their ingenuity in appropriating it for new uses; we expect, however, that the information for studying the latter phenomenon is contained in this index.

Once launched into manuscript circulation, most poems, especially shorter lyrics, whether or not associated with a named author, were subject to various forms of revision: lengthening, shortening, restructuring, etc. One cannot always be sure of the direction of the alteration. At least three kinds of relationship may obtain between two or more evidently related texts. They may be variant textual states of one poem (close verbal and formal congruence, limited differences); examples are some poems of Wyatt shared by three manuscripts. They may be alternate "versions" of one poem (much shared content, but perhaps different arrangements of it), such as the copies of a carol by Wyatt entered as TM 85. Or they may be different poems altogether, such as TM 85 and the song on which it appears to be based, TM 84. Judgments on the validity of these distinctions, and on how to apply them, can differ, but the examples cited illustrate our procedure here. Variant textual states and alternative "versions" are placed under one numbered entry, but this should not be taken to imply that the first listed is an "original" from which variant forms derive, or that the variant forms are textually "corrupt" rather than deliberate efforts by copyists to reshape their material.

Dates, whether specific or approximate, are given for transcriptions, both in the manuscript bibliography and in the first-line index. In general, three designations should be recognized: (1) An unspecific notation, such as "early 16th century" or "second quarter of the 16th century," is usually based on palaeographic evidence and should be regarded as no more precise than such judgments can in the nature of things be. (2) A specific date or dates, e.g., "1512" or "1503–04," is based on evidence in the document, such as a copyist's note or reference to a datable historical event. (3) A range of years, e.g., "1532–39" or "1534+," is based on internal evidence from the texts collected in the manuscript, inferring *termini post* and/or *ante quem* from the date at which the earliest text became available for copying and the latest text's year of composition. Where dates of composition for poems are given, these are derived from evidence in the text or from extant transcription before 1501 (dates given in the *Middle English Dictionary* are usually accepted). Where no date of composition is given, it is safest to assume that the date of the poem approximates the date of its earliest transcription (or printing). This is particularly important to note even when a poem was included in the Brown–Robbins–Cutler indexes. We give the BR number for all poems listed there, but enclose that number in parentheses when there is no ground for placing its composition before 1501; there are over 500 such poems in the early Tudor manuscript corpus.[7]

The identification of authors is based on documentary evidence. This principle largely affects the many poems copied without attribution into miscellanies which editors in more recent periods have included in one or another poet's canon, especially in those of Dunbar and Wyatt. Where no early ascription is to be found, the poem is left unattributed in its first-line entry, but printing information given in the manuscript bibliography will show the modern editorial attributions. Names in manuscript headings or subscriptions are given, with notes in brackets only if they can be shown to be mistaken. But we do index false or doubtful ascriptions. Few students, for example, credit a single manuscript's attribution of TM 256 to Skelton, but the poem's number is given with his name in the index of authors as a record of that one early ascription; false or speculative attributions within the early Tudor period are useful information about poetic reputations. We do not, however, include the names of copyists in the index of authors; rather, we index them separately, as a name subscribed to a piece of verse is not always a claim of authorship. Book owners (or borrowers) often enough signed their names below a transcription of verse they clearly had from elsewhere—the overwhelming number of instances concerns proverbial or gnomic verse—most probably to express agreement with the poem's sentiment. In the case of musical settings of poems, an attribution, where present, is regularly to the composer, not to the poet.

In efforts to generalize about early Tudor manuscript transcription, we deal with three quantities: the number of poems, the number of copies of each poem, and the number of lines in the poem. The number of poems and the total number of lines transcribed in each document are given in its entry in the manuscript bibliography. The number of lines in a poem is given in its entry in the first-line index, and, where there are multiple copies, is given also for each copy if there are differences between them.

3. The manuscripts

The index records verse transcriptions from nearly 400 extant documents listed in the bibliography. Cumulatively, these contain 2,446 copies (in whole or part, and often with substantial variation) of 2,045 poems. The total volume of transcription amounts to almost 567,000 lines of verse, about a third of which is accounted for by second and subsequent copies of the same poem. Of the documents, 342 are manuscripts, 43 are printed books, and 8 are inscriptions on funeral monuments. The last, of course, contain only one poem each, of a memorial nature (86 lines altogether), while the verse entered in printed books (some sixty transcriptions totalling under 600 lines) ranges from ownership rhymes to poems on any number of subjects, sometimes connected with the book's contents, sometimes not. In generalizing about the nature of manuscript transmission proper, some limitations apply. While the manuscripts fall into certain broad categories susceptible to distinction and analysis, the contents of any one manuscript may sometimes fit more than one categorical definition. Therefore, any numerical information given about the proportion of categories within the entire corpus of manuscripts should be regarded as suggestive rather than as a precise statistical representation of the material. Other systems of classification might yield different descriptive results. In the second place, we deal here only with what is extant, and we cannot always infer the amounts or kinds of poetry that have been lost; the picture we have is not necessarily the one we would have if more manuscript verse had survived, especially when comparisons are made with the corpus of printed verse in the same period. In the third place, a certain amount of the manuscript material is fragmentary, sometimes amounting to no more than a leaf or two of indeterminable origin or context bound into a composite volume; such instances of transcription are impossible to categorize.

The largest proportion, about seventy percent, of the manuscripts falls roughly into three categories: (1) older books with verse (and much else) added to them by their owners or borrowers in the early Tudor period; (2) manuscripts of single works; (3) miscellanies, whether of verse or of prose and verse together. Those in the first category comprise about one-third of all the manuscripts. These books contain all sorts of medieval texts in Latin, English, and French transcribed from the 12th through the 15th centuries, though most are 15th-century compilations and about a third of those are manuscripts of single works or collections of English poetry by Chaucer, Lydgate, and other Middle English writers. As is to be expected, Tudor verse entries in older books are mostly few and brief, accounting for a small proportion of the number of copies (about 330) and the number of lines (about 6,400) copied in the period; over half of these manuscripts contain ten or fewer lines, and only thirteen have more than a hundred lines. The kinds of verse entered largely resemble those copied in the printed books: ownership rhymes, moral tags, fugitive scraps, and, occasionally, the record of an early 16th-century reaction to what was read in the manuscript (e.g., TM 1482, 1949). But there are interesting exceptions to the norm, an instance being L: Additional 18,752, a miscellaneous volume of Latin and English prose begun in the 14th century, onto whose blank pages were copied twenty-eight courtly lyrics in the 1530's. This book is one example of a manuscript added to over a long period of time, and there are many others that show continued use, even into the 17th century. This illustrates at least one factor that makes categorization problematic; L: Additional 18,752 could as warrantably be classed a verse miscellany.

Measured by the volume of poetry copied, most verse transcription from 1501 through 1558 is found in the second category of manuscripts, those devoted to a single work in verse, often a large one, or to a collection of closely related poems by one author (Wyatt's collection of 123 of his own poems, L: Egerton 2711, is an example). There are over sixty such books in our period; they transcribe fifty titles ranging in length from the 58 lines of TM 1588, Skelton's congratulatory poem for Henry VIII's accession, to the 24,560 lines of Douglas's translation of the *Aeneid* (TM 879 and 1497). Altogether, these manuscripts account for about 400,000 lines, five complete copies of Douglas's *Aeneid* alone registering nearly 123,000 of them.[8]

The third category, miscellanies compiled in the early Tudor period, comprises about seventy-five manuscripts. More than fifty collect both verse and prose, with a total of some 340 copies of poems and over 33,750 lines transcribed. Many contain just one or very few poems, perhaps randomly entered, of a sort comparable to those found copied in printed books and in older manuscripts. Others, however, show a certain consistency over their prose and verse contents, as in collections emphasizing legal or alchemical or medical or religious material. At least six of these mixed miscellanies carry between ten and fifty poems, with between 2,000 and 5,000 lines of verse, and so count as important sources of poetry. Examples are L: Harley 2252, compiled by the London merchant John Colyns, O: Tanner 407, compiled by Robert Reynys in Norfolk, L: Arundel 285, a devotional collection made in Scotland, and L: Additional 60,577, a manuscript begun in the late 15th century and added to over some seventy-five years. Miscellanies devoted exclusively to verse are rarer. Even if this category is defined generously enough to include any collection of contiguous poems (as few as five, totalling under 100 lines), there are still no more than twenty-one verse miscellanies extant from the early Tudor period. But these few manuscripts transmit almost 900 copies of poems (about 37% of all the copies of poems preserved), amounting to about 96,000 lines. About half of those lines are found in three miscellanies (E: Asloan, L: Additional 29,729, and O17: Balliol 354) which contain much narrative verse. More typical are collections of exclusively lyric poems, such as the principal sources of Henrican court poetry, L: Additional 17,492 (the "Devonshire MS") and D: TCD 160 (the "Blage MS"), each with under 4,000 lines. There are also verse miscellanies (e.g., L: Harley 7578 and LONG: Longleat 258) which collect shorter poems by Chaucer and 15th-century poets.

The remainder of classifiable manuscripts containing early Tudor verse transcription falls into two small categories. The more important comprises musical manuscripts. There are seventeen of these extant, with settings for over 300 poems totalling over 5,000 lines.[9] Over 60 percent of the poems and lines is accounted for by four principal sources of early Tudor lyric, the songbooks recording musical composition at the courts of Henry VII and Henry VIII (L: Additional 5465, 5665, and 31,922, and L: Royal Appendix 58). The second category comprises twenty-eight manuscripts of prose works with verse attached to them (prologues, dedications, etc., and short poems or extracts quoted in historical works). These total about 90 copies of poems and 4,700 lines, over half the poems and a third of the lines accounted for by two manuscripts of Robert Fabyan's *Chronicle*. There are, finally, thirty manuscripts, most of them fragments and loose sheets, carrying fewer than forty poems and 3,000 lines, which fall in none of the categories described above.

4. Manuscript and print

The extant corpus of early Tudor printed verse is preserved in 982 editions of 632 titles. These contain 2,785 poems (not including second and subsequent printings) amounting to some 553,000 lines of verse.[10] That the manuscript corpus for the period is smaller—2,045 poems with 383,650 lines—is for the most part due to the accidents of preservation. Only one copy of the hundreds in one edition of a printed book need survive to preserve one or more poems; the printer's manuscript copy for those poems is in virtually every case lost,[11] and other manuscript copies may be equally lost. Further, we have scarce information from which to infer lost manuscripts of poems never printed. But there appears little to suggest that the introduction and expansion of printing in England worked to slow manuscript transcription of poetry to any significant degree. The many Tudor entries in margins and blank leaves of 15th-century Chaucer and Lydgate manuscripts show that earlier poetry was still read in manuscript even if it was available in print. Only one popular print genre, the verse romance, is minimally represented in the manuscript corpus.[12] Copying *in extenso* of long classics like the *Troilus* and *The Fall of Princes* ceased, but any number of shorter English works by Chaucer, Lydgate, and their contemporaries continued to be transcribed even after their appearance in printed editions. Certain lengthy and important Middle English poems still depended on manuscript transmission, e.g., Lydgate's *Siege of Thebes* (TM 1851, printed in 1497? and not again) and Gower's *Confessio Amantis* (TM 1279, printed in 1483 but not again until 1533). Small printings in the late 15th century failed to satisfy an evidently continuing demand from readers. Other important works, notably *Piers Plowman* (TM 754, not printed until 1550), were to be had only in manuscript until late in the period. Comparisons appear to indicate a somewhat higher concern for the preservation of anonymous Middle English poetry in manuscript than in print. Between 1501 and 1558, 186 Middle English poems were printed, about 7.5 percent of all poems in print and, because many were lengthy works, forty percent of the total lines in print. Figures for manuscript verse in the period show a slightly smaller proportion of lines (36%), but many more poems, about 330, or 16 percent of all poems transcribed. There can be no coincidence in the fact that the printed corpus and the manuscript corpus each records twenty-five Middle English poets; the likely inference is that more earlier poems in manuscript means more anonymous poems preserved, the sorts of less prestigious verse (devotional, practical, "popular") unattached to the major works or poets that appealed to the early printers' clientele.

The difference is not large enough to conclude that manuscript readers were markedly more backward in their preferences. We can assume they also read the printed poetry of their contemporaries. But they do seem to have felt the need to supplement what could be had in print with other, older poems they wished to have on hand. Among these are certain specialized categories of poetry which printers wanted nothing to do with. Interest in alchemical verse is attested to by some forty copies of 21 poems (including multiple copies of Ripley's *Compend*, TM 577, and Norton's *Ordinal*, TM 1752), amounting to about 19,000 lines of verse in manuscript between 1501 and 1558. Alchemy is altogether unrepresented in the printed corpus. Political prophecies in verse are another example; over a hundred copies of more than eighty prophecies, totalling over 8,000 lines, were transcribed, whereas the printed corpus has but one short poem (TP 2160.5 = TM 1857) that fits this category.[13] Comparisons on the incidence of religious poetry appear to bear out these observations. Both print and manuscript contain significant proportions of verse primarily religious in aim and content, but with interesting differences in amounts and kinds. Perhaps half the poems and a quarter of the lines in the printed corpus are religious. The discrepancy between the large proportion of poems and the relatively small proportion of lines owes to the preponderance of short forms: prayers and prologues attached to devotional prose, and the many translations of psalms, other scriptural passages, and liturgical pieces; these short forms account for some forty percent of religious poems in print. Further, the overwhelming proportion of religious verse in print was contemporary. In manuscript, we find religious verse accounting for less, under thirty percent of the poems and about twenty percent of the lines (again, with a preponderance of the same sorts of short forms found in print). Within the manuscript religious category, about a third of the poems and forty percent of the lines were composed before 1501, rather a larger proportion of earlier religious verse than is to be found in print. Of religious poems in both print and manuscript, twelve are Middle English works and 36 are contemporary (Wyatt's *Penitential Psalms*, STC 2726, accounts for much of the contemporary total).

For most contemporary verse, comparison reveals a limited difference between print and manuscript. Ringler observed during the period a certain "time lag" between the composition of new poetry and its printing (p. 9), meaning that multiplication of manuscript copies was for a while the only means of transmission, insuring slightly better chances of survival. Douglas's *Aeneid* (not printed until 1553) and almost all Wyatt's verse (not printed until 1557, apart from the *Psalms* in 1549) are examples. Further, certain kinds of work copied were evidently not intended for the press, such as dramatic scripts (TM 1116, 2024, et al.), records of verse written for private edification (e.g., Thomas Smith's psalms in L: Royal 17.A.17, or Francis Stacy's prayers and didactic verse in L: Additional 33,974), and work composed exclusively for restricted circles of patrons (e.g., TM 211).[14] Mention of Wyatt's verse illustrates the most prominent contrast, the category of contemporary lyric, both secular and (psalm translations excepted) religious; these remained in the province of manuscript throughout almost the entire period.

The small degree of overlap between the two modes of transmission needs to be considered. Only 266 numbered poems in this index (13%) are found printed during the same period; thus less than ten percent of printed poems appear also in manuscript. The figures suggest that manuscript and print went their separate ways after 1500, and certainly confirm the importance of both media as contributors to the total picture we have of poetic taste and poetic composition in the early Tudor period. But at least three factors argue that we must measure these figures circumspectly. First, much of the printed Middle English poetry was reprinted from editions appearing between 1476 and 1500, and that printed for the first time after 1500 must, for the most part, have used 15th-century manuscripts as copy. Except for those major Middle English poems printed relatively late in the period, we should not expect much overlap between print and manuscript in this category of extant verse. Second, obviously enough, are the manuscript losses to be reckoned with. Some idea of this can be had from the following: The 416 short poems printed in STC 13860, Heywood's *Epigrammes* (1550), are represented in extant manuscripts by a few scattered copies. The same holds for all but Wyatt's of the 271 poems printed in STC 13860–61, the first and enlarged second editions of Tottel's *Songes and sonnettes* (both 1557); most of Surrey and the "Uncertain auctores," and all of Grimald, are absent in manuscript before 1558.[15]If copies of just Heywood's epigrams and 170 poems printed in the *Songes and sonnettes* had survived, the overlap between printed and manuscript verse would be at least forty percent. Were the manuscript survival rate near perfect, at least those poems not printed from 15th-century manuscripts would be included as well, and the overlap might rise to as high as eighty percent, with much of the remainder accounted for by work produced for immediate printing rather than manuscript circulation.[16] In this respect, print and manuscript verse begin to look more alike. In the third place, where a poem is extant in both modes of transmission, congruence between corresponding entries in the print and manuscript indexes is not necessarily to be expected. The four editions of Stephen

Hawes, *The Pastime of Pleasure*, listed under TP 1531 have 5,800 lines each; the corresponding poem in manuscript, TM 1368, comprises extracts in two sources amounting to 140 lines. Although shorter poems found in both print and manuscript are typically entries of equal volume, printed editions of mammoth and medium-sized works tend to dwarf their entries in the manuscript index, and we have no examples of a full text in manuscript represented in print only by brief extracts or a truncated copy.[17] Thus for many poems of size, the numerical overlap between print and manuscript, even if small, turns out to be exaggerated. Finally, we note one frequently overlooked corollary of the manuscript-to-print phenomenon. Sometimes the direction is reversed, and what might have been lost in manuscript is resupplied by transcription from print. The pseudo-Lydgatean *Assembly of Gods*, TM 1883, is an example of a sizable poem copied from print, as are several longer poems entered in O17: Balliol 354. And we have any number of instances in which short, gnomic pieces were copied from print to manuscript (see DUR5: Cosin V.iii.9, for example).

After consideration of the origins, kinds, and subject matters of poems, most of the remaining measures of comparison suggest more similarity than difference between verse in manuscript and verse in print. Records of authorship are in the main comparable. The printed corpus preserves the names of 227 English poets. The manuscript corpus preserves work by some 142 authors identified by names or initials (plus work by almost thirty other poets whose names can be supplied from other sources). The list of course includes some eponyms (like Merlin and Thomas of Erceldoune as authors of prophecies), a few persons whose only verse efforts might be ownership rhymes, and a few who may be copyists rather than authors, but the number shows, proportionally, about the same incidence of recorded authorship as is to be found in print, given the smaller size of the manuscript corpus. Manuscript does seem to have been more tolerant than print of anonymity. Only about a fifth of the poems in print are anonymous; the figure is closer to two-thirds in manuscript. A principal source of the difference appears to be the larger proportion of anonymous Middle English verse in manuscript noted above; only nine percent of the pre-1501 religious verse copied appeared also in print. Still, the proportion of identified work parallels the growing interest in authorship seen in the printed corpus of the earlier 16th century, an importance further displayed by a certain amount of speculative or fanciful attribution, as well as by a large number of copyists who subscribed their names or initials to what they copied. There appears to have been a desire to "authorize" poems, to insure that some person be responsible for the pieces of verse transcribed. Only four women poets are identified with printed verse, Dame Julyans Barnes, whose verses on sport appeared in the *Boke of huntyng*, the Protestant martyr Anne Askewe, Lady Jane Dudley (one couplet suffixed to her *Epistle to a Learned Man*), and Queen Elizabeth I (a doubtful attribution). The number doubles in manuscript, although the poems total no more than eighty lines, many fewer than the 600 by women in print.[18] Twenty-five of the identifiable authors of manuscript verse are Middle English poets, the same number recorded in print, and they are very nearly the same poets. Of earlier authors with large bodies of work in manuscript, the alchemists Ripley and Norton, the Scottish chronicler Andrew of Wyntoun, and the didact Peter Idley were not printed. Correspondingly, the chronicler John Harding does not appear in manuscript.[19] Of authors writing between 1501 and 1558, thirty-four appear both in print and manuscript, a number that might grow if printed verse from the 1560's and 1570's were taken into account.

The proportions of translation differ to a degree. Ringler calculated nearly fifty percent of the lines printed between 1501 and 1558 as translation or adapation; the figure for manuscript is only about fifteen percent, but this would double if complete copies of certain long Middle English works which are counted as translations (among them *The Fall of Princes*, the *Troilus*, and Walton's Boethius) survived from the period. Also wanting in manuscripts of our period are almost 9,000 lines of Virgilian translation by contemporary poets, Surrey and Thomas Phaer. Three-quarters of the lines of manuscript translation are from Latin, classical, scriptural, and ecclesiastical; Italian is next, with twenty percent, followed by French, with six percent. Corresponding figures for print are 64 percent from Latin, 30 percent from French (a figure inflated by Lydgate's *Fall*, from Laurent de Premierfait's version of the ostensible source, Boccaccio's Italian), and 5 percent from Italian. In style, as defined by the verse forms employed, manuscript and print are close. Perhaps fifty more verse forms are recorded in manucript than in print, due in part to the tentativeness or lack of finish in much amateur manuscript verse, and in part to the greater variety of stanza patterns in the lyric verse that never reached print (especially in the songbooks and one large collection of carols). But the same two Middle English forms, couplets and rhyme royal, predominate in manuscript as much as in print, accounting for almost two-thirds of the lines in each corpus, owing in large measure to their use in long narrative poems. Other older forms (Monk's Tale stanzas, cross-rhymed quatrains, and tail-rhyme stanzas) bring the proportion of forms conventionalized in Middle English to about eighty percent in each corpus. Medieval Italian forms introduced into English in the 16th century (ottava rima, terza rima, and the sonnet), together with early Tudor inventions (blank verse, poulters measure, and the sixain), account for less than two percent of lines in each corpus. As in print poets, Wyatt is by far the most inventive in verse forms among manuscript poets.

Statistics on forms tend to confirm the observation that, in manuscript as in print, the earlier 16th century was "preeminently the age of Lydgate" (Ringler, p. 11), whose stylistic dominance was relieved by Tottel's publication of the *avant garde* only very late in the period. That this *avant garde*

(Surrey, Wyatt, et al.) appeared earlier in manuscript does little to qualify the observation, given the relatively small circle of readers who had access to their poems and, it seems, the small number of poets interested in them as models.[20] The kinds of contemporary poems that circulated exclusively in early Tudor manuscripts, especially both secular and religious lyrics preserved in songbooks and miscellanies, are in fact more marked by 15th-century tradition than by innovation in either form or subject. Therefore, to generalize as broadly as possible, the outcome of manuscript transcription between 1501 and 1558 was about that of print: preservation of the old and, perhaps a little more narrowly, dissemination of the new. Manuscript copying kept available certain categories of older poetry that had no appeal to printers, and it preserved certain categories of newer work, especially secular lyric, which were either unavailable to printers or of no interest to them until late in the early Tudor period. It seems at any rate warranted to claim that, with respect to poetry in England, the first seventy-five years of printing affected the literary culture of manuscript at most in minor ways. This is not meant to ignore the effects of printing upon writers who used it to disseminate their work, and certainly not to minimize the effect of print on the formation of an expanded reading public for poetry. Neither is it meant to revise the arguments of Elizabeth Eisenstein in *The Printing Press as an Agent of Change* (1979), though it seems fair to say that the more significant changes wrought upon English verse production by the printing revolution would not be felt until later in the 16th century, when the efforts of Gascoigne and Spenser had established a place in the culture for poets as professional and public men of letters. However, as matters of both literary and social history, the consequential differences between the fields of manuscript and of print are likely to be found in contrasting the respective uses of the two media among readers and writers of the period, an analysis requiring different and more detailed comparisons than can be given here.

Notes

[1]Carleton Brown and Rossell Hope Robbins, *The Index of Middle English Verse* (1943); Robbins and John L. Cutler, *Supplement to the Index of Middle English Verse* (1965).

[2]William A. Ringler, Jr., *Bibliography and Index of English Verse Printed 1476–1558* (1988).

[3]Among the sources, apart from the Brown–Robbins–Cutler indexes: Carleton Brown, *A Register of Middle English Religious and Didactic Verse*, 2 vols. (1916–20); Margaret Crum, *First-Line Index of the English Poetry 1500–1800 in Manuscripts of the Bodleian Library*, 2 vols. (1960); the list of early Tudor songs in John Stevens, *Music and Poetry in the Early Tudor Court* (1961); Peter Beal, *Index of English Literary Manuscripts*, vol. 1 (1980); Nancy Gutierrez, *English Historical Poetry 1476–1603: A Bibliography* (1983); first-line indexes on cards in several libraries.

[4]For example, *Jack Upland*, transcribed in C: Ff.6.2; see Ringler, *Index*, pp. 2, 68.

[5]What scholars of earlier French poetry call *mouvance*; see, for example, Paul Zumthor, *Essai de poétique médiéval* (1972), pp. 64–73.

[6]As in this case, where no complete transcript of a poem is extant in our period, its first line is given in square brackets. Acepahalous transcripts (even those inferentially complete before manuscript damage) are treated the same way; this should facilitate complementary use of this index with the print index, with the Brown–Robbins–Cutler indexes, and with the forthcoming Elizabethan verse index. A further reason for conformity with the print index is the need for commensurable information on which to base comparisons betweeen the corpus of manuscript verse and that of printed verse.

[7]Ringler, *Index*, pp. 4–5, estimated that perhaps 15% of the poems in Brown and Robbins and 50% of those added in Robbins and Cutler were written in the 16th century, meaning that, of nearly 6,000 poems with BR numbers, fully one quarter are early Tudor rather than Middle English. These figures are of course rough, owing, first, to the arbitrariness of the cutoff date, and second, to the uncertainty in dating transcriptions in the very early 16th-century manuscripts.

[8]Accidents of preservation skew the totals in favor of Scots poetry; in addition to the five Douglas MSS, there are two nearly complete copies of Wyntoun's *Chronicle* (TM 203), c. 29,000 lines each, and one copy of the Scottish *Alexander* romance (TM 1488), c. 18,000 lines. But the preponderance is partially redressed by substantial losses to one important Scottish verse MS (E: Asloan), and to the fact that much Scots poetry written between 1501 and 1558 is preserved only in the Bannatyne MS (E: Advocates 1.1.6), compiled ten years after our terminal date.

[9]The figure given for the number of poems in music MSS is something of an overrepresentation, since it includes a good many settings whose texts are no more than an incipit. Each of these counts as a copy of a poem, but as only one verse in the line count.

[10]See Ringler, *Index*, pp. 5–15.

[11]The exceptions are HD: Eng f766 (Fabyan's *Chronicle,* STC 10659) and LONG: Longleat 258 (certain pieces in Thynne's edition of Chaucer, STC 5068).

[12]About a dozen of these, more than 30,000 lines of verse, were printed 1501–1558, but of them only versions of the pseudo-historical *Alexander* (TM 1488 and 2029) are extant in manuscript.

[13]The subject assigned to TP 351 (= TM 359) should be revised to "practical" (a poem on writing wills). It seems clear that the large number of prophecies in manuscript led Ringler eventually to discriminate more carefully between "prophecies" and "prognostications" (e.g., weather, lucky days). TP 37, 93, 308, 500, and 1665, indexed as prophecies, are more properly classed as prognostications.

[14]On the vexed question of writers' attitudes toward dissemination of their work in print, see J. W. Saunders, "The Stigma of Print: A Note on the Social bases of Elizabethan Poetry," *Essays in Criticism* 1 (1951), 139–64, and, for a contrary view, Steven May, "Tudor Aristocrats and the Mythical Stigma of Print," *Renaissance Papers 1980* (1981), 11–18.

[15]The major manuscript source of Surrey's poems, L: Additional 36529, was copied in the 1560's.

[16]Robert Crowley's 121 printed poems are an example; see his bibliography in Ringler, *Index*, pp. 72–73. None appear in manuscript.

[17]The one exception might be TM 370, with a 31-line text preserved in D: TCD 160; the corresponding TP 356 (attributed to Wyatt) has only the first stanza, but it is possible that the longer text in manuscript reflects two poems conflated by a copyist, deliberately or in error. Compare TM 133.

[18]Attributions are, of course, problematic, but, among the anonymous verse, there are quite a few poems either certainly or possibly authored by women.

[19]"Herdinge," compiler of a 44,000-line verse chronicle, TM 1993, is not to be identified with John Harding, though the latter was one of his sources.

[20]Compare the decided preference for earlier forms and themes found in the miscellanies compiled during the years of Wyatt's and Surrey's activity, O: Rawlinson C.813 and O17: Balliol 354, or the traditionalism reflected in miscellanies as late as the 1550's, L: Additional 15,233 and O: Ashmole 48.

Guide to the Use of the Index

1. Bibliography of manuscripts

The bibliography is arranged alphabetically by sigla assigned to the libraries and other depositories which hold documents containing verse transcribed from 1501 through 1558; in almost all cases the sigla correspond to those used in the second edition of the STC. Beneath the sigla, printed books, alphabetized by shelfmarks, precede manuscripts, which are alphabetized by their collection titles and/or shelfmarks (or, in some cases, by standard catalogue numbers). Example:

> [1]L: [2]Cotton Titus A.xxiv. [3]Composite volume of papers from the 15th, 16th, and 17th centuries. Twelve poems on fols. 79–97v in a single mid-16th-century hand; five poems on fols. 91v–99v in different mid-16th-century hands. [4]TM 1033, 1134, 1186, 1777, 1919 ptd. Leicester Bradner, *The Life and Poems of Richard Edwardes* (1927), pp. 102–09; TM 26 ptd. Norman Ault, *Elizabethan Lyrics* (1925), pp. 30–31. [5]SEVENTEEN [6](473): [7]26, 176, 658, 876, 1033, 1036, 1134, 1186, 1231, 1461, 1610, 1777, 1900, 1919, 1920, 1941, 1945.

[1]Siglum for collection.
[2]Manuscript shelfmark (or other designation).
[3]Description of manuscript contents.
[4]Citations of printings (consult the list of abbreviations for frequently cited sources).
[5]Total number of poems transcribed 1501–1558 in the manuscript.
[6]Total number of lines of verse transcribed 1501–1558 in the manuscript.
[7]Sequential list of poems, by TM number, transcribed 1501-1558.

2. Index of first lines

First lines are alphabetized according to modern spelling conventions. Those without TM number are cross-references to numbered poems. First lines preceded by an ellipsis are acephalous poems with no complete copy extant; their last lines are given as unnumbered cross-references in the alphabetical sequence. Inclusion of unnumbered cross-references is intended to assist the identification of poems in extant manuscripts, in modern printings of manuscript texts, and in yet to be discovered manuscripts. Example:

> [1]TM 489 [2]God that deyde ffor us All.
> [3]C: Ee.4.35, [4]early 16, [5]ff. 6v–13v. [6]"Expleycet the cheyld & hes stepdame." [7]480:[8]80 x 6 aabccb4*. [9]O17: Balliol 354, 1503–04, ff. 98–100v. "Jak & his Step Dame, & of the Frere." 426 lines. [10]BR 977, comp. a 1475; TP 500.5. [11]Nar., fabliau, humorous.

[1]Poem number.

[2]First line literatim (with some abbreviations expanded) as it appears in the manuscript first cited. Pointed brackets (<>) indicate illegibility owing to manuscript damage. A first line given in square brackets indicates a poem for which no complete transcript is extant 1501–1558, or, in the case of acephalous texts, the first line of an earlier extant complete text of the poem. Poems of two lines are transcribed completely.

[3]Collection siglum and manuscript shelfmark (or other designation).

[4]Date of transcription (16 = 16th century; a notation such as "1511+" means in that year or after; 1/4 16, 2/4 16, 1/2 16 = respectively, first quarter, second quarter, first half of the 16th century. On the dating of transcripts, see Introduction, p. xiv).

[5]Inclusive folios of the transcript (in the case of printed books, signatures).

[6]Identification of the poem. Words in quotation marks are found in the manuscript (except, usually, for names, which are given as they appear, not in normalized spelling); words in parentheses are inferential from the manuscript; any material is square brackets is information supplied from elsewhere.

[7]Number of lines in the copy.

[8]Verse form, stanza form (if in square brackets, an inferential reconstruction). Refrain rhymes are given in upper case in the rhyme-scheme notation. Number following the rhyme indicates the verse measure; a number without an asterisk indicates syllables in accentual-syllabic verse, a number followed by an asterisk indicates the accents in stress-based verse, on average, since the number of stresses per verse is not always consistent through a poem.

[9]Siglum, etc., of second manuscript copy. Where information given for the first copy is not repeated (e.g., lines and verse forms), this is the same as for the first citation.

[10]Bibliographical identification of the poem, by BR number (together with composition date, if before 1501) and TP number. A BR number given in parentheses indicates that the poem is neither extant before 1501 nor inferentially datable before 1501; a BR number followed by a plus sign (e.g.,

TM 40 = BR 97.5+) indicates the placement in the BR alphabetical sequence of a poem composed before 1501 but not recorded in the Brown–Robbins–Cutler indexes.

[11] A selection of the subject and genre categories under which the poem is indexed (see list of abbreviations).

Bibliography of Manuscripts Containing English Verse Transcribed 1501–1558

ALW: DUKE OF NORTHUMBERLAND, ALNWICK CASTLE

ALW: Alnwick 79. (BMP F316) William Peeris, "a tretes of the noble pedegrew of the lords perses sith the conquest," illuminated vellum roll with portraits of the English kings from William the Conqueror through Henry VIII, c 1520. Ptd. from O: Dodsworth 50 by J. Besley, *Reprints of Rare Tracts and Imprints* (1845), pp. 9–43. ONE (366): 313.

ALW: Alnwick 82. (BMP F319) William Peeris, "treatice...of the descente of the lordes percis," c 1520. ONE (651): 313. For print, see MS listed above.

BO: BOSTON PUBLIC LIBRARY, Boston, Mass.

BO: f. Med. 94. Lydgate, *Siege of Thebes*, 74ff., transcribed c 1430; poems entered in a hand of the mid-16th century in Scotland. FIVE (51): 143, 504, 760, 1108, 1443.

C: CAMBRIDGE UNIVERSITY LIBRARY

Incunabula are listed here by numbers in J. C. T. Oates, *A Catalogue of the Fifteenth-Century Printed Books in the Cambridge University Library* (Cambridge, 1954).

C: Ptd. book Oates #2117, Ovid, *Fasti* (Venice, 1497). Ownership verse entered in the early 16th century by Joannes Terry. ONE (2): 828.

C: Ptd. book Oates #3234, Cicero, *Epistolae ad familiares* (Lyons, n.d.). Ownership verses entered in the early 16th century by Thomas Feckynham. ONE (2): 828.

C: Ptd. book Oates #4059 (STC 15383), Caxton, *The history of Jason* (1477). Ownership verses entered in the early 16th century by Thomas P. and Johannes D. ONE (4 + 2): 828.

C: Ptd. book Oates #4065 (STC 3303), *The Book of curtesye* (1477–78). Poem entered on the verso of the last leaf in a hand of the early 16th century by "F. S."; facsimile ed. Francis Jenkinson (1907). ONE (14): 586.

C: Ptd. book Oates #4178, *Abbreviamentum statutorum* (London, n.d.). Ownership verses entered in the early 16th century by Johannes Melsham. ONE (2): 828.

C: Ptd. book Syn. 6.53.5 (STC 2833), *The newe Testament*, trans. Tyndale (1536). Ownership verse entered in the mid-16th century by Thomas Lynsey. ONE (2): 552.

C: Dd.5.76 (I). (BMP B364) *Liber de diversis rebus et medicinis* and historical notes in English, 26ff., 15th century; one poem entered at the beginning of the book in the first quarter of the 16th century. ONE (60): 151, ptd. Person, *ME Lyrics* #4.

C: Dd.9.31. Historical and moral prose and verse, 30ff., copied in the second and early third quarters of the 16th century. THREE (148): 715, 1611, 1867. TM 715 and 1611 ptd. Furnivall, *Ballads* 1, 417–25.

C: Dd.13.27. Music for masses by English composers, tenor part, 34ff., copied in the early 16th century (the bass part-book is C5: 234). ONE (5): 486, ptd. Agnes Strickland, *Lives of the Queens of England*, 4 (1853), 40.

C: Ee.4.35 (I). (BMP B526) Principally narrative and religious verse, 24ff., copied in the early 16th century. TM 489 ptd. Thomas Wright, *The Tale of the Basyn* (1836); TM 788 and 1991 ptd. Child, *Ballads* 3, 109–13; 5, 78–79; TM 1631 ptd. Joseph Ritson, *Ancient Popular Poetry* (1791), p. 59. THIRTEEN (1,187): 239, 310, 489, 642, 775, 788, 869, 905, 973, 1631, 1691, 1917, 1991.

C: Ee.4.37. Peter Idley, *Instructions to his Son*, 113ff., copied in the later 15th century (ptd. Charlotte D'Evelyn, *Peter Idley's Instructions* (1935)); historical material and verse entered on unused pages, late 16th century; short verses in early and mid-sixteenth-century hands, one copied twice. TWO (4): 558, 869.

C: Ff.2.23. (BMP B621) "The Compende of Alkymye by George ripley canon of brydlington," and accompanying poems (some fragmentary due to MS damage), 32ff., copied by Thomas Knyvet in 1545. FOUR (2,003): 160, 177, 577, 1301.

C: Ff.2.38. (BMP B625) English religious prose and verse and eight metrical romances, 247ff., copied in the late 15th century; one poem (copied twice) added in the early 16th century. Facsimile ed. Frances McSparran and P. R. Robinson (1979). ONE (8): 67.

C: Ff.6.2. *Jack Upland*, copied in the early 16th century; not verse, although listed as BR 3782.5. See P. L. Heyworth, *Jack Upland* (1968).

C: Ff.6.31. (BMP B659) Miscellany of religious prose, 162ff., 15th century. One poem added in an early 16th-century hand. ONE (6): 1217, ptd. R. R. Raymo, ELN 4 (1967), 180.

C: Gg.4.12. (BMP B713) John Capgrave, *Chronicle*, 204ff., author's autograph, before 1464. Short English verses entered on the end flyleaf in the early 16th century. TM 1510 and 1972 ptd. R. H. Robbins, ELN 5 (1968), 245; TM 597 and 1859 ptd. Person, *ME Lyrics*, pp. 53, 41. FOUR (19): 597, 1510, 1859, 1972.

C: Gg.4.31. (BMP B720) *Piers Plowman* (B-Text), 105ff., copied in the mid-16th century, and a verse prayer in a different but contemporary hand. TWO (7,105): 274, 753.

C: Hh.2.6. Legal writings, prose and verse, 266ff., copied in several hands at the beginning of the 16th century. FOUR (62): 814, 1104, 1117, 1979. TM 814 ptd. Robbins, *Sec.* #112; TM 1104 ptd. Robbins, *Hist.* #62.

C: Ii.6.2. *Horae*, 98ff., copied in the 15th century; two poems entered c 1536. TWO (18): 856, 863. TM 856 ptd. R. H. Robbins, MP 40 (1942–43), 137–38.

C: Ii.6.4. *Horae beatae Marise* [sic] *Virginis*, 98ff., copied in the 15th century; two ownership verses entered in the early 16th century. TWO (6): 1930, 1983, both ptd. Robbins, *Sec.* #92 and p. 257 (with different transcription of the first line of TM 1983).

C: Kk.1.5 (VIII). (BMP B873) Poem transcribed in an early 16th-century hand on a leaf independent of the remainder of this gathering. ONE (14): 66, ptd. Joseph Stevenson, *Lancelot of Laik*, Maitland Club (1939), p. xix.

C: Kk.6.16. Geoffrey of Monmouth, *Historia Bruti*, 14th century; political prophecies in Latin verse and prose, 15th century; 186ff.; prophecies in English verse added c 1500. TWO (96): 398, 1203.

C: Kk.6.18. *Psalterium beati Gregorii*, 14th century, 52ff.; ownership verse entered on the inside front cover, first quarter of the 16th century. ONE (6): 495, ptd. Robbins, *Sec.* #91.

C: Ll.1.11. Legal writings, 33ff., 15th century; song added on the end flyleaf, c 1500. ONE (13): 1306.

C: Nn.4.5 (I). *Vox populi vox dei,* 16ff., attributed (erroneously) to "Mr skeltone Lawriate," copied between 1550 and 1558. ONE (815): 676, ptd. Dyce, *Skelton* 2, 400–13.

C2: TRINITY COLLEGE, Cambridge

Listed by shelf mark; numbers in parentheses refer to entries in M. R. James, *The Western Manuscripts in the Library of Trinity College, Cambridge,* 3 vols. (1900–02).

C2: B.15.31 (366). Latin religious prose, 100ff., 15th century; English poems added before 1541. TWO (15): 125, 1117. Both ptd. James 1, 496–97; TM 125 ptd. Robbins, *Sec.* #126.

C2: B.15.39 (181, Vol. III). (BMP C967) Latin and English religious prose, 8ff., early 15th century; poem added in the early 16th century. ONE (32): 299, partially ptd. James 1, 234.

C2: B.16.31 (394). Latin religious prose, 150ff., 15th century; poem added in the early 16th century. ONE (4): 379, ptd. James 1, 530.

C2: B.16.41 (402). 26ff., liturgical calendar, 15th century, with historical memoranda inserted through the 1550's; ecclesiastical *Statuta* signed in 1516 by Richard Fitz-James, bishop of London; poem entered on a flyleaf in the early 16th century. ONE (2): 374, ptd. James 1, 538.

C2: O.1.13 (1037), Part V. Fols. 173–222v, miscellaneous prose on practical subjects, 15th through 17th centuries; poem entered in the early 16th century by Robert Jernegan on a flyleaf. ONE (2): 1842.

C2: O.2.53 (1157). (BMP D67) Miscellany of English and Latin prose and verse, 74ff., 15th through 16th centuries; all English verse entered in the early 16th century. TM 381, 610, 1199, 1685, 1820, 1917 ptd. Person, *ME Lyrics,* pp. 56, 26, 11, 8–9, 20; TM 479 and 485 ptd. James 3, 170, 173, and J. Alsop, NQ 228 (1983), 411; TM 407 ptd. Brown, XV #149; TM 2044 ptd. Greene #379. TWENTY-ONE (300): 381, 387, 407, 479, 485, 567, 610, 1199, 1203, 1505, 1633, 1641, 1685, 1767, 1820, 1917, 1970, 1979, 2012, 2028, 2044.

C2: O.3.12 (1184). "...Virgyll...hys twelf bukes of Eneados compilit and translatit...by...Master Gawyn Dowglas...the first correk coppy nixt efter the translation Wrytin be Master Matho Geddes scribe," 329ff., copied c 1515. Ptd. A. Rutherford and G. Dundas, Bannatyne Club (1839); copy-text for David Coldwell's edition, STS, 3d ser., 25, 27, 28, 30 (1957–64). THREE (24,570): 879, 1273, 1497.

C2: O.3.21 (1193). Scottish *Chronicle* of Hector Boece, trans. John Bellenden, 348ff. (imperfect at the end), copied in the early 16th century. ONE (208): 1690.

C2: O.3.55 (1227). Religious, historical, and liturgical prose in Latin, mostly copied in the 12th century, 69ff.; poem added in the mid-16th century. ONE (4): 674, ptd. James 3, 242.

C2: O.7.31 (1359). (BMP D80) Sarum Breviary, 15th century; a carol copied twice, c 1500. ONE (26 + 15): 1618, ptd. Greene #380a–b

C2: O.8.32 (1407). Alchemical tracts in Latin, 141ff., 15th century, with annotations and verses in English added by Thomas Charnocke in the second and third quarters of the 16th century. ONE (6): 365.

C2: R.3.17 (597). (BMP C1000) The romance of *Partenay*, copied in the early 16th century (123ff., acephalous owing to manuscript damage); ownership verse and one short poem added in the early and mid-16th century. THREE (6,651): 419, 1008, 1975. TM 419 and 1008 ptd. W. W. Skeat, EETS 22 (1866); TM 1975 ptd. James 2, 67.

C2: R.3.33 (613). "The disclosinge of the practyse of Stephen Gardyner byshope of Wynchester...," 149ff., with author's name erased; preface in prose and poem (incomplete at the end), copied between 1547 and 1552. Ed. P. Janelle, *Bull. of the Institute of Historical Research* 6 (1928–29), 12–17, 89–96, 167–74. ONE (5,400): 756.

C2: R.14.39 (911), Part II. (BMP D28) Fragmentary life of St. Augustine of Canterbury and medical treatises in Latin, 15th century; medical recipes in verse added in the early 16th century. TWO (20): 276, 1969.

C2: R.14.41 (913), Part III. (BMP D30) Medical treatises in Latin and recipes, 14th and 15th centuries; ownership verse entered in the early 16th century. ONE (6): 1334.

C3: EMMANUEL COLLEGE, CAMBRIDGE

Listed by shelfmark; numbers in parentheses are those in M. R. James, *The Western Manuscripts in the Library of Emmanuel College* (1904).

C3: IV.1.17 (260). Composite volume of letters, speeches, etc., by and about English protestant martyrs, documents dating from the 1520's through the 1550's. TWO (172): 464, 1526.

C3: IV.3.31 (263). Printed tracts bound with manuscript material; flyleaf entry in the early 16th century. ONE (94): 1505, ptd. James, pp. 166–67.

C5: ST. JOHN'S COLLEGE, Cambridge

C5: K.31 (234). (BMP C886) Music for masses by English composers, bass part, 35ff., copied in the early 16th century (the tenor part-book is C: Dd.13.27). ONE (5): 486.

C7: CORPUS CHRISTI COLLEGE, Cambridge

Cited by numbers in M. R. James, *A Descriptive Catalogue of the Manuscripts in the Library of Corpus Christi College, Cambridge*, 2 vols. (1912).

C7: CCC 31. Stephen Langton, *Super xii prophetas*, 192ff., 13th century; early 16th century entry on the flyleaf. ONE (2): 364, ptd. James 1, 63.

C7: CCC 106. Composite volume of documents relating to Cambridge University, dating from the 1540's and 1550's, compiled by Matthew Parker. TWO (152): 841, 1712. Both ptd. Charles Hartshorne, *Ancient Metrical Tales* (London, 1829), pp. 222–24, 288–92.

C7: CCC 298 (I). "the lyff off Seynt Thomas off Cantorbury...translatyd in to our vulgar tonge...by [Laurentius Wade] a brother off Cristes Churche in Cantorbury...," copied in the early 16th century. ONE (2,303): 1258, ptd. C. Horstmann, *Englische Studien* 3 (1880), 409–69.

C7: CCC 379. Latin treatises on hunting, Old English, geography, etc., 65ff., copied by Robert Talbot, mid-16th century; one entry in English after 1534. ONE (4): 1779, ptd. James 2, 227.

C9: GONVILLE AND CAIUS COLLEGE, Cambridge

C9: 793 (red #828). Miscellaneous papers, mainly in Latin, 87ff., 16th and early 17th centuries; English poem in a hand of the early 16th century. ONE (294): 300.

C10: MAGDALENE COLLEGE, Cambridge

C10: F.4.13 (13). Miscellany of religious, historical, medical, etc., material in English and Latin, 246ff., compiled in 1518 by Jasper Fyllol, Domincan friar at Syon monastery, London. EIGHT (67): 480, 511, 739, 775, 849, 928, 1295, 1970. TM 739, 928, 1295, and 1970 ptd. M. R. James, *Catalogue of the Western Manuscripts in the College Library of Magdalene College, Cambridge* (1909), p. 26.

C10: Pepys 2163. Herdinge, "the Englisshe & ffraunche Cronicles" from William Rufus through Henry VIII, 643ff., transcribed c 1550–55. TWO (43,980): 1993, 2031

C13: CLARE COLLEGE, Cambridge

C13: Kk.3.14 (13). St. Gregory, *Homiliae super evangelia*, 120ff., 15th century; verse added in a margin, c 1500. ONE (2): 14, ptd. M. R. James, *Descriptive Catalogue of the Western Manuscripts in the Library of Clare College, Cambridge* (1905), p. 24.

C14: FITZWILLIAM MUSEUM, Cambridge

C14: 56. *Horae*, 162ff., 15th century; verses entered by Margaret Sussex and Mary Sussex, before 1542. TWO (6): 492, 1055. Both ptd. M. R. James, *Catalogue of the Manuscripts in the Fitzwilliam Museum* (1895), p. 141.

C14: Music 784. Single sheet, with two fragmentary poems with musical settings, early 16th century. TWO (11): 1452, 1724.

C15: PEMBROKE COLLEGE, Cambridge

C15: 307. (BMP C769) Gower, *Confessio Amantis*, 202ff., transcribed in the 15th century; later verse entered in the mid-16th century. TWO (14): 1141, 1776. Both ptd. Person, *ME Lyrics*, #45, #52; TM 1776 ptd. J. R. Kreuzer, *RES* 14 (1938), 322, and Robbins, *Sec.* #110

C15: Folder of musical fragments, early 16th century. ONE (1): 230.

C17: SIDNEY SUSSEX COLLEGE, Cambridge

C17: 39. Collection of prophecies in prose and verse, 69ff., compiled in the first quarter of the 16th century. ONE (2,000): 1617.

CANT: CANTERBURY CATHEDRAL

CANT: Christchurch Letters, II, no. 173 (formerly S.B.b.34). Damaged single leaf, c 1500. ONE (47): 97, ptd. Greene #443.

CANT: Christchurch Letters, II, no. 174 (formerly S.B.b.185). Damaged single leaf, c 1500. ONE (26): 1486, ptd. Greene #444.

COP: ROYAL LIBRARY, COPENHAGEN

COP: GL. kgl. Saml. 1551, 4°. Notebook compiled 1520–1535 by Paul Helie (c 1480–c 1535). ONE (6): 844, ptd. Denton Fox, NQ 216 (1971), 204.

COP: Old College 3500. Collection of alchemical writings in English, 15th and 16th centuries. Poem entered on front flyleaf, mid-16th century. ONE (4): 1135, ptd. George Stephens, *Retrospective Review* 2 (1854), 415.

COV: ST. MARY'S HALL, COVENTRY CORPORATION MSS

COV: City Records Office, Clothiers and Broad Weavers Company MS. The Coventry Weavers' Pageant, transcribed by Robert Croo, 2 March 1534/35, plus two leaves containing parts of the pageant in a 15th-century hand. Ptd. Thomas Sharp, *The Presentation in the Temple: A Pageant* (1836); ed. Hardin Craig, EETSes 87 (1902; 2d ed. 1957), 33–71, 119–22. ONE (1,192): 2024.

CU: COLUMBIA UNIVERSITY (New York City, N. Y.)

CU: Plimpton 276. Commonplace book of Agnes Bower, 63ff.; verse and prose entries from 1554 through the 1570's. TWO (18): 1737, 1805.

D: TRINITY COLLEGE, Dublin

Numbers cited according to T. K. Abbott, *Catalogue of the Manuscripts in the Library of Trinity College, Dublin* (1900); shelfmarks in parentheses.

D: 45 (A.4.8). Latin prose, 12th and 14th centuries; ownership verse of Robert Wellburn entered in the early 16th century. ONE (2): 552.

D: 49 (A.1.13). Book of Job with gloss, 12th century; ownership verse of Arthur Symcock added in the early 16th century. ONE (2): 172.

D: 160 (D.2.7). Composite volume whose first two parts contain a lament of the virgin and Peter Idley's *Instructions*, 15th century. The third part (fols. 57–186) is the Blage Manuscript, a verse miscellany compiled by John Mantell, c 1534 through 1541, and George Blage, c 1545 through c 1548; see Helen Baron, *English Manuscript Studies 1100–1700* 1 (1988), 85ff. Most of the contents ptd. by Kenneth Muir, *Unpublished Poems...from the Blage Manuscript* (1961), abbreviated "U" in the list below, and Muir and Patricia

Thomson (eds.), *Collected Poems of Sir Thomas Wyatt* (1969), abbreviated "MT" in the list below. (For poems printed in both, only the MT number or page reference is given.) "W" indicates a poem printed by Muir and Thomson from another source, with Blage MS variants collated. ONE HUNDRED THIRTY-FOUR (3,356): 8 (MT cxviii), 37, 46, 55, 56 (MT cxi), 59 (MT cxvi), 77 (MT cxvii), 83 (MT cxiii), 88, 93 (MT cix), 91, 96 (MT cxii), 103 (MT cxix), 106, 108 (W), 112 (MT p. 403), 124 (MT cxv), 139 (MT cx), 217 (MT cxiv), 218 (W), 231, 259 (MT cxxi), 281, 283, 297 (MT cxx), 323 (MT cxxiii), 329 (MT cxxii), 340 (MT p. 395), 341 (MT pp. 397–98), 346 (MT cxxvii), 348, 351 (MT cxxvi), 353 (MT cxxxi), 356 (MT cxxxii), 361 (MT cxxv), 363, 366 (MT cxxx), 370 (MT cxxviii), 371 (MT cxxix), 372 MT cxxiv), 380, 386 (MT cxxxviii), 440 (MT clxi), 446, 450 (W), 505 (MT cxxxiii), 519 (MT cxxxv), 526 (MT cxxxvi), 549 (MT p. 414), 608 (MT cxxxiv), 624 (MT cxl), 631 (MT cxxxix), 644 (MT cxlv), 653 (MT cxliv), 671 (MT cxli), 696 (MT cxliii), 707, 709, 713, 722 (MT cxlii), 733 (MT p. 414), 778 (MT cxlvi), 787 (MT pp. 402–03), 805, 825, 842 (W), 881, 888 (MT pp. 404–05), 897 (W), 907 (MT cxlix), 919 (W), 927 (MT cxlvii), 948 (MT cxlviii), 960 (MT p. 403), 968 (MT cli), 969 (W), 1002 (MT cliii), 1027 (MT cl), 1052 (MT p. 405), 1061 (W), 1068, 1071 (MT cliv), 1081 (W), 1137 (MT clvii), 1143 (MT p. 406), 1170 (MT p. 398), 1188, 1249 (MT clv), 1268 (ptd. G. F. Nott, *Poems of Wyatt* (1816), p. 77), 1297 (MT clvi), 1310 (MT clix), 1314 (W), 1316 (W), 1322 (MT clviii), 1346 (MT clx), 1361, 1366 (MT p. 409), 1402 (MT clxii), 1406 (MT pp. 411–12), 1410, 1414 (W), 1422 (MT clxvi), 1424 (MT clxiv), 1445, 1460 (MT clxiii), 1466, 1468 (MT clxv), 1470 (MT p. 411), 1491 (MT clxxiii), 1546 (MT clxxii), 1636 (W), 1692 (MT clxvii), 1703 (MT p. 414), 1704 (MT clxix), 1706 (MT clxviii), 1711 (W), 1745 (MT clxxi), 1761 (MT clxx), 1795 (MT clxxvii), 1815, 1826, 1844 (MT clxxv), 1878, 1893 (MT p. 390), 1895, 1922, 1927, 1942 (MT clxxvi), 1947, 1973 (W), 2008 (MT clxxiv), 2032, 2040 (MT clii), 2042 (MT cxxxvii).

D: 223 (C.1.1). Augustine, *Ennarationes in psalmos*, 15th century; ownership verse added in the early 16th century. ONE (2): 1975.

D: 389 (D.2.8). Composite volume, 103ff.; alchemical works in English and Latin, c 1550. ONE (196): 1478, vv. 1–11 ptd. G. W. Dunleavy, *Ambix: Soc. for the Study of Alchemy and Early Chemistry* 13 (1965), 27–28.

D: 423 (D.4.3). English religious verse and prose, 148ff., 15th century; additions in the early 16th century. ONE (6): 287, ptd. R. H. Robbins, ELN 5 (1968), 246.

D: 484 (E.1.26). Historical and heraldic material, preceded on fols. 1–11 by a prose chronicle through 1531 ("A Remembraunce of auncient thinges") and a verse chronicle, copied in the second quarter of the sixteenth century. ONE (160): 1593.

D: 490 (E.2.15). English prose "Brute," 183ff., 15th century; additions in mid- and later-16th century hands. ONE (20): 699.

D: 537 (E.2.12). Composite volume; in the second part (52ff.), early 16th-century entries in at least two hands include verse copied from STC 22409, *Kalender of Shepherdes* [1516]. SIX (492): 169, 600, 736 (copied twice), 1207, 1839, 1960.

D: 652 (F.4.20), Part VI. "the play of the conuersyon of ser Ionathas the Iewe by myracle of the Blyssed sacrament" (the Croxton *Play of the Sacrament*), 20ff., transcribed by R. C., c 1546. Ptd. [Whitley Stokes], *Transactions of the Philological Soc.*, 1860–61, supplement, pp. 101–42; ed. J. Q. Adams, *Chief Pre-Shakespearean Dramas* (1924), pp. 243–62; ed. Norman Davis, EETS, Suppl. Texts 1 (1970), 58–89. ONE (1,007): 1116.

DOR: DORCHESTER ABBEY

DOR: Funeral brass of Abbot Richard Beauforest, died 1512. ONE (2): 584.

DUR5: UNIVERSITY OF DURHAM

DUR5: Cosin V.iii.9. Hoccleve, *Complaint* and *Dialogus cum amico*, 15th century, with missing material supplied by John Stowe (before 1605); short verses entered in margins of the 15th-century transcript, c 1555, some of which were copied from STC 1730.5 (1510?), STC 7635 (1531), STC 10443 (1542), and STC 13296 (1555). TWENTY-SIX (72): 41, 220, 250, 267, 432, 540, 558, 598, 639, 738, 854, 874, 906, 1085, 1259, 1408, 1441, 1506, 1528, 1658, 1669, 1738, 1835, 1932, 1950, 1951.

E: NATIONAL LIBRARY OF SCOTLAND, Edinburgh

E: Advocates 18.3.2 "...the traduction of titus liuius be Maister Iohanne Ballantyne [i.e., John Bellenden], Archde[aco]n of Murray" (composed 1533), transcribed c 1540; ed. W. A. Craigie, STS 47 (1901) and 51 (1903). ONE (140): 171, ptd. Craigie, pp. 1–5.

E: Advocates 19.1.11. Composite volume of 15th-century verse and prose, 222ff.; poems added in Part I after 1525, and in Part III in the early and mid-16th century. FOUR (12): 552 (in part I), 552 (another copy in part III), 646 (in part III; ptd. Brown XV #111), 1876 (in part III).

E: Advocates 19.2.4. Wyntoun's *Chronicle of Scotland*, copied in the first quarter of the 16th century. ONE (29,600): 203.

E: Advocates 34.7.3. Miscellany compiled by James Gray from the last quarter of the 15th through the second quarter of the 16th centuries, 82ff.; seven poems (ptd. George Stevenson, STS 65 (1918), 41–56), five of which were copied before 1500. TWO (10): 737, 779.

E: Asloan Manuscript. Miscellany of Scottish prose and verse, 306ff., compiled by John Asloan some time between 1513 and 1542. Originally contained 52 poems (plus verse at the end of a prose piece), of which 35 are now lacking; missing items are inferrable from table of contents (titles not indexed here). Ed. W. A. Craigie, *The Asloan Manuscript*, STS, n.s. 14 (1923) and 16 (1925). NINETEEN (11,451): 70, 144, 147, 159, 213, 296, 317, 516, 525, 777, 782, 792, 1083, 1087, 1162, 1374, 1453, 1574, 1650.

E: Gaelic 37. The Book of the Dean of Lismore, miscellany of historical material and poetry in Scottish Gaelic, compiled in the first half of the 16th century. ONE (8): 1812, ptd. R. H. Robbins, *Manual of the Writings in Middle English*, ed. A. Hartung, 5 (1975), 1457.

E2: EDINBURGH UNIVERSITY LIBRARY

Listed by shelfmark; numbers in parentheses are entries in Catherine Borland, *A Descriptive Catalogue of the Western Mediaeval Manuscripts in the Edinburgh University Library* (1916).

E2: Db.II.18 (Borland 186). Johannes de Fordun, *Scoticronicon* and other historical material, mainly in Latin, ii+346ff., copied in 1510. ONE (62): 572, ptd. Laing, *Select Remains of Ancient Popular Poetry of Scotland* (1822), p. 186, and W. A. Craigie, *Anglia* 21 (1899), 359–63.

E2: Dc.I.43. The Ruthven Manuscript of Douglas's translation of the *Aeneid*, 301ff., transcribed in 1527, with mid-16th century additions. TM 165 ptd. Denton Fox, Henryson's *Testament of Cresseid* (1968), p. 131; TM 206 variants and unique second stanza ptd. E. Bennett, *MLR* 33 (1938), 403. FIVE (24,650): 165, 206, 879, 1273, 1497.

E2: Dk.VII.49. Douglas's translation of the *Aeneid*, transcribed by James Elphynstoune, 1515–1520, with works of Sir David Lyndsay entered later, 513ff. The text in *Works of Douglas*, ed. John Small (1874) is based on this MS. TWO (c 24,560): 879, 1497.

E2: Laing 149 (Borland 205). 203+iiiff; Latin notes on Aristotle's logical treatises, copied by Magnus Makulloch in 1477; Scots verse added on blank pages before 1525, perhaps by I[ohn] perde. All the poems ptd. George Stevenson, STS 65 (1918), 3–37; TM 131 ptd. Brown XV #53. THIRTEEN (707): 131, 309, 326, 420, 513, 523, 691, 821, 975, 1238, 1374, 1696, 1856.

E2: Laing II.318. Two-leaf fragment of a poem, acephalous and incomplete at the end, possibly early 16th-century. ONE (134): 173.

E2: Laing II.655. Fragment of three leaves containing parts of Douglas's translation of the *Aeneid*, copied before 1550. ONE (198): 1497.

E2: Laing III.164. "Liber Thomas Norton"; alchemical poems, 116ff., transcribed in the early 16th century. FIVE (2,194): 177, 577, 1343, 1752, 1915.

E5: ROYAL COLLEGE OF PHYSICIANS, Edinburgh

E5: Anonyma 2, Vol. V. Part II, 28ff., alchemical material copied in the mid-16th century. TWO (1899): 177, 577.

E COL: COLUMBA HOUSE, SCOTTISH CATHOLIC ARCHIVES, Edinburgh

E COL: Johannes de Fordun, *Scotichronicon*, with the continuation by W. Bower, 219ff., transcribed in the early 16th century with marginal additions in English. ONE (14): 1293.

ETON: ETON COLLEGE, Windsor, Berkshire.

ETON: 98. William of Lyndewode, *Provinciale*, with other ecclesiatical prose in Latin, 345ff., 15th century; fragment of verse added in the early 16th century on the first flyleaf. ONE (5): 1638.

F: FOLGER SHAKESPEARE LIBRARY, Washington, D.C.

F: Ptd. book, STC 12721 (copy 2), Halle, *The vnion of the two noble and illustrate famelies* (1548). Two poems entered by Mary Sidney on sigs. R8 and 3K7v, and one by Sir Henry Sidney on sig. 3K7v, in 1551. THREE (8): 731, 1763, 1790. TM 731 ptd. William Ringler, *The Poems of Sir Philip Sidney* (1962), p. xvi.

F: L.b.554. Fragment of two leaves in the Loseley collection, copied c 1550. Ptd. G. R. Proudfoot, *Malone Soc. Collections* 9 (1977), 52–57, and (with facsimile) by L. A. Cummings, *REED* 1977:2, pp. 2–15. ONE (118): 137.

F: V.a.198 (1). Single sheet in a composite volume; copied early in the 16th century. ONE (35): 1585.

F: V.a.354. Composite volume containing the three Macro plays (middle and late 15th century); entries in blank spaces and margins in the text of

Wisdom (fols. 1–13) made in the first quarter of the 16th century. Facsimile ed. John S. Farmer, *Wisdom* (1907). FOUR (16): 234, 1639, 1723, 2004. All four ptd. Mark Eccles, EETS 262 (1969), xxviii–ix.

F: V.b.135. Single sheet (verso blank) copied in the mid-16th century. ONE (42): 1643, ptd. Joseph Ritson *Ancient Songs* (1790), p. 134.

F: X.d.532. Vellum strip headed "Oratio deuotissima Thomae More quondam Cancellarij Anglie," transcribed after 1535, with prayers in prose and verse attributed (probably in error) to Thomas More. TWO (23): 1350, 1598.

FLAMB: FLAMBOROUGH CHURCH, Yorkshire.

FLAMB: Funeral brass with epitaph of Sir Marmaduke Constable, died 1518. ONE (26): 582, ptd. P. M. King, NQ 226 (1981), 495.

G: HUNTERIAN MUSEUM, University of Glasgow

Numbered according to entries in John Young and P. H. Aitken, *Catalogue of the Manuscripts in the Library of the Hunterian Museum* (1908), with shelfmarks in parentheses.

G: Hunterian 83 (T.3.21). Trevisa's translation of Higden, *Polychronicon*, and carols with music, 148ff., 15th century; ownership rhyme added in the early 16th century. ONE (2): 552, ptd. Young & Aitken, *Catalogue*, p. 89.

G: Hunterian 230 (U.3.3). Chronicle of England ("Brut"), 248ff., copied in the early 15th century; early 16th-century additions on the last leaves. TWELVE (31): 23, 28, 47, 242, 265, 833, 834, 875, 980, 1223, 1368, 1974. TM 242 ptd. Young & Aitken, *Catalogue*, p. 175.

G: Hunterian 232 (U.3.5). Extracts from Lydgate's *Life of Our Lady*, 104ff., 15th century; verses added in the first and second quarters of the 16th century. THREE (16): 222, 1115, 1565. TM 222 and 1565 ptd. Young and Aitken, *Catalogue*, p. 185.

G: Hunterian 258 (U.4.16). English translation of Richard of St. Victor, *De praeparatione animi*, 12ff., 15th century; poem added in the early 16th century. ONE (10): 587, ptd. Young & Aitken, *Catalogue*, p. 210.

G: Hunterian 400 (V.2.20). John Harding, *Metrical Chronicle of England* and *Itinerary of Scotland*, 183ff., 15th century; additions through the mid-16th century. ONE (2): 540, ptd. Young & Aitken, *Catalogue*, p. 320.

G: Hunterian 409 (V.3.7). *The Romaunt of the Rose*, 151ff., verse translation attributed to Chaucer, 15th century; short rhymes entered in the mid-16th century. TWO (9): 619, 642. Both ptd. Young & Aitken, *Catalogue*, pp. 329–30.

GRAN: GRANTHAM CHURCH, Wobern, Buckinghamshire

GRAN: Funeral monument for an unnamed person, c 1520. ONE (12): 931, ptd. P. M. King, NQ 226 (1981), 496.

HD: HARVARD UNIVERSITY, Cambridge, Mass.

HD: fMS Eng 752. Lydgate, *Troy Book*, 365ff., damaged at the beginning and end, 15th century. Verse entered early in the 16th century by Thomas Kynton. ONE (2): 220.

HD: fMS Eng 766. Robert Fabyan, *Chronicles of England and France*, Part II, 438ff., transcribed after 1504; printer's copy for Part II in Pynson's edition of 1516 (STC 10659). TWENTY-NINE (496): 308, 442, 583, 716, 892, 910, 913, 923, 971, 1201, 1228, 1264, 1265, 1323, 1375, 1507, 1522, 1544, 1549, 1569, 1579, 1642, 1672, 1773, 1841, 1890, 1905, 1934, 2007.

HN: HENRY E. HUNTINGTON LIBRARY, San Marino, California

HN: Ptd. book 60363. Iohannes de Burgo, *Pupilla oculi* (Paris, 1510). Poem entered, c 1530, on a blank leaf at the end. ONE (6): 216, ptd. R. Hanna, PBSA 74 (1980), 257.

HN: Ptd. book 61866 (STC 14546). *A contemplacyon...of the shedynge of the blood of our lorde* (?1500). Poem entered in the early 16th century on sig. b4v. ONE (8): 1970.

HN: Ptd. book 69485 (STC 22615). Skelton, *Why come ye not to court* (1545?). Couplet entered in the mid-16th century on sig. D8v. ONE (2): 1428, ptd. Robert Kinsman and Theodore Yonge, *Skelton: Canon and Census* (1967), p. 75.

HN: Ptd. book 69798 (STC 24875). Caxton (?), tr. Jacobus de Voragine, *Legenda aurea* (1493). Extracts of poems entered in the first quarter of the 16th century on sig. gg4v. TWO (6): 1218, 1939.

HN: Ptd. book 82241 (STC 19767.3). Perottus, *Grammatica* (1512). Poem entered sig. A1v in the mid-16th century. ONE (16): 314, ptd. R. Hanna, PBSA 74 (1980), 258.

HN: EL 26.A.13. Composite volume, 133ff.; Middle English poems and extracts of poems (Chaucer, Lydgate, and others); part 3 (fols. 121–132) contains a poem transcribed after 1534. ONE (933): 195, ptd. H. N. MacCracken, *JEGP* 9 (1910), 226–64.

HN: EL 26.C.9. The Ellesmere Manuscript of *The Canterbury Tales*, 242ff., transcribed c 1410, with additions on blank leaves through the 15th and 16th centuries. Verses entered in the early 16th century on a preliminary leaf. Facsimile ed. Alix Egerton, 2 vols. (1911). TWO (5): 425, 1482. Both ptd. J. M. Manly & E. Rickert, *The Text of the Canterbury Tales*, 1 (1940), 152.

HN: EL 34.B.7. *Processionale*, with prayers in Latin and English, ii+86ff., early 16th century. Entire contents ed. J. W. Legg, *The Processional of the Nuns of Chester*, Bradshaw Soc., 18 (1899); TM 1239 ptd. Brown XV, #134. FIVE (225): 858, 1130, 1165, 1167, 1239.

HN: EL 34.B.60. Legal treatises in French and English, 132ff., c 1500; poems added on blank leaves with an indenture dated 1532. TWO (42): 670, 1185. Both ptd. Robbins *Sec.* #20, #26; TM 1185 ptd. Greene #456.1.

HN: HM 1. The Towneley Corpus Christi Cycle, 132ff., transcribed c 1480. Facsimile ed. A. C. Cawley and Martin Stevens (1976). The last pageant, "Suspencio Iude," entered in the early 16th century; ptd. James Raine, *The Towneley Mysteries*, Surtees Soc. (1836); ed. George England and A. W. Pollard, EETSes 71 (1897), 93–96. ONE (96): 90.

HN: HM 3. John Bale, *Kyng Iohn*, 35ff., partially holograph, c 1538, revised between 1546 and 1560. Facsimile ed. W. Bang, *Materialien* (1909); ed. J. P. Collier, Camden Soc. 2 (1838); ptd. J. H. P. Pafford, Malone Soc. 64 (1931); ed. Barry Adams (1969); ed. Peter Happé, *Complete Plays of John Bale* 1 (1985). One song in the text indexed separately. TWO (1,814; revised to 2,693): 1318, 1735.

HN: HM 58. English herbal and medical recipes, 95ff., 15th century; poem added in the early 16th century. ONE (8): 861, ptd. R. Hanna PBSA 74 (1980), 247–48.

HN: HM 121. "A mirroure of myserie...by Myles Huggarde," 24ff., copied in 1557. ONE (895): 174.

HN: HM 131. Scribble added c 1550; prose, but recorded as verse by R. Hanna, PBSA 74 (1980), 253.

HN: HM 136. *Brut* in English, 172ff., 15th century; ownership rhymes and moral tags entered on various leaves by Dorothy Helbartun in the early

16th century. TM 290, 1010, 1011, 1012 ptd. R. Hanna PBSA 74 (1980), 241, 249. TWELVE (37): 220, 248, 290, 373, 687, 929, 1010, 1011, 1012, 1659 (four copies), 1664, 1940.

HN: HM 140. Poems by Lydgate and others, 169ff., copied in the mid-15th century; ownership rhyme entered in the early 16th century. ONE (4): 1649, ptd. J. M. Manly and E. Rickert, *The Text of the Canterbury Tales* 1 (1940), 436.

HN: HM 183. Composite volume collected by Joseph Haslewood in the 19th century; papers from the 15th to the 18th centuries, with Haslewood's transcripts of earlier verse. Early Tudor transcripts on fols. 3v (early 16th century), 7–9 (c 1540), and 11v (on the blank side of an inventory dated 1552). THREE (266): 616 (ptd. R. H. Bowers, MLN 67 (1952), 332–3), 1583 (ptd. R. Kinsman, HLQ 42 (1979), 279–312), 1688.

HN: HM 502. Devotional treatises in English, 90ff., 15th century; proverbs in verse entered in the early 16th century. TWO (3): 540 (ptd. H. C. Schulz, *Ten Centuries of Manuscripts in the Huntington Library* (1962), p. 16), 546 (ptd. R. Hanna, PBSA 74 (1980) 256).

HN: HM 1087. *Horae*, 147ff., mid-15th century; presentation verse by "A W" entered in the early 16th century. ONE (4): 1009, ptd. H. C. Schulz, *Ten Centuries of Manuscripts in the Huntington Library* (1962), p. 6.

HN: ST 36. Account book of Peter Temple, 1541–1555. ONE (2): 1088, ptd. N. W. Alcock, *Warwickshire Grazier and London Skinner 1532–1555* (1981), p. 229.

L: BRITISH LIBRARY, London

L: Ptd. book 1379.a2(7) (STC 10987). Fitzherbert, *Offyce of Shyryffes* (1545). Poem entered in the mid-16th century. ONE (2): 267.

L: Ptd. book 6190.a18(1) (STC 10969). Fitzherbert, *The newe Boke of Iustices of the peas* (1538). Verses entered by James Colbrond in the mid-16th century. ONE (2): 1741.

L: Ptd. book C.15.c.7 (STC 24877). Jacobus de Voragine, *Legenda aurea* (1503). Poem entered in the mid-16th century. ONE (6): 1958.

L: Ptd. book C.18.e.1(48) (STC 14077c.99). Indulgence of Leo X (1520). Single sheet; poem entered on the verso in the mid-16th century. ONE (6): 829.

L: Ptd. book C.21.d.7 (STC 24762). Caxton, *Mirrour of the World* (1481). Entry dated 1520 on verso of the end flyleaf. ONE (34): 708, ptd. *Rel. Ant.* 1, 250–51.

L: Ptd. book C.24.a.3 (STC 2834). *The newe Testament* (1536). Entries on sig. A1v in the mid-16th century. TWO (10): 17, 153.

L: Ptd. book C.35.a.4 (STC 15985). *Prymer* (1534). Entry on sig. A8v in a mid-16th-century hand. ONE (2): 1715.

L: Ptd. book IA 2856(13). Pius II, *Dyalogus...contra bohemos* (c 1470). Entry on fols. 270v–71v before 1542. ONE (46): 10, ptd. C. Bühler, *JEGP* 58 (1959), 248–50, where the shelfmark is incorrectly identified as IA 3420.

L: Ptd. book IB 49408. Petrus Alliaco, *Meditationes circa...psalmos poenitentiales* (1480?). Entries on fol. 34v, c 1500; all ptd. C. Bühler, *ELN* 1 (1963), 81–84. THREE (25): 170, 400, 1956.

L: Ptd. book IB 49437. *Cordiale quattuor novissimorum* (before 1476). Entries on fol. 1, c 1500; all ptd. C. Bühler, *ELN* 1 (1963), 81–84. FOUR (14): 1622, 1779, 1954, 1957.

L: Ptd. book IB 55242 (STC 1536). *Bartholomaeus de proprietatibus*, trans. Trevisa (1495). Entry on fols. 477v–78v, early 16th-century. ONE (26): 1880, ptd. F. L. Utley, *PMLA* 60 (1945), 346–47.

L: Additional 5140. Chaucer, *The Canterbury Tales*, and Lydgate, *The Siege of Thebes* (imperfect at the end), ii + 422ff., copied between 1501 and 1503 for Henry Deane, Archbishop of Canterbury. TWO: (22,500): 1851, 1897.

L: Additional 5465. The Fayrfax Manuscript, ii+124ff., songbook compiled for Robert Fayrfax, written in a single hand 1501–1504; lyrics and musical settings for two or three voices by Gilbert Banastir (d. 1497), John Browne (d. 1498), William Cornysh (d. 1523), Richard Davy (d. 1516), Robert Fayrfax (d. 1529), Hamshere, William Newark (d. 1509), Sir Thomas Phelyppis, Sheryngham, Edmund Turges, Tutor, and unnamed composers. Texts ptd. Bernhard Fehr, *Archiv* 106 (1901), 48–70, and John Stevens, *Music and Poetry in the Early Tudor Court* (1961), pp. 351–85; see also Gustav Reese, *Music in the Renaissance* (1954), p. 768, n. 25, for other early prints. Nine carols ptd. or collated by Greene (#s 146A, 165, 263a, 264, 432–34, 436, 464). Words and music ed. Stevens, *Early Tudor Songs and Carols*, Musica Britannia 36, (1975). FORTY-EIGHT (847): 78, 79, 80, 81, 95, 100, 192, 232, 253, 256, 261, 293, 311, 327, 345, 626, 660, 662, 673, 750, 836, 887, 949, 954, 966, 987, 1013, 1075, 1117, 1133, 1216, 1232, 1378, 1423, 1431,

1452, 1457, 1492, 1493, 1514, 1652, 1724, 1730, 1733, 1789, 1814, 1952, 2038.

L: Additional 5665. The Ritson Manuscript, i+149ff., songbook transcribed in one main and several other hands, shortly before 1511. Thirty-eight pieces in Latin and one in French in addition to the English texts, with settings for two and three voices by T. B. (B. T.?), John Cornish, Sir William Hawte, J. Norman, W. P., Sir Thomas Packe, Henry Petyr, Richard Smert, Edmund Sturges (=Turges?), John Trouluffe, Henry VIII, and unnamed composers. English texts ptd. Bernhard Fehr, *Archiv* 106 (1901), 262–85; carols ptd. by Greene (indicated by "G" in the list below), and nineteen songs by John Stevens, *Music and Poetry in the Early Tudor Court* (1961), pp. 338–50 (indicated by Stevens's designation, "R" plus a number, in the list below). FIFTY-FIVE, with two poems entered twice (889 + 20): 3 (G 58), 15 (G 13), 34 (G 31c), 57 (R4), 135 (R14), 136 (R10), 244 (R3), 263 (G 186), 301 (G 59), 352 (G 109), 354 (G 6), 394 (R9), 454, (G 118), 469 (G 277), 488 (G 387), 588 (G 111), 591 (R19), 604 (G 337c), 643 (R1), 647 (G 306), 651 (G 259), 803 (G 99), 812 (R15), 853 (G 435), 857 (two copies, G 91A–B), 974 (G 359B), 996 (G 85), 1040 (R11), 1076 (R2), 1101 (R8), 1111 (G 14c), 1118 (G 354), 1129 (G 96), 1131 (R6), 1138 (G 2), 1157 (G 307), 1222 (G 1), 1274 (G 89), 1302 (G 116), 1312 (R12), 1437 (R13), 1503 (G 133), 1505 (R16), 1536 (R5), 1538 (G 348), 1676 (G 367), 1689 (R7), 1727 (G 57), 1753 (two copies, G103Ad–e), 1785 (R18), 1864 (G 110), 1875 (G 131a), 1877 (G 330), 1933 (G 375), 2401 (R20).

L: Additional 5947. *Terrae et possess[iones] Ric[ardi] Southwell Militis*, 76ff., compiled 1545–1546; poem added in a different but contemporary hand on the final leaf. ONE (3): 607.

L: Additional 10,303. (BMP 121) "The death of Blaunche the Dutchesse of Lancaster...written by that honorable Englyshe Poet Geoffrey Chaucer Esquier", i.e., Anon., *The Isle of Ladies*, 9ff., copied after 1550. Collated in the editions cited for the text in LONG: Longleat 256. ONE (2,237): 1860.

L: Additional 10,336. *Tractatus de arte musicae*, transcribed by Iohannes Tucke, 1500; ownership verse entered by William Tucke, early 16th century. ONE (4): 1660, ptd. *Rel. Ant.* 2, 164.

L: Additional 14,997. (BMP 274) Collection of Welsh poems, Latin grammar rules, etc., 115ff., late 15th through the early 16th centuries. THREE (52): 826 (ptd. Robbins, *Sec.* #60), 1105 (ptd. Greene #10; K. Hammerle, *Archiv* 166 (1935), 203), 1292 (ptd. Hammerle, p, 204).

L: Additional 15,233. John Redford, "the play of wyt & science," imperfect at the beginning, and fragments of two other interludes, probably also by Redford, Master of the Choristers at St. Paul's, with 35 songs by him and his associates; 65ff., transcribed in three hands between 1554 and 1558. Entire contents ed. J. O. Halliwell, *The Moral Play of Wit and Science and Early Poetical Miscellanies*, Shakespeare Soc. 37 (1848); dramatic pieces and three songs assigned to *Wit and Science* ed. Arthur Brown, Malone Soc. 87 (1951). THIRTY-EIGHT (2,868): 75, 92, 127, 241, 257, 289, 324, 392, 408, 592, 728, 740, 816, 831, 885, 920, 924, 972, 989, 998, 1038, 1172, 1191, 1266, 1285, 1358, 1397, 1542, 1620, 1657, 1798, 1809, 1862, 1918, 1924, 1925, 1953, 1962.

L: Additional 17,492. The Devonshire Manuscript, 124ff., transcribed in several hands between 1532 and c 1539, with one poem entered c 1562. Miscellany of verse by Wyatt and other members of the court of Henry VIII; includes extracts from Chaucer and other Middle English verse (see Ethel Seaton, *RES* 7 (1956), 55–56), copied from STC 5068, Chaucer's *Workes* (1532). Descriptions of and conjectures on the compilation of the MS are by G. F. Nott, *Poems of Wyatt* (1816); E. A. Bond, *Athenaeum*, 27 May 1874, 654–55; Agnes K. Foxwell, *A Study of Sir Thomas Wyatt's Poems* (1911), pp. 125–35; Foxwell, *The Poems of Sir Thomas Wiat*, 2 (1913), 241–46; Raymond Southall in *RES* n.s. 15 (1964), 142–50, and *The Courtly Maker* (1964), pp. 15–25; Richard Harrier, *The Canon of Sir Thomas Wyatt's Poetry* (1975), pp. 23–54. Poems from the MS, most of them unattributed, have been regularly printed in editions of Wyatt since those of Nott and Foxwell: Kenneth Muir (1950), sixty-five poems on pp. 91–155; Muir and Patricia Thomson (1969), fifty-five on pp. 189–236; Joost Daalder (1975), thirty-three on pp. 145–82. Most of those not printed in Wyatt editions were ptd. by Muir, "Unpublished Poems in the Devonshire Manuscript," *Proc. of the Leeds Philosophical Soc.* 6 (1947), 253–82. In the list below, "M" with a number indicates the printing in Muir's edition of 1950; "U" with a number indicates the printing in Muir's "Unpublished Poems." For poems appearing also in D: TCD 160 and L: Egerton 2711, collations of variants are found in the Muir and Thomson edition of Wyatt and in Harrier, *Canon*. ONE HUNDRED SIXTY-FOUR (3,974). 55 (M 161), 83 (M 150), 85, 104 (M 112), 105 (10), 108, 117, 118 (M 133), 123 (U 5), 161 (U 20), 164 (M 113), 175 (U 18), 217 (M 104), 218, 254, 272 (M 132), 279 (U 3), 304, 325, 339 (U 43, 44, 48), 342 (M 166), 350, 357 (M 145), 370 (M 159), 376, 399 (U 34), 401 (M 108), 402, 418 (M 116), 428, 431 (M 130), 434 (M 149), 453 (M 124), 465 (M 144), 471, 501 (M 152), 517 (U 46, 47), 526 (M 151), 532, 569 (M 217), 570, 618 (M 160), 624 (M 167), 629 (U 38), 640, 648, 663 (M 106), 669 (U 12), 682 (U 16), 713, 717, 724, 732 (U 22), 735 (U 36), 742 (M 136), 763, 766 (M 119), 783 (U 35), 824 (M 111), 843 (M 121), 877 (M 142), 897, 914 (M 126), 915 (U 28.9–16), 926 (M 155), 948 (M 156), 962 (M 141), 991, 994 (U 4), 995 (M 138), 1002 (U 39), 1005, 1006 (U 33), 1034 (U 1), 1039, 1042 (U 37), 1046, 1056 (M 127), 1059 (M 153), 1061, 1063, 1067, 1078 (M 148, Greene #467), 1079, 1081, (M 103), 1090 (M 123),

1110 (U 7), 1112 (M129), 1093 (M 158), 1114 (U 42), 1160, 1205 (M 131), 1296, 1313 (M 162), 1314, 1315 (M 118), 1316, 1322 (M 134), 1362, 1389 (U 45), 1400, 1407 (M 125), 1409 (M 128), 1413, 1415 (M 137), 1432, 1439 (M 122), 1446 (U 27), 1447, 1449 (M 117), 1459 (M 147), 1465, 1468 (M 107), 1479 (M 102), 1483 (M 154), 1491 (M 114), 1510 (U 14, 31, 50–54), 1523 (M 135), 1532 (M 109), 1543 (M 140), 1546 (M 120), 1554, 1561 (M 146), 1580 (U 41), 1586 (M 115), 1595 (U 34) 1607, 1632 (U 17), 1636, 1644, 1668 (U 24), 1684 (U 49), 1686, 1700, 1725 (U 15), 1731, 1734 (U 40), 1739 (U 21), 1743 (M 164), 1744 (U 32), 1745 (M 216), 1748 (M 139), 1761 (M 105), 1762, 1765 (U 13), 1768 (U 30), 1794, 1816, 1819 (U 23), 1824 (M 110), 1827 (U 19), 1829, 1831 (M 143), 1836 (U 9), 1866 (U 28.1–8), 1901 (M 163), 1937, 1938 (U 11), 1989 (M 165), 1995 (U 29), 2008 (M 157), 2010 (U 8), 2025, 2039 (U 2).

L: Additional 17,802–05. (BMP 381, 382) Four part-books of masses and motets by English composers, copied in the 1550's. The only items in English are an incipit and a title. ONE (1): 243.

L: Additional 18,752. Prose and verse from the 14th through the 16th centuries in Latin and English, 216ff. Early Tudor verse transcribed (not contiguously) by several hands in the 1530's; all except TM 163 ptd. E. B. Reed, *Anglia* 33 (1910), 344–62. TWENTY-EIGHT (788): 163, 355, 418, 683, 721, 883, 952, 1027, 1029, 1044, 1045, 1049, 1054, 1102, 1174, 1241, 1261, 1307, 1308, 1320, 1324, 1396, 1448, 1487, 1501, 1740, 1808, 1898.

L: Additional 20,059. *Registrum brevium cancellariae*, 14th century; English religious verse, 15th century; poems on fol. 2 in two early 16th-century hands. SIX (12): 544, 786, 1489, 1515, 1529, 1965.

L: Additional 22,718. Anthony Woodville, trans. *The Dicts or Sayings of the Philosophers*, copied from Caxton's 2d edn. (STC 6828, c 1480); entries in early 16th-century hands. FOUR (27): 491, 542, 670, 1975. TM 491 ptd. C. Bühler, *The Library*, 4th ser., 15 (1934), 318.

L: Additional 23,971. Thomas Audley, ["An Introduction or ABC to the warre"], mid-16th century, 40ff.; verse epitaph on Audley added in a contemporary hand. ONE (46): 1850.

L: Additional 24,663. Prophecies in English and Latin verse and prose, compiled in the 1550's. SEVEN (381): 43, 810, 1203, 1429, 1509, 1857, 1907.

L: Additional 24,844. Legal precedents, pardons, grants in English and Latin, 108ff., compiled by various hands before 1547; poem inserted on a single folded sheet in the second quarter of the 16th century. ONE (72): 781.

L: Additional 25,001. Law cases and precedents; 227+ff., compiled 1535–1579. ONE (22): 1979.

L: Additional 29,729. (BMP 433) "dan [John] Lidgate monke of Burye his Woork written by [John] stow And a translation [not extant] of Virgils Aneyd dedicated to prince Arthur." Stow's collection of poems by Lydgate and his contemporaries, 288ff., transcribed by him and others; colophon: "...wryten in the yere of owr lord 1558." Fols. 132–179 were copied from "an owld booke...wrytten by Iohn sherlye," identifiable as C2: 600. The text of TM 1728 was copied from O: Fairfax 16. Other sources cited by Stow are "mr stantons booke" and "mr blomfelds book." Seven poems printed from this MS in H. N. MacCracken's edition of Lydgate's *Minor Poems*: TM 258, 1235, 1253, 1435 in EETSes 107 (1911), 290, 209, 297, 159; TM 1387, 1630, 1996 in EETS 192 (1934), 800, 809, 724; other Lydgate texts are collated. TM 1080 and 1255 ptd. Hammond, *Chaucer–Surrey*, pp. 189–90, 196–97. TM 1311 ptd. M. Förster, *Archiv* 101 (1898), 50–51; TM 1485 ptd. A. S. G. Edwards, ELN 8 (1970), 89–92; TM 1548 ptd. Robert Spindler, *The Court of Sapience* (1927); TM 1728 collated in the ed. of E. Sieper, EETSes 84 (1901). FIFTY-THREE (19,421): 99, 121, 223, 235, 252, 258, 302, 332, 331, 375, 429, 445, 510, 556, 726, 767, 773, 818, 890, 912, 1007, 1016, 1017, 1018, 1019, 1080, 1132, 1164, 1212, 1235, 1253, 1255, 1294, 1311, 1380, 1387, 1435, 1485, 1494, 1548, 1568, 1621, 1623, 1630, 1654, 1656, 1677, 1718, 1728, 1788, 1851, 1996, 2005.

L: Additional 30,513. English keyboard music compiled by Thomas Mulliner, 129+iiiff., c 1550; 120 pieces, of which 24 are English songs (two of Elizabethan date) with only their incipits given. Ed. Denis Stevens, *The Mulliner Book*, Musica Britannica no. 1 (1951). TWENTY-TWO (22): 181, 347, 415, 657, 686, 768, 894, 895, 1036, 1160, 1187, 1242, 1256, 1284, 1412, 1500, 1563, 1614, 1853, 1865, 1891, 1963.

L: Additional 30,981. "A boke of certen chosen psalmes [plus Ecclesiastes chapt. 1 and the *Gloria patri*] translated into ynglyshe meter by Iohn Croke esquyer my father when he was one of the six Clarkes of Chauncery," 78ff., transcribed between 1522 and 1529; title added by Thomas Croke. Ptd. P. Bliss, Percy Soc. 11 (1844). FIFTEEN (868): 130, 273, 378, 470, 559, 563, 611, 866, 935, 940, 943, 1000, 1179, 1329, 1562.

L: Additional 31,922. The Henry VIII Manuscript, 129ff., a collection of 109 vocal and instrumental pieces; English songs have settings for three or four voices by Henry VIII, Kempe, Doctor Cooper, William Cornysh, T. Faredynge (= Farthyng), Wyllyam Daggere, Rysbye, J. Fluyd (= Lloyd), Pygott, and unnamed composers. Probably compiled some time after 1513 by Sir Henry Guilford, Controller of the King's Household. Words ptd. E.

Flügel, *Anglia* 12 (1889), 226–56, and John Stevens, *Music and Poetry in the Early Tudor Court* (1961), pp. 388–425; words and music ed. Stevens, *Music at the Court of Henry VIII*, Musica Britannia 18 (1962). Five carols ptd. by Greene are marked "G" plus a number in the list below. FIFTY-SEVEN (838): 42, 50, 63, 64, 65, 76, 84, 86, 88, 110, 138, 154, 210 (G 448), 344, 349, 367, 403, 518 (G 465), 594 (two copies), 595, 665, 667, 721, 729, 776, 838, 886, 964, 965, 1051, 1057, 1070, 1074, 1092, 1103, 1218, 1312 (G 437), 1335, 1452, 1455, 1545 (G 463), 1570, 1599, 1602, 1666, 1707, 1708, 1774, 1929 (G 466), 1931, 1976, 1977, 1978, 2009, 2014, 2037.

L: Additional 33,974. Meditations and prayers in verse and prose by Francis Stacy, 78ff. (damaged, resulting in much illegibility); transcribed c 1550 perhaps by Stacy himself. FIFTY-TWO (2,743): 51, 53, 54, 149, 228, 260, 270, 319, 330, 423, 443, 481, 562, 633, 636, 705, 706, 755, 772, 819, 820, 1023, 1024, 1096, 1099, 1127, 1136, 1168, 1169, 1175, 1213, 1250, 1267, 1353, 1388, 1530, 1541, 1560, 1571, 1575, 1613, 1695, 1697, 1818, 1852, 1863.5, 1948, 1959, 1966, 1967, 1980, 2017.

L: Additional 34,791. William Forrest, *Ioseph the chaiste*, dedicated to William [Parr] Earle of Eastsex, 116ff., transcribed between 1543 and 1547. ONE (6,694): 1351.

L: Additional 35,179. Legal material in Latin, 91ff., early 14th century; verse entry on a flyleaf, second quarter of the 16th century. ONE (3): 575, ptd. British Museum, *Catalogue of Additions 1894–1899* (1901), p. 202.

L: Additional 35,290. The York Corpus Christi Cycle, 1430–1440, 254ff.; additions by the scribe John Clerke in 1558, and one couplet in a different 16th-century hand. FOUR (586): 60, 128, 917, 918. All ptd. Lucy Toulmin Smith, *York Plays* (1885), 18–21, 433–47, 37–38, xv resp.

L: Additional 38,666. *Stanzaic Life of Christ* and the *Dialogue between a Clerk and a Husbandman*, 189ff., copied in the mid-15th century; one entry in a hand before 1550. ONE (12): 661, ptd. J. Boffey, NQ 226 (1981), 21.

L: Additional 40,732. (BMP 539) "The buike of King allexander the conqueroure," iv+282ff., transcribed in the mid-16th century in Scotland, with later 16th-century entries. TWO (18,002): 1488, 1961.

L: Additional 41,503. Formulary of ecclesiastical deeds, etc., i+185ff., from diocese of Bath and Wells, 15th century, with additions from 1490 through 1519; poem added in the early 16th century. ONE (5): 493.

L: Additional 45,102. Composite volume, 15th through 19th centuries; single sheet, art. S(1), transcribed shortly after 1513. ONE (42): 1233, ptd. C. Wright, BMQ 12 (1938), 13–18.

L: Additional 48,031. Lydgate, *The Serpent of Division*, iv+208ff., 15th century; verse additions in the mid-16th century. TWO (28): 913, 2001.

L: Additional 57,335. Peter Idley, *Instructions to his son*, 94ff., transcribed in the early 16th century with three unique sections (indexed separately) added. FOUR (6,464): 789, 1276, 1552, 1606.

L: Additional 60,577. English, French, and Latin prose and verse, including vocal and keyboard music; 226ff., the earlier portion in a single hand of the late 15th century, the rest in several hands from the early 16th century through the third quarter of the 16th century. Middle English and early Tudor verse, some with musical settings, entered 1549–1558. Facsimile ed. Edward Wilson, *The Winchester Anthology* (1981). TM 189, 1292, 1576, 1781 ptd. Sotheby Sale Catal., 19 June 1979, #57. TM 16, 438, 1232, 1438, 1493, 1984 ptd. Wilson, *NQ* 225 (1980), 293–95. TM 1369 ptd. Wilson, *Middle English Studies Presented to Norman Davis*, ed. Douglas Gray & E. G. Stanley (1983), pp. 137–42. FIFTY (2,826): 16, 28, 157, 189, 255, 312, 328, 358, 438, 463, 478, 538, 596, 632, 672, 703, 727, 753, 845, 873, 890, 899, 903, 944, 980, 988, 1190, 1232, 1237, 1288, 1292, 1357, 1369, 1373, 1438, 1456, 1493, 1567, 1568, 1576, 1767, 1781, 1807, 1832, 1874, 1876, 1916, 1984, 1999, 2030.

L: Arundel 26. Historical collection of 15th- and 16th-century material, 75ff., compiled by Sir William Dethecke, early 16th century. TWO (49): 605, 840. TM 605 ptd. H. N. MacCracken, *PMLA* 26, 179–80.

L: Arundel 285. Scottish religious poetry and prose, 224ff., transcribed in one or more hands, c 1540; illustrated with woodcuts from printed books pasted in. Ed. J. A. W. Bennett, *STS*, 3d ser., 23 (1955); TM 509, 515, 523, 1817 also ptd. Brown XV, #s 22, 21, 102, 94. TWENTY (4,866): 144, 326, 508, 509, 514, 515, 523, 675, 851, 855, 1164, 1178, 1214, 1234, 1476, 1650, 1693, 1757, 1758, 1817.

L: Cotton Cleopatra C.iv. (BMP 793) Composite volume, 220ff.; historical, political, and religious prose in Latin and English, Latin verse, English poetry in several hands in different fascicles from the early to mid-16th century. TM 830 ptd. Joseph Ritson, *Ancient Songs* (1829) 1, 94–105, Child, *Ballads* 6, 295, and Robbins, *Hist*, #26; TM 1462 and 1888 ptd. Thomas Wright, *Political Poems and Songs* 2 (1861), 125–27, 249; TM 1462 ptd. Charles Kingsford, *Chronicles of London* (1905), pp. 120–22; TM 1773 ptd. H. N. McCracken, EETS 192 (1937), 630–48; TM 1903 ptd. Helen Sandison, *The Chanson d'Aventure in Middle English* (1913), pp. 123–26. EIGHT (1,009): 387, 690, 830, 1203, 1462, 1773, 1888, 1903.

L: Cotton Julius A.v. French verse and prose, one English poem on Scottish Wars, 184ff., copied in the later 14th century; one entry in an early 16th-century hand. ONE (56): 197.

L: Cotton Nero C.xi. (BMP 997) Robert Fabyan, *Chronicles of England and France*, Part II, 255ff., transcribed after 1506. TWENTY-NINE (577): 148, 308, 442, 583, 716, 892, 910, 913, 923, 971, 1121, 1228, 1264, 1265, 1323, 1507, 1522, 1544, 1569, 1579, 1642, 1672, 1773, 1841, 1890, 1905, 1934, 1971, 2007.

L: Cotton Titus A.xxiv. Composite volume of papers from the 15th, 16th, and 17th centuries. Twelve poems on fols. 79–87v in a single mid-16th-century hand; five poems on fols. 91v–99v in different mid-16th-century hands. TM 1033, 1134, 1186, 1777, 1919 ptd. Leicester Bradner, *The Life and Poems of Richard Edwards* (1927), pp. 102–09; TM 26 ptd. Norman Ault, *Elizabethan Lyrics* (1925), pp. 30–31. SEVENTEEN (473): 26, 176, 658, 876, 1033, 1036, 1134, 1186, 1231, 1461, 1610, 1777, 1900, 1919, 1920, 1941, 1945.

L: Cotton Titus D.xi. (BMP A179) Miscellaneous prose of the 15th century, 56ff.; final two originally blank leaves have an early 16th-century entry of music and incipits for three songs (one in Latin). TWO (2): 318, 1349.

L: Cotton Titus D.xii. (BMP 180) Religious and historical prose in French and Latin, 93ff., 15th century; addition in the mid-16th century on the final leaf. ONE (4): 1778, ptd. *Rel. Ant.* 1, 205.

L: Cotton Vespasian A.xxv. Parts of several manuscripts bound together, 205ff., dating from the mid-15th century to c 1578, including 56 items of 15th- and 16th-century English verse, some with musical settings. Ptd. K. Böddeker, *Jahrbuch für romanische und englische Sprache und Literatur* 2 (1875), 3 (1876), superseded by Peter Seng, *Tudor Songs and Ballads from MS Cotton Vespasian A–25* (1978). Early Tudor copies of verse are on fols. 37v–40v (four poems, c 1555) and 125–26v (two poems, c 1525); TM 196 and 1434 ptd. *Rel. Ant.* 1, 238–40, all ptd. Seng, pp. 1–7. SIX (145): 72, 196, 410, 880, 1434, 1849.

L: Cotton Vespasian E.vii. (BMP A291) Latin historical treatises and prophesies, 135ff., 15th century; later entries between 1548 and 1552. TWO (6): 1539, 1906.

L: Cotton Vitellius A.xvi. "Cronicon regum Angliae et Series Maiorum... London... ad Annum primum Hen[rici] 8ui," 213ff., the latter portions copied shortly after 1509. Ed. Charles L. Kingsford, *Chronicles of London* (1905), pp. 152–163. TWO (434): 652, 922.

L: Cotton Vitellius C.xiii. (BMP A356) *Pilgrimage of the Life of Man*, 311ff., 15th century; early 16th-century additions at the end. TWO (9): 397, 951.

L: Cotton Vitellius E.x. (BMP A386) 242ff.; among papers of various dates from the late 15th to the late 16th centuries, damaged by fire, an imperfect copy of Skelton, *The Garland of Laurell*, transcribed in the second quarter of 16th century. ONE (245): 384, ptd. Hammond, *Chaucer–Surrey*, pp. 342–46.

L: Egerton 2402. G[eorge]. C[avendish]., *Life of Wolsey* (prose) and *Metrical Visions*, 154ff., transcribed and corrected by the author, 1556–1558. ONE (2,327): 793, ed. S. W. Singer, *Cavendish's Life of Cardinal Wolsey* 2 (1825), 1–172; ed. A. S. G. Edwards, *Metrical Visions by George Cavendish* (1980).

L: Egerton 2711. 110ff.; collection of 123 poems (one copied twice) entered before 1558, with 19 added in Elizabethan hands. Twenty-five poems and corrections in three others are in the hand of Sir Thomas Wyatt; one and some revisions of Wyatt poems are in the hand of Nicholas Grimald (c 1549); 73 of the pre-1558 entries are signed with a "TV" (or "VT") monogram, or "Tho" perhaps in Wyatt's hand, and 15 others are signed "Wyatt" in a later 16th-century hand. The manuscript was copied for and partly by Wyatt, some time before his death in 1542, as a collection of his own poems, and was evidently used by Grimald in preparing Wyatt's *Penitential Psalms* for the press in 1549 (STC 2726). The major source of Wyatt's poetry in the editions of G. F. Nott (1816), A. K. Foxwell (1913), Kenneth Muir (1950), Muir and Patricia Thomson (1969), Joost Daalder (1975), and R. A. Rebholz (1981). Pre-1558 poems ptd. literatim by E. Flügel, *Anglia* 18 (1896), 263–90, 455–516, and 19 (1897), 175–210, 413–50, and by Richard Harrier, *The Canon of Sir Thomas Wyatt's Poetry* (1975), though Harrier #109 is not in Wyatt's hand (see W. H. Siek, NQ 222 (1977), 496), and this transcription should be dated after 1558. ONE HUNDRED TWENTY-THREE (3,263): 39, 69, 73, 85, 101, 108, 116, 140, 155, 218, 246, 254, 292, 304, 325, 350, 376, 388, 402, 406, 428, 447, 450, 451, 471, 532, 565, 570, 574, 615, 640, 648, 655, 710, 713, 717, 724, 725, 741, 762 (two copies), 765, 842, 881, 896, 897, 900, 919, 933, 947, 959, 969, 991, 1004, 1005, 1022, 1037, 1039, 1046, 1061, 1063, 1081, 1158, 1159, 1177, 1184, 1262, 1263, 1275, 1296, 1314, 1316, 1339, 1340, 1362, 1370, 1376, 1400, 1413, 1432, 1444, 1447, 1464, 1465, 1477, 1496, 1512, 1525, 1554, 1555, 1586, 1607, 1636, 1637, 1644, 1671, 1675, 1686, 1700, 1702, 1711, 1731, 1749, 1762, 1783, 1794, 1799, 1816, 1828, 1829, 1830, 1840, 1843, 1854, 1855, 1926, 1937, 1947, 1968, 1973, 2027, 2025, 2035.

L: Egerton 2862. Seven English metrical romances, iv+148ff., c 1400. Marginal entries in the mid-16th century. ONE (2) 496, ptd. British Museum, *Catalogue of Additions 1906–10* (1912), p. 239.

L: Egerton 3002. Volume 25 of the Heath and Verney Papers, 161ff., 16th through 18th centuries. Poem on the verso of a single sheet of financial memoranda dated 1507. ONE (6): 812.

L: Egerton 3537. Thoresby Park papers, vol. 21; memorandum book of William Rayne, ii + 75ff., compiled 1552–1578; poems (one copied twice) among memoranda of rents and Latin exercises, c 1553–1554. FOUR (26 + 9): 4, 154, 1025, 1705.

L: Harley 43. Extracts from Burgh's *Cato Maior* and Walton's trans. of Boethius, *De consolatione*, 92ff., copied in the late 15th century; additions in two early 16th-century hands. TWO (175): 1547, 1825.

L: Harley 45. 15th-century English religious verse, 168ff.; ownership rhyme entered in the early 16th century. ONE (3): 552, ptd. *Rel. Ant.* 2, 163.

L: Harley 78. Composite volume of papers of various dates, 15th and 16th centuries, collected by John Stow, containing historical notes and poems. Poems of Wyatt and contemporaries on fols. 15–30v, transcribed in the mid-16th century; 15th-century verse transcribed on fols. 54–72 in different mid-16th century hands; the "Tale of the Prioress and her Suitors" copied in an early 16th-century hand on fols. 74ff. TM 696 ptd. Kenneth Muir, *Collected Poems of Wyatt* (1950), #218; TM 898 ptd. Ewald Flügel, *Neuenglisches Lesebuch* (1895), p. 389; TM 1117 ptd. B. Fehr, *Archiv* 106 (1901), 54, and J. Kreuzer, *RES* 14 (1938), 321–23; TM 1146 ptd. J. O. Halliwell, Percy Soc. 2 (1841), 107–17; TM 1605 ptd. F. Taylor, *Bull. of the John Rylands Library* 24 (1940), 376–77, 383ff.; TM 1722 ptd. Alexander Chalmers, *The English Poets* 2 (1810), 389, and Agnes Foxwell, *Poems of Wiat* 1 (1913), 363. TWENTY-SEVEN (1,969): 6, 115, 208, 224, 689, 697, 701, 898, 957, 1081, 1117, 1146, 1158, 1160, 1281, 1404, 1447, 1605, 1722, 1780, 1794, 1797, 1834, 1893, 1895, 1994, 2021.

L: Harley 116. Verse and prose by Lydgate, Hoccleve, and others, 170ff., copied in the late 15th century; gnomic verses added at the end in an early 16th-century hand. FIVE (24): 25, 533 (ptd. Greene, p. 420), 537 (ptd. *Rel. Ant.* 1, 316), 642 (ptd. Robbins, *Sec.* #81); 868 (ptd. *Rel. Ant.* 1, 316).

L: Harley 293. Historical collection of 16th- and 17th-century papers, some of the earlier material with notes by John Stow; one poem (art. 9, fol. 31) copied in the mid-16th century. ONE (49): 1321.

L: Harley 372. Poems of Lydgate and others copied in the 15th century, 114ff.; one poem added on the last leaf in the mid-16th century. ONE (64): 761.

L: Harley 424. Papers of John Foxe of various dates through the 16th century, 167ff. TWO (144): 950 (ptd. Edward Arber, *English Garner* 4, 72), 1195 (ptd. Furnivall, *Ballads* 1, 431).

L: Harley 559. Historical collections and prophecies in prose and verse, 68ff., compiled 1554. SEVENTEEN (610): 166, 387, 603, 757, 757, 810, 1028, 1203, 1317, 1403, 1589, 1845, 1847, 1858, 1888, 1907, 1981.

L: Harley 838. Heraldic and historical material, 121ff. One poem copied in the mid-16th century. ONE (973): 1537, ptd. James Gordon, *The Epistle of Othea to Hector* (1942).

L: Harley 984. (BMP A468) Wyclifite trans. of the Gospel of Matthew; one poem added in the early or mid-16th century. ONE (6): 377.

L: Harley 1197. Prose tracts in different hands of the 15th and 16th centuries; two poems added in the early to mid-16th century. TWO (38): 225, 620.

L: Harley 1304. Lydgate, *Life of Our Lady*, and didactic verse, 104ff., late 15th century; prose and verse added through the first half of the 16th century. THREE (63): 266, 1803, 1982.

L: Harley 1317. Digest of the laws of England in Latin and French, 101ff., copied in the 15th century; one carol added c 1500 and incipits of two songs entered in the early 16th century. THREE (24) 154, 963, 1787. TM 1787 ptd. Greene #462.

L: Harley 1587. Grammatical treatises and penmanship exercises, 15th century and second quarter of the 16th centuries. TWO (6): 344, 1998.

L: Harley 1717. Metrical chronicle of the dukes of Normandy in French, 252ff., 15th century; poems added in the early 16th century. TWO (76): 18, 1907.

L: Harley 2250. (BMP A484) Religious prose and verse, 108ff., late 15th century; one poem added in the early 16th century. ONE (8): 1117, ptd. Kreuzer, *RES* 14 (1938), 322.

L: Harley 2252. (BMP A485) 166ff.; *Ipomedon* and the stanzaic *Morte Arthur*, late 15th century, bound with a notebook of historical material and poems compiled by John Colyns, mercer of London; his entries are dated from 1517 to 1539. See L. Bessemann, G. Gilman, and V. Weinblatt, *NM* 71 (1970), 212–38, who print TM 1210, 1910, 2026 from this MS; Carol M. Meale, "The Compiler at Work...BL MS Harley 2252," in Derek Pearsall (ed.), *Manuscripts and Readers in Fifteenth-Century England* (1982), pp. 82–103; Meale, SB 35 (1982), 156–71. TM 484, 606, 748, 1094, 1425, 1682 ptd. Furnivall *Ballads* 1, 333–35, 338–39, 409–13, 158–66, 352–61; TM 551, 1206, 1442 ptd. *Rel. Ant.* 1, 316, 255, 258–59; TM 1026, 1206, 1442, 1698 ptd. Ewald Flügel, *Neuenglisches Lesebuch* (1895), pp. 139–40. Copies of TM 1065 and 1813 in this MS collated in the texts of *Speke Parrot* and *Colin Clout* ed. Dyce, *Skelton*, 2, 125, 1, 311–60, and ed. John Scattergood, *Complete English Poems of Skelton* (1983), pp. 230–78. Other prints are given in parentheses in the list below. TWENTY-NINE (2,520): 109 (ptd. Morfill, *Ballads* 2 (1873), 62–65), 152, 185 (ptd. J. O. Halliwell, *Palatine Anthology* (1850), p. 208), 221 (ptd. F. J. Furnivall, EETSes 8 (1869), 68–70), 420, 484, 536 (ptd. R. H. Bowers, *ELN* 1 (1964), 164), 551, 606, 714 (ptd. M. A. Denham, Percy Soc. 20 (1846), 69–70), 748, 869, 945 (ptd. Thomas Wright, Percy Soc. 4 (1841), 20), 1026, 1065, 1094, 1206 (ptd. Robbins, *Sec.* #137), 1209 (ptd. Robbins, *Studia Neophilologica* 26 (1954), 61–64), 1210, 1230, 1350, 1425, 1442, 1682, 1698, 1813, 1910, 1996, 2026.

L: Harley 2259. Treatises on heraldry, 15th century, 191ff.; poem added in the early 16th century. ONE (36): 573, ptd. F. J. Furnivall, NQ, 7th ser. 8 (1889), 22–23.

L: Harley 2320. Astrological poems of the 15th century, 74ff.; ownership verse added in the early 16th century. ONE (2): 1649.

L: Harley 2321. Principally Latin verse and prose, copied in the early 16th century, with additions in the later 16th. SIX (14): 21, 201, 1342, 1365, 1870, 1914. All ptd. *Rel. Ant.* 1, 207–08.

L: Harley 2341. *Calendarium* and other Latin prose, 215ff.; English poem entered c 1500. ONE (4): 1645, ptd. Robbins, *Sec.* #68.

L: Harley 2383. Religious tracts in Latin and English, 15th century; incipit of a song entered in the mid-16th century. ONE (1): 1990.

L: Harley 2407. Alchemical verse and prose in Latin and English, 111ff., compiled from the late 15th through the early 16th centuries. FOUR (157): 580, 1282, 1481, 1627. TM 580 ptd. Elias Ashmole, *Theatrum Chemicum* (1651), pp. 348–49; TM 1627 ptd. *Rel. Ant.* 1, 309.

L: Harley 3118. Sermons in Latin, 15th century; ownership verse added in the early 16th century. ONE (4): 1681, ptd. *Rel. Ant.* 2, 164.

L: Harley 3362. Grammatical and historical collections with some verse, 91ff., 15th century; additions in the early 16th century. THREE (24): 220, 1049, 1751. TM 1049 ptd. Joseph Ritson, *Ancient Songs* (1790), p. 114.

L: Harley 3444. Myles Huggarde, *Marie hath brought home christe agayne*, 24ff., author's presentation copy to Queen Mary (printed in 1554, STC 13560.5). ONE (921): 1032.

L: Harley 3725. (BMP A511) Latin chronicle and register of monasteries of Hayles and Abercoonwey, 81ff., 14th century; additions in early 16th-century hands. TWO (676): 826, 1517. TM 826 ptd. Robbins, *Sec.*, p. 229.

L: Harley 3835. *Horae beatae Mariae*, 14th century; verse added in the mid-16th century. ONE (4): 847, ptd. H. Littlehales, EETS 109 (1897), xlix.

L: Harley 4011. Lydgate, *Life of Our Lady*, *The Libel of English Policy*, and other English verse copied in the late 15th century; 189ff.; poems added in early 16th-century hands. TWO (128): 1007 (ptd. Brown XV #159), 1066 (ptd. J. Boffey, NQ 226 (1981), 20).

L: Harley 4012. Religious prose and verse, 153ff., copied c 1505 in several hands. FIVE (1,223): 256, 860, 1379, 1458, 1782. TM 256 and 1782 ptd. Brown XV #103, #104.

L: Harley 4294. *Sydrac and Boctus*, 82ff., copied in the late 15th century; last three leaves written in the early 16th century. FIVE (116): 981 (ptd. *Rel. Ant.* 1, 316), 1421 (ptd. Greene #343), 1524, 1753 (ptd. Greene #103B), 1760 (Greene #396).

L: Harley 4826. (BMP A523) Poems by Lydgate and Hoccleve, 146ff., late 15th century; poems added at the end in a mid-16th-century hand; one poem of Elizabethan date. TWO (86): 133, 1355. TM 1355 ptd. A. S. G. Edwards, ELN 11 (1973), 92.

L: Harley 5401. (BMP A530) Latin and English medical and culinary prose and verse, 207+ff., late 15th century; poems entered in the early 16th century. TWO (77): 420, 627.

L: Harley 6919. [William of Touris,] "Contemplacioun peccatorum," with six illustrations, 49ff., copied c 1550. ONE (1,560): 1650, ptd. J. A. W. Bennett, *STS*, 3d ser., 23 (1955), 65–169.

L: Harley 7332. Composite volume, 280ff.; one fragmentary leaf in a hand c 1500. ONE (60): 1398.

L: Harley 7578. Composite volume; second fascicle, fols. 2–20v, poems by Chaucer, Lydgate, and anonymous writers, copied in the early 16th century. TM 122 and 1269 ptd. W. W. Skeat, respectively in *Oxford Chaucer* 4 (1894), xxvii, and 2d ed. 4 (1924), xxix–xxxi; TM 126 ptd. F. J. Furnivall, *Supplementary Parallel Texts: Minor Poems*, Pt. 2, Chaucer Soc. (1880), pp. 29–31; TM 285 ptd. R. H. Robbins, *PQ* 35 (1956), 93–95, and R. H. Bowers, MLN 70 (1955), 397–98; TM 835 ptd. E. P. Hammond, MLN 19 (1904), 38; TM 1021 and 1451 ptd. *Rel. Ant.* 1, 227–28; TM 1326 ptd. Furnivall, *Odd Texts: Minor Poems*, Pt. 2, Chaucer Soc. (1880), pp. 252–60; TM 1451 and 1518 ptd. Furnivall, *Parallel Texts: Minor Poems*, Chaucer Soc. (1879), pp. 435–37. NINETEEN (1,612): 122, 126, 285, 556, 835, 967, 1021, 1269, 1326, 1451, 1518, 1568, 1601, 1612, 1678, 1729, 1833, 1904, 2020.

L: Lansdowne 210. Mainly extracts from English chronicles, 88ff., transcribed by William Smyth or his father John in Walden, Essex, 1553–1558. SEVEN (463): 452, 815, 984, 1426, 1490, 1661, 1662. TM 984 and 1490 ptd. *Rel. Ant.* 1, 251–52.

L: Lansdowne 379. Miscellaneous papers of the 16th and 17th centuries, 86ff.; two carols copied in the early 16th century . TWO (34): 29, 1928. Both ptd. Greene, #94, #43; TM 1928 ptd. Brown XV #82.

L: Lansdowne 762. Moral, religious, and historical verse, 99ff., copied 1524–1529, with one Elizabethan verse entry. Political prophecies TM 193 and 1810 ptd. J. A. H. Murray, EETS 61 (1875), 3–47, 52–61; fifteen shorter poems ptd. *Rel. Ant.* 1 (indicated by R plus a page number in the list below). Other printings given in parentheses. THIRTY-FOUR (2,105): 87, 146, 170 (ptd. R, p. 233, and F. J. Furnivall, EETS 32 (1868), 359), 191 (ptd. W. Skeat, EETS 30 (1867), 69–72), 193, 387, 400 (R, p. 233); 407 (R, p. 228), 441, 457 (R, p. 288), 499 (R, p. 275), 702 (R, p. 289), 767 (R, p. 260, and Brown XV #162), 800 (R, p. 287), 922 (R, pp. 205–07), 1203, 1271 (R, p. 288), 1283 (ptd. C. Bühler, *RES* 12 (1936), 237), 1305, 1535, 1553, 1615 (ptd. V. J. Scattergood, *Politics and Poetry in the Fifteenth Century* (1971), pp. 386–89), 1662, 1759 (R, p. 288), 1779 (R, p. 233), 1810, 1813 (ptd. Dyce, *Skelton* 1, 329), 1846, 1907, 1954 (R, p. 233), 1955 (R, p. 288), 1956 (R, p. 233), 1979, 1964 (R., p. 291).

L: Lansdowne 794. "The Image of Ipocrysy," 155ff., composed 1533. Ptd. Furnivall, *Ballads* 1, 181–296, and Dyce, *Skelton* 2, 413–47. ONE (2,576): 1791.

L: Lansdowne 858. Heraldic and historical material, 44ff., compiled in the 1520's. ONE (259): 2006.

L: Royal 7.C.ix. *Revelations* of St. Bridget in Latin, 193ff., 15th century; verses added in the second quarter of the 16th century. THREE (8): 813, 1386, 1746.

L: Royal 7.F.xiv. Composite volume; art. 6 (fols. 53–55), Edwarde Leibourne prest, "A declaracion of the xxti [21st] psalme of David resemblinge...our moost gracious kinge Henry," copied before 1547. ONE (147): 1405.

L: Royal 8.C.xii. Sermons of Jacobus de Voragine and Miracles of the Virgin in Latin, 158ff., early 15th century; verse added in the early 16th century. FIVE (59): 113, 396, 645, 698, 1917. TM 396 ptd. G. F. Warner & J. P. Gilson, *Catalogue of the...Royal and King's Collection* 1 (1921), 238; TM 645 ptd. Brown, *Register* 1, 212.

L: Royal 9.C.ii. *Decretales*, 147ff., 13th century; verses added in the hand of Thomas Lower after 1531. FIVE (19): 540, 818, 1710, 1892, 1932. TM 818 ptd. Brown XV #164; TM 1710 ptd. Brown *Register* 1, 362–63.

L: Royal 12.E.xvi. Treatises on the calendar, prognostications, etc., 186ff., 15th century; verses added in margins by Thomas Willes in the mid-16th century. THREE (8): 33, 47, 1750.

L: Royal 17.A.xvii. "Certaigne Psalmes or Songues of David Translated into Englishe meter by Sir Thomas Smith Knight then Prisoner in the Tower of London, with other prayers and Songues by him made to pas the tyme there. 1549," 27ff, transcribed after 1551. Ed. Bror Danielsson, *The Literary and Linguistic Works of Sir Thomas Smith*, Part 1 (1963). FOURTEEN (786): 275, 280, 360, 391, 564, 798, 799, 999, 1331, 1616, 1754, 1823, 1873, 1987.

L: Royal 17.A.xxi. "Certaigne Psalmes of Dauyd in Meeatre, added to maister Sterneholdes, and oothers, by William Forreste, 1551," 83ff. FIFTY-FIVE (3,306): 321, 498, 527, 528, 529, 566, 614, 796, 797, 817, 832, 867, 934, 937, 938, 939, 941, 1069, 1107, 1123, 1124, 1125, 1126, 1149, 1150, 1152, 1153, 1155, 1156, 1180, 1181, 1183, 1226, 1227, 1246, 1286, 1300, 1303, 1336, 1384, 1416, 1511, 1520, 1533, 1556, 1557, 1558, 1559, 1609, 1687, 1755, 1756, 1784, 1806, 2022.

L: Royal 17.A.xxxii. Astrological and medical treatises, 132ff., 15th century; additions in the early and mid-16th century. ONE (10): 808, ptd. R. H. Robbins, *MP* 36 (1939), 338.

L: Royal 17.B.xxxvii. Iohn mardeley, "A brefe declaracioun...," 36ff., 1558. ONE (937): 71.

L: Royal 17.C.vii. Iohn Hart, "The unreasonable writing of our inglish toung," 1551, 117ff. ONE (10): 409, ptd. Bror Danielsson, *John Hart's Works on English Orthography and Pronunciation*, Part 1 (1955), p. 111.

L: Royal 17.D.iii. William Forrest, "The pleasaunt poesye of princelie practise...muche parte collecte owte of a booke entiteled, The gouernaunce of noblemen, which...Aristotele wrote to discyple Alexandre [i.e., *Secreta secretorum*]," 1548; 78ff. Ed. M. A. Manzalaoui, *EETS* 276 (1977), 390–534. ONE (3,857): 211.

L: Royal 17.D.xiv. Works and letters of Sir Thomas More, 1534–1535, i+455ff, copied before 1550. TWO (14): 393, 925.

L: Royal 17.D.xx. Wyntoun's *Chronicle of Scotland* and other historical prose, i+312ff, copied in the late 15th century; ownership verses added by George Barclay and Patrick Barclay in the early and mid-16th century. TWO (24): 1419, 1648. Both ptd. G. F. Warner & J. P. Gilson, *Catalogue of the...Royal and King's Collection* 2 (1921), 257.

L: Royal 18.A.xv. "The exposition of the XXXVI Psalme of Dauid...by the great and excellent dyuyne Iohannes de Turrecremata [Torquemada]," trans. into English by Henry Parker, Lord Morley, before 1547; 9ff. ONE (15): 1299, ptd. E. Flügel, *Anglia* 13 (1891), 73–75, and Hammond, *Chaucer–Surrey*, p. 391.

L: Royal 18.A.lxiv. "...diuers and sundry verses as well in latin as in Englishe deuised and made partely by Jhon Leland and partely by Nicholas Vuedall [i.e., Udall]" for the coronation of Anne Boleyn (1533), 16ff, copied in the mid-16th century. Ptd. John Nichols, *Progresses of Queen Elizabeth* 1 (1788), ix–xx, and Furnivall, *Ballads* 1, 378–401. ONE (207): 1014.

L: Royal 18.B.xvii. *Pierce the Ploughman's Creed* and *Piers Plowman* (C-text), i+123ff, copied in the second quarter of the 16th century. TWO (7,855): 336, 753.

L: Royal 18.B.xxii. *The boke of noblesse*, i+45ff, copied c 1475; verses added in the early 16th century. TWO (6): 33, 522. Both ptd. G. F. Warner & J. P. Gilson, *Catalogue of the...Royal and King's Collection* 2 (1921), 275; TM 522 ptd. Robbins, *Sec.*, p. 256.

L: Royal 18.C.ix. Vol. 2 of an English translation of Polydore Vergil, *Anglica historia*, 81ff, copied in the 1540's; ed. Henry Ellis, Camden Soc. 36 (1846). TWO (4): 226, 2013. Both ptd. Ellis, pp. 20, 21.

L: Royal 18.D.ii. Miscellany of English poetry, i+212ff, compiled from c 1450 through c 1520. TM 168, first stanza of 313, 369, 385, 429, 545, 1341, 1360, 1547, 1596, 1909 ptd. E. Flügel, *Anglia* 14 (1892), 472–97; other printings given in parentheses. SIXTEEN (4,955): 168, 313 (see ALW: Alnwick 79), 369, 385, 429, 545, 678 (ptd. G. F. Warner & J. P. Gilson, *Catalogue of the...Royal and King's Collection* 2 (1921), 310), 693 (ptd. Dyce, *Skelton* 1, 6–14, and J. Scattergood, *Complete English Poems of Skelton* (1983), pp. 29–35), 801, 1164, 1341, 1360, 1547 (ptd. John Hollander, *Untuning of the Sky: Ideas of Music in English Poetry* (1961), pp. 433–36); 1596, 1883, 1909.

L: Royal 18.D.vi. Lydgate, *Troy Book*, 217ff, copied in the late 15th century; presentation verses to Henry VIII by Iohn [Touchet, baron] of Audelay added c 1512. ONE (105): 209.

L: Royal Appendix 56. Songbook, 32ff, compiled after 1508; incipits only to settings of English lyrics. FOUR (4): 20, 439, 497, 1003.

L. Royal Appendix 58. Songbook of liturgical, religious, and secular pieces, 60ff., begun after 1507, added to in the 1520's, and completed some time after 1547; full texts, single stanzas, or incipits with musical settings composed during the reign of Henry VIII. All but eight (TM 320, 497, 570, 712, 813, 958, 1312, 1399) ptd. E. Flügel, *Anglia* 12 (1889), 256–72; carols TM 872, 1411, 1673 ptd. Greene #458, #449, #150D. THIRTY-FOUR (520): 86, 134, 294, 320, 367, 424, 444, 497, 570, 712, 721, 790, 813, 872, 958, 1053, 1073, 1097, 1220, 1312, 1325, 1347, 1399, 1411, 1455, 1573, 1608, 1651, 1673, 1701, 1709, 1742, 1811, 1861.

L: Royal Appendix 74–76. Part-books for religious songs, 53, 36, 52ff, resp.; Tudor portion copied c 1547–48. NINE (396): 36 119, 612, 1182, 1192, 1332, 1333, 1534, 1891.

L: Sloane 96. Collection of medical recipes, 15th century; verse copied in the early 16th century. ONE (11): 494.

L: Sloane 747. (BMP A592) Register of Missenden Abbey, Buckinghamshire; verse added c 1501–1506. SEVEN (289): 28 (ptd. Brown, *Register* 1, 373), 170, 180, 561 (Brown, *Register* 1, 373), 851 (ptd. R. H. Robbins MP 36 (1938–39), 337–38), 1436 (ptd. Dyce, *Skelton* 2, 200–3), 1822 (ptd. Robbins, *Sec.* #65).

L: Sloane 1118. (BMP A621) Alchemical treatises in Latin, recipes in English; one English poem copied in the early 16th century. ONE (26): 524.

L: Sloane 1207. Miscellaneous prose and verse, 54ff, copied mainly in the mid-16th century. TM 911 and 1611 ptd. Furnivall, *Ballads* 1 435–37, 420–

25. ELEVEN (220): 129, 156, 306, 483, 774, 874, 911, 1280, 1377, 1611, 1732.

L: Sloane 1313. (BMP A628) Herbal, medical notes and treatises, 148ff, early 16th century. TWO (57): 1095, 1691.

L: Sloane 1584. Religious prose in English and Latin, medical recipes, legal forms, 96ff, compiled by John Gysborn, Canon of Coverham, 1520–1531. SIX (330): 167 (ptd. *Rel. Ant.* 1, 116), 467 (first stanza ptd. R. H. Robbins, SP 36 (1939), 471), 502 (ptd. *Rel. Ant.* 1, 70–73, and Robbins, *Sec.* #206), 1147, 1148, 1277 (ptd. Greene #446).

L: Sloane 1710. Historical and other tracts in several hands, from the early 16th through the 17th centuries. ONE (624): 517.

L: Sloane 1825. Hoccleve, *De regimene principium*, 15th century; additional verse entered at the beginning of the 16th century. FOUR (111): 556, 1257, 1287, 2036.

L: Sloane 1873. Norton, *Ordinal of Alchemy*, 85ff, copied in the early 16th century; additional entries in the later 16th century. ONE (2,994): 1752, collated in the edition of J. Reidy, EETS 272 (1975).

L: Sloane 2232. "The boke called Sydrac," i.e., *Sydrac and Boctus*, 117ff, subscribed "Explicit quod Robertus Wakefelde" and dated 4 May 1502; one short poem entered in a different early 16th-century hand. TWO (6,110): 997, 1084.

L: Sloane 2578. Collection of prophecies in prose and verse, 117ff, c 1557; see S. L. J. Jaech [Jansen], *Manuscripta* 29 (1985), 30–41. TM 193 ptd. J. H. A. Murray, EETS 61 (1875), 18–46); TM 1888 ptd. R. Haferkorn, *Beiträge zur englische Philologie* 19 (1932), 114–15. SEVENTEEN (964): 35, 62, 145, 193, 269, 303, 387, 723, 1359, 1540, 1591, 1604, 1857, 1881, 1888, 1896, 1907.

L: Sloane 3292. Composite volume of medical, practical, and religious material; art. 3, The Short Charter of Christ prefaced by 6 unique verses, early 16th century. Ptd. Caroline Spalding, *Middle English Charters of Christ* (1914), p. 1. TWO (38): 848, 1999.

L: Sloane 3501. "the book of hunttyng...cleped maistere of game," 55ff, 15th century; vellum flyleaf, second quarter of the 16th century, contains texts and incipits for English songs. TM 568 and 1058 ptd. B. Fehr, *Archiv* 107 (1901), 52–53. SEVEN (39): 107, 272, 568, 670, 1058, 1224, 2019.

L: Sloane 3809. Alchemical material, including Ripley's *Compend of Alchemy*, early 16th century. TWO (1,938): 577, 628.

L: Sloane 4031. Lydgate, *The Fall of Princes*, 190ff, copied in the late 15th century; later verse entered on a flyleaf (not part of the original MS) in the early 16th century. TWO (150): 1495 (ptd. Robbins, *Hist.* #97), 1907 (partially ptd. H. Bergen, EETSes 124 (1927), 59).

L: Stowe 38. Wycliffite "treatise compiled for a pore caitif," 161ff, 15th century; verse added on the first flyleaf in an early 16th-century hand. ONE (16): 970.

L: Stowe 389. Statutes from 1 Henry IV through 12 Henry VI, 125ff; at the end, lute tablatures for songs with incipits, entered in 1558 by Raphe Bowie. TWO (2): 712, 1041.

L: Stowe 850. Miscellaneous papers of the 15th and 16th centuries, 341ff; verse copied on the back of a certificate dated 2 Oct. 1522 (art. 8). ONE (11): 170.

L2: LAMBETH PALACE (London)

Entries according the numbering in M. R. James and Claude Jenkins, *Descriptive Catalogue of the Manuscripts in the Library of Lambeth Palace* (1930).

L2: Lambeth 117. Gavin Douglas, trans., "the buke of virgill writtin be the hand of Johanne mude with master thomas bellenden...2 feb xlv [i.e., 1545]." TWO (24,560): 879, 1497.

L2: Lambeth 159. Saints lives in Latin collected by Richard Stone at Canterbury, i+286ff, after 1507; three poems c 1535–1537; two poems on an event of 1556. TM 98 and 1245 partially ptd. James & Jenkins, *Cat.*, pp. 255–56; TM 1198 and 1804 ptd. Furnivall, *Ballads* 1, 281–89, 93–100. FIVE (814): 98, 1198, 1245, 1395, 1804.

L2: Lambeth 223. *South English Legendary*, i+297ff, late 14th-century; poem added in the early 16th century. ONE (2): 1876, ptd. Brown, *Register* 1, 432.

L2: Lambeth 259. "Brut" chronicle in prose, 132ff, 15th century; ownership verse and other poems added in the early 16th century. THREE (17): 359, 552, 2000. TM 359 and 552 ptd. James & Jenkins, *Cat.*, p. 405; TM 2000 ptd. R. H. Robbins, PQ 35 (1956), 92.

L2: Lambeth 265. Anthony Woodville, trans. *The Dictes and Sayings of the Philosophers*, 109ff, copied after 1477; verse epilogue added on the last leaf in the mid-16th century. ONE (14) 2034, ptd. C. Bühler, MLN 72 (1957), 5–6.

L2: Lambeth 491, Part II (fols. 295–329). Latin and English religious prose and verse, 15th century; poem added in an early 16th-century hand. ONE (4): 642.

L6: VICTORIA AND ALBERT MUSEUM, London

L6: Dyce 45. Collection of prose and verse, mainly Roman Catholic religious material; fols. 1–48 transcribed in the second quarter of the 16th century. TM 288 ptd. Dyce, *Skelton* 1, vii. THIRTEEN (889): 7, 233, 271, 288, 503, 692, 752, 771, 1385, 1472, 1629, 1653, 1988.

L8: CITY OF LONDON, GUILDHALL LIBRARY

L8: Guildhall 3035. Legal materials, 338ff, 16th century; poems entered in the early and mid-16th century. THREE (37): 449, 719, 1979.

L8: Guildhall 3313. [Robert Fabyan?], The "Great Chronicle" of London, copied shortly after 1512; ed. A. H. Thomas and I. D. Thornley, *The Great Chronicle of London* (London, 1938). NINE (1,667): 383, 652, 913, 922, 986, 1015, 1204, 1619, 1773.

L11: GREAT BRITAIN, PUBLIC RECORD OFFICE, London

Citations of *LP* are to *Letters and Papers, Foreign and Domestic, of the Reign of Henry VIII*, ed. J. S. Brewer et al., 21 vols. + addenda, 2d. ed. (1920–1932).

L11: E 36/228. Single folded sheet (fols. 7–8), autograph copy of John Skelton, congratulatory poem on the accession of Henry VIII, 1509. Ptd. Dyce, *Skelton* 1, ix–xi; John Scattergood, *Complete English Poems of Skelton* (1983), pp. 110–12; facsimile and transcript in P. J. Croft, *Autograph Poetry in the English Language* (1973) 1, 6–8. ONE (56): 1588.

L11: E 163/22/1. Document of 1457; carol with music on the verso, c 1530. Ptd. John Saltmarsh, *Antiquaries Journal* 15 (1935), 12–14; Robbins, *Sec.* #163; Greene #450.1. ONE (30): 1086.

L11: SP 1/115. Document of 2 February 1537. ONE (33): 19, six lines ptd. *LP* 12:1 (1890), 146.

L11: SP 1/121. Document of 1537. ONE (6): 1427, ptd. *LP* 12:2 (1891), 61.

L11: SP 1/220. Verse quoted in the examination of Richard Laynam, 9 June 1546. TWO (26): 249, 1771. Both ptd. *LP* 21:1 (1908), 513–14.

L11: SP 1/232. Political prophecies in verse, entered in 1520 on fol. 19. All ptd. Furnivall, *Ballads* 1, 316–18, and *LP Addenda* 1:1 (1929), 81–82. FIVE (71): 387, 1203, 1260, 1884, 1888.

L11: SP 1/244. Document of 1543. ONE (16): 1600, ptd. *LP Addenda* 1:2 (1932), 459–60.

L11: SP 1/246. Fols. 16–29v, partbook (bassus) with texts or incipits for English songs, mid-16th century; see Denis Stevens, *Music Survey* 2 (1950). Fol. 37, a verse prophecy in a document of 1546. Songs ptd. *LP Addenda* 1:2 (1932), 614–16, in modern spelling; TM 1484 ptd. Furnivall, *Ballads* 1, 319–20. TWENTY-THREE (131): 433, 589, 720, 743, 823, 865, 990, 1036, 1160, 1161, 1193, 1394, 1467, 1484, 1500, 1516, 1793, 1798, 1801, 1879, 1943, 1944, 2003.

L16: WELLCOME INSTITUTE FOR THE HISTORY OF MEDICINE, London

L16: 41. Latin and French prose, English historical material, 16ff, 15th century; verse added in 1502. ONE (4): 58, ptd. S. A. J. Moorat *Catalogue of Western Manuscripts...in the Wellcome Historical Medical Library* 1 (1962), 27.

L22: LINCOLN'S INN, London

L22: Hale 73. Historical material, 210ff, begun in the 15th century and continued through 1534 in the hand of William Wymondham. ONE (4): 1885, ptd. *Rel. Ant.* 1, 315.

L30: UNIVERSITY OF LONDON

L30: 278. Robert of Gloucester's *Chronicle,* 151ff, c 1440; verse added 14 Sept. 1516 on a preliminary leaf. ONE (34): 1350, ptd. J. H. Pafford, *Studies Presented to Hilary Jenkinson,* ed. J. C. Davies (1957), pp. 313–14.

L37: COLLEGE OF ARMS, London

L37: 1st M.13. Composite volume; fols. 27–74v contain a contemporary copy of "the note and tretise of the...receyt of the Ladie Kateryne...yoven in mariage gainct to Prince Arthure, son and heir unto...King Henry the vijth, in the xvij yere of his reign," i.e., 1502. Ed. Gordon Kipling, EETS 296 (1990). TWO (426): 652, 1582.

LINC: LINCOLN CATHEDRAL

LINC: Ptd. book RR.4.20 (STC 16106). *Hore beate Marie Virginis* (1536). Ownership verse entered c 1540 ONE (3): 1975, ptd. C. Wordsworth, *Horae Eboracenses*, Surtees Soc. 132 (1920), xvi.

LINC: 105. *Daretis historia Troiae* and medieval Latin poetry, 117ff, 13th and 14th centuries; English verse entered in early 16th-century hand. ONE (8): 1119, ptd. R. M. Wooley, *Catalogue of the Manuscripts of Lincoln Cathedral Chapter Library* (1927), p. 68.

LINC: 129. Poems of Lydgate, 89ff, 15th century; verse added at the end in the early 16th century. ONE (8): 1354, ptd. Wooley, *Catalogue*, p. 90.

LINC: 189. *Gesta romanorum* and other Latin prose, 138ff, 15th century; English rhyme copied twice in the early 16th century. ONE (2 + 2): 220, ptd. Wooley, *Catalogue*, p. 138

LONG: MARQUESS OF BATH, LONGLEAT (Warminster, Wilts.)

LONG: Longleat 29. Miscellany of English verse, compiled from the mid- to late-15th century; one verse addition in the mid-16th century. ONE (32): 1475.

LONG: Longleat 53. Prose chronicle of London through the reign of Henry VI; verse entered at the end in the early 16th century. ONE (156): 1773, ptd. Ralph Flenley, *Six Town Chronicles* (1911), pp. 99–101.

LONG: Longleat 96. Hector Boece, *The Chroniklis of Scotland*, translated by John Bellenden, copied before 1544. ONE (200): 1690.

LONG: Longleat 252A. "Virgill...twelf bukes of Eneados compilit by...gawin douglas," copied "be me henry aytoun notare publict and endit 22 Nov. 1547". TWO (24,560): 878, 1497.

LONG: Longleat 254. Lydgate, *The Fall of Princes*, 185ff, 15th century; poem added in the early 16th century ONE (7): 338, ptd. Henry Bergen, EETSes 124 (1927), 19.

LONG: Longleat 256. "The Temple of glasse Compilid by Geoffray Chaucer," an attribution in a later hand of Anon., *The Isle of Ladies*, transcribed c 1550; the same hand added a final couplet to the envoy. Ed. Jane B. Sherzer, *The Ile of Ladies* (1903); ed. Anthony Jenkins, *The Isle of Ladies or the Isle of Pleasaunce* (1980). ONE (2,237): 1860.

LONG: Longleat 258. Poems by Chaucer, Lydgate, and others, 147ff, transcribed in the first quarter of the 16th century, with additions of Elizabethan date; see E. P. Hammond, *MLN* 20 (1905), 77–79. Probably served as printer's copy for *The Assembly of Ladies*, *Annelida and Arcite*, *The Complaint of Mars*, and the envoy of *La Belle Dame sans Merci* in STC 5068, Chaucer's *Workes* (1532); see J. E. Blodgett, *The Library*, 6th ser., 1 (1979), 102–04. TM 466, 1551, and 1684 ptd. F. J. Furnivall, *Supplementary Parrallel Texts of Chaucer's Minor Poems*, part 2, Chaucer Soc. (1880), pp. 143–52, 1–26, 39–46; other printings given in parentheses in the list that follows. NINE (4,816): 426 (collated by J. Schick, EETSes 60 (1891)), 466, 517, 785 (collated by Derek Pearsall, *The Floure and the Leafe and the Assembly of Ladies* (1962), 153–71), 791 (ptd. E. P. Hammond, *Anglia* 34 (1911), 237–64), 1326 (ptd. Furnivall, *Odd Texts of Chaucer's Minor Poems*, part 2, Chaucer Soc. (1880) pp. 253–61), 1338 (ptd. Hammond, *Chaucer–Surrey*, pp. 104–110), 1551, 1684.

M: JOHN RYLANDS LIBRARY (Univ. Library of Manchester)

M: Rylands English 955, Part I. "The bible of pollicie," i.e., *The Libel of English Policy*, transcribed in the mid-16th century (27ff, imperfect copy); see F. Taylor, *Bulletin of the John Rylands Library* 24 (1940), 376–77, 387–88, 406–409. TWO (986): 472, 1605.

M2: CHETHAM LIBRARY, Manchester

M2: Chetham 6696 (Mun. A7.48). Gower, *Confessio Amantis*, copied with omissons (131ff, imperfect at the beginning), c 1540. ONE (33,700): 1279.

NLW: NATIONAL LIBRARY OF WALES, Aberystwyth

NLW: 734B (Plas Power 19). Georgius Rypla [Ripley], "the compownde off alkeny," transcribed before 1550. ONE (1,976): 577.

NLW: 369B (Hengwrt 178). Medical and religious prose in Latin and English, 15th century; early 16th-century additions. ONE (46): 654, ptd. John Simons, *ELN* 22 (1984), 1–5.

NLW: 3567B (Puleston 7). Chaucer, *Treatise on the Astrolabe*, transcribed by Iohn Edw[ards] in 1551. ONE (4): 1244.

NOR3: NORFOLK RECORD OFFICE, Norwich

NOR3: ANW 1/1. Norwich Archdeaconry Visitation Book, 1533–1551; poem entered on a visitation record of 1548. ONE (49): 1208, ptd. David Galloway, *REED* 1979:1, pp. 10–13.

NY: NEW YORK PUBLIC LIBRARY, New York City, N. Y.

NY: Drexel 4180–4185. Part-books of 17th-century songs whose bindings (except for 4182) preserve fragments of texts and settings of early Tudor songs copied in the second quarter of the 16th century. See John Stevens, *Music and Poetry in the Early Tudor Court* (1961), pp. 426–28. Some texts are reconstructed from other copies. TM 1869 ptd. F. W. Sternfeld, *Music in Shakespearean Tragedy* (1963), pp. 50–52. Drexel 4180, FIVE (66): 79, 337, 427, 836, 1352. Drexel 4181, ONE (2): 1720. Drexel 4183, TWO (15): 1452, 1724. Drexel 4184, THREE (43): 955, 1802, 1869. Drexel 4185, THREE (26): 548, 932, 1802.

O: BODLEIAN LIBRARY, Oxford

Manuscripts listed by shelfmarks; numbers in parentheses are those of F. Madan et al., *A Summary Catalogue of Western Manuscripts in the Bodleian Library*, 7 vols. (1897–1953).

O: Ptd book 8°.70.Th.Seld. (STC 16018). *Prymer* (1540?). Poems entered in a mid-16th century hand on sigs. 2L7v, 2L8v. FIVE (23): 461, 541, 623, 1328, 2018.

O: Ptd. book Arch. A.b.8 (10) (STC 15472). Indulgence of Pope Leo X (28 Aug. 1515). Single sheet, poem copied at the bottom of the text in the early 16th century. ONE (6): 487.

O: Ptd. book Arch. G.d.34 (STC 17958). Mirk, *Liber festivalis* (1486). Moral couplets entered in the hand of Thomas Myhell of Peterborough, early 16th century. THREE (6): 27, 540, 557.

O: Ptd. book Arch. G.e.39 (STC 15898). *Hore beate marie virginis* (1502). Poem entered on the back flyleaf early in the 16th century. ONE (10): 850.

O: Ptd. book Douce A.314 (STC 782). "Arnold's Chronicle" (1503?). Poem on the flyleaf in a 16th-century hand; two others in later hands. ONE (8): 1970.

O: Ptd. book Douce BB.200 (STC 15816). *Breviarium... ad vsum... ecclesie Sarisburiensis* (1519). Poem in a contemporary hand on sig. F4v. ONE (3): 953.

O: Ptd. book Douce L.645 (STC 15127). *Prognosticum Magistri Gasparis* (1529). Poem entered in a contemporary hand on fols. 2v–3. ONE (4): 1513.

O: Ptd. book Gough Missals 145 (STC 15925). *Hore beatissime virginis Marie* (1520). Verse entered in two early 16th-century hands. TWO (7): 1372, 1474.

O: Ptd. book Mason H169 (STC 16009). Hilsey, *Manual of Prayers* (1539). Poems entered on preliminary leaves in mid-16th century hand. TWO (8): 1001, 1736.

O: Ptd. book Vet. A1.e.127 (STC 15948). *Hore beatissime virginis Marie* (1526?). Poem in a contemparary hand entered on sig. Q3. ONE (4): 520.

O: Arch. Selden B.8 (3338). Composite volume; fols. 266–303v contain a collection of verse prophecies copied in the mid-16th century, with one poem entered later in a contemporary hand and one added in the later 16th century. TWENTY-SIX (1,272): 2, 5, 30, 31, 44, 52, 268, 387, 555, 621, 758, 795, 804, 806, 807, 870, 1498, 1521, 1577, 1603, 1635, 1858, 1863, 1882, 1908, 1911.

O: Arch. Selden B.10 (3356). 214ff, Harding's *Chronicle*, late 15th century; *The Proverbs of Lydgate*, partial text copied from STC 17027 (1520?). FIVE (624): 414, 556, 638, 1680, 1772.

O: Arch. Selden B.24 (3354). (BMP F980) *Troilus* and other poems by Chaucer, *The Kingis Quhair*, *The Cuckoo and the Nightingale*, and other pieces copied in Scotland in the last quarter of the 15th century; poems at the end of the MS entered in the mid-16th century. TWO (55): 1173 (ptd. Robbins, *Sec.* #196), 2043 (ptd. P. J. Frankis, *Anglia* 73 (1955), 301–02).

O: Ashmole 48 (6933). Verse miscellany compiled in 1557–58, with additions through c 1565; 141ff; see H. E. Rollins, *MLN* 34 (1919), 340–51. Seventy-seven poems, 41 of which were transcribed after 1558; entire manuscript ed. Thomas Wright, *Songs and Ballads...Chiefly of the Reign of Philip and Mary* (1860). THIRTY-SIX (3,583): 74, 75, 120, 141, 186, 187, 227, 229, 315, 333, 334, 650, 659, 700, 747, 752, 770, 1035, 1048, 1082, 1144, 1151, 1251, 1270, 1272, 1356, 1480, 1550, 1578, 1584, 1663, 1713, 1868, 1886, 1946, 2016. (TM 1713 + 1251 ptd. as one poem (#23) by Wright.)

O: Ashmole 176 (III). (BMP F998) Part III of a composite volume, fols. 97–101; a collection of poems (most composed in the 1520's) copied in the second quarter of the 16th century. TM 1349 ptd. *Rel. Ant.* 1, 258; others, except TM 64, 712, 882, 1505, and 1785, ptd. B. M. Wagner, *MLN* 50 (1935), 452–55. EIGHTEEN (360): 64, 68, 82, 102, 109, 635, 712, 749, 882, 946, 1050, 1248, 1309, 1349, 1383, 1505, 1714, 1785.

O: Ashmole 191 (IV) (6668). Fols. 191–211, a collection of songs with musical settings, early 16th century. Words and music ptd. *Early Bodleian Music*, ed. J. Stainer, 2 (1901), 66–74; all but TM 1122 ptd. Robbins, *Sec.*, #s 152–156. SIX (53): 94, 473, 961, 1122, 1171, 1721.

O: Ashmole 759 (6954, 7568–9). (BMP G8) Alchemical writings in Latin and English, ii+151ff, early 16th century. SEVEN (895): 212, 411, 1113, 1278, 1478, 1655, 1894.

O: Ashmole 1152 (7861). Legal writings, 292ff, 15th century; one poem added in the early 16th century. ONE (7): 2015, ptd. W. H. Black, *Catalogue of the Manuscripts... [of] Elias Ashmole* (1845), p. 1017.

O: Ashmole 1379 (7683). (BMP G14) Prose treatise on the herb rosemary and poems copied in the early 16th century, 19ff. TWO (204): 200, 1674. TM 1674 ptd. Greene #170.

O: Ashmole 1416 (7611). (BMP G22) Composite volume, 150+iff, mainly alchemical material, from the early 15th to the mid-16th centuries. THREE (142): 158, 871, 1278.

O: Ashmole 1438 (I) (7776). (BMP G26) Composite volume of medical tracts and recipes copied in the 15th century; one poem entered in Part I (86ff) in the early 16th century. ONE (6): 1634.

O: Ashmole 1448 (7627). Alchemical material, 288pp, 15th century; poem added in the early 16th century. ONE (4): 521.

O: Ashmole 1451 (II) (8343). Part II, 66ff, of a composite volume, alchemical tracts in English and Latin, compiled in the 1550's and the later 16th century. ONE (62): 628.

O: Ashmole 1479 (7731). Alchemical writings copied through the 1560's, 324ff; fragment of a song with music on a preliminary leaf, c 1550. ONE (7): 1391.

O: Ashmole 1486 (Ib [7727], III [7653]). Composite volume of alchemical material, 15th through early 17th centuries; parts Ib (ii+40ff) and III (75ff) contain verse entered in the early 16th century. FOUR (20): 158, 839, 1278, 1478.

O: Ashmole 1524 (VI) (8180). (BMP G42) Composite volume of 15th-century texts; Part VI, 11ff, Rolle, *The Form of Living*, with verse added in the early 16th century. TWO (58): 864, 1986.

O: Bodley 120 (27643). (BMP G69) Lydgate, *Life of Our Lady* and other poems, v+106ff, late 15th century; additions in an early 16th century hand. TWO (28): 264, 1098. TM 1098 ptd. Robbins, *Sec.* #202.

O: Bodley Rolls 1 (2974). Alchemical scroll copied in a single hand of the early 16th century; English material recopied in a later 16th-century hand. ONE (138): 1278.

O: Digby 133 (1734). Scientific prose, 16th and 17th centuries, and the Digby Mystery Plays: *The Conversion of St. Paul, Mary Magdalene, The Massacre of the Innocents and the Purification*, and *Wisdom*; transcribed, each play in a different hand, 1512 to c 1525, with one passage in the *Conversion* entered c 1550; iii+169+iiff. Facsimile, *The Digby Plays*, ed. Donald Baker & John Murphy, Leeds Texts and Monographs, Medieval Drama facsimiles 3 (1976). Ptd. Thomas Sharp, *Ancient Mysteries from the Digby Manuscripts* (1835); ed. Baker, Murphy, & Louis Hall, EETS 283 (1982), 1–140. FOUR (4,124): 637, 744, 1364, 1670.

O: Digby 145 (1746). *Piers Plowman* (A- and C-Texts conflated) and proverbs in verse, 180ff, transcribed by Sir Adrian Fortescue, 1532–34. TWO (7,060): 753, 985. TM 985 ptd. Lord Clermont, *History of the Family of Fortescue* 2 (1869), 177–78.

O: Douce 54 (21628). (BMP G302) Latin verse, religious prose, and recipes, 86ff, transcribed in several hands from the late 15th through the early 16th centuries. TWO (24): 1471, 1979. TM 1979 ptd. Robbins, *Sec.* #74.

O: Douce 84 (21658). (BMP G307) Three 15th-century medical MSS, vi+55ff; couplet entered in the early 16th century by Iohan Crowe on a flyleaf. ONE (2): 921.

O: e Musaeo 52 (3510). (BMP G510) Medical, astrological, and practical prose in English, i+80ff, copied in the first quarter of the 16th century; poem entered as prose. ONE (80): 420.

O: e Musaeo 63 (3652). (BMP G513) Two manuscripts, the first, fols. 1–96, alchemical verse and prose, English and Latin, compiled in the early 16th century; Welsh verse in the second. SIX (4,941): 335, 577, 628, 1278, 1508, 1752.

O: e Musaeo 160 (3692). Collection of religious narrative, meditative, and dramatic verse, v+176+iiiff, compiled in 1520 or shortly after; see Donald Baker, John Murphy, & Louis Hall, EETS 283 (1982), lxxiv–lxxxiii.

Facsimile, *The Digby Plays*, ed. Baker and Hall, Leeds Texts and Monographs, Medieval Drama facsimiles 3 (1976). TM 38 and 1243 ptd. *Rel. Ant.*, 2, 124–61; ed. Baker, Murphy, & Hall, EETS 283 (1982), 141–93. TM 1418 ptd. M. C. Seymour, *Jnl. of the Australasian Universities Language and Literature Assn.* 21, 42–50. SIX (9,109): 38, 61 (last 43 vv. ptd. *Rel. Ant.* 2, 117–18), 507, 852, 1243, 1418.

O: English Poetry e.59. Autograph copy of Robertus Parkyn, "The Life of Christ," 191ff, copied 1548–1554; ONE (4,982): 247.

O: Greaves 60 (3832). (BMP G394) Notes on Latin poetry, and portions of the romance of *Alisaunder*, copied c 1551–1552 by Nicholas Grimald; see T. Turville-Petre, *ELR* 27 (1977), 180–86. ONE (1,247): 2029, ptd. W. W. Skeat, EETSes 1 (1867), 177–218.

O: Hatton 105 (4054). Lydgate, *Fall of Princes*, 166ff, 15th century, with poems added in the 1550's. TWO: 207, 482. Both ptd. H. Bergen, EETSes 124 (1927), 75; TM 482 ptd. Brown XV #56.

O: Latin misc. c.66. The Capesthorne Manuscript, 130ff, the collection of Humfrey Newton begun in the late 15th century, containing poems by him and others, entered c 1500; ptd. R. H. Robbins, *PMLA* 65 (1956), 249–81. TWENTY-THREE (1,053): 89, 245, 291, 298, 389, 390, 405, 430, 474, 475, 576, 677, 855, 1020, 1064, 1077, 1254, 1291, 1330, 1767, 1857, 1921, 1979.

O: Latin misc. e.85. Poem entered in an early 16th-century hand. ONE (53): 199, ptd. Robbins, *Hist.* #81.

O: Latin Th. d.15. Religious tracts and poems 157ff, copied by Robert Parkyn, curate of Adwick-le-Street, near Doncaster, 1551–1555; see A. G. Dickens, *EHR* 62 (1947), 58–83. FIVE (538): 420, 688, 979, 1163, 1992.

O: Lyell 16. Petrus Ruffensis, *Summula viciorum*, i+140ff, late 14th century; ownership verses entered in the mid-16th century by Iohn Bracke. TWO (8): 862, 1319.

O: Lyell 24. Liturgical material, ii+100ff, 15th century; early 16th-century entry on the last leaf. ONE (15): 256, ptd. Quaritch & Co., *Catalogue of Illuminated and Other Manuscripts* (1931), no. 66.

O: Rawlinson A.338 (11224). (BMP G702) English translations of Chartier, *Le Quadrilogue invective* and *Curial*, 111ff, 15th century; addition in an early 16th-century hand. ONE (4): 554, ptd. R. H. Robbins, *Manual of the Writings in Middle English*, ed. A. Hartung, 5 (1975), 1456.

O: Rawlinson C.86 (11951). (BMP G729) *The Northern Passion*, an English translation of the introduction to Higden's *Polychronicon*, and Middle English poetry, 189ff, transcribed in the late 15th century; verse entered on fol. 31 in an early 16th-century hand. Poems ptd. F. J. Furnivall, EETS 32 (1868, rpt. 1969), 332. SIX (19): 344, 416, 540, 837, 1792, 1821.

O: Rawlinson C.448 (12299). (BMP G739) Lydgate, *The Fall of Princes*, ii+183ff, 15th century; additional verse entered on the inside cover and flyleaves, after 1534. TWO (158): 1949 (ptd. H. Bergen, EETSes 124 (1927), 69), 1992.

O: Rawlinson C.813 (12653). (BMP G747) Fols. 1–98, a collection of secular poems (one in Latin) followed by political prophecies in verse and prose, compiled c 1520 through c 1535 by Humphrey Wellys of Staffordshire; see Edward Wilson, *RES* 41 (1990), 12–44, the edition of the entire manuscript by Sharon L. Jansen and Kathleen L. Jordan, *The Welles Anthology*, Medieval & Renaissance Texts & Studies 75 (1991), and, on the dating, Jansen, *Manuscripta* 25 (1981), 141–50. TM 1176 and 1716 ptd. J. O. Halliwell, *Nugae Poeticae* (1844), pp. 42–44; TM 1716 ptd. Child, *Ballads* 2, 478–9. Fragment of Skelton's *Why come ye not to court* (TM 1770) ptd. J. Zupitza, *Archiv* 85 (1890), 429–36; TM 322 ptd. Zupitza, *Archiv* 87 (1891), 433–35. All the lyrics ptd. F. M. Padelford and A. R. Banham, *Anglia* 31 (1908), 309–97, rpt. *Bulletin of the Univ. of Washington* 1 (1909), 1–89. Robbins, *Sec.*, prints TM 194 (#200), 404 (#204) 859 (#129), 1142 (#130), 1229 (#207). TM 1030 ptd. Robbins, *Hist.* #74. FIFTY-NINE (4,150): 32, 111, 114, 178, 194, 197, 219, 236, 322, 327, 382, 404, 417, 500, 571, 664, 666, 679, 751, 859, 878, 908, 1030, 1043, 1060, 1072, 1109, 1139, 1142, 1145, 1176, 1194, 1196, 1197, 1215, 1219, 1221, 1229, 1236, 1240, 1260, 1327, 1367, 1368, 1371, 1401, 1473, 1590, 1716, 1764, 1770, 1775, 1810, 1838, 1845, 1871, 1899, 2002, 2011. (TM 236, 1260, 1590, 1845 are printed as one long prophecy, #62, by Jansen and Jordan; their #61 was judged by Ringler to be prose.)

O: Rawlinson D.913 (13679). (BMP G767) Composite volume of papers from the 14th to the 16th centuries; fol. 5, poem, partially effaced, on the recto of a vellum leaf, copied before 1547. ONE (14): 1247, ptd. W. D. Macray, *Catal. Codicum Manuscriptorum Bibl. Bodleianae* 5:4 (1898), 137.

O: Rawlinson Poetry 36 (14530). Nine Middle English poems, iv+124ff, late 15th century; quatrain entered on the final leaf, c 1500. ONE (4): 711, ptd. Caroline Spurgeon, *Five Hundred Years of Chaucer Criticism and Allusion*, Chaucer Soc., 2d ser. 48 (1908), 65.

O: Tanner 110 (9936). (BMP H52) Composite volume, 246ff, of papers from the 14th to the 16th centuries; fols. 238–245 contain verse copied in the early 16th century. THREE (276): 1345, 1381, 1417. TM 1345 and 1417 ptd. H. N. MacCracken, EETSes 107 (1911), 284, 140.

O: Tanner 407 (10234). (BMP H337) Prose pieces, recipes, historical notes, and verse, 64ff, compiled by Robert Reynys of Acle (Norfolk), in the first quarter of the 16th century. TM 11 ptd. R. H. Robbins, *Anglia* 83 (1965), 44; TM 630 ptd. Robbins, *Sec.* #176; TM 909 and 1120 ptd. G. Colderhead, MP 14 (1916–17), 6–9; TM 1120 ptd. R. H. Robbins, ES 30 (1949), 134–35; TM 1166 and 1624 ptd. Brown XV #169, #177; TM 1420 ptd. R. W. Tryon, PMLA 38 (1923), 374–78; TM 1458 ptd. R. E. Parker, EETS 174 (1928), 110–26; TM 1694 ptd. Joseph Ritson, *Remarks on the Last Edition of Shakespeare* (1783), and I. Gollancz, *The Parlement of the Thre Ages* (1915), app. xiii; TM 1970 ptd. H. M. R. Murray, EETS 141 (1911), 37. TWENTY-THREE 1,023): 11, 368, 422, 630, 794, 871, 889, 909, 916, 942, 978, 1120; 1166, 1199, 1393, 1420, 1458, 1587, 1624, 1625, 1694, 1917, 1970.

O: Wood Empt. 2 (8590). "the Historye of Grysilde the seconde, onlye meanynge Queene Catharyne [of Aragon], . . . fynysched the 25 daye of Iune . . . , 1558, by . . . Syr Wyllyam fforrest, preeiste, propria manu," i+77ff. ONE (3,465): 204, ptd. W. D. Macray, Roxburghe Club 101 (1875).

O5: CORPUS CHRISTI COLLEGE, Oxford

O5: Ptd. book. Bartholomaeus Anglicus, *De proprietatibus rerum* (1488). Notes and verse in the hand of Richard Kaye, c 1550. TWO (114): 162, 622. TM 622 ptd. J. Milne & E. Sweeting, *MLR* 40 (1945), 87–89.

O5: Ptd. book ø.c.1.1.1. F. Griffolini, trans., *Epistolae Phalaris* (1485). Poem entered in the early 16th century on sig. M6v. ONE (7): 1202.

O5: 237. Religious prose and verse, principally saints' lives, 15th century; short verses added in an early 16th-century hand on preliminary leaves. TWO (7): 477 (ptd. R. H. Robbins, *MP* 36 (1939), 338), 551 (ptd. Robbins, *Sec.* #86).

O17: BALLIOL COLLEGE, Oxford

O17: Balliol 353. Collection of Welsh poetry and other material in Latin and Welsh, 159ff., compiled by Sir John Prise (Sion ap Rhys, d. 1555), c 1539–1550. ONE (20): 132.

O17: Balliol 354. "a boke of dyueris tales and balettes and dyueris Reconyngs etc.," collected by Richard Hill, grocer of London; contains English and Latin prose, verse, historical material, notations on Hill's family, etc. Entries were made chronologically from the front of the book to the back; fols. 7–178v, including most of the narrative verse and prose material, were copied 1503–04, the remainder between 1505 and 1536; nearly all the verse is copied in Hill's hand. See the description and bibliography in R. A. B. Mynors, *Catalogue of the Manuscripts of Balliol College Oxford* (1963), pp. 352–54. Twenty-five poems ptd. J. A. Froude, *Fraser's Magazine* 58 (1858), 127–44; twenty-six ptd. Ewald Flügel, *Neuenglisches Lesebuch* (1895), and 38 by the same in *Anglia* 26 (1903), 94–285. Roman Dyboski, *Songs and Carols*, EETSes 101 (1907), prints most of the shorter poems and gives (pp. xxxiv–lix) the fullest list of contents. The 77 carols are printed or collated by Greene ("G" plus number in parentheses in the list that follows). Not ptd. in Greene or Dyboski are TM 379 (Robbins, *Sec*, p. 253); TM 458 and 1433 (R. H. Robbins, *ELN* 1 (1963), 2); TM 489, 904, and 1504 (Flügel, *Anglia* 26 (1903), 105–32, 151–56, 100, resp.); TM 490 (H. Huscher, *Kölner Anglistische Arbeiten* 1 (1927)); TM 780 (collated by K. Brunner, EETS 191 (1933)). ONE HUNDRED SEVENTY-SIX (17,519): 1 (G 152), 9, 12, 13, 22 (G 408), 24 (G150C), 28, 45 (G 45), 48, 49 (G 79Ab), 150 (G 346), 170, 179 (G 77), 182, 183, 188 (G 234D), 190 (G 370B), 198, 205, 214 (G 424A), 215 (G 361), 237, 238, 240, 262, 267, 278 (G 162), 286, 307 (G 52), 316, 343, 359, 362, 377, 379, 395 (G 178), 407, 413, 421 (G 48), 437, 448 (G 240), 455 (G 238), 456 (G 237B), 458, 459 (G 230a), 460 (G 233), 462 (G 421), 467, 468, 489, 490, 506, 512, 520, 522 (G 175B), 530 (G 322A), 531, 534, 535, 539, 540, 543, 547, 550, 551, 553, 560, 578, 579 (G 141), 585, 601, 602 (G 136B), 609, 617, 634, 641, 649, 680 (G 471), 681, 684 (G 419Aa), 685 (G 241), 694 (G 166), 695 (G 350), 704 (G 413), 718 (G 351), 745 (G 372), 746, 754, 759 (G 21A), 764, 767, 780, 802 (G 27C), 809 (G 374), 811, 822 (G 50), 827 (G 420), 869, 874, 884 (G 11), 891 (G 120), 901, 902 (G 114D), 904, 905, 922, 930, 936, 976 (G 359A), 977, 982 (G 319), 983 (G 410), 992 (G 46), 993 (G 232C), 1031, 1089, 1106 (G 51), 1128, 1140, 1200 (G 373), 1252 (G 273), 1257, 1279, 1289, 1290 (G 321), 1304 (G 126), 1337 (G 355B), 1338, 1344 (G 187B), 1382, 1390, 1392, 1430 (G 153), 1433, 1440 (G 401 Aa), 1454, 1499, 1502 (G 132A), 1504, 1519, 1564 (G 331b), 1572, 1592 (G 78), 1594 (G 49), 1626 (G 123A), 1628 (G 122C), 1640 (G 20), 1646, 1647 (G 158), 1665 (G 35B), 1679, 1683 (G 105), 1705, 1717 (G 389b), 1719, 1726 (G 259), 1753 (G 103c), 1766, 1786 (G 183), 1796 (G 386b), 1800, 1848, 1872, 1875 (G 131b), 1880 (G 402b), 1889 (G 100), 1902 (G 163a), 1912, 1913, 1935, 1936, 1974, 1979, 1997, 1998, 2023.

O23: OXFORD CATHEDRAL (Christ Church)

O23: Allestree Fragments. Single leaf, c 1555. ONE (35): 1470.

PEN: UNIVERSITY OF PENNSYLVANIA, Philadelphia

PEN: Latin 35. Latin sermons by John Felton, 182ff, mid-15th century; poem entered on a front flyleaf in the early 16th century; see J. Morford,

Library Chronicle of the Friends of the University of Pennsylvania Library 25 (1959), 80–83. ONE (18): 656, ptd. Greene #468.1.

PFOR: CARL H. PFORZHEIMER LIBRARY, New York City

PFOR: 40A. [Nicholas Udall?], "A mery entrelude entitled Respublica made in... 1553," 28ff, copied shortly after 1553. Facsimile ed. John S. Farmer, *Tudor Facsimile Texts* (1908); ptd. J. P. Collier, *Illustrations of Old English Literature* 1 (1866); ed. W. W. Greg, *EETS* 226 (1952). Incipits to four songs indexed separately. FIVE (2,068): 282, 412, 590, 593, 1566.

PML: PIERPONT MORGAN LIBRARY, New York City

PML: Ptd. book 691 (STC 4853). *The book callid Caton*, tr. Caxton (1483?). Poem added on the flyleaf in the mid-16th century. ONE (7): 599, ptd. C. Bühler, *Renaissance News* 8 (1955), 10.

PML: Ptd. book 698 (STC 21429). Caxton, *Book named Ryal* (1488?). Poem entered by Thomas Archer in the early 16th century on sig. b2v. ONE (10): 1298.

PML: Ptd. book 775 (STC 3199). Boethius, *De consolacione philosophiae* (1478?). Poem entered before 1550 on the last leaf. ONE (8): 956, ptd. C. Bühler, MLN 53 (1938), 246.

PML: Ptd. book 776 (STC 24762). Caxton, *Myrrour of the worlde* (1481). Poem entered on MS leaves inserted at the end of the book, c 1540. ONE (8): 1469, ptd. C. Bühler, *Isis* 33 (1942), 614.

PML: Ptd. book Checklist 1787 (STC 25853). *Lyf of saynt Wenefryde* (1485). Poem entered on first flyleaf, c 1540. ONE (48): 1225, ptd. C. Bühler, *Anglia* 72 (1954), 420–21.

PML: Glazier MS 39 (on deposit). Illustrated prayer roll in Latin and English, written by "Percevall," canon of Coverham (Yorkshire), c 1500. ONE (20): 1091 ptd. W. H. Legge, *The Reliquary & Illustrated Archaeologist* 10 (1904), 111–12; C. Bühler, *Speculum* 39 (1964), 278.

PML: M 527. "The Cronikillis of Scotland compylit be ... hector boece And translatit ... by ... Iohane Bellantyne [i.e., Bellenden]," 315ff, transcribed between 1531 and 1536. ONE (200): 1690.

PML: MA 717. Two leaves formerly bound with STC 5758, Caxton, *Cordyale* [1479]; poem entered c 1501–09. Facsimile ed. Klynkenberg,

Cahoon, and Ryskamp, *Morgan Library British Literary Manuscripts*, ser. 1 (1981), no. 10. ONE (56): 922, ptd. C. Bühler, RES 13 (1937), 8–9.

PN: PRINCETON UNIVERSITY LIBRARY, Princeton, New Jersey

PN: Ptd. book Robert H. Taylor Collection, Inc. B 741. *Boetius de disciplina scholarium* (1496). Manuscript gathering contains liturgical matter in Latin, notes, and two poems entered by Ioannes Symson in the second quarter of the 16th century. TWO (80): 256, 1325. Both ptd. W. deG. Birch, *Athenaeum*, 29 Nov. 1873, p. 6.

R: RIPON MINSTER

R: Ptd. book, Gerson, *De consolatione theologie* (Cologne, 1488) bound with other books. Poems with musical settings entered on blank leaves in the second quarter of the sixteenth century. TWO (44): 295, 769. Both ptd. J. T. Fowler, *Yorkshire Archaeological Jnl.* 2 (1873), 396–97.

SHIP: SHIPTON-UNDER-WYCHWOOD, Oxfordshire

SHIP: Cadaver tomb, 1548, memorial of Elizabeth Thame. ONE (12): 1667, ptd. P. M. King, NQ 226 (1981), 496.

STALB: ST ALBANS CATHEDRAL

STALB: Wooden tablet with three epitaphs dated 1547, 1613, 1619. ONE (12): 581.

STU: UNIVERSITY OF ST ANDREWS, Scotland

STU: T.T.66. Wyntoun's *Chronicle of Scotland*, transcribed before 1550 (imperfect at the beginning). ONE (29,000): 203.

TEX: HUMANITIES RESEARCH CENTER, UNIVERSITY OF TEXAS, Austin

TEX: Ptd. book Stark +6451 (STC 5068). Chaucer, *Workes* (1532). Eight leaves containing the *Plowman's Prologue* and *Tale* inserted after The Parson's Tale, copied in the early 16th century; see A. S. Irvine, *Univ. of Texas Studies in English* 12 (1932), 27–56. TWO (1379): 40, 1581.

THORN: THORNHILL CHURCH, Wakefield, Yorkshire

THORN: Funeral monument of a member of the Savile family, erected 1537. ONE (2): 277, ptd. Thomas Hearne, *Guilielmi Neubrigensis Historia* (1719), p. 763.

TOK2: TOSHIYUKI TAKAMIYA, Tokyo

TOK2: Takamiya 6 (formerly Helmingham Hall LJ.I.10). Hardyng's *Chronicle*, vi+181ff, late 15th century; poems on three added leaves copied with notes of events in the 1530's. TWO (216): 284, 476. Both ptd. Brown Rel XV, #109, #118; TM 476 ptd. Greene #95b.

WADDE: WADDESDON, Buckinghamshire

WADDE: Cadaver tomb in Waddesdon Church; memorial of Hugh Brystowe, 1548. ONE (16): 1450, ptd. P. M. King, NQ 226 (1981), 496.

Y: YALE UNIVERSITY, New Haven, Connecticut

Y: Beinecke 337. Three works by Anthony Ascham, 106ff, copied c 1527: "a boke off astronomy," a calendar for 1524–35, and (in verse) "The complaynt off Sanct Cipriane the grett nigromancer." ONE (91): 1211, ptd. Fred C. Robinson, RES, n.s., 27 (1976), 261–65.

Y: Osborn music 13. The Braye Lute Book, 57ff., compiled after 1553 (the latest datable text is on the death of Edward VI); lute tablatures by R.C., T.C., R. K., and T.W. for twenty-nine full or partial texts and nine giving incipits only (one duplicated). TM 1527 ptd. J. Osborn, *Times* (London), 17 Nov. 1958, p. 11, and Peter Seng, *Vocal Songs in the Plays of Shakespeare* (1967), pp. 62–63. THIRTY-SEVEN (1,284): 142, 184, 202, 251, 305, 435, 436, 613, 668, 712, 730, 734, 784, 813, 846, 893, 919, 1047, 1062, 1100, 1154, 1189, 1322, 1348, 1363, 1463, 1527, 1531, 1597, 1643, 1699, 1747, 1769, 1837, 1887, 1985, 2033.

YORK: YORK MINSTER

YORK: Funeral monument of Thomas Dalby, Archdeacon of Richmond, died 26 Jan. 1525/6. Poem given under a Latin epitaph. ONE (4): 1007, ptd. A. F. Leach, Surtees Soc. 108 (1903), xcv.

YORK2: YORKSHIRE MUSEUM

YORK2: Sykes MS (property of the Yorkshire Philosophical Soc.). York Scriveners' play, The Incredulity of Thomas, 4ff, copied in the second quarter of the sixteenth century. Ptd. *History and Antiquities of the City of York* (1785), 2, 128–32; ed. A. C. Cawley, *Leeds Studies in English and Kindred Languages* 7–8 (1952), 45–80. ONE (196): 625.

First-line Index of English Verse in Manuscript, 1501–1558

A (exclamation). Alphabetized as Ah.

A< > upon astrawe. See TM 196.

A. A. [anno?] 1550 2 and 1. See TM 43.

TM 1 A babe is born, to blys us brynge.
O17: Balliol 354, 1505–36, f. 225v. 46: 2 burd. (aa) + 11 x 4 aaab8 (burd. Now synge we with angelis). BR 22, comp. a 1475. Rel., carol, lullaby, Virgin Mary, Jesus.

TM 2 A blacke cowe of a true lyne agayne shall Ryse.
O: Arch. Seld. B.8, mid 16, f. 294. 49: 12 x 4 abab5*. Prophecy.

TM 3 A childe ys born of a mayde.
L: Add. 5665, bef. 1511, ff. 34v–5. "De nativitate," music by Smert. 10: 2 burd aa + 2 x 4 abab4* (burd. Nascitur ex virgine). BR (31). Rel., carol, nativity.

A cok sum tyme with fetherem frech & gay. First fable in TM 1696.

TM 4 A cumly reson now have rede.
L: Egerton 3537, c 1553, f. 3. 12: 3 x 4 abab4*. Moral, manners.

TM 5 A dead man shall ryse which was buryed in syght.
O: Arch. Seld. B.8, mid 16, f. 275r–v. "The Prophecy of Marlian"; cf. TM 555 on f.271v. 28: abab4* + irreg. Prophecy.

TM 6 A doble wyll in the begane | When Adam fyrst deserved blame.
L: Harley 78, mid 16, f. 30. "Answer" (to TM 701). 2: aa8. Moral.

TM 7 A dreadfull payn to mie ys broghte.
L6: Dyce 45, 2/4 16, ff. 16v–17. 38: aabb8. Rel., prayer.

TM 8 A face that shuld content me wonders well.
D: TCD 160, 1535–48, f. 72. 8: abababcc10. TP 11. Women, description.

TM 9 A fastyng bely | may never be mery.
O17: Balliol 354, 1505–36, f. 200. Tr. "Jeiunus venter..." 2:aa2*. BR (33.9). Proverb.

TM 10 A for Alyn Mallson that was armyde in a matt.
L: Ptd. book IA 2856(13), bef. 1542, ff. 270v–71v. "Explicit the crosse rowe." 46: aa4*. BR (0.1). ABC, humorous.

TM 11 A fryer an heyward a fox and a fulmer sittyng on a rewe | a tapster hym sittyng by to fylle the cumpany the best is ascrewe.
O: Tanner 407, 1/4 16, f. 52. 2: aa5*. BR (35.5). Humorous.

TM 12 A good beginning | makith a good endinge.
O17: Balliol 354, 1505–36, f. 191v. 2: aa2*. BR 37.5, comp. a 1500. Proverb.

TM 13 A good scoler yf thou wilt be | Arise erly and worship the trinite.
O17: Balliol 354, 1505–36, f. 200. 22 rhymed proverbs among 55 otherwise unrhymed, with Latin originals; tr. "Surge sub aurora ..." 44: aa4*. BR (39.5). Proverb, moral .

TM 14 A Jake Juggelar that guggyll with a cake | Etying up fleche blode bonse i besh[r]ew your pate.
C13: Clare MS 13, c 1500, f. 36v. 2: aa4*. BR (49). Humorous.

TM 15 A kynges sone and an emperoure.
L: Add. 5665, bef. 1511, ff. 39v–40. "De Nativitate," with music. 21: 5 burd abbbb + 4 x 4 aaaR4* (burd. Proface welcome wellcome; ref. ...proface). BR (54.5). Rel., carol, nativity.

TM 16 A lady bryght fayre and gay.
L: Add. 60577, 1549–58, f. 115v. 8: aaabcccb4*. Song, love.

TM 17 A lady gawe me a gyfte she had not.
L: Ptd. book C.24.a.3, mid 16, sig. A1v. [Wyatt.] 8: mono4*. TP 23. Love, riddle.

TM 18 A Lepard engandres of natyf kynd.
L: Harley 1717, early 16, f. 250. 4: abab4*. Prophecy.

TM 19 A litle boke was made in dede.
L11: PRO SP 1/115, 1537, f. 177. Quoted in a document dated 2 Feb. 1537. 33: aa4* and irreg. Prophecy, Thomas Cromwell.

TM 20 A litell god fayth yn all e[n]gland.
L: Royal App. 56, 1508+, f. 32. Incipit only, with music. Song.

TM 21 A little in the morninge nothing at noone | And a light supper doth make to live longe.
L: Harley 2321, early 16, f. 147. 2: aa4*. BR (63.8). Moral, proverb.

TM 22 A lytill tale I will you tell.
O17: Balliol 354, 1505–36, f. 249. 58: 2 burd. (aa) + 14 x 4 aaa3B2* (burd. Alas sayd the gudman thys ys an hevy lyf; ref. Att the townys end). BR (65). Carol, marriage, humorous.

TM 23 A lordes purpose and a ladyes thoghtt | In a yer schouyth full offtt.
G: Hunt. 230, early 16, f. 248. Fifth of nine proverbs entered by Rychard Wylloughbe. 2: aa4*. Moral.

TM 24 A lovely lady sat & songe.
O17: Balliol 354, 1505–36, f. 226r–v. (3 verses missing in 6th stanza; cf. TM 1673.) 73: 6 burd. (aabccb) + 7 x 10 abab8cc4b6dd4B8 (burd. This enders nyght (aabccb); ref. ...syng By by lully lulley). BR 3627, comp. a 1500. Lullaby, rel., Virgin Mary, carol.

TM 25 A man may a while nature be gile.
L: Harley 116, early 16, f. 170v. 6: aabccb4*. BR (68). Moral.

TM 26 A man may live thrise Nestors lyfe.
L: Cott. Titus A.24, 1550's, f. 80v. [Thomas] "Norton." 14: ababcdcd-efefgg8. TP 30. Satire, women.

TM 27 A man that will lyve in rest | must here & see & say the best.
O: Ptd. book Arch. G.d.34, early 16, sigs. k6, m5, q3v. Copied three times in the hand of Thomas Myhell of Peterborow. (Cf. TM 557.) 2: aa4*. Moral.

TM 28 A man without mercy mercy shall mysse | He shall have mercy that mercifull ys.
L: Sloane 747, bef. 1506, f. 58v. 2aa4*. L: Add. 60577, 1549–58, f. 91v. O17: Balliol 354, 1505–36, f. 213v. Variant first line "For man withowt mercy..." G: Hunt. 230, early 16, f. 248v. Last of nine proverbs entered by Rychard Wylloughbe. BR 77, comp. a 1500 (also appears as vv. 5–6 in TM 221). Moral, proverb.

TM 29 A mervelus thyng I hafe musyd in my mynde.
L: Lansd. 379, early 16, f. 38. 14: 2 burd + 3 x 4 abab4* (burd. Mirabilem misterium). BR (78). Rel., carol, nativity.

TM 30 A Mary be tyed at a banke.
O: Arch. Seld. B.8, mid 16, f. 277v. "An other [prophecy]." 4: abab3*.

A myghtie mars that marre mony a wight. Variant first line of TM 1203.

TM 31 A Moole shall come and overthrowe with her snowte.
O: Arch. Seld. B.8, mid 16, f. 275v. 6: aa4*. Prophecy.

A mornynges when I am callide to scole. Variant first line of TM 1292.

TM 32 A newe songe anewe | unto yow lovers blynde.
O: Rawl. C.813, 1520–35, f. 14v. 16: 4 x 4 abab3*. BR (79.5). Love, complaint.

TM 33 A nyce wyfe A backe dore | Makyth oftyn tymys a ryche man pore.
L: Royal 12.E.16, mid 16, f. 34v. Copied by Thomas Willes. 2: aa4*. L: Royal 18.B.22, 1554–58, f. 44v. BR 81.5, comp. c 1450; also appears as vv. 33–34 of TM 219. Women, satire, proverb.

TM 34 A patre unigenitus.
L: Add. 5665, bef. 1511, ff. 28v–9. "De nativitate," with music. 10: 2 burd ab + 2 x 4 aabB4* (burd. Now make we joye in this feste; ref. Veni Redemptor gencium). BR 18, comp. c 1450. Rel., carol, macaronic.

TM 35 A peace shalbe dissembled.
L: Sloane 2578, c 1557, f. 107. 30: aa3*. Prophecy.

TM 36 A saving helth victorious.
L: Royal App. 74–76, c 1548, ff. 14–15. "Benidictus," with music. 38:6 x 6ababcc4* + 2aa4*. Rel., hymn.

TM 37 A sobre maide asswrde of looke and mynde.
D: TCD 160, 1535–48, f. 70. 6: ababcc10. Moral.

TM 38 A soule that list to singe of love.
O: e Musaeo 160, 1520+, ff.140–56v. "this tretye or meditation off the buryalle of Criste and mowrnyng therat." 862: MT4*, RR4*, aa4*, aa4b3cc4b3*, and irreg. (ref. Remembre myn awn son that ye sowket my brest). BR (95). Rel., nar., Jesus, Virgin Mary, dramatic meditation.

TM 39 A spending hand that alway powreth owte.
L: Egerton 2711, bef. 1542, ff. 56–7v. [Wyatt.] 91: terza rima10. TP 47. Letter, satire, moral.

TM 40 A Sterne striffe ys stered newe.
TEX: Ptd. book Stark +6451, 1532+, ff. 1–8v. "[The plowman's] Tale" (omits line 1276). Included in BR 3448, composed in the early 15th century, except for vv. 205–28, which are early 16th; see A. N. Wawn, *Yearbook of Engl. Stud.* 2 (1972), 21–40. See TM 1581 for the Prologue. 1,327: 166 x 8 abababab4*. BR 95.7+, TP 47.5. Rel. controversy, dialogue, satire.

TM 41 A sufficyent salve foe eache disease.
DUR5: Cosin V.iii.9, c 1555, f. 83. 4: abab8. BR (95.8). Moral.

TM 42 A thorne hath percyd my hart ryght sore.
L: Add. 31922, 1513+, f. 108v–9v. With music. 11: 2 burd aa + 3 x 3 aaa4* (burd. What remedy what remedy). BR (98.5). Carol, love.

TM 43 A. A. 1550 2 and 1.
L: Add. 24663, 1550's, ff. 35v–6v. Preceded by title verse "To judge the trewthe as befor it hath been | So many judge of all that hear after shalbe seen." 48: aa4*. Prophecy.

TM 44 A trety of a peace there shalbe a tyme.
O: Arch. Seld. B.8, mid 16, f. 284r–v. "A prophecye." 79: aa2* + irreg.

A tr[u]sty frende ys hard to fynde. Lines 58–9 of TM 221; 7–8 of TM 219.

TM 45 A virgyn pure | this is full sure.
O17: Balliol 354, 1503–04, f. 178. 30: 2 burd. (aa) + 4 x 7 aa2b3aaa2C3* (burd. Now let us syng both more and lesse; ref. Deo Gracias). BR (103). Rel., carol, nativity.

TM 46 A voyce I have and yk a will to wayle.
D: TCD 160, 1535–48, ff. 101–03. Subscribed "G. B." [George Blage]. 140: 35 x 4 abab10. Rel., faith, protestant.

TM 47 A welde best a man may meyke | A womanes answere is never for to seke.
G: Hunt. 230, early 16, f. 248. Fourth of nine proverbs entered by Rychard Wylloughbe. 2: aa4*. L: Royal 12 E.16, mid 16, f. 34v. Variant copied by Thomas Willes: "A wyld beast a man may tame | A womans tunge will never be lame." BR 106.5. comp. a 1500. Proverb, moral, women, satire.

TM 48 A woman oftymes will do | that she is not bede to do.
O17: Balliol 354, 1505–36, f. 200v. Tr. "Femina prona..." 2: aa4*. BR (108.5). Proverb.

TM 49 A-bowt the feld they pypyd ryght.
O17: Balliol 354, 1505–36, f. 222. 22: 2 burd. (aa) + 5 x 4 aaa4B2* (burd. Tyrly tirlow tirly terlow, ref. Terly terlow). BR 112, comp. a 1500. Rel., carol, nativity.

TM 50 Aboffe all thynge | now lete us synge.
L: Add. 31922, 1513+, ff. 24v–5. With music by Ffaredynge (perhaps celebrating the birth of Prince Henry, 1511). 6: aa2b3aa2b3*. BR (112.5). Song, hist.

TM 51 Above al thinges have stedfast faythe of all good workes the grownde.
L: Add. 33974, c 1550, ff. 16v–7. (Francis Stacy), "The howse of Justyce by the letteres of the Alphabethe." 26: aa14. Rel., ABC, moral.

TM 52 Above all thynges Marlyan maketh mention.
O: Arch. Seld. B.8, mid 16, ff. 294v–5. 82: 21 x 4 abab5* and irreg. Prophecy.

TM 53 A bove all thinges pray first to god his grace to us to send.
L: Add. 33974, c 1550, f. 28r–v. (Francis Stacy), "An alphabeth to clym to Christe." 42: aa14. Rel., ABC.

TM 54 A bove all thynges remember thys.
L: Add. 33974, c 1550, f. 43v. (Francis Stacy), "A chrystyan Alphabethe." 24: aa4*. Rel., ABC.

TM 55 Absens absenting causeth me to complaine.
L: Add. 17492, 1532–39, f. 81v. 24: 6 x 4 abab4*. D: TCD 160, 1535–48, f. 59. Incipit only from table of contents. Love.

TM 56 Absence alas.
D: TCD 160, 1535–48, f. 64. 32: 4 x 8 aaabcccb2*. Love.

TM 57 Absens of you causeth me to sygh and complayne.
L: Add. 5665, bef. 1511, ff. 67v–8. With music. 7: RR5*. BR (113.5). Love, song.

TM 58 Accipe that longeth to the.
L16: Wellcome MS 41, 1502, f. 5. 4: aaaa3*. BR (113.8). Rel., macaronic.

Acompany with them that be oneste. Lines 72–75 of TM 221; 21–24 of TM 219.

TM 59 Accusyd thoo I be without desert.
D: TCD 160, 1535–48, f. 70. 12: ababababab cc10. TP 61. Love.

TM 60 Adam and Eve this is the place.
L: Add. 35290, 1558, ff. 13v–4v. Verses added to the York Adam and Eve play (BR 1273); line lacking after 44. 99: 10 x 10 aa4b3cc4bdbdb3*. Rel. drama.

TM 61 Adame prince of all mankind.
O: e. Mus. 160, 1520+, ff.1v–108v. History of the world from Adam to 1518, with digressions and prayers to Old Testament heroes and Christian saints; prose prologue. 6,000: abab4* linked. BR (119). Nar., world hist., rel., prayer.

TM 62 Adam spake to seathe his sonne.
L: Sloane 2578, c 1557, f. 108r–v. 60: aa4*. Prophecy.

TM 63 Adew adew le company.
L: Add. 31922, 1513+, f. 74v. With music; celebrates birth of Henry VIII's first son, Prince Henry, 1511. 4: abaa4*. BR (120.4). Song, macaronic, hist., Prince Henry.

TM 64 Adew adew my hartis lust.
L: Add. 31922, 1513+, ff. 23v–4. With music by [William] Cornysh. 4: abab4*. O: Ashm. 176, 2/4 16, f. 100. BR (120.5). Song, love.

TM 65 Adew corage adew | hope & trust.
L: Add. 31922, 1513+, f. 42v. With music by W. Cornyshe. 4: a3b2a3a4*. BR (120.6). Song, love.

TM 66 Adew dear hart | be man depart.
C: Kk.1.5, pt. 8, early 16, s.sh. (Cf. TM 1742, TM 1057, and TP 2229.) 14: 2 burd (aa) + 2x6 [imperf. rhyme] aa4b6cc4b6 (burd. My luf mornes for me for me). BR (120.7). Love, carol, Scots.

TM 67 Adewe my prettye pussey.
C: Ff.2.38, early 16, f.147, f.165. Copied twice. 8: ababccca3*. Song, love.

TM 68 Adewe pleasure welcome mournynge.
O: Ashm. 176, 2/4 16, f. 99. 4: abab4*. Love.

TM 69 Avysing the bright bemes of these fayer Iyes.
L: Egerton 2711, bef. 1542, f. 22. "Wyat[t]," tr. Petrarch, *Rime* 173. 14: abbaabbacddcee10. TP 203. Love.

TM 70 Isope myn auctor makis mencioun.
E: Asloan, 1513–42, ff. 236–40. [Robert Henryson] "The tale of the uplandis

mouss and the borowstoun mouss." (Included in BR 3703; see also TM 1696). 228: 28 x 7 RR10, 2 x 8 MT10. Nar., fable, Scots, moral.

After all thys I wyll you understond. "Premonicion" in TM 577.

TM 71 After Christe oure lorde, hadd thoroughlie fulfilled.
L: Royal 17.B.37, 1558, ff. 3v–32. "A brefe declaratione of the Institucione and trewe effecte off the lordes supper with the aduochement aswell by the holie scripture as by dyverse doctores with sounde abbuses in the masse and also the like abuse in Gyveing of orders and a Invectyve also Agaynst the papistes set fourth by John mardeley 1558." 937: aabccb4*, abab3*, aaaabccccb3*, MT4*. Rel. controversy, protestant.

TM 72 After droght commythe rayne.
L: Cotton Vespasian A.25, c 1525, f. 125. 5: aa4b3a4b3*. Moral.

TM 73 After great stormes the cawme retornis.
L: Egerton 2711, bef. 1542, f. 55v. [Wyatt]. 20: 5 x 4 abaB8 (ref. ...happy). Love.

TM 74 After man had broken the preseptes of the lord.
O: Ashmole 48, bef. 1558, ff. 3–4v. 96: 12 x 8 MT5*. Rel., prayer, thanksgiving to Christ, feast of the circumcision.

TM 75 After mydnyght when dremes do fall.
L: Add. 15233, 1554–58, ff. 48–9. 82: 2 burd aa + 20 x 4 abaB4* (burd. Aryse, Aryse, Aryse I say; ref. ...aryse I say). O: Ashmole 48, bef. 1558, ff. 21v–3. No burden, 72 vv. only. Carol, rel. instruction.

TM 76 Ageynst the frenchmen.
L: Add. 31922, 1513+, ff. 100v–2. With music, text perhaps incomplete, probably composed in 1513 for Henry VIII's expedition to France. 7: 2 burd aa + 1 x 5 aaaa5R4* (burd. Englond be glad pluk up thy lusty hart; ref. Help now thi kyng & tak his part). BR (134.5). Carol, hist.

TM 77 Agaynste the Rock I clyme both hye and hard.
D: TCD 160, 1535–48, f. 71. (One line lacking.) 13: abba[a]bbacddcee5*. Love.

TM 78 A a my herte I knowe yow well.
L: Add. 5465, 1501–04, ff. 3v–4. With music perhaps by William Newark. 8: ababbccb4*. BR (0.2). Song, love, lament.

Ah beshrew you by my fay. See TM 232.

TM 79 A blessid Jhesu hough fortunyd this.
L: Add. 5465, 1501–04, ff. 82v–6. Music by Richard Davy. 28: 4 x 7 aabbc5CC7* (ref. Sicut domino placuit ita factum est). NY: Drexel 4180, 2/4 16, f. 1v. Aceph. fragment, voice II, beginning with the second line, "My mood is changed". BR (1). Song, rel., prayer, Jesus.

TM 80 A man I have yeven and made a graunt.
L: Add. 5465, 1501–04, f. 118v–22. Carol version of the "Short Charter of Christ"; cf. BR 4184. 39: 9 burden aaabbccdd + 3 x 10 aabbccddee4* (burd. Be hit knowyn to all that byn here). Rel., carol, monologue of Christ.

TM 81 A myn hart remembir the well.
L: Add. 5465, 1501–04, ff. 86v–9. With music by Richard Davy. 16: 2 burd. aa + 2 x 7 RR4* (burd. A[h] my hert remembir the well; ref. I crye God mercy I will amend). BR (13). Rel., carol.

TM 82 Ah my hart ah this ys my song.
O: Ashmole 176, pt. 3, 2/4 16, f. 99v. 28: 7 x 4 aaa4B3* (ref. That ah my hart ah). BR (13.5). Love.

TM 83 A my herte a what aileth the.
L: Add. 17492, 1532–39, f. 78v. 20: 5 x 4 aaaB8 (ref. A my herte a what aileth the). D: TCD 160, 1535–48, f. 66. Love.

TM 84 A robyn gentyl robyn.
L: Add. 31922, 1513+, ff. 53v–4. Music by Cornysh (cf. TM 85). 7:abc3* + 2 x 2 aa7*. Song, love.

TM 85 A Robyn | Ioly Robyn.
L: Egerton 2711, bef. 1542, f. 37v. Subscribed "Wyat[t]" in a later hand (omits vv. 17–20 of next copy). 24: 6 x 4 a4b3a4b3*. L: Add. 17492, 1532–39, ff. 24r–v. Variant first line "Hey Robin Joly Robin"; vv. 1–8 copied also on ff. 22v–3. 28 lines. BR (13.8). Love, dialogue.

TM 86 A the syghes that cum fro my hart.
L: Add. 31922, 1513+, ff. 32v–3. With music by W. Cornysshe. 16: 4 x 4 a4b3a4b3*. L: Royal App. 58, 1507+, f. 3. With music. BR (14.5). Song, love.

TM 87 A woo worth that false strong parlyament.
L: Lansd. 762, c 1529, ff. 96, 97. Copied twice. 20: aa4*. Prophecy.

TM 88 Alac alac what shall I do.
L: Add. 31922, 1513+, f. 35v. With music by "The Kyng H.viii" (probably incomplete). 3: aba4*. D: TCD 160, 1535–48, f. 59. Incipit only, in table of contents. BR (135.5). Song, love.

TM 89 Alas a thousand sith alas.
O: Latin misc. c.66, c 1500, f. 94v. (Humfrey Newton.) 56: 7 x 8 ababcdcd4*. BR (137). Love.

TM 90 Alas Alas and walaway.
HN: HM 1, early 16, ff. 131v–2. "Suspencio Jude," added to the Towneley Corpus Christi Cycle, BR 715. 96: 16 x 6 aaa4b2a4b2*. Rel. drama.

TM 91 Alas all Sorofull.
D: TCD 160, 1535–48, f. 59. Incipit only, from table of contents. Love.

TM 92 Alas by what mene may I make ye to know.
L: Add. 15233, 1554–58, f. 46r–v. Jhon Heywood, "A Ballad of the Green Willow." 42: 2 burd ab + 8 x 5 aaaaR4* anapestic (burd. All a grene wyllow wyllow; ref. For all a grene wyllow is my garland). Carol, love.

TM 93 Alas dere harte what happe had I.
D: TCD 160, 1535–48, f. 62. 20: 5 x 4 abaB4* (ref. ...love me agayne). Love.

TM 94 Alas departynge is ground of woo.
O: Ashmole 191, pt. 4, early 16, ff. 194v–5. With music. 8: MT4*. BR (146). Song, love.

TM 95 Alas for lak of her presens.
L: Add. 5465, 1501–04, ff. 30v–1. With music by Robard ffayrfax. 7: RR3*. BR (146.5). Song, love.

TM 96 Alas fortune what alith the.
D: TCD 160, 1535–48, f. 65. 20: 5 x 4 aaa4R2* (ref. Thow wyl not chaunge). Love.

TM 97 Alas good man most yow be kyst.
CANT: Christ Church Letters 2, bef. 1550, No. 173. Subscribed "I. Wolstane." 47: 3 burd aaa + 11 x 4 aaaR4* (burd. I pray yow now come Kyss me; ref. ...ye shall not kyss me). BR (150). Carol, love.

TM 98 Alas I wayle the wofull harme by treason don of late.
L2: Lambeth 159, 1556+, f. 278v–9. "Ane Epitaphe upon the death of John Hartgyll" (murdered 1556), signed "Thomas H[artgill?]". 48: poulters + 1 x 6 ababcc8. Hist., epitaph.

TM 99 Alas I wofull creature.
L: Add. 29729, 1558, ff. 160–61. "A balade sayde by a gentill woman which loved a man of gret estate made by lidgate." 56: 7 x 8 MT4*. BR 154, comp. a 1449. Ballad, love.

TM 100 Alas it is I that wote nott what to say.
L: Add. 5465, 1501–04, ff. 17v–19. With music by [Edmund] Turges. 7: RR5*. BR (155.5). Song, love.

TM 101 Alas madame for stelyng of a kysse.
L: Egerton 2711, bef. 1542, f. 31. "Tho[mas Wyatt]", paraphrase of Serafino, "Incolpa donna amor." 8: abababcc10. TP 87. Love.

TM 102 Alas myne eye whye doost thou bringe.
O: Ashmole 176, 2/4 16, f. 99. 4: abab8. BR (158.2). Love.

TM 103 Alas my dere the word thow spakest.
D: TCD 160, 1535–48, f. 75. Serpentine rhyme; last line begins next stanza and last stanza ends with opening line. 35: 5 x 7 ababcb4c2*. Love

TM 104 Alas poore man what hap have I.
L: Add. 17492, 1532–39, ff. 15v–16. 28: 7 x 4 abab8. Love.

TM 105 Alas that men be so ungent.
L: Add. 17492, 1532–39, f. 27v. [?by Lord Thomas Howard, d. Oct. 1537.] 24: 6 x 4 abab8. Love.

TM 106 Alas that same Swete face.
D: TCD 160, 1535–48, f. 59. Incipit only, from table of contents. Love.

TM 107 Al[a]s the gren wylloy.
L: Sloane 3501, 1530's, f. 2v. Incipit only. Song, love.

TM 108 Alas the greefe, and dedly wofull smert.
L: Egerton 2711, bef. 1542, ff. 5v–6v. [Wyatt.] 30: 5 x 6 aababb10. D: TCD 160, 1535–48, f. 74. L: Add. 17492, 1532–39, f. 2v. Acephalous, vv. 13–30; begins "O cruel causer of undeserrved chaynge." Love.

Alas the woo that we are wroght. See TM 625.

TM 109 Alas to whom shuld I complayne.
L: Harley 2252, 1517–38, ff. 2v–3. "of Edward [Stafford,] duke of Bokyngham" (executed 1521). 88: 22 x 4 abaB4* (ref. And am exiled remedyles). O: Ashm. 176, 2/4 16, f. 100. Lines 1–4 only. BR (158.9). Elegy, hist.

TM 110 Alas what shall I do for love.
L: Add. 31922, 1513+, ff. 20v–1. With music by 'The Kynge H. viii.' 6: ab4cc2b3d1*. BR (159.5). Song, love.

Alas what shuld yt be to yow prejudyce. Extract from TM 517.

TM 111 Alas what thing can be more grevous payne.
O: Rawlinson C.813, 1520–35, ff. 13v–14. 42: 6 x 7 RR10 (ref. I am yours unto my lyves ende). BR (159.8). Love.

TM 112 Alas your ffondnes makys me smyll.
D: TCD 160, 1535–48, f. 121. "The Answer" to TM 960. 7: RR5*. Love.

TM 113 Alle crysten men lystenyt and hyre.
L: Royal 8.C.12, early 16, f. 2. (Prologue only to the Life of St. Erasmus.) 38: aa4*. BR 173, comp. a 1450. Rel.

TM 114 All Crysten men that walke me by.
O: Rawl. C.813, 1520–35, ff. 4v–6v. Prologue to "The Adulterous Falmouth Squire," vv. 45–48 lacking. 92: 12 x 8 MT8. BR 172, comp. a 1500. Rel., hell.

TM 115 All hast ys odyus whereas dyscrecyoun.
L: Harley 78, mid 16, ff. 77v–9. Attributed incorrectly to "lydgatt" by John Stow. 112: 14 x 8 MT5*. BR 186, comp. c 1475. Moral.

TM 116 All hevy myndes.
L: Egerton 2711, bef. 1542, f. 58r–v. "Tho[mas Wyatt]". 60: 15 x 4 a4ba6b4. Love.

TM 117 <A>wel I have at other lost.
L: Add. 17492, 1532–39, f. 22v. Signed "Mary Shelton" in a different hand. 4: abbb8. Love.

TM 118 All yn thi sight my lif doth hole depende.
L: Add. 17492, 1532–39, f. 69. [Wyatt,] based on Serafino, "Viuo sol di mirarti." 8: abababcc10. TP 104. Love.

TM 119 All men rejoyse, and prayse the lord.
L: Royal App. 74–76, c 1548, 13v, 6v–7, 15v–16. Tr. Jubilate deo, with music (setting in Royal App. 74 has stanzas 1 and 3 only). 60: 15 x 4 abab2*. Rel., hymn.

TM 120 All men the do wysshe unto them selfe all goode.
O: Ashmole 48, bef. 1558, f. 10. "Henry [Parker], Lord Morley" (on Petrarch's *Trionfi*). 22: aa12. Moral, on the good, human wishes.

TM 121 All rightwysnes now dothe procede.
L: Add. 29729, 1558, f. 10r–v. "John lydgate written out of Mr Phyllipps

boke." 56: 7 x 8 MT5* (ref. Conveyed by lyne rycht as a rammes horne). BR 199, comp. a 1449. Moral, satire.

All thoo that been, Enemyes to the Kyng. Extract from TM 1773.

All to my harme. Acephalous copy of TM 2025.

TM 122 Al holly youres with outhen others parte.
L: Harley 7578, early 16, f. 15. [Speculatively attributed to Chaucer by Skeat.] 32: 4 x 8 MT10. BR (231). Love.

TM 123 All women have vertues noble & excelent.
L: Add. 17492, 1532–39, f. 18v. "Rychard Hattfeld" (punctuation poem). 21: 3 x 7 RR5*. BR (232). Women.

TM 124 Alle ye that knowe of care and hevynes.
D: TCD 160, 1535–48, f. 69. 35: 5 x 7 ababacc10. Complaint against fortune.

TM 125 Alle ye that passe bi thys holy place.
C2: TCC B.15.31 (366), bef. 1541, f. 1. (Leaf dated 1541 on verso.) 7: RR4*. BR 237, comp. a 1500. Epitaph.

TM 126 Almighty and a merciable Queene.
L: Harley 7578, early 16, f. 20v. [Chaucer, "ABC," lines 1–48.] 48: 6 x 8 MT5*. BR 239, comp. a 1400. Rel., ABC, Virgin Mary.

TM 127 Almyghty god | doth shake hys rod.
L: Add. 15233, 1554–58, ff. 60–1v. John Heywood, ["A ballad against slander and detraction," 1544?]. 126: 6 burd + 20 x 6 a4b6cc4b6 (burd. Gar call hym downe). Carol, moral, ballad.

TM 128 Almyghty God in heven so hy.
L: Add. 35290, 1558, ff. 211–6. Verses added to York Purification play (BR 1273). 459: abab4a2bbb4a2*, aaa4b2ccc4b2*, abab4*, and irreg. Rel. drama.

TM 129 Almyghty god in trynyte.
L: Sloane 1207, mid 16, f. 12v. 5: mono3*. Rel., prayer, trinity.

TM 130 All myghty god lorde eternall.
L: Add. 30981, 1522–29, ff.11v–14v. John Croke, tr. Miserere mei deus (Ps. 51). 80: abab4*. Rel.

TM 131 Almychty god our fader of hevynnis abuf.
E2: Laing 149, 1/4 16, f. 87. Paraphrase of Pater noster. 8: MT5*. BR (254). Rel., prayer, Scots.

TM 132 Almeghtie Ladie Leding to have.
O17: Balliol 353, c 1539, ff. 1, 63, 87v. Lines 1–10, 19–20, 91–102 of a hymn in English copied in Welsh orthography, subscribed "Howel Surdevall sang it" [i.e., Jevan ap Hywel Swrdwal]; vv. 1–4 repeated on f. 120: 12 mono4* + 2 x 4 abab4* allit. BR 2514, comp. a 1500. Rel, prayer, Virgin Mary.

TM 133 Almes dystrybuted unto the indygent.
L: Harley 4826, mid 16, ff. 145v–6. [Lines 1–4 are William Baldwin, tr. Socrates (TP 126).] 66: aa5*. Moral.

TM 134 Alone alone alone alone alone alone | Alone in wyldernes.
L: Royal App. 58, 1507+, f. 8. Two-line burden only, with music. 2: ab3* (burd. Alone alone alone alone alone alone). BR (263.3). Carol, love.

TM 135 Alone alone | here y am my sylf Alone.
L: Add. 5665, bef. 1511, f. 140v. With music. 8: 2 x 4 aaBB4* (ref. Pyteusly my own sylf Alone). BR (263.5). Song, love.

TM 136 Alone Alone | mornyng Alone.
L: Add. 5665, bef. 1511, ff. 133v–5. With music. 48: 6 x 8 aaabaaab2*. BR (263.8). Song, love.

TM 137 ...Alone and only in a wrong scole.
F: L.b.554, c 1550, ff. 1–2v. "Part of a playe" (title entered in a later hand), acephalous fragment; last line: "Bothe promise and m[er]cy conteyned theryn"; not dramatic, an argument against justification by faith alone. 11: abab4* and irreg. Rel., controversy.

TM 138 Alone I leffe alone.
L: Add. 31922, 1513+, f. 22. Burden only, with music by Doctor Cooper. 6: 3 x 2 aa3* (burd. Alone I leffe alone). BR (266.5). Carol, love.

TM 139 Alone musyng | Remembryng.
D: TCD 160, 1535–48, f. 63. 18: 3 x 6 aa2b3cc2b3*. Love, complaint.

Also wyckyd tonges byn so prest. Excerpt from TM 1510.

TM 140 Altho thow se thowtragius clime aloft.
L: Egerton 2711, bef. 1542, f. 65v. Wyatt, Penitential Psalms, tr. Psalm 37. 36: 12 x 3 terza rima10. Rel.

TM 141 Amyddes my myrth and pleasantnes.
O: Ashmole 48, bef. 1558, f. 1r–v. 49: 7 x 7 ababcc8R4 (ref. So often warnd). Complaint, fortune.

TM 142 Among the ashes wheer the lye.
Y: Osborn music 13, 1553+, f. 20. With music. 28: 4 x 7 RR8 (ref. So nere the asshes as I lye). Song, love.

TM 143 Amang the ost of greekis as we hard.
BO: f. Med. 94, mid 16, f. ii. (Translation of Juvenal, Sat. 8.269–71.) 8: 2 x 4 abab5*. Scots.

TM 144 Among thir freris within a closter.
L: Arundel 285, c 1540, ff. 168–74v. [William Dunbar,] "The Passioun of Crist" (omits vv. 73–80, 90, 121–8). 127: 16 x 8 MT4* (ref. O mankind for the lufe of the; 2nd ref: Thy blis[si]t salviour Jesu). E: Asloan, 1513–42, ff. 290v–2. "Heir begynnis the passioun of Jhesu... quod Dunbar." 96 vv. only. BR (276.5). Rel., dream, nar., cruxifixion, Scots.

TM 145 An Egle shall flye.
L: Sloane 2578, c 1557, f. 64r–v. 42: 7 x 6 aabaab2*. Prophecy.

TM 146 An Egyll shall ryse with a bore bold.
L: Lansd. 762, 1524–29, ff. 53v–4. 58: irreg. BR (285.5). Prophecy.

TM 147 Ane emprious in tymes bygane.
E: Asloan, 1513–42, f.167–209v. "Heir begynnis the buke of the sevyne sagis [of Rome]," D-version; cf. TM 780. 2,782: aa3*. Frame nar., tr. French, women, Scots.

TM 148 An ende of this book, or of this Rude werk.
L: Cotton Nero C.11, 1506+, f. 462r–v. Robert Fabyan, tr. "Limas adest, precessit opus," his Latin envoy to the Chronicle. 56: 8 x 7 RR4* (ref. And wyth compassion, axe ffor us mercy). TP 143. Envoy.

TM 149 An heretyke he ys most sure who dothe the church of god forsake.
L: Add. 33974, c 1550, f. 47r–v. (Francis Stacy), "What an heretyke ys." 24: aa7*. Rel. instruction.

TM 150 An old said sawe: On-knowen, on-kyste.
O17: Balliol 354, 1505–36, f. 231. 22: 2 burd. (aa) + 4 x 5 aaabB4* (burd. An old sawe hath be fownd trewe; ref. ...elles most we drynk as we brew). BR (294). Carol, moral .

TM 151 ...And as thy worde <came on> this wyse.
C: Dd.5.76, 1/4 16, ff. 1–2. Acephalous, illegible in part; last line: "Mayden mari mylde amen." 60: 10 x 6 aabccb4*. BR (296.6). Rel., prayer, Jesus, Virgin Mary.

And ever in welth be ware of woo. Lines 47–48 of TM 221.

TM 152 And he that swerythe tyll no man tryste hym.
L: Harley 2252, 1517–38, f. 2. 4: mono4*. BR (301). Moral.

TM 153 And he that wrote this for Ryme | He is but A clouneshe swyne.
L: Ptd. book C.24.a.3, mid 16, sig. A1v. 2: aa3*. Epigram.

TM 154 And I war a mayden as many one ys.
L: Add. 31922, 1513+, ff. 106v–7. With music. 12: 3 x 4 abab3*. L: Egerton 3537, c 1554, f. 59. Tr. "Non me aurum midecriciner opes violarent si virginitas immaculata forit." Lines 1–4 only. L: Harley 1317, early 16, f. 94v. Incipit only. BR 302.5, comp. a 1500. Song, love, moral.

TM 155 And if an Ie may save or sleye.
L: Egerton 2711, bef. 1542, ff. 65, 62v. [Wyatt]; 28-line text cancelled on f. 62v. 42: 6 x 7 RR8 (ref. for the Iye is traitor of the herte). Love.

And yff on party wold fayne be Awreke. Lines 19–20 of TM 221.

And yf thou wylte be owt of sorow and care. Lines 43–44 of TM 221.

TM 156 And yff thow wylt lyve puerly.
L: Sloane 1207, mid 16, f. 12v. 5: mono4* in –ly. Moral.

TM 157 And yf thou wyst whatt thyng yt were.
L: Add. 60577, 1549–58, ff. 59–60v. Thomas Dakcomb, "ABC," dated 1549; preceded by title verse "Here folowyth the propre treatyse." 96: 4 abab4* + 23 x 4 aabb4*. Moral.

TM 158 And yf ye will to this medcyn applie.
O: Ashmole 1416, mid 16, f. 150v. Verses added to an earlier transcript of BR 2656. 10: aabbccaabb4*. O: Ashmole 1486, early 16, f. 18v. Variant beginning "Iff thou will this medesin a plye"; lines 1–6 only. Alchemy.

TM 159 ...And in this fair way persaif I wele a thing.
E: Asloan, 1513–42, ff.229–35v. "The talis of the fyve bestis," acepahlous due to MS damage; last line "Eternale god the ground of every gud." 422: aa5*. BR (303.3). Nar., beast fable, Scots.

And know thy self wysely I rede. Last line of acephalous TM 1640.

And menes king in the south arte. Acephalous text of TM 203.

And never I mot do that thynge. See TM 855.

TM 160 And now he hathe donn and made a mend.
C: Ff.2.23, 1545, f. 32. Thomas Knyvet, "To the Reader," envoy to TM 577. 6: aa4*. Alchemy.

And now my pen alas wyth wyche I wryte. Extract from TM 1510.

And sure I thynke yt ys best way. Stanzas 3–5 of TM 766 (ptd. by Muir as a separate poem).

TM 161 And thys be thys ye may.
L: Add. 17492, 1532–39, f. 44. 4: ab6a8b6. Love.

And thou wedde mercury to mercury wyth hyr wyfe. Variant first line of TM 1481.

TM 162 And thow wyst what thyng yt were.
O5: Ptd. book, Bartholomaeus Anglicus, *De proprietatibus rerum* (1488), c 1555, sig. DD7–6. An ABC poem transcribed in the hand of Richard Kaye. 82: aa4*. BR (312.5). Moral.

And tho that Y be < > hym fro. Stanzas 3 and 4 of TM 1042.

TM 163 And whan you hawe red this same.
L: Add. 18752, 1530's, f. 114v. Rhyming close to the draft of a letter. 4: a4b3a4b3*.

And who that sayth that for to love ys vyce. Extract from TM 1510.

TM 164 And wylt thow leve me thus.
L: Add. 17492, 1532–39, f. 17. Subscribed "W[yatt]." 24: abbba6R4 (ref. Say nay say nay). Love.

TM 165 [Ane] doly sassone onto ane cayrfull dit.
E2: Dc.1.43, mid 16, f. 301v. [Robert Henryson, *Testament of Cresseid*, vv. 1–21 only]. 21: 3 x 7 RR10. BR 285, comp. a 1492; TP 156.9. Nar., classical, Scots.

TM 166 Anno Domini 1554.
L: Harley 559, 1554, f. 34v. 12: 3 x 4 abab4*. Prophecy.

[An]noye nott thy neghbure in worde nor dede. Lines 49–52 of TM 219.

TM 167 Ante ffinem termini baculus portamus.
L: Sloane 1584, 1531+, f. 33. 14: aa6*. BR (320.5). Schoolboy's lament, macaronic, humorous.

Apostles martyrs and confessores all. Part of TM 467.

TM 168 Apply to the best gyftis geven to the.
L: Royal 18.D.2, c 1520, f. 205v. "The counsell of Aristotell...to Alexander kinge of Macedony [inscribed] in the syde of the garet of the gardynge in Lekyngfelde" [Leconfield]. 68: aa4*. BR (321). Moral.

Arectynge my sight. See TM 384.

TM 169 Aries is good, taurus is not so.
D: TCD 537, 2/4 16, p. 76. "Of the xii signes which be good or bad." 7: ababcdd4*. TP 160. Calendar, astrology, prognostication.

TM 170 Aryse early | Serve God devoutly.
L: Ptd. book IB 49408, early 16, f. 34v. 16: mono2* in –ly. L: Sloane 747, bef. 1506, f. 65v. (11 lines.) L: Stowe 850, 1552+, f. 1. (11 lines.) L: Lansd. 762, 1524–29, f. 16v. (16 lines, written as prose.) O17: Balliol 354, 1503–04, f. 159v. (11 lines.) BR 324, comp. c 1475; TP 160.5. Moral instruction.

TM 171 Armipotent Lady Bellona serene.
E: Adv. 18.3.2, 1540, ff. i–v. Johane Ballantyne [Bellenden], "proloug apoun the translation of titus livius." 140: RR5*. Prologue, Scots.

TM 172 Arthure Symcocke ys the trwe possessor of this boocke | God geve him good minde well thereon to loocke.
D: TCD 49, early 16, f. 33v. (A version of TM 1659.) 2: aa5*. Ownership rhyme.

TM 173 As clerkis may se that wil it luke.
E2: Laing II.318, early 16, ff. 1–2v. Acephalous fragment. 134: aa4*. Rel. instruction, Scots.

TM 174 As farre as guyfte, maie goode will expresse.
HN: HM 121, 1557, ff. 1–24v. Myles Huggarde, "A mirroure of myserie." 895: a8b6a8b6, RR4*. Nar., dream vision, social criticism.

TM 175 As ffor my part I crave no thyng.
L: Add. 17492, 1532–39, f. 41r–v. 12: 3 x 4 abab4*. Love.

TM 176 As frendes to frendes so gretinge we yow sende.
L: Cotton Titus A.24, 1550's, ff. 98v–9. Subscribed "finis Cr." 49: 7 x 7 RR10. Greeting.

As from theys hylles when that a spryng doth fall. See TM 450.

TM 177 As holy scripture maketh mention.
E2: Laing III.164, early 16, pp. 109–11. George Ripley, verses attached to a diagram in TM 577. 28: 4 x 7 RR4*. E5: Anonyma 2, vol. V, c 1550, f. 28v. C: Ff.2.23, 1545, f. 32. Transcribed by Thomas Knyvet, 1545; first two stanzas only. Alchemy.

TM 178 As I came by a bowre so fayr.
O: Rawlinson C.813, 1520–35, ff. 1v–2. 32: 4 x 8 ababbcb8C6 (ref. ...almes for our lady sake). BR (340.5). Love.

TM 179 As I cam by the way.
O17: Balliol 354, 1505–36, f. 231. 34: 2 burd (aa) + 4 x 8 ababbcbC4* (burd. Man, move thy mynd, and joy this fest; ref. Veritas de terra orta est). BR 343, comp. c 1475. Rel., carol, nativity.

TM 180 As y can walke upon a day.
L: Sloane 747, bef. 1506, f. 95–6. 132: 11 x 12 abababab bcbC4* (ref. And gyffe me ban to lyve in ease). BR 373, comp. a 1500. Moral.

TM 181 As I deserve.
L: Add. 30513, c 1550, f. 113. Incipit only, with music. Song.

TM 182 As I fared thorow a forest free.
O17: Balliol 354, 1505–36, f. 206. 56: 7 x 8 MT8 (ref. Welfare hath no sykernes). BR (346). Moral.

TM 183 As I gan wandre in on evenyng.
O17: Balliol 354, 1503–04, f. 156. 48: 6 x 8 MT4* (ref. To kepe ther shepe well in fold). BR (350). Rel. instruction, prelates.

TM 184 As I lay drowsie in my dreames.
Y: Osborn music 13, 1553+, ff. 53v–5. "R. C." (probably composer), with music. 120: 20 x 6 ababcc8. Dream, nar., allegory, animals.

TM 185 As I lay musyng my selfe a lone.
L: Harl 2252, 1525, ff. 43v–4v. "The Lamentacion of the Kyng of Scottes" [on the Scottish loss of the Battle of Flodden Field, 1513]. 120: 15 x 8 MT4* (ref. Miserere mei Deus absolva me). BR (366.8). Lament, James IV of Scotland.

TM 186 As I lay of lat musyng in my bede.
O: Ashmole 48, bef. 1558, ff. 39v–42. Subscribed "Amen quoth T. S. P." 136: 17 x 8 MT5*. Vision, moral, fortune.

TM 187 As I lay slombrynge In manner of a trans.
O: Ashmole 48, bef. 1558, ff. 55–7v. "by harry sponer." 136: 17 x 8 MT5* (ref. The all straynyde curtesie who shulde first begynne). Vision, moral.

TM 188 As I me lay on a nyght.
O17: Balliol 354, 1505–36, f. 222. 18: 2 burd. (aa) + 4x4 aaaB3* (burd. Now syng we all in fere; ref. Alma redemptoris mater). BR 354, comp. a 1450. Rel., carol, annunciation.

TM 189 As I me walkid in a may morning.
L: Add. 60577, 1549–58, f. 221. Incomplete, with music. 3: aa3b1*. Song.

TM 190 As I me walked on mornyng.
O17: Balliol 354, 1503–04, f. 176v. [The version in TP 170.5 differs considerably from this text.] 18: 2 burd. (aa) + 4 x 4 aaaB4* (burd. In what state that ever I be; ref. Timor mortis conturbat me). BR 375, comp. a 1500; TP 170.5. Rel., carol, death.

TM 191 As I me walked over feldis wide.
L: Lansd. 762, 1524–29, ff. 5–6v. "A process or an Exortation to tendre the Chargis of the true husbandys." 96: 12 x 8 MT4* (ref. I pray to god spede wele the plough). BR (363). Political exhortation, husbandry.

TM 192 As I me walkyd this endurs day.
L: Add. 5465, 1501–04, ff. 48v–50. With music. 22: 2 burd (aa) + 5 x 4 aaa4R2* (burd. Alone alone alone alone alone; ref. ...a lone). BR (364). Rel., carol, dialogue, Jesus, Virgin Mary.

TM 193 As I me went this thender day.
L: Lansd. 762, 1524–29, ff. 24–31. [Thomas of Erceldoune's Prophecy.] 549: MT4*, ababc, and irreg. L: Sloane 2578, c 1557, ff. 6–11v. "the iid [2nd] fytt of sir thomas of Arseldon," beginning "Farewell thomas I wend my waye." 332 lines. BR 365, comp. c 1440. Prophecy.

TM 194 As I myselfe lay thys enderz nyght.
O: Rawlinson C.813, 1520–35, ff. 54–5. 48: abab4* and irreg. BR (366). Love, epistle.

TM 195 As I on hilly halkes logged me late.
HN: EL 26.A.13, 1534+, ff. 121–32. [The story of Joseph and Asneth, omissions after vv. 100 and 265.] 933: RR5* and abab5*. BR 367, comp. a 1475?. Rel., nar.

TM 196 A<s I sat?> upon astrawe.
L: Cotton Vespasian A.25, c 1525, f. 126v. Verses lacking in first and sixth

stanzas. 26: 2 burd aa + 6 x 4 a4b3a4b3* (burd. Newes newes newes newes). BR (102.3). Carol, nonsense, humorous.

TM 197 <A>s I stode in A park streght by a tre.
L: Cotton Julius A.5, early 16, f. 131v. [John Lacy, "Testament of a Buck," enumerating the parts of a deer]. 56: 8 x 7 RR5*. O: Rawlinson C.813, 1520–35, ff. 30–1v. "The testament of the bucke." 70 lines. BR (368). Testament, practical, hunting, description.

TM 198 As I walked here by west.
O17: Balliol 354, 1503–04, ff. 145–6. 88: 11 x 8 MT4* (ref. ...marcy Lorde and gramarcy). BR 374, comp. c 1390. Rel., prayer, penitence.

TM 199 As I walkyd my self alone.
O: Lat. misc. e.85, early 16, f. 83. "Of kynge Herry the vi" (incomplete at the end). 53: abab4*. BR 372, comp. 1464. Hist.

TM 200 As in a booke wretyn y fownd.
O: Ashmole 1379, early 16, pp. 19–28. (Incomplete.) 160: aa4*. BR 3754, comp. c 1425. Medical.

TM 201 As long as I am riche reputed.
L: Harley 2321, early 16, f. 146. 4: aabb4*. BR (397). Moral.

TM 202 As love requiryth eche ffaythffull hart.
Y: Osborn music 13, 1553+, ff. 48v–9. "R. K." (probably composer). 40: 5 x 8 a8b6a8b6c8d6c8d6. Song, love.

TM 203 <As> men ar be thair qualiteis.
E: Adv. 19.2.4, 1500–1525, ff. 8–434v. Andrew of Wyntoun, *Chronicle of Scotland*. 29,600: aa4*. STU: St. Andrews Univ. T.T.66, bef. 1550, ff. 1–end. Acephalous, begins at 1.509, "And menes king in the South arte." BR 399, comp. c 1420. Nar., hist. Scots.

TM 204 As nature hathe an Inclynation.
O: Wood Empt. 2, 1558, ff. 1–69v. Wyllyam Forreste, "The seconde Griselede." 3,465: RR10. Nar., hist., Katherine of Aragon.

TM 205 [As often as I consider, these old noble clerks].
O17: Balliol 354, 1503–04, ff. 103–6. [Sir Thomas More] "The wordis of Fortune to the peple," partial text beginning "Myne high estate power and auctorytye." 259: 37 x 7 RR5*. BR (2183.5); TP 180. Moral, fortune.

TM 206 As phebus brycht In speir meridian.
E2: Dc.1.43, mid 16, f. 1. Headed "Lib 12." (damaged text). 63: 9 x 7 RR10. Love, Scots.

As poverte causithe sobernes. Lines 83–90 of the prologue to TM 818.

TM 207 As Right to rule is reason | so tyme doeth trye out treason.
O: Hatton 105, c 1550, f. 165v. 2: aa7. BR (404.5). Proverb.

TM 208 As shipe escaped the powre of tyde and wynde.
L: Harley 78, mid 16, ff. 25v–6. "The Epitaphe of Sir A[nthony] Dennie" (d. 28 Oct. 1549). 42: 6 x 7 RR10.

As solen as so pretty as strange toward me. Acephalous text of TM 1724.

TM 209 As the bryght beames of phebus Illumyneth the worlde universall.
L: Royal 18.D.6, c 1512, ff. 1–2v. John [Touchet, baron] of Audelay (presenting a late 15th-cent. MS of Lydgate's *Troy Book* to Henry VIII). 105: RR5*. Dedication.

TM 210 As the holy grouth grene.
L: Add. 31922, 1513+, ff. 37v–8. With music signed 'The Kyng H. viii'. 20: 4 burd (aaaa3) + 4 x 4 abab3* (burd. Grene growith the holy). BR (409.5). Carol, love.

TM 211 As the olde feeldis bringeth forthe our new corne.
L:Royal 17.D.3, 1548, ff. 2–78. Sir William Forrest, preeiste,"The pleasaunt poesye of princelie practise...collecte owte of...The governaunce of noblemen, which...Aristotle wrote too his discyple Alexandre." Dedicated to Edward, Duke of Somerset, and King Edward VI, 1548. [Tr. of 12th cent. Latin pseudo-Aristotelian *Secreta Secretorum*]; incomplete, prologue and 24 of 37 chapters. 3,857: RR5*. Moral, political.

TM 212 As the philosopher in metheours doith write.
O: Ashmole 759, early 16, ff. 103–5v. 176: 22 x 8 MT4*. BR 410, comp. a 1500. Alchemy.

TM 213 As yung aurora with his cristall hale.
E: Asloan, 1513–42, ff.211v–2v. [Dunbar,] "Off the fenyeit falss frer of tungland" (incomplete text). 69: 8 x 8 aaabcccb10 + 1 x 5 aaabc . BR (417.5). Nar., satire, Scots.

TM 214 At a place where he me sett.
O17: Balliol 354, 1503–04, f. 178. 17: 2 burd. (aa) + 3 x 5 aaaRR4* (burd. As I walked by a forest side; ref. We shall have game and sport ynow). BR (418); TP 193. Carol, nar.

TM 215 Att domys day, whan we shall ryse.
O17: Balliol 354, 1505–36, f. 221. 22: 2 burd. (aa) + 5 x 4 aaab8 (burd. Mary moder I you pray). BR (425); see also BR 3658. Rel., carol, last judgment.

TM 216 At her hed I wyl begyn.
HN: Ptd. book 60363, c 1530, sig. s10. 6: 2 burd (aa) + 1 x 4 aaab4* (burd. With fye and fy with fy|ffy my lady marg). Carol, women, satire.

TM 217 At last withdrawe yowre cruelltie.
L: Add. 17492, 1532–39, f. 4r–v. 36: 4 x 9 a8b6a8bccddd6. D: TCD 160, 1535–48, f. 67. Love complaint.

TM 218 At most myscheffe.
L: Add. 17492, 1532–39, f. 12. "ffynys q Wyatt." 48: 6 x 8 aaabcccb4. D: TCD 160, 1535–48, f. 68. L: Egerton 2711, bef. 1542, f. 34r–v. "Tho[mas Wyatt]," imperfect at the end, vv. 1–41 only. Love.

TM 219 Att my begynning Criste me spede.
O: Rawlinson C.813, c 1523, ff. 9–11. Series of moral and proverbial couplets and quatrains, beginning with TM 220; one couplet (TM 496) appears independently, others are included in TM 221. Proverbs are cross-referenced without numbers. 80: aabb4*. BR (430). Moral, father's advice to son.

At my commyng the ladys everychone. Excerpt from TM 517.

TM 220 At owre beginynnyng God be my spede | Wyth grace and vertue to procede.
L: Harley 3362, early 16, f. 89. Written three times as pen practice. 2: aa4*. HD: Eng 752F, early 16, f. 184. Subscribed "Thomas Kynton." LINC: Lincoln Cath. 189, early 16, f. 5v. Copied twice, begins "In my begenning..." DUR5: Cosin V.iii.9, c 1555, f. 17. Begins "In the begynnyng..." HN: HM 136, mid 16, f. 112. Copied by Dorothy Helbartun; begins "Yn my begenneng..." BR 430.5. Rel., prayer.

TM 221 At owur begynny[n]ge god be owur spede.
L: Harley 2252, 1517–38, f. 3. Series of moral and proverbial couplets beginning with TM 220; includes TM 28, 33, 496, 540, and others appearing in TM 219. Each proverb is cross-referenced without numbers. 85: aa4*. BR (432). Moral, father's advice to son.

TM 222 At shoteres hyll in the shyre of kent.
G: Hunt. 232, early 16, f. 96. 4: mono4*. Thievery.

TM 223 At the reverence of saynt margret.
L: Add. 29729, 1558, ff.170v–7v. "the lyffe of saynt margret translated [from French] in to englysshe by...lidgate...at the request of my lady of huntingeton..." 532: 76 x 7 RR4*. BR 439, comp. 1430. Rel., nar.

TM 224 Att westmyster william crownyd was.
L: Harley 78, mid 16, ff. 69v–72. The Kings of England from William I to Henry VI. 212: aa4*. BR 444, comp. c 1450. Hist.

TM 225 Attende my people unto my law and to my words enclyne.
L: Harley 1197, early 16, ff.212v–3v. [Portion of Thomas Sternhold, tr. Ps. 78.] 26: aa7*. TP 201. Rel.

Avysing. See Advising.

TM 226 Avoyd all sharpe and thornie wooddis, if care thow take of wooll.
L: Royal 18.C.9, 1540's, f. ?. Tr. from Vergil, *Georgics* III, in an English trans. of Polydore Vergil, *English History*, Bk. 1. 2: poulters. Husbandry.

TM 227 A wak all fethfull harttes a wake.
O: Ashmole 48, bef. 1558, ff. 62v–4. Subscribed "sponer" 91: 13 x 7 abab4c2d4c2*. Rel. exhortation.

TM 228 Awake my soule thinke on my synnes.
L: Add. 33974, c 1550, f. 23. (Francis Stacy), "< > by the letters of the Alphabethe." 12: aa7*. Rel., ABC.

TM 229 A wak Rych men for shame and here.
O: Ashmole 48, bef. 1558, ff. 67v–9. Subscribed "Henry Sponar." 96: 24 x 4 a4b3a4b3*. Moral.

TM 230 Awake synner out of thi slepe.
C15: Folder of musical fragments, early 16, unfol. (Fragment; uncertain number of lines.) BR (455.5). Song, rel.

TM 231 Away all care and payne.
D: TCD 160, 1535–48, f. 59. Incipit only from table of contents.

TM 232 Ay be shrewe yow be my fay.
L: Add. 5465, 1501–04, ff. 96v–9. [Skelton, "Mannerly margery"] with musical setting by William Cornish. 28: 4 x 7 aaaaaRR4* (ref. ...With manerly margery mylke and ale). BR 456.5, comp. a 1500. Song, love, dialogue.

TM 233 Aye hathe made hys complainte.
L6: Dyce 45, 2/4 16, ff. 18–19v. 96: 12 x 8 ababbcbC3* (ref. for gogg hathe geven hys governaunce). Rel. instruction.

TM 234 B for a stondyng aye.
F: V.a.354, 1/4 16, f. 121v. Robert Oliver (explanation of his cipher). 6: aaabbb4*. Cipher.

TM 235 Bacchus which is god of the glade vyne.
L: Add. 29729, 1558, ff.135v–6v. "a balade made by...Lidgate at elltham...ffor a momyng to fore the kynge and the Quene." 84: 12 x 7 RR4* (ref. Pees with your leges plente and gladness; 2d ref. Ay by encresse Joye gladness of harte). BR 458, comp. c 1428. Ballad, mumming, pageant, myth.

TM 236 Bar[o]nes In battell birkling shalbe.
O: Rawl. C.813, c 1535, f. 90. 13: allit., with some rhyme. Prophecy.

TM 237 Be it better or be it worse | do after hym that berith the purse.
O17: Balliol 354, 1505–36, f. 200. Tr. of "Seu bene siue..." 2: aa4*. BR 465.5, comp. a 1500. Proverb.

TM 238 Be it right or wronge | Thes men amonge | on wymen do complayn.
O17: Balliol 354, 1505–36, ff.210v–3v. ["The Nutbrown Maid," prob. copied from a lost print of 1520 or earlier; earliest text 1503?; see W. A. Ringler, ELR 1 (1971), 27–51.] 180: 30 x 6 aaaabB7* (ref. He is a banysshed man; 2nd ref. She loved but hym alone). BR (467); TP 209. Nar, dialogue, proto-dramatic, women (defense).

TM 239 Be meke & meylde yn hert & loving.
C: Ee.4.35, early 16, f. 5v. "The vii vertuys Agyn the vii dedley synys." 16: aa4*. BR (469). Rel. instruction.

TM 240 Be mery & suffer as I the vise.
O17: Balliol 354, 1505–36, f. 231. 22: 2 burd. (aa) + 5 x 4 aaab4* (burd. He is wise, so most I goo). BR (470). Carol, moral.

TM 241 Be merye frendes take ye no thowghte.
L: Add. 15233, 1554–58, ff. 56–7. Subscribed "Heywood." 70: 14 x 5 aaaa8B4 (ref. Be mery frendes). Convivial.

TM 242 Be milde and Jentyll | And have all at thy wyll.
G: Hunt. 230, c 1500, f. 246. "q[uod] Zowche" 2: aa2*. Proverb, Scots.

TM 243 Be not A fraide.
L: Add. 17802–5, bef. 1554, f. 63. Incipit only, with music by "mr sheperde" (fl. 1554). Song.

Be not to bold for to blame. Lines 17–18 of TM 221.

TM 244 Be pes ye make me spille my Ale.
L: Add. 5665, bef. 1511, ff. 66v–7. With music. 24: 3 x 8 MT4*. BR (474.5). Song, love, dialogue, flyting.

Be petuus and eke merciabyll. Lines 3–4 of TM 221.

TM 245 Beaute of you burne in my body abydis.
O: Lat. misc. c.66, c 1500, f. 93v. (Humfrey Newton.) 7: RR4*. BR (481). Love.

TM 246 Bicause I have the still kept fro lyes & blame.
L: Egerton 2711, bef. 1542, f. 20. "Wyat," tr. Petrarch, *Rime*, 49. 14: abbaabbacddcee10. TP 221. Love.

TM 247 Bycause my master and frende goode.
O: Engl. Poetry e.59, 1548–54, ff. 1–191v. Robertus Parkyn, ["Life of Christ"]. 4,982: RR8. Rel., nar.

TM 248 By cause thys ys her boke | she may the beter in ym loke.
HN: HM 136, early 16, f. 89. Ownership rhyme of Dorothy Helbartun. 2: aa3*.

TM 249 Beade did in book make.
L11: PRO SP 1/220, 1546, f. 64. Quoted by Richard Laynam, 9 June 1546. 4: abab4*. Prophecy.

TM 250 Before thou pretend any evill in thyn harte | Remember the end when thow shalt departe.
DUR5: Cosin V.iii.9, c 1555, f. 55v. "quod [Thomas] carter." 2: aa4*. BR (484.5). Proverb, death.

TM 251 Begin all agayne a gallyard.
Y: Osborn music 13, 1553+, f. 12v. Incipit or title only, with lute tablature. Song, dance.

TM 252 Beholde and se this gloriows fygure.
L: Add. 29729, 1558, ff. 9v–10. "A balade made by John lydgate of the image of our lady."' 40: 5 x 8 MT4*. BR 490, comp. a 1449. Rel., indulgence, Virgin Mary.

TM 253 Beholde he saide my creature.
L: Add. 5465, 1501–04, ff. 122v–4. With music. 11: 4 burd abab + 7 RR4* (burd. In a slumbir late as I was). BR (490.5). Rel., carol, crucifixion, dream.

TM 254 Behold, love, thy power how she dispiseth.
L: Eger. 2711, bef. 1542, f. 4. "Tho[mas Wyatt]," tr. Petrarch, *Rime* 121. 15: aabbaaab10C3aabba10C3 (ref. Behold love). L: Add. 17492, 1532–39, f. 69v. TP 227. Love, women.

Behald man lift up thy ene and see. Extract from TM 1164.

TM 255 Be hold man what thou arte.
L: Add. 60577, 1549–58, f. 115. 8: abab4c1dd2c3*. Rel., memento mori.

TM 256 Beeholde me y pray thee with all thyn hoole reeson.
PN: Ptd. book Taylor Coll. Inc. B71, 2/4 16, MS gathering bound in. Subscribed "Explicit quod Skelton." 56: 6 burd (abbaba) + 5 x 10 aaaa4bbb2cc4D2*, anapestic (burd. Woyfully arrayed; ref. Woyfully a rayd). L: Harl 4012, c 1505, f. 109r–v. 46: 6 + 4 x 10 (same form). L: Add. 5465, 1501–04, ff. 63v–67. With music by William Cornish; variant with another musical setting on ff. 73v–77. 36: 6 + 3 x 10 (same form). O: Lyell 24, early 16, f. 100. Variant burden and stanza two, beginning "I naked am nayled." 15: 6 burd + 1 x 9 aaaa4bbb2cc4* (burd. Woefully A rayde, the sone of A mayde). BR (497). Rel., carol, monologue of Christ.

TM 257 Behowlde of pensyfnes the pycture here in place.
L: Add. 15233, 1554–58, f. 47r–v. "Finis Thomas [Prideaux]" (on Dido). 30: 5 x 6 aaaabb4*. Myth, love lament.

TM 258 Be holde thys greate prynce edwarde the seconde.
L: Add. 29729, 1558, f. 169r–v. "seven balades mad by...lydgate of the sodeine fall of certain princes of ffraunce and engelond now late in our dayes" (on Edward II, Richard II, Charles of France, the Duke of Orleans, Thomas, Duke of Gloucester, John, Duke of Burgundy, and the Duke of Ireland). 49: 7 x 7 RR5*. BR 500, comp. a 1449. History, fall of princes.

TM 259 Beyng as noone ys I doo complayne.
D: TCD 160, 1535–48, f. 77. 21: 3 x 7 RR5* (ref. paciens parforce content thy self with wrong). Love, complaint.

TM 260 Bende downe thyne eares o lorde and heare my wordes and crye consyder.
L: Add. 33974, c 1550, ff. 8v–10v. (Francis Stacy), "< > and amendymente of lyfe < >." 100: aa7*. Rel., prayer.

TM 261 Benedicite what dreamyd I this nyght.
L: Add. 5465, 1501–04, ff. 13v–15. With music by Fayrfax. 7: RR4*. BR (506.5). Love, dream, song.

TM 262 Benedicta sit sancta trinitas.
O17: Balliol 354, 1503–04, f. 146r–v. 56: 7 x 8 MT4*. BR (506). Rel. instruction, marriage, macaronic.

TM 263 Benyng lady blessed mote thow be.
L: Add. 5665, bef. 1511, ff. 4v–5. "[D]e sancta maria," with music. 14: 2 burd aa + 3 x 4 aaaR4* (burd. Syng we to this mery company; ref. Regina celi letare). BR (507). Rel., carol, Virgin Mary.

TM 264 Besecheth you of moderly pete.
O: Bodley 120, early 16, f. 95. 21: 3 x 7 RR4*. BR (511). Rel., prayer, Virgin Mary.

Better ys to have vertu and Connynge. Lines 78–79 of TM 221; 27–28 of TM 219

TM 265 Bettyr it ys a lye be mad by Reson | Thann throgth be spoken owtt off seyssonn.
G: Hunt. 230, early 16, f. 247. Third of nine proverbs entered by Rychard Wylloughbe. 2: aa4*. Moral.

TM 266 Better yt ys a poore house to houlde | [than] to Lye in prysone wyth feta[r]s of goulde.
L: Harley 1304, early 16, f. 103. 2: aa4*. Proverb, moral.

Better hyt his serten to abyde. Variant of TM 267.

TM 267 Better yt ys to soffer and fortune to a byde | then hastlye to clymbe & sodinly to slyde.
L: Ptd. book 1379.a2(7), 1544, sig. Li. Subscribed "martin pollard anno 1544." 2: aa4*. DUR5: Cosin V.iii.9, c 1555, f. 85v. Variant first line: "Better hyt his serten to abyde." 2: aa3*. O17: Balliol 354, 1503–04, f. 160. BR 513, comp. a 1450; TP 241.5. Moral, proverb.

TM 268 Betwene fyfty & v, It ys to understond.
O: Arch. Seld. B.8, mid 16, f. 273r–v. (Continues to f. 275 as prose.) 45: aa4* and irreg. Prophecy.

TM 269 Betwixt ix and xi all thinges fynished shalbe.
L: Sloane 2578, c 1557, f. 107v. 10: aa4* and irreg. Prophecy.

TM 270 Bewayle and morne here lett us all who in thys worlde ar plaste.
L: Add. 33974, c 1550, f. 60r–v. (Francis Stacy), "A remembrance of this wyckyde worlde." 30: aa7*. Rel. instruction.

Beware my son ever of had I wyste. Lines 56–59 of TM 221; 5–8 of TM 219.

TM 271 Blame me not reader thowthe I speak playne.
L6: Dyce 45, 2/4 16, ff. 44–8. "A commendation and exhortation of willfull heresye to hys fryndes. with hys laste will and testamente... quod Smythe." 203: 29 x 7 RR5*. Rel. exhortation, personification of heresy.

TM 272 Blame not my lute for he must sound.
L: Add. 17492, 1532–39, f. 64r–v. Subscribed "W[yatt]." 42: ababcc8R4 (ref. Blame not my lute). L: Sloane 3501, 1530's, f. 2v. Incipit only, no music. Love, complaint.

Blessyd & meke mary mawdeleyne. Part of TM 467.

Blessed be... Extract from TM 1524.

TM 273 Blessed be they that may obteyne.
L: Add. 30981, 1522–29, ff. 5–7. John Croke, tr. Beati quorum (Ps. 32). 56: 14 x 4 abab4*. Rel.

TM 274 Blessed god: sovereange goodnes.
C: Gg.4.31, mid 16, ff. 104–5v. "A goodly preaer." 105: 15 x 7 RR4*. BR 532, comp. a 1500. Rel., prayer.

TM 275 Blessid is he that considereth the poore.
L: Royal 17.A.17, 1551+, ff. 8v–9v. Sir Thomas Smith, tr. "Psalme 40" [41]. 52 (as 26 long lines): 13 x 4 a4b3a4b3*. Rel.

Blessyd John that callyd was Baptyst. Part of TM 467.

Blessyd mare virgyne off nazareth. Part of TM 467.

TM 276 Bolnyng of genytras of a man.
C2: TCC R.14.39 (911), early 16, f. 1v. "for bolnyng of mannys genythrottes" [included in BR 1408]. 14: aa4*. Medicine

TM 277 Bonys emonge stonys lys ful steyl | Qwylste the sawle wonderis were that god wyleth.
THORN: Thornhill Church, 1537. Funeral monument of one of the Savils, dated 28 Henry VIII (1537). 2: aa4*. Epitaph.

TM 278 Bowght & sold full traytorsly.
O17: Balliol 354, 1505–36, f. 230. 22: 2 burd. (aa) + 5 x 4 a8b6a8b6 (burd. To see the mayden wepe her sones passion). BR (548). Rel., carol, passion, Virgin Mary.

TM 279 Bound am I now and shall be styll.
L: Add. 17492, 1532–39, ff. 8v–9. 35: 7 x 5 ababb8. Love.

TM 280 Bow down thine eare to me o Lorde and harken to my crie.
L: Royal 17.A.17, 1551+, ff. 5v–6v. Sir Thomas Smith, tr. "Psalme 85" [86] 64: a4b3a4b3*. Rel.

TM 281 Bragg not of goodes put gg [=goods] unto ther flyght.
D: TCD 160, 1535–48, f. 153v. 4: abab5*. Riddle?

TM 282 Bring ye to me and I to ye.
PFOR: MS 40A, 1553+, f. 368v. [Nicholas Udall?], incipit only of song at end of Act II (after line 598) of *Respublica*. Song.

TM 283 Brome yf you wante yet ought to be loved.
D: TCD 160, 1535–48, ff. 78–9. Subscribed "I John" [probably a draft.] 29: RR4* and irreg. Friendship.

TM 284 Brother abyde I the desire and pray.
TOK2: Takamiya MS 6, 1531, ff. 117–9. "Here begynnyth a lamentable complaynt of our saviour cryst kyng eternall to sinfull mane his brother naturall." 196: 28 x 7 RR4*. BR (550). Rel., monologue of Christ.

TM 285 Burgeys thou haste so blowen atte the Cole.
L: Harley 7578, early 16, f. 16r–v. 56: 7 x 8 MT4*. BR (551). Bawdy, love.

TM 286 Besy in stody be thou child.
O17: Balliol 354, 1505–36, f. 200. Tr. "sidulus in studio..." 4: aabb4*. BR (552.5). Proverb.

TM 287 But god that good may geve.
D: TCD 423, early 16, f. 203. 6: aa3*. BR (553.5). Rel., prayer.

TM 288 But yf that I | maye have trwly.
L6: Dyce 45, 2/4 16, ff. 23v–25. 100: 4 burd abca + 16 x 6 aa2b3cc2b3* (burd. Back and syde goo bare goo bare). BR (554.5). Carol, conviviality.

TM 289 But late in place.
L: Add. 15233, 1554–58, f. 30r–v. 63: 3 burd aab + 10 x 6 aa4b7cc4b7 (burd. How should I rock the cradle). Carol, moral, woman's lament.

TM 290 But now I se even then.
HN: HM 136, early 16, f. 73. Ownership rhyme of Dorothy Helbartun. 4: abab3*.

TM 291 Bot on thynge mastres greves me ful sore.
O: Lat. misc. c.66, c 1500, f. 94. (Humfrey Newton.) 32: 8 x 4 abaB4* (ref. ...my hert wold berst). BR (556). Love.

TM 292 But sethens you it assay to kyll.
L: Egerton 2711, bef. 1542, f. 7. [Wyatt], acephalous; last line: "Slain have I by unfaithfulnes." 10: 2 x 5 ababa8. Love.

TM 293 But why am I so abusyd.
L: Add. 5465, 1501–04, ff. 20v–22. Music by William Newarke. 7: RR3*. BR (557.5). Song, love.

TM 294 By a bancke as I lay.
L: Royal App. 58, 1507+, ff. 10v–11. With music. 21:3 x 7 abcaabd4*. BR (558.5). Song, love.

TM 295 By a forest as I can passe.
R: Ptd. book, Gerson, *De consolatione theologie* (1488), 1530+, sig. ?. "A ballet of the deth of the Cardynall" [Wolsey, d. 1530], with music. 24: 4 x 6 ababc4C3* (ref. Miserere mei deus). Song, hist., lament.

TM 296 By a palace as I couth pass.
E: Asloan, 1513–42, inlaid p. 4. First line only in table of contents.

TM 297 Be belstred wordes I am borne in hand.
D: TCD 160, 1535–48, f. 76. (Later copy of vv. 1–8 in a different hand on the same page.) 14: abbaabbacddcee4*. Love.

TM 298 By god of love set I lothyng.
O: Lat. misc. c.66, c 1500, f. 93r–v. (Humfrey Newton.) 64:16 x 4 abab5*. BR (572). Love.

TM 299 By hym that all dothe imbrase.
C2: TCC B.15.39 (181), early 16, f. 172. Verses for a lord mayor's pageant. 32: aa3*, aa4*, RR4*. BR (1547.5). Pageant, allegory.

By mercye and mekenes all thynge chevythe. Lines 7–8 of TM 221.

TM 300 By the grace of our lord omnipotent.
C9: G&C MS 793, early 16, pp. 161–71. An English metrical version of the Biblia Pauperum. 294: 42 x 7 RR4*. BR (576.5). Rel., nar., Bible.

TM 301 By thi burthe ye blessed lord.
L: Add. 5665, bef. 1511, ff. 52v–3. Music by [Smert]. 10:2 burd aa + 2 x 4

aabB4* (burd. Blessed mote ye be swete jhus; ref. Qui hodie natus es nobis). BR (581). Rel., carol, nativity.

TM 302 By wytte of man: a thyng that is contryved.
L: Add. 29729, 1558, ff. 123–4. "by Iohn lidgate...the songe of ...iust mesure." 104: 13 x 8 MT5* (ref. Nothyng commendyd but it in measure be). BR 584, comp. a 1449. Moral.

TM 303 Cadar and Sibell bothe of them sayes.
L: Sloane 2578, c 1557, ff. 12–15v. 203: 51 x 4 abab4*. Prophecy.

TM 304 Cesar when that the traytour of Egipt.
L: Egerton 2711, bef. 1542, ff. 4v–5. Wyatt, tr. Petrarch, *Rime* 102. 14: abbaabbacddcee10. L: Add. 17492, 1532–39, f. 70. Variant first line: "Ceasar whom the traytor of ejipte." TP 295. Love.

Ceasar whom the traytor of ejipte. Variant first line of TM 304.

Care not to myche for ony thynge. Line 61–62 of TM 221.

TM 305 Care who so wyll.
Y: Osborn music 13, 1553+, f. 32. Incipit only, with lute tablature. Song.

Chylde of this discipline inclyne to me thinne eare. Prologue to TM 577.

TM 306 Crist com nere and toke hym by the hand.
L: Sloane 1207, mid 16, f. 12v. 4: mono4*. Rel., Jesus.

TM 307 Cryst kepe us all, as he well can.
O17: Balliol 354, 1505–36, f. 241v. 18: 2 burd. (aa) + 4 x 4 abab8 (burd. Now syng we syng we). BR (608). Rel., carol, nativity, macaronic.

TM 308 Cryste of the theeff, whych on thy Rygth hand was.
L: Cotton Nero C.11, 1506+, f. 47v. Robert Fabyan, tr. "criste tue calicis," verses on Richard I. 21: 3 x 7 RR4*. HD: Eng 766F, 1504, f. 18r–v. TP 307. Hist.

TM 309 Criste qui lux es et dies.
E2: Laing 149, 1/4 16, f. 120v. (Cf. BR 1614–1619.) 56: 7 x 8 MT4*. BR (612). Rel., prayer, macaronic, Scots.

TM 310 Cresyt that was cruciffeyed ffor sunys on kynd.
C: Ee.4.35, early 16, ff. 3–5. [The lady who buried the Host.] 136: 17 x 8 MT4*. BR 622, comp. a 1450? Rel., Jesus, nar., miracle.

TM 311 Crist that was of Infynyt myght.
L: Add. 5465, 1501–04, ff. 53v–8. With music by [John] Browne. 25: 5 burd ababa + 4 x 5 ababR4* (burd. Jhesu mercy how may this be; ref. Jhesu mercy how may this be). BR (1731). Rel., carol, crucifixion.

TM 312 Chrystys crosse be oure spede | With grace mercye in all oure nede.
L: Add. 60577, 1549–58, f. 56v. Couplet introducing TM 1767. 2: aa4*. Title verse, rel., prayer.

TM 313 Cronykillis and Annuall bookis of kinges.
L: Royal 18.D.2, c 1520, ff. 186–95. "...the discente of the lorde percis [Percys]...by me william peeris clerke & preste secretory to...henry 5th Erle [of Northumberland, 1478–1527]..." 679: 97 x 7 RR4*. ALN: Alnwick Castle 79, c 1520, unfol. vellum roll. William Peeris, "a tretes of the noble pedegrew of the lords perses." 366: 53 x 7 RR4*. ALN: Alnwick Castle 82, c 1520, ff. 1–8. "tretice...of the descente of the lordes percis maid and compiled by me William Perrs clerke and secretary to the right noble erle Henry of northumberland." 651: aa4*, ababbccdd4*, MT4*, RR4*, irreg. BR (631.8). Hist., nar., genealogy.

TM 314 <Circum>stant lye thre kynges came by nyght.
HN: Ptd. book 82241, mid 16, sig. A1v. 16: 4 x 4 aabb5*. BR (633.5); TP 310. Rel., calendar, mnenomic, tr. French.

TM 315 Cleane witheowt feare truthe dothe me constrene.
O: Ashmole 48, bef. 1558, ff. 7–8v. "quod Thomas Watertonne." 84: 14 x 6 aaa5b2ab5*. Love, complaint.

TM 316 Clime not to hie | lest chipis fall in thin eie.
O17: Balliol 354, 1505–36, f. 191v. (Cf. TM 539.) 2: aa2*. Proverb.

TM 317 Cloister of crist riche recent flour delyss.
E: Asloan, 1513–42, ff. 301v–3. [Walter] Kennyde, "Ane ballat of our lady." 72: 9 x 8 MT5*. BR (636). Rel., Virgin Mary, macaronic, Scots.

TM 318 Coll standyth.
L: Cotton Titus D.11, early 16, f. 56v. Incipit only, with music. Song.

TM 319 Come all ye wyghtes on earth that dwell And heare my penne declare.
L: Add. 33974, c 1550, ff. 7v–8. (Francis Stacy), "A remembrance of the <mercyes of god>." 32: aa7*. Rel instruction.

TM 320 Cum home swet hart cum home cum home.
L: Royal App. 58, 1507+, f. 8v. With music (cf. burden of Greene #270). 24: 4 x 6 abccca4–3*. Song, love.

TM 321 Come, let us singe unto the lorde.
L: Royal 17.A.21, 1551, ff. 5–6v. William Forreste, tr. Ps 94: Venite. 60: 15 x 4 a8b6a8b6. Rel.

TM 322 Come over the woodes faire & grene.
O: Rawl. C.813, 1520–35, ff. 58v–60. 80: 10 x 8 MT4* (ref. for conforth ys non alone to be; 2nd ref. ...alone). BR (642.5). Love, dialogue.

TM 323 Comeforthe at hand pluck up thy harte.
D: TCD 160, 1535–48, f. 81. (Parodied by TM 324.) 25: 5 x 5 a4bab3B2* (ref. Pluck up thy hart; 2nd ref. Comfort at hand). Love.

TM 324 Comfort at hand | pluck up thy hart.
L: Add. 15233, 1554–58, ff. 28v–9. (Religious parody of TM 323.) 45: 9 x 5 a4bab3B2* (ref. Pluck up thy heart). Rel., grace.

TM 325 Comfort thy self my wofull hert.
L: Eger. 2711, bef. 1542, f. 48v. "Tho[mas Wyatt]." 24: 6 x 4 abaB8 (ref. Why sighes thou then and woult not breke). L: Add. 17492, 1532–39, f. 74. Love.

TM 326 Compatience persis reuth and marcy stoundis.
L: Arundel 285, c 1540, ff.159v–61. "The passioun of Christ." 64: 8 x 8 MT5*. E2: Laing 149, 1/4 16, f. 86v. BR (648). Rel., nar, passion, Scots.

TM 327 Compleyn I may wher soo ever I goo.
O: Rawl. C.813, 1520–35, f. 46v. 21: 3 x 7 RR4*. L: Add. 5465, 1501–04, ff. 46v–8. First stanza only, with music; variant first line "Complayne may wher evyr I go." BR (649). Song, love.

TM 328 Complayne we maye miche ys a mise.
L: Add. 60577, 1549–58, ff. 57v–8v. "Totus mundus in maligno est positus," dated 1549. 64: 16 x 4 abab4*. TP 320. Complaint.

TM 329 Complaynyng alas without redres.
D: TCD 160, 1535–48, f. 80. 24: 6 x 4 abab4* (ref. Wherefore Alas I dy Alas; 2nd ref. Wherefore alas I dy I dy). Love, complaint.

TM 330 Conscyence by readinge this I fynde.
L: Add. 33974, c 1550, f. 57v. (Francis Stacy), "Of Conscyence." 32: 8 x 4 abab4*. Rel. instruction.

TM 331 Consider well with every circumstaunce.
L: Add. 29729, 1558, f.149v–51v. "a balad of good counsayle translated out of the vercis in latine...[by] lidgate" [incorrect attribution]. 133: RR5* (ref. A

wycked tonge wolle allwaye deme amys). BR 653, comp. a 1500; TP 327.5. Moral.

TM 332 Considring effectually the grete diversite.
L: Add. 29729, 1558, ff. 3–4v. 136: 17 x 8 MT5* (ref. Allas quid eligam ignoro). BR 655, comp. a 1500. Rel., trust in god, choice of profession.

TM 333 Consideryng Godes mercye greate.
O: Ashmole 48, bef. 1558, ff. 66–7v. "A songe Exortinge to the laude of God," subscribed "[Henry] Sponer." 72: 12 x 6 ababcc8. Song, rel., God's mercy.

TM 334 Considerynge this worlde and the Incres off vice.
O: Ashmole 48, bef. 1558, ff. 45–7. "quoth T. S. P." 112: 14 x 8 MT4*. Moral, against lies and flattery.

Coventes off monkes channo[n]s of charthous. Portion of TM 467.

TM 335 Counsaill which afterward is sought is like the untimely showers | distillinge from the duskish cloudes when heath hath parched ye flowers.
O: e Musaeo 63, mid 16, f. 146v. Copied three times. 2: aa6*. Proverb, moral.

Cover allway from cold thi hede. See TM 420.

TM 336 Crose and curtys crist, thys begynyng spede.
L: Royal 18.B.17, 2/4 16, ff. 1–13v. [Pierce the Ploughman's Creed.] 855: allit. BR 663, comp. c 1395?; TP 332.5. Nar., rel. controversy.

TM 337 ...< c>rowne of thorne so scharpe and kene.
NY: Drexel 4180, 2/4 16, f. 1. Acephalous fragment, with music; last line: "...ytt were I lothe that yow shuld spyll." 6: aabbcc4*. BR (664.3). Song, rel., Jesus.

Cruell desire my [master] & my foo. See TM 350.

TM 338 Cunnyng and Vertu is not sett by.
LONG: Longleat 254, early 16, last leaf. 7: RR4*. BR (665). Moral.

TM 339 [Cupido unto whos commandement].
[Thomas Hoccleve, "The letter of Cupyde," comp. 1402, tr. from the French of Christine de Pisan; BR 666, TP 333.5.] L: Add. 17492, 1532–39, ff. 89v, 91. Extracts, vv. 344–50, 64–77, 302–8, copied from STC 5068, Thynne's *Chaucer* (1532), beginning "Woman's herte unto no crueltye," "Ys thys afayre avanture," and "How frendly was Medea to Jason." 28: 4 x 7 RR5*. Love, epistle, women.

TM 340 Cursyd be he that furst began.
D: TCD 160, 1535–48, f. 82r–v. 42: 14 x 3 aba and terza rima4*. Love.

TM 341 Danger thy selff led for nothyng.
D: TCD 160, 1535–48, f. 91r–v. 35: 5 x 7 RR4*. Moral, adversity.

Disceite disceyvyth and shall be disceyved. Extract from TM 556.

TM 342 Deme as ye list uppon goode cause.
L: Add. 17492, 1532–39, f. 84v. 32: 4 x 8 ababcacB8 (ref. I wolde I thought yt ware not). Love.

TM 343 Deme no thyng that is in dowt | till the trowth be tred owt.
O17: Balliol 354, 1505–36, f. 200v. [Listed under BR 675.5 (TM 344), but a separate poem.] 2: aa4*. Proverb.

TM 344 Deme the best of every dowt | tyll the trowth be try[ed] owt.
L: Add. 31922, 1513+, f. 79v. With music by J. ffluyd [Lloyd]. 2: aa4*. L: Harl 1587, 2/4 16, f. 212. Copied twelve time as pen practice; variant first line: "Deme the best in every dowte"; tr. "In dubiis servi..." O: Rawl. C.86, early 16, f. 31. Begins "Deame the best in every dowte." BR 675.5, comp. 14th century (see Joan Evans, *English Art* (1949), p. 90); cf. TM 343. Moral, proverb.

TM 345 Demyd wrongffully | In absent | & wote not why.
L: Add. 5465, 1501–04, f. 9v. With incomplete musical setting (3 leaves lacking). 28: 4 x 7 a3baccc2A3* (ref. ...demyd wrongfully). BR (675.8). Song, love.

TM 346 Defamed gyltynes by sylens unkept.
D: TCD 160, 1535–48, f. 86. 12: 3 x 4 aabb4* (ref. ...never do soo agayne, forgyve me this). Love.

Defend me saynt mychaell archaungell. Part of TM 467.

TM 347 Defyled is my name ffull wroungfullye.
L: Add. 30513, c 1550, ff. 78v–9v. Incipit only, with music by Johnson. Song.

TM 348 Degrese of lyghtnes lefte be hy<nd>.
D: TCD 160, 1535–48, f. 176v. Subscribed "H" [Muir attributes to Surrey]. 6: mono8. Women, dispraise.

TM 349 Departure is my chef payne | I trust ryght wel of retern agane.
L: Add. 31922, 1513+, ff. 60v–1. With music by "the Kyng H. VIII." 2: aa4*. BR (676.5). Song, love.

TM 350 Desire alas my master & my foo.
L: Egerton 2711, bef. 1542, f. 50. [Wyatt]. 8: abababcc10. L: Add. 17492, 1532–39, f. 73. Variant first line "Cruel desire my master and my foe." TP 344. Love.

TM 351 Desyre to sorow doth me constrayne.
D: TCD 160, 1535–48, f. 85. 16: 4 x 4 aaa4R2* (ref. But paciens). Moral.

TM 352 Dic [H]erode impie.
L: Add. 5665, bef. 1511, ff. 6v–7. "De innocentibus," with music. 17: 2 burd aa + 3 x 5 ababR4* (burd. Sonet laus per secula; ref. ...milicia). BR (680). Rel., carol, Holy Innocents, macaronic.

TM 353 Dydo am I the fownder furst of cartage.
D: TCD 160, 1535–48, f. 90. [Based on an epigram attributed to Ausonius.] 8: abababcc5*. Myth, hist.

TM 354 Dieus vous garde byewsser tydynges y yow bryng.
L: Add. 5665, bef. 1511, ff. 8v–9v. "In die nativitatis," with music. 19: 7 burd abaccca + 3 x 4 aaaR4* (burd. Nowell nowell nowell nowell; ref. Nowell). BR (681). Rel., carol, advent.

TM 355 Dysdayne me not wythout desert.
L: Add. 18752, 1530's, f. 163v. [Wyatt.] 25: abab8C4 (ref. Refuse me not). BR (681.5); TP 348. Love.

TM 356 Dysdayne not madam on hym too louke.
D: TCD 160, 1535–48, f. 92. 24: 4 x 6 a4b3a4b3cc4*. Love, complaint.

TM 357 Dyvers dothe use as I have hard & kno.
L: Add. 17492, 1532–39, f. 77v. 14: abbaabbacddcee10. Love.

TM 358 Dives and lazarus the scripture saythe plaine.
L: Add. 60577, 1549–58, f. 216. 14: aa4*. Rel. instruction.

TM 359 Do sum good man by thy lyffe.
O17: Balliol 354, 1503–04, f. 147v. 4: mono4*. L2: Lambeth 259, early 16, f. 234v. BR (686); TP 351. Practical (on wills).

TM 360 Do thou o Lorde | My prayer heare.
L: Royal 17.A.17, 1551+, ff. 12,14. Sir Thomas Smith, tr. "Psalme 54" [55] 144: 24 x 6 ab2c3ab2c3*. Rel.

TM 361 Do way do way ye lytyll wyly prat.
D: TCD 160, 1535–48, f. 84. 28: 4 x 7 RR5*. Love.

TM 362 Do woll whill thou art here | and thou shalt have well els wher.
O17: Balliol 354, 1505–36, f. 200. Tr. "Fac bene dum..." 2: aa4*. BR (687.5). Proverb.

Do what they wyll and do the worst. See TM 1042.

TM 363 Do what you Lust.
D: TCD 160, 1535–48, f. 60. Incipit only from table of contents.

TM 364 Docter Rest and docter quyett | Docter myrthe and docter dyett.
C7: Corpus Christi 31, early 16, flyleaf. "Master Skeltons docters of cownsell" [erroneous attribution.] 2: aa4*. Moral.

TM 365 Dorn, Norten Rippley and no more.
C2: TCC O.8.32 (1407), 1557?, f. 128v. "T[homas] Charnock." 6: aa4*. Alchemy, satire.

TM 366 Dobbell dyverse soleyn and straunge.
D: TCD 160, 1535–48, f. 89. Written twice in different hands. 16: ababbbbccccccdeffe4*. Love.

TM 367 Downbery down | now am I exiled my lady fro.
L: Add. 31922, 1513+, f. 25. With music by Wyllm. Daggere. 8: abbc4d2cca4*. L: Royal App. 58, 1507+, f. 4v. "A Rownde" with music; begins "Downbery down down hay down." BR (688.8). Song, love.

TM 368 Drede god and alle thyng schal drede you.
O: Tanner 407, 1/4 16, f. 36v. 5: aaabb5*. BR (690). Rel. instruction.

TM 369 Drede god and fle from syn.
L: Royal 18.D.2, c 1520, f. 204v. "The proverbes in the roufe of my lordis library at Lekyngefeld [Leconfield]." 92: aaaa4*. BR (691). Moral, proverbs.

Drede owur lord god bothe nyght and day. Lines 66–69 of TM 221; 13–14 of TM 219.

TM 370 Dryven bye desire I dede this dede.
L: Add. 17492, 1532–39, f. 81v. [Wyatt.] 7: RR4*. D: TCD 160, 1535–48, f. 87. 31: 7 RR4* + 3 x 8 MT4*. TP 356 (vv. 1–7 only). Moral, love.

TM 371 Dryven to desyre a drad also to dare.
D: TCD 160, 1535–48, f. 88. 14: abbaabbacdcdee5*. Love.

TM 372 Dwrese of paynes & grevus smarte.
D: TCD 160, 1535–48, f. 83. 24: 6 x 4 abab8 (ref. Why syest thou, hart, and will not brake). Love, complaint.

TM 373 E and now thys letel D.
HN: HM 136, early 16, f. 66. Ownership rhyme of Dorothy Helbartun. 4: abab3*.

TM 374 Eche day that schyneth persuade the latter stowre | happy befalleth soo the unhoped houre.
C2: TCC B.16.41 (402), early 16, flyleaf. 2: aa5*. Proverb.

TM 375 Eche man folowith his owne fantasie.
L: Add. 29729, 1558, ff. 124v–6. "Iohn lydgat." 136: 17 x 8 MT4*. BR 698, comp. a 1449. Rel., moral.

TM 376 Eche man me telleth I chaunge moost my devise.
L: Egerton 2711, bef. 1542, f. 11v. "Tho[mas Wyatt]." 14: abbaabbacd-dcee5*. L: Add. 17492, 1532–39, f. 75v. Variant first line "Eche man telles me..." TP 359. Moral.

Erly in the dawny[n]ge of the day. Lines 69–71 of TM 221; 18–19 of TM 219.

TM 377 [Erthe owte of erthe is wondyrly wroght].
L: Harl 984, early 16, f. 72. (B-version, begins "How schulde erthe upon erthe be prud and gay.") 6: aaaa4*. O17: Balliol 354, 1505–36, f. 207v. (Also B-version; begins "Erth owt of erth is worldly wrought.") 64: 16 x 4 aaaa4*. BR 704, comp. c 1450. Rel., death, moral, ubi sunt.

TM 378 Ecclesiastes Salomon | Son of David that worthy kynge.
L:Add. 30981, 1522–29, ff. 39–41v. John Croke, tr. Ecclesiastes, chap. 1. 84: RR4*. Rel.

TM 379 8 is my trew love do beffore 9.
O17: Balliol 354, 1505–36, f. 219. Numerical riddle [HIESUS = Jesus] 4: mono4*. C2: TCC B.16.31 (394), early 16, f. 4v. BR 717, comp. a 1450? Riddle, rel., Jesus.

TM 380 Ely the elect on the Sabathe dothe praye.
D: TCD 160, 1535–48, f. 153v. 6: ababcc4*. Rel., satire.

TM 381 Enforce thy wyttes for to lere.
C2: TCC O.2.53 (1157), early 16, f. 60. 4: abab4*. BR (726). Moral.

TM 382 Entierly belovyd & most yn my mynde.
O: Rawl. C.813, 1520–35, f. 52r–v. 32: 8 x 4 abab4*. BR (729). Love, epistle.

TM 383 Or I begyn | my threde to spyn.
L8: Guildhall 3313, c 1510, f. 329–30v. "A Balad of Knave Baptist" [John Baptist de Grimaldis, extortionist], with verse title: "The legend of Baptyst here Afftyr ensuyth | Of whom all good men, the long lyffe Ruyth." 167: 2 aa11 + 28 x 6 aa4b6cc4b6, some anapestic. Satire, nar., hist.

TM 384 Arectynge my syght towarde the zodyake.
L: Cott. Vitellius E.10, 2/4 16, ff. 223–40v. [John Skelton, *The Garland of Laurel*, damaged copy, vv. after 245 illegible.] 245: 35 x 7 RR10. BR (729.5); TP 366. Nar., allegory, praise.

TM 385 Esperaunce en dyeu | Truste in hym he is moste trew.
L: Royal 18.D.2, c 1520, ff. 201–2. "The proverbis in the...chambre in the gardinge at Lekingfelde [Leconfield]". 60: aa4*. BR (730). Rel., proverbs.

Eternale god the ground of every gud. Last line of acephalous TM 159.

Evyn as you lyst my wyll ys bent. Variant first line of TM 418.

TM 386 Even when you lust ye may refrayne.
D: TCD 160, 1535–48, f. 105. "The answer" (to TM 2042). 32: 8 x 4 abaB4* (ref. Hit ys naught but your fantasy). Love.

TM 387 Ever is 6 the best chaunce of the dice.
L: Harley 559, 1554, f. 39r–v. Begins "Even six ys the..." 48: aa4* + abab4*. L: Cott. Cleopatra C.4, mid 16, f. 123v. 12 lines. C2: TCC O.2.53 (1157), early 16, f. 41. Begins "When six is the best cast of the dyse." 11 lines. O: Arch. Seld. B.8, mid 16, f. 271r–v. "The chaunces of dyce"; begins "Off all chaunces six ys moste at the dyce." 46 lines. L: Lansd. 762, 1524–29, f. 96r–v. 10 lines. L11: PRO SP 1/232, 1520, f. 219. Begins "Whan sise ys the best Caste of the dyesce." 13 lines. L: Sloane 2578, c 1557, f. 45v. Repeated on ff. 64, 67, 52v. 10 lines. BR 734.8, comp. a 1500. Prophecy.

TM 388 Ever myn happ is slack and slo in comyng.
L: Egerton 2711, bef. 1542, f. 22v. Wyatt, tr. Petrarch, *Rime* 57. 14: abbaabbacddcee10. TP 374. Love.

Ever 6 ys the best chance at the dyce. Variant first line of TM 387.

TM 389 Ever sovereyn swete, swettist in sith.
O: Lat. misc. c.66, c 1500, f. 93v. (Humfrey Newton.) 4: abab4*. BR (737). Love.

Ever the ferther I goo the ferther I am behynde. Variant first line of TM 1568.

TM 390 Everlastynge lof to me I have tane.
O: Lat. misc. c.66, c 1500, f. 92v. (Humfrey Newton.) 4: abab4*. BR (735). Love.

TM 391 Everie man knoweth his own faulte.
L: Royal 17.A.17, 1551, ff. 26v–7v. Sir Thomas Smith, "An other Psalme" (against political opponents of Warwick when he made himself Duke of Northumberland, 1551). 32: a4b3a4b3*. Hist.

TM 392 Exceedyng mesure wyth payne continewall.
L: Add. 15233, 1554–58, f. 44v. [John Redford.] 14: 2 x 7 RR4*. Song, moral.

TM 393 Ey flatteringe fortune looke thow never so faire.
L: Royal 17.D.14, mid 16, f. 453. [Sir Thomas More], "Lewes the loste lover." 7: RR5*. TP 385. Rel., personal.

TM 394 Fayre and discrete fresche wommenly figure.
L: Add. 5665, bef. 1511, ff. 72v–3. With music. 9: aabaabbab5*. BR (753.8). Song, love.

TM 395 Fayre maydyn who is this barn.
O17: Balliol 354, 1503–04, ff. 176–8v. 20: 4 burd. (aaaa) + 4 x 4 aabb3* (burd. Mater ora filium). BR (755). Rel., carol, Virgin Mary.

ffayrest of fayer and godleste on lyve. Introductory stanza to the Envoy of TM 1860.

TM 396 Fayrnes and yong blood.
L: Royal 8.C.12, early 16, f. 1v. 4: aabb4*. BR (756). Moral.

TM 397 Fals hert may | Trwe lufe betray.
L: Cott. Vitellius C.13, early 16, f. 311. 2: aa2*. Love.

TM 398 False love when vi setteth against viii.
C: Kk.6.16, c 1500, f. 153v. Nearly illegible. 20: ? BR (757). Prophecy.

TM 399 Fancey framed my hart furst.
L: Add. 17492, 1532–39, ff. 61v–2. 21: 3 x 7 RR8. Love.

TM 400 ffer fro thi kynsmen caste the.
L: Ptd. book IB 49408, early 16, f. 34v. 4: mono3*. L: Lansd. 762, 1524–29, f. 16v. BR 761, comp. a 1486; TP 389.5. Moral.

TM 401 ffarewell all my wellfare.
L: Add. 17492, 1532–39, ff. 9v–10. 36: 6 x 6 abab6cc8. Love.

TM 402 ffarewell Love and all thy lawes for ever.
L: Egerton 2711, bef. 1542, f. 13. "Tho[mas Wyatt]." 14: abbaabbacddcee10.
L: Add. 17492, 1532–39, f. 75. Begins "Now fare well..." TP 390. Love.

ffare wele my frendis the tide abideth no mann. Last stanza of TM 407.

TM 403 Farewell my Joy and my swete hart.
L: Add. 31922, 1513+, ff. 66v–8. Music by D[r]. Cooper. 8: 2 x 4 a8b6a8b6. BR (765.5). Song, love.

Fayre wele my Joye my comfort and solace. See TM 1098.

TM 404 Farewell now my lady gaye.
O: Rawl. C.813, 1520–35, ff. 52v–3. 32: 4 x 8 MT4* (ref. I take my leve agaynst my wyll). BR (767). Love.

TM 405 Fare-well, that was my lef so dere.
O: Lat. misc. c.66, c 1500, f. 93v. (Humfrey Newton.) 24: 3 x 8 MT4*. BR (768). Love.

TM 406 ffarewell the rayn of crueltie.
L: Eger. 2711, bef. 1542, f. 12. [Wyatt.] 16: 4 x 4 aaaa8. TP 391. Love.

TM 407 Farewell this world I take my leve for ever.
O17: Balliol 354, 1505–36, f. 199r–v. (Incorporates BR 765 as 5th stanza.) 35: 5 x 7 RR5*. C2: TCC O.2.53 (1157), early 16, f. 67. 26 lines. L: Lansd. 762, 1524–29, f. 19v. "Epitaphum"; last stanza only, begins "Fare wele my frendis the tide abideth no mann." 7 lines. BR (769). Rel., death, epitaph.

ffarewell thomas I wend my waye. See TM 193.

TM 408 Father I am thine onlye soone.
L: Add. 15233, 1554–58, ff. 35–7v. Subscribed "Mr. [John] Redford." 138: 23 x 6 ababcC4* (ref. Nolo mortem peccatoris). BR (782.5). Rel., nar., monologue of Christ.

TM 409 Father, keep me still with the, I the pray.
L: Royal 17.C.7, 1551, f. 1v. John Hart, "The booke to the Author" and "The author to the boke," prefacing "The unreasonable writing of our inglish toung," 1551. 10: 1 x 4 abab5* + 1 x 6 abbaba5*. Author's preface, orthography.

TM 410 Fyll the cuppe phylyppe and let us drynke a drame.
L: Cott. Vespasian A.25, c 1555, f. 37. 6: poulters. Song, convivial.

TM 411 ffyrst calcyon and after that putrfie.
O: Ashm. 759, early 16, f. 78r–v. 20: 5 x 4 irreg. rhymes. BR 801, comp. a 1500. Alchemy.

TM 412 First helth and successe with many a good newe yeare.
PFOR: MS 40A, 1553+, ff. 360–87. [Nicholas Udall?] "A mery entrelude entitled Respublica made inn 1553." (Prologue and five Acts divided into scenes; includes incipits of four songs plus "content et extant" at the end without words. Songs indexed separately.) 2,063: abab6*, aa5–6*. Drama, morality play, political.

TM 413 First two and then one then three and then five.
O17: Balliol 354, 1503–04, f. 178v. "Seynt Thomas Lottis," also copied on f. 221v. 2: aa4*. BR (805). Riddle.

Flaunders and England shall fall at decensyon. Lines 25–36, 41–52 of TM 1260.

TM 414 Fle from the prece and dwell with sothfastnes.
O: Arch. Seld. B.10, c 1520, ff. 201v–2. "Ecce bonum consilium galfredi chaucers contra fortunam" [Chaucer's "Truth," without envoy, incorporated in *The Proverbs of Lydgate*]. 21: 3 x 7 RR5* (ref. And trouthe the shall delyver it is no drede). BR 809, comp. c 1390; TP 404.5. Moral.

TM 415 Fonde youthe is a bubble.
L: Add. 30513, c 1550, f. 29v. Incipit only with music by Thomas Tallys. Song.

TM 416 Folys lade polys, wisemen ete the fysshe | Wisemen hath in their hondes ofte that folys ofte wyssh.
O: Rawl. C.86, early 16, f. 31. 2: aa5*. Moral, proverb.

TM 417 [For age is a page].
O: Rawl. C.813, 1520–35, ff. 36v–42v. [Skelton, *Why Come Ye Not to Court*, vv. 841–1217, beginning "Ytt were greate Ruythe"; introduced by TM 1770, followed by epilogue, TM 1109.] 356: skeltonics. BR (813.3), comp. 1522; TP 411. Satire, hist., Cardinal Wolsey, rel. controversy.

TM 418 For as ye lyst my wyll ys bent.
L: Add. 17492, 1532–39, f. 20. 37: 2 burd aa + 7 x 5 aaaa8B4 (burd. As power and wytt wyll me assyst; ref. Evyn as ye lyst). L: Add. 18752, 1530's, ff.

89v–90. Without burden; begins "Even as you lyst..." 35 lines. BR (813.6). Carol, love.

TM 419 ...For full fayne I wold do that myght you please.
C2: TCC R.3.17 (597), 1501–25, ff. 2–124v. [Romance of *Partenay*, from the French abridged metrical version of Melusine by La Coudette, c. 1400. Acephalous, first leaf lacking; last line: "yut excusith me besech you hertely."] 6,615: 945 x 7 RR5*. BR (819.5)*. Nar., romance.

TM 420 For helthe of Bodye kepe from cold thyne hede.
L: Harley 2252, 1517–38, f. 1v. [Lydgate, "Dietary".] 24: 3 x 8 MT5*. L: Harl. 5401, early 16, ff. 103–4. "Bonum concilium," begins "Cover allway from cold thi hede." 61 lines. O: e Musaeo 52, 1/4 16, ff. 80v–1. Run into text as prose. 80 lines. O: Lat. theol. d.15, 1551, ff. 132–3. "Dietarium salutis," copied by Robert Parkyn. 80 lines. E2: Laing 149, 1/4 16, f. 190r–v. (In Scots dialect.) 80 lines. BR 824, comp. a 1449; TP 415.5. Medical.

TM 421 For his love that bowght us all dere.
O17: Balliol 354, 1505–36, f. 229. 18: 2 burd. (aa) + 4 x 4 aaaB8 (burd. Synge we all for tyme it is; ref. ...can the flowr de lyce). BR (825). Rel., carol, nativity.

For love ys yet the moste stormy lyfe. See TM 1510.

TM 422 For love of god and drede of peyne.
O: Tanner 407, 1/4 16, f. 35v. 4: aabb4*. BR (832). Moral.

For man withowt mercy of mercy shall misse. See TM 28.

TM 423 For mercy lord to the I call.
L: Add. 33974, c 1550, f. 53. (Francis Stacy), "A prayer to obtayne the mercy of god." 36: 9 x 4 abab4*. Rel., prayer.

TM 424 ffor my pastyme upon A day.
L: Royal App. 58, 1507+, f. 4. With music. 20: 2 burd aa + 4 x 4 abab4* (burd. Colle to me the rysshes grene). BR (835.5). Carol.

TM 425 For of all Tresure Learnynge is the flower.
HN: EL 26.C.9, early 16, f.ii. One line of verse, following (or meant to be part of?) TM 1482. Moral.

For thylke grounde that bearyth the wedes wyck. See TM 1510.

For though I had yow tomorrow agayne. See TM 1684.

TM 426 For thought constraint and grevous hevynesse.
LONG: Longleat 258, 1500+, f. 1–32. [John Lydgate], "the Temple of Glas." 1,403: RR5*, aa5*. BR 851, comp. c 1420; TP 434.5. Nar., allegory, love, dream.

TM 427 ...for thi sake man to whom yf thou call at an< >.
NY: Drexel 4180, 2/4 16, f. 1v. Fragment, with music. 4: ? (burd. In a f<orest?> laytt as I was I...). BR (851.3). Rel., carol, monologue of Christ.

TM 428 ffor to love her for her lokes lovely.
L: Egerton 2711, bef. 1542, f. 14. [Wyatt.] 15: aabbaaab10C4aabba10C4 (ref. ffor to love her). L: Add. 17492, 1532–39, f. 75. Love.

TM 429 [For why that God is inwardly the wit].
[Benedict Burgh, *Cato Major*, BR 854, comp. a 1440?; TP 428.5.] L: Royal 18.D.2, c 1520, ff. 207–9. "The proverbes in the sydis of the innere chamber...at Wresill [Wressel, Yorks.]" (Stanzas 1, 3–4, 6–10, 12–17, 19–21 are extracted from *Cato Major*; begins "When it is tyme of coste and greate expens." 168: RR5*. L: Add. 29729, 1558, f. 288v. Fragment (stanza 104) of *Cato Major*; begins "sum wemen wepyn." 7 lines. Moral, proverbs, attack on women.

TM 430 For you my lady i am negh slayn.
O: Lat. misc. c.66, c 1500, f. 94v. (Humfrey Newton.) 16: 4 x 4 abaB4* (ref. For ye have my hert for ever more). BR (855). Love.

TM 431 fforget not yet the tryde entent.
L: Add. 17492, 1532–39, f. 54v. 20: 5 x 4 aaa4R2* (ref. fforget not yet). Love.

TM 432 Fortunate is he who hathe the happe | To bewarre by another mans clappe.
DUR5: Cosin V.iii.9, c 1555, f. 82v. Tr. "Felix quem faciunt aliena pericula cantum" 2: aa4*. BR (859.5). Moral.

TM 433 Fortune Alas is this thy chaunce.
L11: PRO SP 1/246, mid 16, f. 26. With music. 4: abab4*. Song, love.

TM 434 ffortune dothe frown.
L: Add. 17492, 1532–39, f. 78v. 4: ab4a3b4. Fortune.

TM 435 Fortune hathe fayled alas why so.
Y: Osborn music 13, 1553+, ff. 47v–8. 40:10 x 4 abab8, linked. Song, love, lament.

TM 436 Fortune is nowe my foe.
Y: Osborn music 13, 1553+, f. 27. 35: 4 x 8 aaabaaab3* + 3 aaa3*. Song, fortune.

TM 437 Fortune ys varyant ay tornyng her whele | He ys wyse that ys ware or he harm fele.
O17: Balliol 354, 1503–04, f. 160. 2: aa4*. BR 860.3, comp. a 1477; TP 435.5. Proverb, fortune.

TM 438 Fortune unfrendly thou art unto me.
L: Add. 60577, 1549–58, f. 116v. 5: abbcc4*. Rel., moral, fortune.

TM 439 Fortune unkynde.
L: Royal App. 56, 1508+, f. 22. Incipit only, with music. Song.

TM 440 ffortune what aylith the.
D: TCD 160, 1535–48, f. 151. [imperfect text.] 20: 3 x 6 aabccb3*, + 2 aa3*. Love.

Foure poyntis my will or I hence depart. See TM 767.

TM 441 ffraunce and fflaundrs than shall aryse.
L: Lansd. 762, 1524–29, f. 53v. 4: abab4*. BR (864.5). Prophecy.

TM 442 ffre freteth this world and de confoundyth alle.
L: Cott. Nero C.11, 1506+, f. 77. Robert Fabyan, tr. "Fre fremit in mundo," verses on the Emperor Frederick, 1250. 7: RR4*. HD: Eng 766F, 1504, f. 48. TP 438. Hist.

TM 443 Free wyll thow haste gywyne me lord to chuse.
L: Add. 33974, c 1550, f. 78. Francys Stacy, "< > as before." Acrostic: "Francys Stacy a sinnefull creature." 30: aa4*. Rel.

TM 444 ffrere gastkyn wo thou be.
L: Royal App. 58, 1507+, ff. 24v–5v. With music by Raff Drake. 28: 7 x 4 abab4*. BR (870.5). Song, macaronic, friars, satire.

TM 445 ffreshe lusty beaute Joyned with gentyllnesse.
L: Add. 29729, 1558, f. 157r–v. "A Balade which lydgate made at the request of a squyer that served in loves courte." 49: 7 x 7 RR5*. BR 869, comp. a 1449. Love.

Frend and we ar ffer in det. See TM 826.

TM 446 From Adams fall to noees noyfull floudd.
D: TCD 160, 1535–48, f. 93v. 24: 3 x 8 ababccdd10. Love, praise of mistress.

TM 447 ffrom depth off sin & from a diepe dispaire.
L: Egerton 2711, bef. 1542, f. 97. Wyatt, Penitential Psalms, tr. "de profundis clamavi" [Ps. 130]. 31: terza rima10. TP 441. Rel.

TM 448 From hevyn was sent an angell of light.
O17: Balliol 354, 1505–36, f. 219v. 37: 2 burd. (aa) + 7 x 5 aaa8b4b8–10 (burd. Now we shuld syng and say Newell). BR (878). Rel., carol, annunciation, macaronic.

TM 449 From thence, almost, comes everie cause of mischief for no vice.
L8: Guildhall 3035, c 1550, f. 102v. "concupiscence." 7: aa14bcbcd8. Moral, greed.

TM 450 From thes hye hilles as when a spryng dothe fall.
L: Egerton 2711, bef. 1542, f. 66. "Tho[mas Wyatt]" (holograph). 8: abababcc10. D: TCD 160, 1535–48, f. 73. Begins: "As from these hylles." TP 444. Love.

TM 451 From thowght to thowght from hill to hill love doth me lede | clene contrary from restfull lyff thes comon pathes I trede.
L: Egerton 2711, bef. 1542, f. 70. [Wyatt], tr. Petrarch, *Rime* 129.1–3. 2: poulters. Love.

TM 452 From tyme of Brewte awctors do specyfye.
L: Lansd. 210, 1553–58, ff.14v–17v. "Versus of John Lydgate monke of bery" [Kings of England, 5 of 15 stanzas]. 35: 5 x 7 RR5*. BR 882, comp. c 1475. Hist.

TM 453 ffull well yt maye be sene.
L: Add. 17492, 1532–39, f. 51. 35: 5 x 7 RR8. Love.

TM 454 Gabriell brygth[er] then the sonne.
L: Add. 5665, bef. 1511, ff. 12v–13. "In die circumcisionis," with music. 14: 2 burd aa + 3 x 4 abab4* (burd. Make us meri this new yere). BR (887). Rel., carol, New Year.

TM 455 Gabriell of hygh degre.
O17: Balliol 354, 1505–36, f. 219v. 34: 2 burd. (aa) + 8 x 4 aaa4B1* (burd. Nova Nova | Ave fit ex Eva; ref. Vith noua). BR 889, comp. a 1500. Rel., carol, annunciation, macaronic.

TM 456 Gabryell that angell bryght.
O17: Balliol 354, 1505–36, f. 221v. 18: 2 burd. (aa) + 4 x 4 aaa4*R8 (burd. Now synge we syng we; ref. Regina celi letare). BR 890, comp. a 1500. Rel., carol, annunciation.

TM 457 Galauntis purse penyles per vicos ecce vagrantur | yf it be as I ges male solunt quod mutuantur.
L: Lansd. 762, 1524–29, f. 92. 2: aa6*. BR (892.5). Macaronic, moral.

TM 458 Gardeyn ways Comfort of flowres | so hight my leman what high[t] yowrs.
O17: Balliol 354, 1505–36, f. 219. Riddle [answer = "Alison" (included in BR 597.5)]. 2: aa4*.

TM 459 Gaude Maria Cristis moder.
O17: Balliol 354, 1505–36, f. 219. "Explicit de quinque gaudia" [by John Audelay]. 50: 2 burd. (aa) + 6 x 8 ababcdc8c7 (burd. Ave Maria now say we so). BR 895. comp. a 1500. Rel., carol, Five Joys of Mary, macaronic.

TM 460 Gaude to whom Gabryell was sent.
O17: Balliol 354, 1505–36, f. 228v. 22: 2 burd. (aa) + 5 x 4 abab4* (burd. Gawde for thy joyes five). BR (898). Rel,, carol, Virgin Mary.

TM 461 Gay cotes grayceles | longe berdes hartles.
O: Ptd. book 8°C.70.Th. Seld., 1540+, sig. 2L7v. 6: aaaa3bb4*. Moral.

TM 462 Jentill butler, bellamy.
O17: Balliol 354, 1505–36, ff. 251v–2. 27: 2 burd. (aa) + 5 x 5 aaaBB3* (burd. How, butler, how Bevis a towt; ref. ...and let the cup rowght). BR (903). Carol, convivial.

TM 463 [Gifte hys made domesman].
L: Add. 60577, 1549–58, ff. 75v–6. [Variant of "Four Philosophers on the Evils of the Age", *Gesta Romanorum* #144 (English version), begins "Wyt ys treachery luff ys lechery."] 12: aa2* (ref. Wyt ys trechery, Wysse men ar blynd). BR 906, comp. c 1450. Moral.

TM 464 Geve yere my childres to my wordes.
C3: Emmanuel 4.1.17(260), mid 16, ff. 1v–2. "Thomas Mathews to his wiffe and childres." 18: aa14. Rel. instruction.

TM 465 Gyve place all ye that dothe rejose.
L: Add. 17492, 1532–39, f. 77v. 36: 6 x 6 ababbb8. Love.

Gyve thow trewe weyghte mete and measure. Lines 15–16 of TM 221.

TM 466 [Gladeth ye foules of the morowe gray].
LONG: Longleat 258, 1500+, ff. 49–54v. [Chaucer], "the Complaint of Mars," acephalous, begins at line 43. 254: 17 x 7 RR5*, 15x9 aabaabbcc5*. BR 913, comp. a 1400; TP 466.3. Love, myth.

TM 467 [Glorieux crosse that with the holy blood].
L: Sloane 1584, 1520–31, ff. 16v–8. [Litany to the cross, stanzas 6–15 only; stanzas individually cross referenced.] 70: 10 x 7 RR5*. O17: Balliol 354, 1505–36, f. 209r–v. Partial text; begins "O most blessid Fader omnipotent". 105 lines. BR 914, comp. c 1424; TP 466.5. Rel., prayer, Holy Cross.

TM 468 Glorious God had grete pyte.
O17: Balliol 354, 1505–36, ff. 226v–7. 44: 2 burd. (aa) + 6 x 7 aaa8bccb4 (burd. Synge we with myrth joye and solas). BR (916). Rel., carol, nativity.

TM 469 Glorius god in trinite.
L: Add. 5665, bef. 1511, ff. 32v–3. "De nativitate," music by Smert. 14: 2 burd aa + 3 x 4 aaaR4* (burd. Jhesu fili dei; ref. Miserere mei). BR (918). Rel., carol.

TM 470 Glorye be to god all myghtye.
L: Add. 30981, 1522–29, f. 24v. John Croke, tr. Gloria patri. 8: 2 x 4 abab4*. Rel., hymn.

TM 471 Goo burnyng sighes unto the frosen hert.
L: Egerton 2711, bef. 1542, f. 16v. Wyatt, tr. Petrarch, *Rime* 153. 15: aabbaaab10C4aabba10C4 (ref. Goo burning sighes). L: Add. 17492, 1532–39, f. 61v. TP 468. Love.

TM 472 Go forth litle boke & mekly sheue thy face.
M: Rylands 955, mid 16, f. 2. Envoy to "The Libel of English Policy," TM 1605. 16: 2 x 8 MT5*.

Go forthe myn owne trewe harte innocent. Envoy to TM 1860.

TM 473 Go hert hurt without adversite.
O: Ashmole 191, pt. 4, early 16, ff. 192v–3. With music. 5: ababb4*. BR (925). Love, song.

Go kys the steppes of them that were fartherynge. Extract from TM 556 in *The Proverbs of Lydgate*.

TM 474 Go litull bill and command me hertely.
O: Lat. misc. c.66, c 1500, f. 94. (Humfrey Newton.) 22: aa3*. BR (926). Love, letter.

TM 475 [Go lityll quayere and swyft thy prynses dresse].
O: Lat. misc. c.66, c 1500, ff. 107–11. [Lydgate, "Nightingale", acephalous], subscribed "Humfrey Newton"; begins "Meved of courage by vertew of the season" (line 22). 437: 63 x 7 RR4*. BR 931, comp. 1446. Rel., allegory.

TM 476 God ageynst nature iii thyngys hath wrought.
TOK2: Takamiya MS 6, 1531, f. 119v. "A carolle" (miracles of creation and salvation). 20: 2 burd aa + 2 x 9 ababbcc4b2b4* (burd. By resone of ii and powur of one). BR (933). Rel., carol, nativity.

God all mytty fader of bliss. Part of TM 852.

TM 477 God allmyghte Rewe all wylfull.
O5: Corpus Christi 237, early 16, f. i. (Cf. BR 981.) 3: aaa3*. Rel., prayer.

TM 478 God almyghti save & conse[r]ve oure Kynge.
L: Add. 60577, 1549–58, ff. 24v–37v. "the boke of the governaunce of kynges and princes" [Lydgate, tr. pseudo-Aristotle, *Secreta Secretorum*, imperfect at end]. 737: 105 x 7 RR5*. BR 935, comp. a 1449; TP 482. Moral, political.

TM 479 God & hovre blyssyd lady | safe & kepe Rowland and mare.
C2: TCC O.2.53 (1157), early 16, f. 24v. Prayer for Rowland Rampston, d. 1549, and his wife. 2: aa4*. Rel., prayer.

TM 480 God be in my hedde and in my understandyng.
C10: Magdalene F.4.13, 1528, f. 27v. [Tr. "Jesus soit en ma teste."] 6: mono6*. BR (940); TP 483. Rel., prayer.

TM 481 ...god had incresyde the worlde wythe men.
L: Add. 33974, c 1550, f. 77r–v. (Francis Stacy), "< >" 60: abab4*. Rel. instruction.

TM 482 God is a substaunce forever dureable.
O: Hatton 105, 1548+, f. 165v. [William Baldwin, "The sum of all"]. 7: RR5*. BR (952); TP 491. Rel. instruction.

TM 483 God passeth gold & precyous stone | god shall be god whane gold ys gone.
L: Sloane 1207, mid 16, f. 11v. Repeated on f. 12. 2: aa4*. Moral.

TM 484 God save kyng herry, owur nobyll kyng.
L: Harley 2252, 1525, f. 156r–v. "Of the Cardnell Wolse." 80: 10 x 8 aabbccdd4*. Hist.

TM 485 God safe Kyng hare whare hefer he go or ryde | sent gorge be hys forman hovre blyssed lady be hys gyde.
C2: TCC O.2.53 (1157), early 16, f. 24v. Prayer for King Henry VIII. 2: aa5*. BR (960.3). Rel., prayer, hist.

TM 486 God save king henry wheresoer he be.
C: Dd.13.27, early 16, f. 31. Anthem for marriage of Henry VII and Elizabeth of York (1486) with music by Thomas Ashwell (tenor part). 5: aaaaa5*. C5: St. John's 234, early 16, f. 28. (Bass part.) BR 960.5, comp. 1486. Hist.

TM 487 God save hus all, & well to spede.
O: Ptd. book Arch. A.b.8(10), 1515+, s. sh. Copied on an Indulgence of Pope Leo X, 1515. 6: aa4*. Rel., prayer.

TM 488 God send us pese & unite.
L: Add. 5665, bef. 1511, ff. 50v–1. With music. 26: 2 burd aa + 4 x 6 aabbcC4* (burd. The beste rede that I can; ref. Do well and drede no man). BR (962). Carol, satirical.

TM 489 God that deyde ffor us All.
C: Ee.4.35, early 16, ff. 6v–13v. "Expleycet the cheylde & hes stepdame." 480: 80 x 6 aabccb4*. O17: Balliol 354, 1503–4, ff. 98–100v. "Jak & his Step Dame, & of the Frere." 426 lines. BR 977, comp. a 1475; TP 500.5. Nar., fabliau, humorous.

TM 490 God that dyed upon a tree.
O17: Balliol 354, 1503–04, ff.128–38v. "The siege of Rone" [i.e., Rouen, by John Page]. 1,300: aa4*. BR 979, comp. c 1420. Nar., hist., Henry V.

TM 491 God wote grete cause these wyffys have a mong.
L: Add. 22718, early 16, f. 86v. 20: 5 x 4 aaa4R2* (ref. In besenysse). BR (994.5). Women.

TM 492 Good my lord I schall you hartely pray.
C14: Fitzwilliam 56, bef. 1542, f. 159v. Signed "Mary Sussex" (1st wife of Robert Ratcliffe, d. 1542) in a different hand. 4: aabb5*. Marriage.

TM 493 Good women I say nolyte timere.
L: Add. 41503, early 16, f. 155. (English version of the Easter trope 'Quem

quaeritis,' fifth line damaged, text incomplete.) 5: ababc5*. BR 1006.5+, comp. a 1500. Rel., liturgy.

TM 494 Good workes are lost in me & cannot be founde.
L: Sloane 96, early 16, ff. 27v–8. 11: 5 aaa5bb2* + 6 aabb5cc2*. Moral.

TM 495 Goodman fool ass lovte.
C: Kk.6.18, 1/4 16, front cover. 6: aa4*. BR (1007). Book motto.

TM 496 Grace and good manears maketh a man | But woe be unto him that no good cane.
L: Eger. 2862, mid 16, f. 50. [Also appears as vv. 75–76 of TM 221 and 25–26 of TM 219.] 2: aa4*. BR 1009.3, comp. a 1500. Moral, proverb.

TM 497 Grace and vertew.
L: Royal App. 58, 1507+, f. 31. Incipit only, with music. L: Royal App. 56, 1508+, f. 20v. Incipit only, with music. Song.

TM 498 Great is the lorde, passinge to tell.
L: Royal 17.A.21, 1551, ff. 45v–7. William Forreste, tr. Psalm 47. 56: 14 x 4 a8b6a8b6. Rel.

TM 499 Grete marvaile & wonder I have in my conceite.
L: Lansd. 762, 1524–29, f. 9v. 7: RR5*. BR 1015, comp. after 1486. Moral.

TM 500 Grene flowryng age of your manly countenance.
O: Rawlinson C.813, 1520–35, f. 53v. 15: abababcadefgcchii5*. BR (1017.5). Love, epistle of a woman to her lover.

TM 501 Greeting to you both yn hertye wyse.
L: Add. 17492, 1532–39, f. 79r–v. 42: 6 x 7 RR10. Moral, epistle.

TM 502 Grevus is my sorowe.
L: Sloane 1584, bef. 1550, ff. 85–7. [Parodied by TM 503.] 112: 14 x 8 aabbcdcd3–4*. BR (1018). Love.

TM 503 Grevouse ys my sorowe.
L6: Dyce 45, 2/4 16, f. 17r–v. [Religious parody of TM 502.] 56: 7 x 8 aabbcdcD3* (ref. Ye wilnot frome synne refrayne). BR (1018.5). Rel., monologue of Christ.

TM 504 Grounde the in paciens.
BO: f. Med. 94, mid 16, f. i verso. 16: 2 x 8 aaabcccb2*. Moral, Scots.

TM 505 Had I wiste that now I wott.
D: TCD 160, 1535–48, f. 96. 14: 2 x 7 RR8. Moral.

TM 506 Hayle be thow Mary moder of Cryst.
O17: Balliol 354, 1503–04, f. 147r–v. 48: 6 x 8 MT5*. BR 1032, comp. c 1450. Rel., prayer, Virgin Mary, macaronic.

TM 507 Haylle benigne lorde crist jesu.
O: e Musaeo 160, 1520+, ff. 118–36. [Verse rendering of *Hundred Meditations on the Passion of Christ*, found as a supplement to Suso's *Horlogium Sapientiae*.] 1,036: aa4*. BR (1035). Rel.

TM 508 Hail cristin knycht haill etern confortour.
L: Arundel 285, c 1540, ff. 6–46v. "The passioun of our Lord Jesu Crist compilit be maister Walter Kennedy." 1,715: 245 x 7 RR5*. BR (1040). Rel., nar., Scots.

TM 509 Haill glaid and glorius.
L: Arundel 285, c 1540, ff. 193–6v. "Ane devoit orisoun To oure lady The Virgin Mary Callit Ave Gloriosa." 115: aaaa3*, abab3*, aabaabb3*. BR (1044). Rel., prayer, Virgin Mary, Scots.

TM 510 Heyl gloryous virgyne ground of all our grace.
L: Add. 29729, 1558, ff. 130v–1. "A hymn onn the Five Joys." 40: MT5*. BR 1046, comp. a 1500. Rel., Virgin Mary, hymn.

TM 511 Hayle holy spirett and joye be unto the.
C10: Magdalene F.4.13, 1528, f. 28r–v. 26: aa4*. BR 1051, comp. c 1450. Rel., prayer.

TM 512 Hayle lovely lady laymand so lyght.
O17: Balliol 354, 1503–04, ff. 146v–7. 56: 7 x 8 MT5* (ref. Salue sancta parens). BR (1055). Rel., prayer, Virgin Mary.

TM 513 Hail mare goddis moder ful of grace.
E2: Laing 149, 1/4 16, f. 87. English version of the Ave maria. 5: mono5*. BR (1065). Rel., Virgin Mary.

TM 514 Haill Mary quhais concepcioun.
L: Arundel 285, c 1540, ff. 188v–9. "Ane devoit orisoun till our Lady callit ave cuius concepio." 22: aa4*. BR (1070.3). Rel., prayer, Virgin Mary, Scots.

TM 515 Haill quene of hevin and steren of blis.
L: Arundel 285, c 1540, ff. 196v–7. 8: 2 x 4 aabb4*. BR (1077). Rel., prayer, Virgin Mary, Scots.

TM 516 Hale sterne superne, hale Ineterne.
E: Asloan, 1513–42, ff. 303–4v. "Ane ballat of our lady, quod Dunbar." 84: 7 x 12 a8b6a8b6a8b6a8b6C10bab8 (ref. Ave maria gracia plena). BR (1082.5). Rel., Virgin Mary.

TM 517 Half in a dreme nat fully wele awaked.
LONG: Longleat 258, 1500+, ff. 120–36. [Sir Richard Ros], tr. Alain Chartier, *La Belle Dame sans Merci*. 856: 8 x 7 RR5*, 100 x 8 MT5*. L: Sloane 1710, early 16, ff.164–76v. Partial text, stanzas 13–18, 25–96; begins "At my commyng the ladys everychone." 624 lines. L: Add. 17492, 1532–39, f. 90. Extract, vv. 717–24, 229–36, beginning "O marble herte and yet more harde perde." 16 lines. BR 1086, comp. c 1475; TP 529. Nar., love, dialogue, complaint.

TM 518 Hange I wyl my nobyl bow upon the grenewod bough.
L: Add. 31922, 1513+, ff. 65v–6. Music by D[r]. Cooper. 19: 4 burd abaa + 5 x 3 aa7B3* (burd. I have bene a foster long and many a day; ref. Yet have I bene a foster). BR (1303.5). Carol, love, bawdy.

TM 519 Happe happith ofte unloked for.
D: TCD 160, 1535–48, f. 99. 33: 3 x 11 ababcdcddee8. Moral, fortune.

TM 520 Happe ys very harde.
O: Ptd. book Vet.A1.e.127, 1526+, sig. Q3. 4: abab3*. O17: Balliol 354, 1505–36, f. 205v. BR 1088.5, comp. a 1500. Proverb, moral.

TM 521 Herde hevy hote and dry.
O: Ashmole 1448, early 16, f. 77. "Thus cold." 4: aabb4*. BR 3721, comp. a 1490. Medical, complexions.

TM 522 Herkyn to me, both old & younge.
O17: Balliol 354, 1505–36, f. 220v. (Cf. BR 1914.) 34: 2 burd. (ab) + 8 x 4 aaab4* (burd. Off a rose a lovely rose). Rel., carol, Virgin Mary.

TM 523 Herkyne wordis wonder gud.
E2: Laing 149, 1/4 16, ff. 200v–1. [Complaint of Christ]; also a damaged fragment of the same, beginning "Me Rewis one mary my modyr," on f. 201. 126: 18 x 7 aaa4b2cc4b2*. L: Arundel 285, c 1540, ff. 164v–8. "The Dollorus complant of our Lorde Apoune the croce crucifyit," begins "Now herkynnis wordis wunder gude." 138: 23 x 6 aaa4b2c4b2*. BR 1119, comp. a 1500. Rel., monologue of Christ, Scots.

TM 524 Herkeneth all that ben hynde.
L: Sloane 1118, 1/4 16, f. 26v. 26: aa4*. BR (1097). Alchemy.

TM 525 Harry harry hobillschowe.
E: Asloan, 1513–42, ff. 240–2v. "Heir followis the maner of the crying of ane play" (incomplete). 165: 16 x 12 aaabcccbdddbeeeb4*. BR (1119.3). Drama, proclamation.

TM 526 Hate whom ye list for I kare not.
L: Add. 17492, 1532–39, f. 78v. 10: mono8. D: TCD 160, 1535–48, f. 100. Love.

TM 527 Have mercye god, and blesse thowe us.
L: Royal 17.A.21, 1551, ff. 57v–8v. William Forreste, tr. Deus misereatur (Ps 66). 28: 7 x 4 a8b6a8b6. Rel.

TM 528 Have mercye (god) on me, I crye.
L: Royal 17.A.21, 1551, ff. 52–3v. William Forreste, tr. Ps 56, Miserere deus miserere. 60: 15 x 4 a8b6a8b6. Rel.

TM 529 Have mercye god, on me poore wrache.
L: Royal 17.A.21, 1551, ff. 50v–2. William Forreste, tr. Ps 55, Miserere mei deus qui. 56:14 x 4 a8b6a8b6. Rel.

Have The moved thoghe I do complayne. Last line of acephalous TM 1720.

TM 530 He bare hym up he bare hym down.
O17: Balliol 354, 1503–04, f. 165v. ["The Corpus Christi carol."] 14:2 burd. (aa) + 6 x 2 aa8 (burd. Lully lulley lully lulley). BR (1132). Rel., carol, eucharist.

He hath need of a long spoone that eateth with the Devill. Prose version of TM 561.

He hathe wysdom at hys wyll. Lines 37–38 of TM 221.

TM 531 He is no good swayn | that lettith his iorney for the rayn.
O17: Balliol 354, 1505–36, f. 200v. Tr. "Qui parcit stille..." 2: aa3*. BR (1136.5). Proverb.

TM 532 He is not ded that somtyme hath a fall.
L: Egerton 2711, bef. 1542, f. 40. "Tho[mas Wyatt]," tr. Serafino, "Sio son caduto interra inon son morto." 8: abababcc10. L: Add. 17492, 1532–39, f. 74. Begins "I am not dead ..." TP 560. Love.

TM 533 He ys wyse that can be war or he be wo.
L: Harley 116, early 16, f. 170v. 5: mono5*. BR 1139, comp. a 1400. Moral.

TM 534 He mai lightli swim | that is hold up by the chin.
O17: Balliol 354, 1505–36, f. 191v. 2: aa3*. BR 1142.5, comp. a 1500. Proverb.

TM 535 He that all coweitith | often all lesith.
O17: Balliol 354, 1505–36, f. 191v. 2: aa2*. Proverb.

TM 536 He that harborythe a ffrere harboryth fesyke.
L: Harley 2252, c 1525, f. 1v. 4: aabb4*. BR (1148). Rel., satire.

TM 537 He that hath a good neyghboure hath a good morow.
L: Harley 116, early 16, f. 170v. 4: mono5*. BR 1149, comp. a 1500. Moral.

TM 538 He that hathe an evyll bylle.
L: Add. 60577, 1549–58, f. 76. 4: aabb4*. Moral.

He that hath thoughte. See TM 1970.

TM 539 He that heweth to hye | the chippis will fall in his ye.
O17: Balliol 354, 1505–36, f. 200v. Tr. "Qui nimis alte..." (cf. TM 316). 2: aa3*. BR (1149.5). Proverb.

TM 540 He that in yowth no vertu will use | In age all honour shall refuse.
O17: Balliol 354, 1505–36, f. 213v. 2: aa4*. O: Ptd. book Arch. G.d.34, early 16, sigs. k6, m5, r1v. Copied three times. O: Rawl. C.86, early 16, f. 31. Begins "Whoso in youthe no vertu usith." DUR5: Cosin V.iii.9, c 1555, f. 79. Adds vv. 78–79 of TM 221. 4: aabb4*. L: Royal 9.C.2, 1525+, f. 130. Copied by Thomas Lower. HN: HM 502, early 16, f. 34v. G: Hunt. 400, mid 16, f. cv. Begins "In youth whoo will no virtue use." BR 1151, comp. a 1500; TP 576.5 (also appears as vv. 11–12 of TM 221). Proverb, moral.

TM 541 He that in youthe to sensualitie.
O: Ptd. book 8° C.70.Th. Seld., 1540+, sig. 2L7v. 7: RR4*. BR (1151.5). Moral.

TM 542 He that ys nought and of ill fame | thinketh Every man to be the same.
L: Add. 22718, early 16, ff. 46v, 49. Copied twice by Cristafer Travylyan. 2: aa4*. Proverb, moral.

TM 543 He that is warned | ys half armed.
O17: Balliol 354, 1505–36, f. 200v. Tr. "Qui premunitur..." (cf. BR 1152.5). 2: aa2*. Proverb.

TM 544 He that is willing pease for to make | Most be indifferent and no partie take.
L: Add. 20059, early 16, f. 2. Fifth of five moral couplets 2:aa4*. Moral, proverb.

TM 545 He that made this hous for contemplacion.
L: Royal 18 D.2, c 1520, ff. 202–4. "The proverbis in the rouf of my lorde Percy closett at Lekyngfelde [Leconfield]". 144: aa5*. BR (1160). Dialogue, youth.

TM 546 He that may thyse and will not.
HN: HM 502, early 16, f. 34v. First line only. 1: [mono3*]. TP 581. Moral, proverb.

TM 547 He that no good can nor non will lern | If he never thrive who shall him warne.
O17: Balliol 354, 1505–36, f. 191v. 2: aa4*. BR (1162.8). Proverb.

He that of wast takys no hede. See TM 1974.

He that owith mych & hath nowght. See TM 551.

TM 548 He that smyth th with a stafe off oke.
NY: Drexel 4185, 2/4 16, f. 1v. Fragment, with music. 4: 1 burd + ?aaba4* (burd. To the nale tryll; ref. card lye downe). BR (1163.5). Carol, spinning.

TM 549 He that spares to speak hathe hardly his entent.
D: TCD 160, 1535–48, f. 176v. Subscribed "H." 4: aabb5*. Moral.

TM 550 He that spareth to speke | ofte spereth to spede.
O17: Balliol 354, 1505–36, f. 200v. Tr. of "Qui parcit fari..." 2: aa2*. Proverb.

TM 551 He that spendes myche and getythe nowght.
L: Harley 2252, 1525, f. 2. 4: mono4*. O17: Balliol 354, 1505–36, f. 208v. Variant first line "He that owith mych and hath nowght." O5: Corpus Christi 237, early 16, f. i. Subscribed "Quothe K L." BR (1163); TP 585. Proverb, moral.

TM 552 He that stellys thys booke.
Ownership rhymes ending "...shall be hung on a hook" (BR 1165, first appearing c 1475). L: Royal 18.B.22, 1554–58, f. 44v. "John Twychener [h]ys book." 4: aa3*. L2: Lambeth 259, early 16, f. iv r–v. "quod Wyllm Bentelee," copied twice; begins "He that thys boke dothe stele." 6: aa3*. L:

Harley 45, early 16, f. 169. Begins: "If ony persone stele this boke" (listed separately as BR 1410). 3: aaa4*. E: Adv. 19.1.11, pt. 3, 1/4 16, f. 150. Begins "John Atkynson Boke." 2: aa3*. D: TCD 45, early 16, f. 122v. Begins: "Robert Welburne This boke." 2: aa3*. G: Hunt. 83, early 16, f. 14. "Thys ys meyster wyllyam Bromwelles boke." 2: aa4*. E: Adv. 19.1.11, pt. 1, bef. 1544, f. 10. "This is William Patrike book." 2: aa4*. C: Ptd. book Syn.6.53.5, mid 16, sig. S6v. Begins "Memorandum that I Thomas lynsey ys the Ryght owner of Thys boke." 2: aa7*.

TM 553 He that swerith till no man trist hym.
O17: Balliol 354, 1505–36, f. 208. [Included in BR 1162.] 4: mono4*. TP 587. Moral, proverb.

He that thys boke dothe stele. See TM 552.

TM 554 He that to women hys credens gyffe.
O: Rawl. A.338, early 16, ff. 111v–2. 4: aabb4*. BR (1166.5). Women (against).

TM 555 He that was deade & buryed in syght.
O: Arch. Seld. B.8, mid 16, f. 271v. "Another" [prophecy]; cf. TM 5. 18: ababacaddeddfghdhd4*. Prophecy.

TM 556 [He that whylom dyde his dilygence].
[Lydgate, *The Fall of Princes*, BR 1168, comp. c 1430–40; TP 588.5.] O: Arch. Seld. B.10, c 1520, ff. 200r–v, 202–05. Incomplete transcript of "The proverbes of Lydgate", copied from STC 17026 (1510?); consists of extracts from *The Fall of Princes* beginning "Go kys the steppes..." (9.3605–28), "Sodeyne departynge..." (1.967–1001), "The unsure gladnes..." (1.4530–57), "Vertue of vertues..." (9.2371–433), "Myne auctoure Bochas..." (6.2948–54), "This tragedye doth naturally..." (5.2509–36), and four separately indexed poems by Chaucer and Lydgate (TM 414, 638, 1680, 1772). 195: 25 x 7 RR5* + 3 x 8 MT5* (five refs.: Unto theyre grace that thou mayst up ascende; Were fyrst brought in by inobedyence; Theyr pompous fygures meynt with bitter gall; Agayne the vyce of ingratytude; Agayne all vyces lengst may endure). L: Add. 29729, 1558, ff. 169v–70v. "a balade ryall...by lydgate...in the tyme of his translation of bocas by the commaundement of my lord of glocester" (extract, 3.1569–1638; begins "This tragedye gyveth a gret warnynge"). 70: 10 x 7 RR5*. L: Sloane 1825, early 16, ff. 90v,91. Extract, 2.4432–8; begins "Deceit deceiveth..." (copied twice). 7: RR5*. L: Harley 7578, early 16, f. 20. Extract, 2.4432–8; begins "Deceit deceiveth..." 7: RR5*. Moral, hist., tragedy, proverbs.

He that wylbe wyse and ys wyllyng to kno. Lines 77–78 of TM 219.

TM 557 He that will lyve in rest must se & / say the best wheare he cum in boure.
O: Ptd. book Arch. G.d.34, early 16, sigs. k6, m5. Copied twice by Thomas Myhell of Peterborow (cf. TM 27). 3 (incomplete): aab3*. Moral.

TM 558 He that will not when he may | When he will he shall have nay.
C: Ee.4.37, mid 16, f. iii verso. Headed "per me Henry Coop." 2: aa7. DUR5: Cosin V.iii.9, c 1555, f. 85v. BR (1173); vv. 1–2 of Heywood, Epig. 2.7, TP 590. Proverb, epigram, moral.

TM 559 He that woll seke a place for reste.
L: Add. 30981, 1522–29, ff. 35–7v. John Croke, tr. Ps 91, Qui habitat. 64: abab4*. Rel.

TM 560 He that will venge every wreth | the longer he levith, the lesse he hath.
O17: Balliol 354, 1505–36, f. 208v. [Included in BR 1162]. 2:aa4*. Proverb.

TM 561 He that wyll with the devyll ete | A longe spone must he gete.
L: Sloane 747, bef. 1506, f. 66. 2: aa4*. BR (1174.5). Proverb, moral.

TM 562 He who dothe for good lyfe care | must fyrste in youthe the same prepare.
L: Add. 33974, c 1550, f. 75v. (Francis Stacy), rhymed conclusion to prose "An Alphabethe <for> yong Chrystyans." 2: aa4*. Moral, proverb.

Helthe onor and vertue longe tyme and spase. Rhymed title to TM 1611.

TM 563 Hear me good lorde for nowe I praye.
L: Add. 30981, 1522–29, ff. 21v–4. John Croke, tr. Domine exaudi (Ps. 143). 56: abab4*. Rel.

TM 564 Heare me o Lorde when I do pray.
L: Royal 17.A.17, 1551+, ff. 3v–4v. Sir Thomas Smith, tr. "Psalme 142" [143]. 40: 10 x 4 aabb4*. Rel.

TM 565 Here my prayer o lord here my request.
L: Egerton 2711, bef. 1542, f. 98r–v. Wyatt, Penitential Psalms, tr. "domine exaudi orationem meam" [Ps 143]. 49: 16 x 3 terza rima10. TP 597. Rel.

TM 566 Heare thowe (o god of thye mercye).
L: Royal 17.A.21, 1551, ff. 54v–5v. William Forreste, tr. Ps 60 Exaudi deus. 36: 9 x 4 a8b6a8b6. Rel.

Hearken. Alphabetized as Harken.

TM 567 Harte be tru & don not a mys.
C2: TCC O.2.53 (1157), early 16, f. 59. 3: aab4*. BR (1176.5). Love, presentation verse.

TM 568 Hartte be trwe and true love kype.
L: Sloane 3501, 1530's, f. 53. 4: aabb4*. BR (1176.8). Love.

TM 569 Hartte aprest with dessparott thoughte.
L: Add. 17492, 1532–39, ff. 47v–8. 18: 3 x 6 ababcc8. Love.

TM 570 Hevyn and erth & all that here me plain.
L: Egerton 2711, bef. 1542, ff. 47v–8. "Tho[mas Wyatt]." 36: 9 x 4 abab10. L: Add. 17492, 1532–39, f. 11. Lines 25–36 only, beginning "If I had suffereth" (preceding leaf lacking). L: Royal App. 58, 1547+, f. 52, 55v. Incipit only, "Heven and erth," with lute tablature. Love.

Hevy of thi herte loke thou not be. Lines 80–81 of TM 221.

TM 571 Hevy thoughtes & longe depe sykyng.
O: Rawlinson C.813, 1520–35, ff. 44v–5. 24: 3 x 8 MT5*. BR (1180). Love, epistle.

TM 572 Hector of troy throu hard feichtynge.
E2: Db.II.18 (186), 1510, f. 343. "De nouem nobilis." 62: aa4*. BR (1181). Hist., Nine Worthies, Scots.

TM 573 Ector that was off all knightes flowr.
L: Harley 2259, early 16, f. 39v. (Arms of the Nine Worthies). 36: aa5*. BR (1181.5). Hist.

Hekhnes [?] speches of manyakyd thyng. See TM 1403.

TM 574 Helpe me to seke for I lost it there.
L: Egerton 2711, bef. 1542, f. 15. [Wyatt] 15: abbaaab10C4aabba10C4 (ref. Helpe me to seke). Love.

TM 575 Henricus Octavus tooke from us.
L: Add. 35179, 2/4 16, f. 3. Epigram on the dissolution of the monasteries. 3: mono4*. Hist., Henry VIII.

TM 576 Her hert I wold I had I-wis.
O: Lat. misc. c.66, c 1500, f. 92v. (Humfrey Newton.) 7: RR4*. BR (1187). Love.

TM 577 Here beginneth the compende of alchemy.
E2: Laing III.164, early 16, pp. 3–104, 115. [George Ripley, *The Compend of Alchemy*.] 1,976: 2 x 8 abababab4* + 280 x 7 RR4*. O: e Musaeo 63, 1550's, ff. 41–65. "Compende of Alkamie...by Sir George Riple." E5: Anonyma 2, vol. V, c 1550, ff. 1–28v. "compende of Alchemy" (lacks the "Admonition"). 1,871 lines. C: Ff.2.23, 1545, ff. 1–33v. "Compende of Alkymye [copied by] Thomas Knyvet 1545." L: Sloane 3809, early 16, ff. 4–34v. Acephalous, lacking prologue; begins "O hygh Incomparabyl and gloryus majeste." 1,869 lines. NLW: 734B, 1/2 16, pp. 2–49. Georgius Rypla, "The compownde off alkeny." BR 595, comp. 1471. Alchemy.

TM 578 Here beside dwellith a riche barons dowghter.
O17: Balliol 354, 1505–36, f. 251. [The juggler and the baron's daughter.] 44: 2 burd. (aa) + 14 x 3 aa5b4* (burd. Drawe me ere, draw me nere). BR (1194.5). Carol, nar., fabliau.

Here folowyth the propre treatyse. Rhymed title to TM 157.

TM 579 Here have i dwellyd with more & lasse.
O17: Balliol 354, 1505–36, f. 224v. 30: 2 burd. (aa) + 7 x 4 aaa8R4 (burd. Now have gud day, now have gud day; ref. Now have gud day). BR (1198). Carol, candlemas.

TM 580 Her ys an erbe, men calle lunayrie.
L: Harley 2407, early 16, f. 7r–v. 44: aa4*. BR 1203, comp. a 1500. Alchemy, practical.

TM 581 Here lyes intoomed a woman worthie Fame.
STALB: Memorial in St. Albans Cathedral, 1547. "To the memorie of Margery Rowlat Wife to [John] Ma[y]nard Esquire," 1547, on a wooden tablet, with two others dated 1613, 1619. 12: aa5*. Epitaph.

TM 582 Here lieth Marmaduke Cunstable of Flaynborght knyght.
FLAMB: Brass in Flamborough Church, Yorkshire, memorial of Marmaduke Constable, d. 1518. 26: 3 x 8 MT5* + 2 aa5*. Epitaph.

TM 583 Here lyeth of Errour, the prynce yf ye wyll ken.
L: Cott. Nero C.11, 1506+, f. 140v. Robert Fabyan, tr. of an English poet's verses, "Hic iacet errorum," answering TM 1265, by a Welshman on Llywelyn ab Gruffydd, d. 1282. 8: aa4*. HD: Eng 766F, 1504, f. 111v. TP 613. Hist., epitaph.

TM 584 Here lyeth sir Richard Bewfforeste | pray jhesu geve his sowle good Rest.

DOR: Dorchester Abbey, memorial brass to Richard Beauforest, d. 1512. 2: aa4*. Epitaph.

TM 585 Here lith the fresshe flowr of Plantagenet.
O17: Balliol 354, 1503–04, f. 176. Tr. "Extinctum jacet hic," epitaph on Queen Elizabeth, d. 1503. 18: aa4*. BR (1206.9). Hist.

TM 586 Here maist thou learne thyselfe howe to behave.
C: Ptd. book Oates #4065, 1/4 16, f. 14. F. S., "To the Reader," entered on the last leaf of Caxton, *The booke of curtesye.* 14:2 x 7 RR5*. Moral, address, preface.

TM 587 Here ye may lerne wisdom ful god.
G: Hunt. 258, early 16, quire 2, f. 7v. 10: aa4*. BR 3848, comp. c 1425. Medical.

TM 588 Herode that was bothe wylde & wode.
L: Add. 5665, bef. 1511, ff. 24v–5. "De innocentibus," with music. 18: 2 burd aa + 4 x 4 aaab4* (burd. Worcepe we this holy day). BR (1212). Rel., carol, Innocents.

TM 589 Hey downe downe &c.
L11: PRO SP 1/246, mid 16, f. 18. Incipit only, with music. Song.

TM 590 Haye, haie, haie, haie | I wilbe merie while I maie.
PFOR: MS 40A, 1553+, f. 383. [Nicholas Udall?] song by Adulacion at end of V.viii (vv. 1661–62) of *Respublica*. 2: aa2*. Song.

TM 591 Hay how the mavys on a brere.
L: Add. 5665, bef. 1511, ff. 146v–8. With music. 30: 3 x 10 aa4aabaaaab2*. BR (1214.5). Song, chanson d'aventure, love.

TM 592 Hey nony nonye.
L: Add. 15233, 1554–58, f. 28. [John Redford], incipit only. Song.

TM 593 Hey noney nony houghe for money etc.
PFOR: MS 40A, 1553+, f. 372v. [Nicholas Udall?], Incipit only of a song by Insolence, Adulacion, Oppression, and Avarice in III.vi (after line 898) of *Respublica.*

TM 594 Hey now now.
L: Add. 31922, 1513+, ff. 21v, 25v. Incipit only, with music by Kempe, on f. 21v; same incipit, with music by ,Thomas Fardyng, on f. 25v. BR (1214.6). Song.

Hey Robin | Joly Robyn. Variant first line of TM 85.

TM 595 Hey troly loly loly.
L: Add. 31922, 1513+, f. 80. With music. 10: abbabbabba4*. BR (1214.7). Song, round, love.

TM 596 Hyghe and almyghtye, creator of alle.
L: Add. 60577, 1549–58, ff. 64v–5. 49: 7 x 7 RR4*. Rel., prayer, praise.

TM 597 Heigh Towers by strong wyndes full lowe be cast.
C: Gg.4.12, early 16, f. 105v. "Tuta paupertas." 4: aabb5*. BR (1218). Moral.

TM 598 Himself by geving receyveth a benefiche | who geveth to a person worthy to have yt.
DUR5: Cosin V.iii.9, c 1555, f. 58v. [Nicholas Udall, tr. Publius Mimus]. 2: aa4*. BR (1218.8); TP 620. Moral.

TM 599 Ho ho who lies heere.
PML: Ptd. book 691, mid 16, flyleaf. Epitaph of Edward Courtney, third Earl of Devonshire, d. 1419. 7: aaaa4bcd2*. Hist., epitaph.

TM 600 Ho ho yow blynd folke darkened in the cloude.
D: TCD 537, 2/4 16, pp. 82–3. 35: 5 x 7 RR5*. TP 623. Rel. instruction.

TM 601 Hogyn cam to bowers dore.
O17: Balliol 354, 1505–36, f. 249. 36: 6 x 6 aaa6B5a6B5 (ref. Hum ha tryll go bell). BR (1222). Song, bawdy, humorous.

Holde over us o lorde thy holly hande. See TM 46.

TM 602 Holy berith beris, beris rede ynowgh.
O17: Balliol 354, 1505–36, f. 251r–v. BR 1226, but different from text in L: Harley 5396 ("Holy stond in hall"). 18: 2 burd. (aa) + 4 x 4 aaaa5* (burd. Nay nay, Ive, it may not be, iwis). BR 1226, comp. a 1475. Carol, holly and ivy.

TM 603 Wholye churche is alwayes In Justes lawes.
L: Harley 559, 1554, f. 10v. Line count and verseform unrecorded. Prophecy.

Holy seyntes Edwarde and seint lowes. Extract from TM 913.

TM 604 Holi write seith wech no thyng ys sother.
L: Add. 5665, bef. 1511, ff. 31v–2. With music. 14: 2 burd aa + 3 x 4 aaaR4* (burd. Y pray you alle with o thoght). BR 1234, comp. c 1450. Rel., carol.

TM 605 Honnour and beaute vertue and gentilnesse.
L: Arundel 26, early 16, f. 32v. "Balade coulourd and Reversid." 28: 1 x 4 abab5* + 3 x 8 MT5*. BR (1237). Love.

TM 606 Honouryd ys the Realme by moste nobyll prudens.
L: Harley 2252, 1/4 16, ff. 33v–4. "By [Edward] northe to the same Cardinall [Wolsey]" (see TM 1094). 42: 6 x 7 RR5*. Hist., complaint.

TM 607 Hoope makethe gladnes.
L: Add. 5947, 1545–46, f. 76. "per me Io." 3: mono2*. Moral.

Hope to fynd a specyll remedy. Fragment of TM 1724.

TM 608 Horrybell of hew hidyus to be hold.
D: TCD 160, 1535–48, f. 97. 28: 4 x 7 RR5*. Dream.

TM 609 Whote wortis | make softe crustis.
O17: Balliol 354, 1505–36, f. 200v. Tr. "Molificant olera..." 2: aa2*. Proverb.

How cometh al ye That ben ybrought. Extract from TM 818.

TM 610 How darest thow swere or be so bold also.
C2: TCC O.2.53 (1157), early 16, f. 66. 7: RR5*. BR 1255, comp. c 1490. Moral.

How frendly was medea to jason. Extract from TM 339.

TM 611 How longe lorde wolt thou me forget.
L: Add. 30981, 1522–29, f. 28r–v. John Croke, tr. Usquequo domine [Ps. 13]. 24: 6 x 4 abab4*. Rel.

TM 612 How long O lord wilt me forget.
L: Royal App. 74–76, c 1548, ff. 19v, 14v–5v, 22v–3v. Tr. Ps. 13, with music. 24: 6 x 4 abab4*. Rel.

TM 613 How longe shall I byte on the byt.
Y: Osborn music 13, 1553+, f. 38. With music. 14: abababababab4ab3*. Song, love, complaint.

TM 614 Howe longe wylte ye forget me (lorde).
L: Royal 17.A.21, 1551, f. 17r–v. William Forreste, tr. Ps 12. 28: 7 x 4 a8b6a8b6. Rel.

TM 615 How oft have I my deere & cruell foo.
L: Egerton 2711, bef. 1542, f. 23v. Wyatt, tr. Petrarch, *Rime* 21. 14: abbaabbacddcee10. TP 694. Love.

TM 616 How schal a mann best in pes abide.
HN: HM 183, 1/4 16, f. 3v. "W. Hichecoke," collection of proverbial couplets and quatrains, including TM 28. 50: aa4*. BR (1261). Moral.

How schulde erthe upon erthe be prud and gay. See TM 377.

TM 617 How that mankynd doth begynne.
O17: Balliol 354, 1505–36, ff. 194–9. "The Myrrour of Mankind." 488: 61 x 8 (imperfect) MT3*. BR 1259, comp. c 1450. Rel. instruction.

TM 618 I abide and abide and better abide.
L: Add. 17492, 1532–39, f. 81v. 14: abbaabbacddcee10. Love.

TM 619 <I a>llway serche & never fynd.
G: Hunt. 409, mid 16, f. 151v. 5: ababb8. Moral.

TM 620 I am a knight | and menes to fight.
L: Harley 1197, early 16, f. 203. 12: 2 x 6 aa2b3cc2b3*. Military, challenge.

TM 621 I am a powre prentis.
O: Arch. Seld. B.8, mid 16, f. 266. 5: aa4*. Song, labor.

TM 622 I am Alexander that conquert to paradise yate.
O5: Ptd. book Bartholomaeus Anglicus, *De proprietatibus rerum* (1488), c 1555, sigs. 2D3v–2CC1. Copied by Richard Kaye. 32: 8 x 4 abab4*. BR (1270.1). Nine Worthies.

TM 623 I am as I am and not as I was.
O: Ptd. book 8° C.70.Th. Seld., 1540+, sig. 2L7v. 4: aabb4*. Moral.

TM 624 I am as I am and so will I be.
L: Add. 17492, 1532–39, f. 85. 40: 10 x 4 aaa8a10. D: TCD 160, 1535–48, f. 107. Acephalous, beginning "I do not rejoice nor yet complain." 32: 8 x 4 aaaa4*. (For a carol version, see TM 656). BR (1270.2). Moral.

TM 625 [I am gracyus and grete god withoutyn begynnyng].
[York Corpus Christi Cycle, BR 1273, comp. a 1500.] YORK2: Sykes MS, 1525–50, ff. 1–4v. York Scriveners' Play on the Incredulity of Thomas, beginning "Alas the woe that we are wroght." 196: 33 x 6 aaa4b2a4b2*. L: Add. 35290. Four early 16th-century additions indexed separately; see TM 60, 128, 917, 918. Rel. drama.

TM 626 I am he that hath you dayly servyd.
L: Add. 5465, 1501–04, f. 20v. Fragmentary, with music by Edmund Turges. 4: abab4*. BR (1273.3). Song, love.

TM 627 I am Mayus that is bothe yong and shene.
L: Harley 5401, early 16, f. 81. Couplets to illustrations of months of year, May to Dec. only. 16: aa5*. BR (1275). Practical, calendar, captions.

TM 628 I am [Mercury] most myghty and flos florum.
L: Sloane 3809, early 16, ff. 2v–3v. 69: aa5*. O: e Musaeo 63, 1550's, ff. 70–1. "Mr Rysppleys woord The Best of Mercurye." 103 lines. O: Ashmole 1451, pt. 2, 1550's, ff. 62v–3v. Variant first line, "I am mercury the myghty flow florum." 62 lines. BR 1276, comp. a 1500. Alchemy.

I am not ded altho I had a falle. See TM 532.

TM 629 I am not she by prowess off syt.
L: Add. 17492, 1532–39, f. 65. 8: abababcc8. Love.

TM 630 I am olde when age doth apele.
O: Tanner 407, 1/4 16, f. 38v. 8: 2 x 4 abab4*. BR (1278). Moral, age.

TM 631 I am redy and ever wyll be.
D: TCD 160, 1535–48, f. 106. 32: 8 x 4 aaaR2* (ref. (varies) But that I have not). Love.

TM 632 I am soore astoned when I remembre me.
L: Add. 60577, 1549–58, ff. 8–22. Headed "franciscus Petrarcha," [tr. Prol. and Bk. I of *Secretum]*. 848: MT5*, aa5*. Dialogue, moral.

TM 633 I am wery o allmightie and mercyfull god and marvylus wery of this | myserable lyfe.
L: Add. 33974, c 1550, ff. 35v–6. (Francis Stacy), "A prayer <shewinge the> mysery of thys lyfe." 22: aa8*. Rel., prayer.

TM 634 I bost & brage ay with the best.
O17: Balliol 354, 1505–36, f. 210. [Cf. BR 4150, the seven deadly sins from *Speculum Christi*.] 28: 7 x 4 aabb4*. BR 1286, comp. a 1456. Rel. instruction.

TM 635 I can be wanton & yf I wyll.
O: Ashmole 176, pt. 3, 2/4 16, f. 98v. 24: 6 x 4 abab4*. BR (1286.5). Love.

TM 636 I can not wryghte I cannot say nor yet in harte thinke more.
L: Add. 33974, c 1550, ff. 30v–2. (Francis Stacy), "The tenne comaundementes of god ar not unpossyble to be kepte." 58: aa7*. Rel. instruction.

TM 637 I command sylyns in the peyn of forfetur.
O: Digby 133, c 1515–25, ff. 95–145. "Explycit oreginale de sancta mari

magdalena." 2,143: abab4*, MT4*, and irreg. BR 1291, comp. a 1500?. Rel. drama.

TM 638 I Counsayll what soever thou be.
O: Arch. Seld. B.10, c 1520, ff. 205–6v. Lydgate, "Counsulo quisquis eris: qv[i] pacis sedera queris...", poem included in *The Proverbs of Lydgate* (see TM 556). 120: 15 x 8 MT5* (ref. Lyke the audyence so utter thy language). BR 1294, comp. a 1449; TP 735.5. Moral, proverb.

TM 639 I count his conquest greate.
DUR5: Cosin V.iii.9, c 1555, f. 83. 4: abab6. BR (1294.3). Moral.

I doo not rejoise not yet complayne. Stanza 3 of TM 624.

TM 640 I fynde no peace and all my warr is done.
L: Egerton 2711, bef. 1542, f. 20v. "Wyat[t]," tr. Petrarch, *Rime* 134. 14: abbaabbacddcee10. L: Add. 17492, 1532–39, f. 82r–v. TP 740. Love.

TM 641 I fynde wretyn a noble story.
O17: Balliol 354, 1503–04, ff.139–40v. "Trentale Sancti Gregorii pape" (1st couplet version; cf. TP 1623.3). 200: aa4*. BR 1653, comp. a 1350?. Rel., nar., saint's life, Pope Gregory I.

I had my frynde And my sylver. See TM 642.

TM 642 I hayde my goode And my frende.
L2: Lambeth 491, early 16, f. 323. 4: mono4*. L: Harley 116, early 16th, f. 170v. Begins "I had my good had my ffrend." 6: aaaabb4*. C: Ee.4.35, early 16, f. 5v. Begins: "I had mey God and mey ffrende." 4: mono3*. G: Hunt. 409, mid 16, f. 27. Begins "I had my frynde and my sylver." 4: mono4*. BR 1297, comp. a 1500. Moral, friendship.

TM 643 Y have ben a foster long and meney day.
L: Add. 5665, bef. 1511, f. 53v. With music. 8: 2 x 4 a5b3a5b3*. BR (1303.3). Song, love, bawdy.

TM 644 I have benne a lover.
D: TCD 160, 1535–48, f. 113r–v. 72: 12 x 6 ababcC3* (ref. Ar tryffylles to the last). Love.

TM 645 I have in harte and ffresche in mynde | The blod of hym that was so kynde.
L: Royal 8.C.12, early 16, f. 1v. 2: aa4*. BR 1307, comp. a 1400. Rel., Jesus.

TM 646 I have laborede sore and suffered deygth.
E: Adv. 19.1.11, 1/2 16, f. 178v. 6: aa4*. BR (1308). Rel., monologue of Christ.

< > I have plesyd my lady now and than. See TM 1869.

TM 647 I have soghfte in many a syde.
L: Add. 5665, bef. 1511, ff. 46v–7. With music. 14: 2 burd aa + 3 x 4 abab4* (burd. To many a will [i.e., well] have y go). BR (1315). Rel., carol, prayer.

TM 648 I have sought long with stedfastnes.
L: Egerton 2711, bef. 1542, f. 45v. "Tho[mas Wyatt]." 24: 6 x 4 abab8. L: Add. 17492, 1532–39, f. 71v. Love.

TM 649 I have xii oxen that be fayre and brown.
O17: Balliol 354, 1503–04, f. 178v. 16: 4 x 4 a5a4B3B5* (ref. ...thow myn oxen thou litill prety boy). BR (1314). Song.

TM 650 I hard latly to a ladye.
O: Ashmole 48, bef. 1558, f. 18v. Subscribed "fynis quod C f," for which another hand has substituted "Christopher Curtis". 16: 2 x 8 a8b4a8b4c8b4c8b4. Love, dialogue.

TM 651 I josep wonder how this may be.
L: Add. 5665, bef. 1511, ff. 10–11. "In die nativitatis," with music. 18: 2 burd aa + 4 x 4 aaa4B2* (burd. Mervel noght josep on mary mylde; ref. Mervell not Joseph). BR (1322). Rel., carol, Joseph and Mary.

TM 652 I kateryn of the Court Celestyall.
L: Cott. Vitellius A.16, 1509+, ff.184v–95. Verses recited at Katherine of Aragon's reception in London, 12 Nov. 1501 (part of a city chronicle). 378: 54 x 7 RR4*. L37: Coll. of Arms,1st M.13, 1503, ff. 34–43. In an account of the reception and the wedding of Katharine of Aragon and Prince Arthur. L8: Guildhall 3313, c 1510, ff.276–85v. BR (1322.8). Hist., pageant.

TM 653 I knowe not where my hevy hartye syghys to hyd.
D: TCD 160, 1535–48, f. 112. 28: 4 x 7 RR5* (ref. Ffor Dethe yet ys owte off thy syght to bee). Love.

TM 654 Y lay alle nyght.
NLW: 369B, early 16, f. 74v. 46: 4 burd abab + 7 x 6 aa2B1ab2B3* (burd. Hegh nony nony; ref. ...hegh). Carol, love, dialogue.

TM 655 I lede a liff unpleasant.
L: Egerton 2711, bef. 1542, f. 62. "Tho[mas Wyatt]." 8: abababcc10. Love.

TM 656 I lede my lyff indifferently.
PEN: Latin 35, early 16, f. iii. (Cf. TM 624.) 18: 2 burd (aa) + 4 x 4 aaaa4* (burd. I ham as I ham and so will I be). Carol, love.

TM 657 I lift my heart.
L: Add. 30513, c 1550, f. 111. Incipit only, with music. Song.

TM 658 I Live that dieth everey houre.
L: Cott. Titus A.24, 1550's, f. 99r–v. 48: 12 x 4 a8b6a8b6. Mortality.

TM 659 I lothe that I dyd love.
O: Ashmole 48, bef. 1558, ff. 23v–4v. "quod lord vaws" [Thomas, Lord Vaux]. 52: 13 x 4 ab6a8b6. TP 762. Love, repentance.

TM 660 I love a floure of Swete odour.
L: Add. 5465, 1501–04, ff. 40v–6. (On the birth of Prince Arthur, 1486) with music by Syr Thomas Philyppes. 35: 5 burd aaabb + 6 x 5 aaa4b2b4* (burd. I love I love & whom love ye). BR (1327). Carol, hist.

TM 661 I love good alle | that ys no fayle.
L: Add. 38666, 1/2 16, f. 173v. Riddle on the beloved's name: 'goodall.' 12: 2 x 6 aa2b3cc2b3*. Love, riddle.

TM 662 I love loved & loved wolde I be.
L: Add. 5465, 1501–04, ff. 28v–30. With music by Robert Fayrfax. 7: RR5*. BR (1328.5). Song, love.

TM 663 I louve lovyd and so dothe she.
L: Add. 17492, 1532–39, f. 6. 24: 6 x 4 abab8. Love.

TM 664 I love so sore I wolde fayne descerne.
O: Rawl. C.813, 1520–35, f. 61r–v. (The four leaves of truȇ love: desire, meekness, audacity, kindness; one line missing in sixth stanza.) 55: 8 x 7 RR5*. BR (1328.7). Love.

TM 665 I love trewly withowt feynyng.
L: Add. 31922, 1513+, ff. 44v–5. With music by T ffardynge [Farthing]. 4: abab4*. BR (1328.8). Song, love.

TM 666 I love on louvyd I wotte nott what love may be.
O: Rawl. C.813, 1520–35, ff. 45–6. 48: 5 x 8 MT5*, 1 x 8 aabbccdd8. BR (1329). Love, epistle.

TM 667 I love unloved suche is myn adventure.
L: Add. 31922, 1513+, ff. 122v–4. With music. 7: ababcaa4*. BR (1329.5). Song, love.

TM 668 I may as well to take in hande.
Y: Osborn music 13, 1553+, f. 36v. With music. 30: 5 x 6 ababa8B4 (ref. A stedfast mynde). Song, moral.

TM 669 I may well say with joyfull harte.
L: Add. 17492, 1532–39, f. 28v. [?by Lady Margaret Douglas, 1515–78, on her secret marriage to Lord Thomas Howard, 1536.] 24: 6 x 4 abab4*. Love.

TM 670 I must go walke the woed so wyld.
HN: EL 34.B.60, c 1532, f. 11v, 107v, 108v, 109. Copied several times. 20: 4 x 5 a4bb3a4R3* (ref. And all ffor [love] of one). L: Add. 22718, early 16, ff. 14, 54. Two fragmentary copies, with variant first lines: "I muste go walke the wood so wyde," "I muste nedes wander her and ther." 3: abb4*. L: Sloane 3501, 1530's, f. 2v. Incipit only, as title, without music. BR (1333); cf. TM 671, a later composition. Song, love, lament.

TM 671 I muste go walke the woodes so wyld.
D: TCD 160, 1535–48, ff. 108–9. (Different verse form and refrain from TM 670; prob. a new poem composed to the same tune.) 75: 15 x 5 abbaB4* (ref. And all for your Love my dere). Song, love.

I muste nedes wander her and ther. See TM 670.

I naked am nayled oo manne for thi sake. See TM 256.

TM 672 I never sawe maden wythe my eye.
L: Add. 60577, 1549–58, f. 57v. 4: abab4*. Love.

TM 673 ...I pray daily ther paynys to asswage.
L: Add. 5465, 1501–04, f. 20. Acephalous, with music; last line: "Without disease or adversity." 3: abb, fragmentary. BR (1339.5). Song, love.

TM 674 I pray god off my behaffe.
C2: TCC O.3.55 (1227), mid 16, f. 4v. 4: aa5*. Epitaph, humorous.

TM 675 I pray thow lady Mary deir.
L: Arundel 285, c 1540, ff. 190v–3. "Obsecre." 122: aa4*. BR 1343, comp. a 1425. Rel., prayer, Virgin Mary, Scots.

TM 676 I pray yow be not wrothe.
C: Nn.4.5, 1550–58, ff. 1–16v. "Mr skeltone Lawriate" [really Anon.], *Vox populi vox dei.* 815: skeltonics. Hist., satire, enclosures.

TM 677 I pray you M to me be tru.
O: Lat. misc. c.66, c 1500, f. 93v. (Humfrey Newton.) 26: 4 abab + 22 aa4*. BR (1344). Love, letter.

TM 678 I receyve noo lighte but of thy beames bright.
L: Royal 18.D.2, c 1520, f. 200. Motto to a picture of Christ holding the sun in the center of a red and white rose. 8: aa3*. BR (1349). Rel., caption, emblem.

TM 679 I recommende me to yow with harte & mynde.
O: Rawl. C.813, 1520–35, ff. 2–3. 52: 13 x 4 abab4*. BR (1349.5). Love, epistle.

TM 680 I sawe a doge sethyng sowse.
O17: Balliol 354, 1505–36, f. 241v. 30: 2 burd. (aa) + 7 x 4 aaaR4* (burd. Hey hey hey hey; ref. I will have the whetston and I may). BR (1350). Carol, humorous.

I saye this is my mystrys boke | god sende her wel on ym to loke. See TM 1659.

TM 681 I say withowt boste | that the smoke stereth the roste.
O17: Balliol 354, 1505–36, f. 200v. Tr. of "Dico sine pompa..." 2: aa2*. BR (1354.5). Proverb.

TM 682 I see the change ffrom that that was.
L: Add. 17492, 1532–39, f. 40v–1. 30: 5 x 6 ababb8R4 (ref. I se the change). Love.

TM 683 I serve where I no truyth can ffynde.
L: Add. 18752, 1530's, f. 138v. 15: 3 x 5 aaaba8. BR (1356.8). Love.

TM 684 I shall you tell a full good sport.
O17: Balliol 354, 1505–36, f. 206. [Gossip's Meeting]. 153: 3 burd (aaa) + 25 x 6 aaa4bb4C2* (burd. How gossip myne, gossip myn; ref. Good gossips mine). BR 1362, comp. a 1500. Nar., humorous, carol.

TM 685 I shall you tell a gret mervayll.
O17: Balliol 354, 1505–36, f. 230v. 20: 2 burd. (aa) + 6 x 3 aaa4* (burd. What hard ye not? The Kyng of Jherusalem). BR (1363). Rel., carol, annunciation.

I shall you tell of Cristes derlyng. See TM 1753.

I shall you tell without leyssinge. See TM 1278.

TM 686 I smyle to see how yow devyse.
L: Add. 30513, c 1550, f. 86v. Incipit only, with music. Song.

I speke by that And mene by this. Last line (perhaps independent?) of TM 783.

TM 687 I tel the playne yt ys my mystrys boke | Who ys yovr mystrys toren over and loke.
HN: HM 136, early 16, f. 101. "Dorothe Helbartun," dialogue between book and reader; cf. TM 929, TM 1940. 2: aa5*.

TM 688 I thanke the lorde wyth gratulacion.
O: Lat. theol. d.15, c 1551, f. 120. Copied by Robert Parkyn. 22: mono10. Rel., prayer.

TM 689 I that ulisses yeres have spent.
L: Harley 78, mid 16, f. 30v. "H[enry Howard, Earl of] S[urrey]." 24: 4 x 6 a8b6a8c6b8c6. TP 784. Love.

TM 690 I thinke yt but folye as this tyme requyers.
L: Cott. Cleopatra C.4, c 1550, ff. 71–2v. 88: 11 x 8 MT4* (ref. Sum fawtt yhey wyll fynd ever wemen to dysprayes). Women (praise).

TM 691 I trow in god the fader almychty.
E2: Laing 149, 1/4 16, f. 87v. [The Creed, see also BR 1284] 21: 3 x 7 RR4*. BR (1376). Rel. instruction.

TM 692 I vowed chastitee long a gooe.
L6: Dyce 45, 2/4 16, f. 1v. [Thomas Martin], tr. "Lupoldus contra coniugium sacerdotum." 4: abab4*. TP 788. Rel. controversy, chastity of priests.

TM 693 I wayle I wepe I sobbe I sigh ful sore.
L: Royal 18.D.2, c 1520, ff. 165–6v. "Skelton laureat upon the dolorus dethe and Muche Lamentable Chaunce of the Most Honorable [Henry Percy, 4th] Erle of Northumberland" (d. 1489). 217: 31 x 7 RR5*. BR 1378, comp. 1489. Elegy.

TM 694 I was born in a stall.
O17: Balliol 354, 1505–36, f. 224. 56: 4 burd. (abab) + 13 x 4 abab3* (burd. Shall I moder shall I). BR (1383). Rel., carol, monologue of Christ.

TM 695 I was with pope & cardynall.
O17: Balliol 354, 1505–36, f. 226v. 18: 2 burd. (aa) + 4 x 4 aaaB4* (burd. Forsooth I hold hym well and withowt woo; ref. That had ynough and cowld say Who). BR (1386). Carol, moral.

TM 696 I wyll all thowe I may not.
D: TCD 160, 1535–48, f. 111. 16: 4 x 4 a7b6a7b6. Love.

TM 697 I will and yet I may not.
L: Harley 78, mid 16, f. 28. "A balad of will." 24: 6 x 4 abab3*.

TM 698 I wyll len[d]e but I no dar.
L: Royal 8.C.12, early 16, f. 1v. 7: aa4*. BR 1400, comp. a 1500. Money, moral.

TM 699 I wyll no more go to the plowe.
D: TCD 490, mid 16, f. 179v. 20: 5 x 4 abab8. Lament, love.

TM 700 I wyll not paynt to purchase prayse.
O: Ashmole 48, bef. 1558, ff. 5–6v. "quod Sponner." 90: 15 x 6 ababcc8. Music, education of girls.

TM 701 I will that I will not howe lyke you that.
L: Harley 78, mid 16, f. 30. "Ridle" (answered by TM 6). 4: aa4*. Riddle.

TM 702 I winked I winked whan I a woman toke.
L: Lansd. 762, 1524–29, f. 92. 4: a5bb2a5*. BR (1392). Women.

TM 703 I wolde be absent day and nyght.
L: Add. 60577, 1549–58, back cover. 4: aabb4*. Love.

TM 704 I wold ffayn be a clarke.
O17: Balliol 354, 1505–36, f. 252. 32: 2 burd. (aa) + 6 x 5 aaaaR3* (burd. Hay, hay, by this day; ref. What avaylith it me though I say nay). BR 1399, comp. a 1500. Carol, complaint of a schoolboy, humorous.

TM 705 I wretchyde man do now complayne And wythe my harte lamente.
L: Add. 33974, c 1550, ff. 37v–8. (Francis Stacy), "A lamentatyon of man." 28: aa7*. Rel.

TM 706 I wretchyde man to the sweitt Chryst In synne here bownd that lye.
L: Add. 33974, c 1550, f. 43. (Francis Stacy), "A prayer to Christ." 22: aa7*. Rel.

TM 707 I yeldid streyghe denyinge quit eche wourde that I had seyde.
D: TCD 160, 1535–48, f. 151v. 4: aabb14. Love.

TM 708 Yff a yong woman had a c. men take.
L: Ptd. book C.21.d.7, 1520, flyleaf. "A good medesyn yff a mayd have lost her madened to make her a mayd ageyn." 34: abba4*, aa4*, and irreg. BR (1409.1). Women, satire, burlesque advice.

Yff all the erthe were parchment scrybable. Extract from TM 1389.

TM 709 If alle were trewe that men do saye.
D: TCD 160, 1535–48, f. 105v. Draft with two versions of v. 8. 8: 2 x 4 abab4*. Love.

TM 710 Yf amours faith and hert unfayned.
L: Egerton 2711, bef. 1542, f. 12v. [Wyatt], tr. Petrarch, *Rime* 224. 14: abbaabbacddcee10. TP 821. Love.

TM 711 Yif eny crafte be in baled makyng.
O: Rawl. Poetry 36, c 1500, last fol.. Praise of Chaucer, Gower, Lydgate. 4: abab4*.

If ony persone stele this boke. See TM 552.

TM 712 If care doo cawse men crie whye doe I not complayne.
Y: Osborn music 13, 1553+, f. 22r–v. [Henry Howard, Earl of Surrey], with music; also, incipit only on f. 32v with lute tablature. 26: poulters. O: Ashmole 176, pt. 3, 2/4 16, f. 97r–v. Variant first line "If care may cause..." 58 lines. L: Royal App. 58, 1547+, f. 52. Incipit only, with music; variant first line "Yf care cause me to cry." L: Stowe 389, c 1558, f. 120. Incipit only, with lute tablature. TP 825. Love, song.

Yf care may cause men crye whye doe I not complayne. See TM 712.

TM 713 If chaunce assyned.
L: Egerton 2711, bef. 1542, ff. 44v–5. "Tho[mas Wyatt]." 42: 6 x 7 aaabcc4B8 (ref. ...libertie). L: Add. 17492, 1532–39, f. 70v. D: TCD 160, 1535–48, f. 109. (Five-line version). 5: aaabB2*. Love.

TM 714 Yf Crystmas day on the Munday be.
L: Harl 2252, 1525, f. 153. 36: 6 x 6 aabccb4*. BR 1411, comp. a 1500. Prognostication, calendar.

TM 715 If ever noble manne were bounde to thanke god.
C: Dd.9.31 (518), bef. 1558, p. 24. "theise sayeings followinge were geuen to the Duke of Somersett for his Newe yeares gifte at his firste beinge Prysoner in the Towre of London [1549/50], By his servaunte [William] Grey." 18: aa4*. Moral, hist., presentation.

TM 716 Iff Excellence of wytt, or Grace of good vertu.
L: Cott. Nero C.11, 1506+, ff. 76v–7. Robert Fabyan, tr. "Si probitas sensus," on the tomb of Emperor Frederick II, d. 1247. 7: RR4*. HD: Eng 766F, 1504, ff. 47v–8. TP 830. Epitaph.

TM 717 If fansy would favor.
L: Egerton 2711, bef. 1542, f. 30r–v. [Wyatt.] 36: 9 x 4 abab6. L: Add. 17492, 1532–39, f. 34v. (Lacks lines 13–16). 32: 8 x 4 abab6. TP 831. Love.

TM 718 Yf God send the plentuowsly riches.
O17: Balliol 354, 1503–04, f. 178. 14: 2 burd. (ab) + 3 x 4 aaa4B3* (burd. Divisie si affluant; ref. Nolite cor apponere). BR (1412). Carol, moral advice, macaronic.

TM 719 If grede gaping after gaine to get another groate | Make usurie dispatch apace to cut the por mans throate.
L8: Guildhall 3035, c 1550, f. 102v. 2: poulters. Moral, greed, usury.

TM 720 Yf I had space now for to write.
L11: PRO SP 1/246, mid 16, f. 28. With music. 8: aaa4b2ccc4b2*. BR (1414.5); also variant first line of TM 721. Song, love.

Yff I had sufferd thys to you unaware. See TM 570.

TM 721 Iff I hade wytt for to endyte.
L: Royal App. 58, 1507+, f. 3v. With music. 24: 6 x 4 abaB4* (ref. Shall no man know hur name for me). L: Add. 31922, 1513+, ff. 34v–5. With music. L: Add. 18752, 1530's, f. 58v. Variant first line "Yf I had space now for to write"; less one stanza. BR (1414.8). Song, love.

TM 722 Yf I myght hav at myne owne wyll.
D: TCD 160, 1535–48, f. 110. 30: 5 x 6 ababcC4* (ref. That fforce perforce I do sustayne). Love.

TM 723 If I syng a newe songe.
L: Sloane 2578, c 1557, f. 89. "of the Cockoo, anno 1272." 12: abababab-bcbc3*. Prophecy.

TM 724 Yf in the world there be more woo.
L: Egerton 2711, bef. 1542, ff. 62v–3. "Tho[mas Wyatt]." 13: a8baa6b8cb10d8cde6de8. L: Add. 17492, 1532–39, f. 53v. Love.

TM 725 Yf it be so that I forsake the.
L: Egerton 2711, bef. 1542, f. 15v. "[Thomas] Wyat[t]." 15: aabb-abba10C4bbaab10C4 (ref. Yf it be so). Love.

Yff yt be so that ye so cruell be. Extract from TM 1510.

TM 726 If it befalle that god the lyst visyte.
L: Add. 29729, 1558, f. 132v. "Balade de bone conseyle." 7: RR4*. BR 1419, comp. a 1449?. Rel., Christ.

TM 727 Iff hit so be tyde | the wyche dowghters over the syde.
L: Add. 60577, 1549–58, f. 76. 4: aabb4*. Moral.

If Love be not o Lord what fele I so. Extract from TM 1510.

TM 728 Yf love for love, of long tyme had.
L: Add. 15233, 1554–58, f. 57r–v. "[John] Haywood." 17: 3 x 6 ababcc8 (ref. And I wyll love her as trewlye). Love, song.

TM 729 If love now reyned as it hath bene.
L: Add. 31922, 1513+, ff. 48v–9. With music by "The kyng H. viii." 14: aa8. BR (1420.5). Song, love.

TM 730 Gyve lawtye be in luve.
Y: Osborn music 13, 1553+, ff. 51v–2. With music. 42: 7 x 6 ababab4*. Song, love.

Yf Luste or anger do Thy mynde assaylle. Lines 13–14 of TM 1710.

TM 731 If not for to spede thou think a pain.
F: Ptd. book STC 12721, 1551, sig. 3K7v. [William Baldwin, tr. "Hermes,"] copied by Mary Sidney, 1551. 4: aabb4*. TP 840. Moral.

TM 732 Yff reason govern fantasye.
L: Add. 17492, 1532–39, ff. 45v–6. "T[homas] H[oward]" (d. Oct. 1537). 50: 6 x 7 RR8 + 1 x 8 ababbcdd8. Love, friendship.

TM 733 Yf Ryght be rakt and over Roon.
D: TCD 160, 1535–48, f. 179. 28: 7 x 4 abab8. TP 846. Moral.

TM 734 Yffe that Appelles nowe dyd rayne.
Y: Osborn music 13, 1553+, f. 57r–v. With music. 42: 7 x 6 ababcc8. Love, song.

TM 735 If that I coulde in versis close.
L: Add. 17492, 1532–39, f. 63v. "E[dward]. K[nyvet]." 14: abbaabbacd-dcee8. Love.

TM 736 If that the day of saint paule be cleare.
D: TCD 537, 2/4 16, p.87, p.86. "the saying of erra pater to the husbandman"; variant transcription on p. 86 begins "If the daye of sainte paule be cleare." 16: abab4*. BR 1426.1, comp. a1500; TP 853. Almanac, weather prognostication.

If thow art young then mary not ekit. See TM 847.

Yff thou be ffamylyer with every man. Lines 75–76 of TM 219.

Yf thou be trobyllyd with ynconvenyens. Lines 82–83 of TM 221.

TM 737 Gyf thou cummis to the flude.
E: Adv. 34.7.3, 2/4 16, f. 27. "Aristoteles Magnus." 6: aabccb6. BR (1429). Practical, weather, Scots.

Yff thou have troble or vexation. Lines 31–32 of TM 219.

Yff thou showe thy counsell to every man. Lines 11–12 and (variant) 75–76 of TM 219.

Iff thou will this medesin a plye. See TM 158.

TM 738 Yf thow wilt eschew Bytter adventure.
DUR5: Cosin V.iii.9, c 1555, f. 64v. [Thomas Elyot, tr.] "Martialis lib 12" [Epig., 12.34]. 4: abab4*. BR (1436.2); TP 862. Moral.

Yf thow wylte leve in peas and Reste. Lines 52–53 of TM 221.

TM 739 If tho[u] wylte lyve purelye.
C10: Magdalene F.4.13, 1528, f. 2. (Cf. TM 1392, 1393.) 5: mono3*. Rel. instruction.

TM 740 Yf vertu sprynge wher as youth raynythe.
L: Add. 15233, 1554–58, f. 31. 24: 3 x 8 ababcddC8 (ref. Servire deo regnare est). Rel., moral, macaronic.

TM 741 If waker care if sodayne pale coulor.
L: Egerton 2711, bef. 1542, f. 66v. "Tho[mas Wyatt]" (cf. vv. 1–4 with Petrarch, *Rime* 224). 14: abbaabbacdcdee10. TP 867. Love.

TM 742 Yf with complaint the paine might be exprest.
L: Add. 17492, 1532–39, f. 73. 12: 2 x 6 abaa10b6b10. Love.

TM 743 Yf writers wordes.
L11: PRO SP 1/246, mid 16, f. 17. Incipit only, with music. Song.

Yf ye be lusty and of age. Second stanza of TM 2036.

TM 744 If ye wylle wete the propyrte.
O: Digby 133, c 1512, ff.158–69v. "Wysdam." 752: 94 x 8 MT4*. BR 1440, comp. c 1470. Rel. drama.

TM 745 Illa juventis that is so nyse.
O17: Balliol 354, 1505–36, f. 229. 22: 2 burd. (aa) + 5 x 4 aaaB4* (burd. Alas

my hart wil brek in thre; ref. Terribilis mors conturbat me.). BR (1444). Rel., carol, death, macaronic.

TM 746 In a busshell of wynnynge | ys not a hondfull of cunnyng.
O17: Balliol 354, 1505–36, f. 200v. Tr. of "In m[o]dico rendi..." 2: aa2*. BR (1445.5). Proverb.

TM 747 In a comly closet when the tyme was.
O: Ashmole 48, bef. 1558, ff. 42v–4v. "quoth T S P." 132: 33 x 4 abab4*. Love, warning against women.

TM 748 In A ffreshe Mornyng Among the flowrys.
L: Harley 2252, 1533–38, f. 155. (On Anne Boleyn's execution, 1533; cf. TM 1900). 100: 25 x 4 aaaR4* (ref. ... fortune). Hist.

TM 749 In a garden underneath a tree.
O: Ashmole 176, pt. 3, 2/4 16, f. 100v. 38: 2 burd (aa) + 6 x 6 aaabaB4* (burd. This nyghtes rest this nyghtes rest; ref. Adewe farewell this nyghtes rest). BR (1449.5). Carol, chanson d'aventure, love.

TM 750 In a glorius garden grene.
L: Add. 5465, 1501–04, ff.108v–11. With music (perhaps in honor of Elizabeth of York, on her marriage to Henry VII, 1486). 16: 4 burd aaab + 2 x 7 aaaabb4C2* (burd. This day day dawes this gentill day dawe; ref. And ever she sang). BR 1450, comp. c 1486. Carol, hist., praise.

TM 751 In a goodly nyght as yn my bede I laye.
O: Rawl. C.813, 1520–35, ff. 47–8. 48: 6 x 8 MT4* (ref. But when I awoke ther was but I alone). BR (1450.5). Love.

TM 752 In a pleasante harbar very quaynt and quadrente.
O: Ashm. 48, bef. 1558, ff. 57v–60. "quod Henry Sponare." 120: 15 x 8 MT4* (ref. ...vice throughe vyolence hathe put vertu to flyght). L6: Dyce 45, 2/4 16, ff. 17v–21v. 96 lines only. BR (1455.5). Moral, vision of evil in society.

TM 753 In a someres seyson when soft was the sonne.
C: Gg.4.31, mid 16, ff. 1–101. *Piers Plowman*, B-text. 7,000: allit. L: Royal 18.B.17, 2/4 16, ff.14–122v. C-text, begins "In somer season whan sett was the sonne." O: Digby 145, 1532–34, ff. 2–130. A-text, Prol.–XI, + C-text, XII.297–XXIII, transcribed by Sir Adrian Fortescue. L: Add. 60577, 1549–58, f. 212. "qd Piers Plowman" (B-text, VI.328–31, entered as a prophecy; begins "When you see the sun..." 4: allit. BR 1459, comp. c 1376; TP 877.5. Allegory, dream, rel. instruction, satire, nar.

TM 754 In a tyme of a somers day.
O17: Balliol 354, 1503–04, f. 155v. "Explicit Revertere." 32: 4 x 8 ababcdcD4* (ref. ...revertere). BR 1454, comp. c 1455. Nar., moral.

TM 755 In all goode worckes who dothe delyghte of thys carefull muste be.
L: Add. 33974, c 1550, f. 59v. (Francis Stacy), '< >'. 18: aa7*. Rel. instruction, good works.

TM 756 In an evenynge last forthe as I walkyde.
C2: TCC R.3.33 (613), c 1547, ff.14–148v. William Palmer (author's name erased), "The disclosinge of the practyse of Stephen Gardyner byshope of Wynchester...," c 1547; preface in prose, poem incomplete at the end. 5,400: abab4*, irreg. Hist.

TM 757 In Anno domine 1552 & one.
L: Harley 559, 1554, ff. 6–7. "Prophetia In Anno 1553 & 1554." 55: aa4*. Prophecy.

TM 758 In anno 1587 I understande.
O: Arch. Seld. B.8, mid 16, ff.297v–9. Prophecies for 1587 to 1591 124: aa5* + irreg. Prophecy.

TM 759 In Bedlem, in that fayer cite.
O17: Balliol 354, 1505–36, f. 222v. 22: 2 burd. (aa) + 5 x 4 aaaa4* (burd. To blis God bryng us all and sum). BR 1471, comp. a 1500. Rel., carol, nativity, macaronic.

TM 760 In Day now amang That presumss qwilichis [?].
BO: f. Med. 94, mid 16, f. 74v. 13: aa4*. Moral, Scots.

TM 761 In December when the Dayes draw to be short.
L: Harl 372, mid 16, f. 114r–v. "The Ballad of Little John Nobody, Who (under that Name) libells the Reformation, under K. Edward 6th" (title added in an 18th-century hand). 64: 8 x 8 MT4* (ref. He sayd he was little John Nobody, that durst not speak). Rel. controversy.

TM 762 In dowtfull brest, whilst moderly pitie.
L: Egerton 2711, bef. 1542, f. 54v. "Tho[mas Wyatt]," tr. "Mentre nel duro..." (based on Josephus, *Jewish War*, VI.2.4; see J. C. Fucilla, RN 9 (1956), 187–88). 8: abababcc10. TP 888. Hist.

TM 763 In eternum I was ons determined.
L: Add. 17492, 1532–39, f. 72v. [Wyatt.] 24: 6 x 4 aaa10R4 (ref. in eternum).
L: Egerton 2711, bef. 1542, f. 46v. Damaged text. Love.

TM 764 In every place ye may well see.
O17: Balliol 354, 1505–36, f. 250. 42: 2 burd. (aa) + 10 x 4 aaaa3* (burd. Of all creatures women be best). BR 1485, comp. a 1500. Carol, ironic praise of women.

TM 765 In faith I wot not well what to say.
L: Egerton 2711, bef. 1542, f. 19. "Tho[mas Wyatt]." 21: 3 x 7 RR8 (ref. Spite of thy hap hap hath well hapt). TP 892. Love.

TM 766 In faythe methynkes yt ys no Ryght.
L: Add. 17492, 1532–39, ff. 21v–2. Subscribed "A. I." 35: 5 x 7 RR8. Love.

TM 767 [In] ffoure poyntis my will or I hence departe.
L: Lansd. 762, 1524–29, f. 3r–v. "Terram terra tegat." 28: 4 x 7 RR4*. O17: Balliol 354, 1505–36, f. 199. Begins "In IIII poyntis or I hens departe. L: Add. 29729, 1558, f. 126r–v. "quod Robertus poet [or "peet"]." BR 1488, comp. a 1500? Rel., testament.

TM 768 In goinge to my naked bedde.
L: Add. 30513, c 1550, ff.79v–80v. Incipit only, with music [text by Richard Edwardes?]. Song, friendship.

TM 769 In grace honor and prospyrite.
R: Ptd. book Gerson *De consolatione theologie* (1488), 1520+, sig. ?. "A lytyll ballet mayde of the yong duk[es] grace" [i.e., of Henry Fitzroy Duke of Richmond, 1519–36], with music. 20: 4 x 5 aaaBB4* (ref. ...joy | And long to preserve hym and henry fyzt roy). Song, hist., praise.

TM 770 In historyes off olde to Rede.
O: Ashmole 48, bef. 1558, ff. 31–5v. On the murder of Lewes West, 1556. 220: 55 x 4 abab8. Hist., nar.

TM 771 In holy churche of Xristys foundacion.
L6: Dyce 45, 2/4 16, ff. 22–3. 50: 2 burd aa + 16 x 3 aaa4* (burd. In towne a in towne a). BR (1494.5). Rel., carol.

TM 772 In holly fathers thys I fynde sett downe for trewe to us.
L: Add. 33974, c 1550, f. 62v. (Francis Stacy), 'Of < >.' 20:aa7*. Rel. instruction.

TM 773 In Juygne | whan tytan was in the crabes hed.
L: Add. 29729, 1558, ff. 161–6. "a saying of the nightengalle...[by] lidgate" (incomplete). 377: 54 x 7 RR5*. BR 1498, comp. a 1449. Rel., dream vision, allegory, nar.

TM 774 In losse of tyme and hopyng for better | maketh many a man to be a dragge Ever after.
L: Sloane 1207, mid 16, f. 12. 2: aa4*. Moral.

TM 775 In marche aftar the furste C.
C10: Magdalene F.4.13, 1528, f. 9. 6: aa4*. C: Ee.4.35, early 16, f. 5. Variant, begins: "Yn Marche take the pryme wher." 3: abb3*. BR 1502, comp. c 1450. Calendar, calculation of Easter.

TM 776 In may that lusty seson.
L: Add. 31922, 1513+, f. 26. With music by T ffaredyng [Farthing]. 9: aa3b3cd4b3ee4b3*. BR (1504.5). Song, love.

TM 777 In maij quhen flora the fresche lusty qwene.
E: Asloan, 1513–42, f.293–300v. "Heir begynnis the mayng and disport of chauceir" [i.e., Lydgate, "Complaint of the Black Knight"]. 667: 93 x 7 RR5*, 2 x 8 MT5*. BR 1507, comp. a 1449; TP 906.5. Nar., allegory, love, complaint.

TM 778 In mornyng wyse syns daylye I Increas.
D: TCD 160, 1535–48, f. 114r–v. On the execution of Anne Boleyn's alleged lovers, Thomas Boleyn (Lord Rochford), Henry Norris, William Brereton, Francis Weston, and Mark Smeaton in May, 1536. 64: 8 x 8 ababcdcd5*. Hist.

In my Beginninge god be my spede. See TM 220.

TM 779 In my defens god me defend.
E: Adv. 34.7.3, c 1550, f. 45. 4: aa8. BR (1509). Rel., prayer.

TM 780 In olde days ther was a man.
O17: Balliol 354, 1503–04, ff. 18–54v. "the VII sages of Rome" [A-version; tr. from early 12th-century French prose *Les Sept Sages de Rome*; cf. TM 147, D-version.] 3,840: aa4*. BR 3187, comp. c 1330. Nar., frame tale, evils of women.

TM 781 ...In paradise he made Adam a pure Innocent.
L: Add. 24844, 1530's, ff. 2v–4. Acephalous, begins at line 3; last line: "Sed libera nos a malo amen." 72: 9 x 8 MT4*. Rel., macaronic, lord's prayer.

TM 782 In Peblis town sumtyme, as I heard tell.
E: Asloan, 1513–42, ff. 257–62v. "The Thrie Tailes of the Thrie Priests of Peblis" (17ff. lacking at end). 1,342: aa5*. BR 1522.5+, comp. a 1492. Frame nar., Scots.

TM 783 In places wher that I company.
L: Add. 17492, 1532–39, f. 62v. Incomplete. 6: 1 x 5 aabba4* + 1. Love.

TM 784 In secrett place this hendres nyght.
Y: Osborn music 13, 1553+, ff. 50v–1. With music [Scots text attributed to "Clerk" in E: Advocates 1.1.6, transcr. 1568; more recently attributed to Dunbar]. 56: 8 x 7 aabbcbc8 (ref. Ye breake my heart my bony ayne). BR (1527). Song, dialogue, bawdy.

TM 785 In Septembre at the falling of the leaf.
LONG: Longleat 258, 1500+, ff. 58–75v. "the book of Assemble De Dames." 756: 108 x 7 RR5*. BR 1528, comp. 1478; TP 912.5. Nar., allegory, love.

TM 786 In seyven foretene and foure | Is all my truste and store.
L: Add. 20059, early 16, f. 2. 2: aa3*. BR (1528.5). Lucky numbers, practical.

In synne yf thou thi lyffe have ledde. See TM 947.

TM 787 In sommer seson as soune as the sonne.
D: TCD 160, 1535–48, f. 115r–v. "Jelosy." 58: allit. Love.

In somer season whan sette was the sonn. See TM 754.

TM 788 In schomer when the leves spryng.
C: Ee.4.35, early 16, ff. 14v–19. "Expleycet Robyn hode." 162: aa7*. BR (1533); comp. a 1525. Nar.

In the begynnyng god be my speede. See TM 220.

TM 789 [In the begynnyng of this litell werke].
L: Add. 57335, early 16, ff. 1–73v. [Peter Idley's *Instructions to his Son*, Bks. I and II. First leaf, vv. 1–49, lacking; begins "Lett not <thy tongue clack> as mylle." Three unique added sections are indexed separately as TM 1276, 1552, 1606]. 5,000: 700 x 7 RR4*. BR 1540, comp. c 1450. Rel. instruction.

TM 790 In the begynnyng off thys yere.
L: Royal App. 58, 1507+, ff. 9, 13. With music; burden only on f. 9. 6: 2 burd. aa + 4 aabb4* (burd. Nay mary I nay maye mary). BR (1540.5). Carol, marriage.

TM 791 In the furst weke of the saison of May.
LONG: Longleat 258, 1501+, ff. 102–19. "the ye and the hert" (tr. of *Le Jardin de Plaisance*, c 1501). 824: 103 x 8 MT4*. BR (1548); TP 918. Dialogue, complaint.

TM 792 In the myddis of may as I went.
E: Asloan, 1513–42, ff.213–28v. [Sir Richard Holland], "Heir begynnis the buke of the howlat." 1,001: 77 x 13 abababab c4dddc2* allit. BR 1554, comp. c 1450–52; TP 923.5. Nar., hist. allegory, parliament of birds, praise, Scots.

TM 793 In the monyth of June, I lyeng sole alon.
L: Eger. 2402, 1556–58, ff. 94–151. "G[eorge]. C[avendish, *Metrical Visions*]., with an added "Epitaphe for Queen Mary in 1558..." (composed 1552–4, 1558). 2,327: 333 x 7 RR4*. Nar., hist., moral, tragedy.

TM 794 In the olde lawe in that lyff. A man hyghte yskar.
O: Tanner 407, 1/4 16, f. 20r–v. The children of St. Anne by her three husbands. 32: aa6*. BR (1560). Rel., nar.

TM 795 In the towne of london one shall peach another.
O: Arch. Seld. B.8, mid 16, f. 279r–v. 31: abab4* + irreg. Prophecy.

TM 796 In the cheef lorde, doe I delyte.
L: Royal 17.A.21, 1551, ff. 15–16. William Forreste, tr. Ps 10 In domine. 36: 9 x 4 a8b6a8b6. Rel.

TM 797 In thee (o lorde) have I trusted.
L: Royal 17.A.21, 1551, ff. 76v–7. William Forreste, tr. Ps 30 In te domine speravi. 28: 7 x 4 a8b6a8b6. Rel.

TM 798 In thee o Lorde I put my trust.
L: Royal 17 A.17, 1551+, ff. 6v–8v. Sir Thomas Smith, tr. "Psalme 30" [31]. 112: 28 x 4 a4b3a4b3*. Rel.

TM 799 In thee o Lorde | I put my trust.
L: Royal 17 A.17, 1551+, ff. 9v–12. Sir Thomas Smith, tr. "Psalme 70" [71]. 56: aa7*. Rel.

TM 800 In thise wordis plus pi been conteyned.
L: Lansd. 762, 1524–29, f. 91. 7: RR4*. BR (1570.5). Rel., tr. of a Latin dispensation from fasting.

TM 801 In this litill tretis men may se and be indusyde.
L: Royal 18.D.2, c 1520, ff. 181–3. [Expanded version of Lydgate's Kings of England (BR 3632) with added introductory stanza and stanzas on Edward IV, Richard III, Henry VII, and Henry VIII]. 160: RR5* and irreg. Hist.

TM 802 In this tyme God hath sent.
O17: Balliol 354, 1505–36, f. 220. 18: 2 burd. (aa) + 4 x 4 aaaB3* (burd.

Make we merry in hall and bowr; ref. God that ys our Saviowr). BR 1575, comp. a 1450. Rel., carol, nativity.

TM 803 In this vale of wretchednesse.
L: Add. 5665, bef. 1511, ff. 22v–3. "Sancti Stephani," with music. 18: 2 burd aa + 4 x 4 aaab4* (burd. Pray ffor us that we saved be). BR (1578). Rel., carol, St. Stephen, macaronic.

TM 804 In those dayes when charytye ys at least & most feble.
O: Arch. Seld. B.8, mid 16, ff. 285–6. 92: aa5* + irreg. Prophecy.

TM 805 In thoughtfull throws when Theatis hadd.
D: TCD 160, 1535–48, ff. 94v–5. 30: 5 x 6 ababcc8. Love.

TM 806 In tyme comyng there shall come an asse.
O: Arch. Seld. B.8, mid 16, ff. 290–1. 100: aa4* and irreg. Prophecy.

TM 807 In tyme to come a ffawcon dryven shall bee.
O: Arch. Seld. B.8, mid 16, ff. 296v–7. 52: aa5* and irreg. Prophecy.

TM 808 In troble & in thraull.
L: Royal 17.A.32, early 16, f. 122v. Lines 1–6 also on f. 122r. 10: aabccbaabc3*. BR (1586). Rel., prayer.

TM 809 In XXti yere of age remembre we everychon.
O17: Balliol 354, 1505–36, f. 210. 22: 6 burd. (aabccb) + 4 x 4 aaaa6* (burd. So dye shall then). BR (1587). Carol, death.

TM 810 In us Judge the truthe as before hathe been.
L: Add. 24663, 1550's, f. 1r–v. (Prophecy for 1553). 52: aa4*. L: Harley 559, 1554, ff. 32v–3. "Prophecia" [for 1552], 48 lines.

TM 811 In welth be ware of woo what so the[e] happes | and bere the[e] evyn for drede of after clappes.
O17: Balliol 354, 1503–04, f. 160. [Possibly copied from STC 17030 (?1477), f.4v (The 3rd of 6 moral maxims).] 2: aa4*. BR 1587.8, comp. 1477; TP 943.5. Proverb, moral.

TM 812 In wyldernes there founde y besse secret Alone.
L: Add. 5665, bef. 1511, f. 141. With music. 48: 8 x 6 aabaab2*. L: Egerton 3002, 1507+, f. 2v. With music, first stanza only. 6 lines. BR (1589.5). Song, love.

TM 813 In wynter[s] Just returne When boryas begon to ream [i.e., reign].
L: Royal 7 C.9, 2/4 16, f. 40. [Henry Howard, Earl of Surrey], vv. 1–2 only. 2:

poulters. L: Royal App. 58, 1547+, f. 52. Incipit only, with music. Y: Osborn music 13, 1553+, f. 41v. Incipit only, with music. TP 944. Song, love complaint.

TM 814 In women is rest peas and pacience.
C: Hh.2.6, early 16, f. 58. 8: MT5*. BR (1593). Punctuation poem, women, satire.

TM 815 In youth in age in wealt[h] in woe | Sing benedicamus Dominoe.
L: Lansd. 210, 1553–58, f. 66. (Cf. burden of TP 1971.5). 2: aa4*. Rel. instruction.

In youth when I did love. see TM 659.

In youth whoo will no virtue use. See TM 540.

TM 816 In youthfull yeares when firste my yonge desiers beganne.
L: Add. 15233, 1554–58, ff. 38v–9. "[Richard] Edwardes." 32: poulters (ref. ...that faire woordes make fooles faine). Moral.

TM 817 Inclyne thyne earys to me (O lorde).
L: Royal 17.A.21, 1551, ff. 62v–4. William Forreste, tr. Ps 85 Inclina domine. 68: 17 x 4 a8b6a8b6. Rel.

TM 818 [Insufficience of cunning and of wit].
[John Walton, tr. Boethius, *De consolatione philosophiae*, BR 1597, comp. 1410; TP 948.5.] L: Royal 9.C.2, early 16, f. 119v. Extract, 3.10, copied by Thomas Lower; begins "How cometh all ye that ben ybrought." 8: MT5*. L: Add. 29729, 1558, f. 288v. Extract, vv. 83–90 of the Prologue, beginning "As poverte causithe sobernes." 8 lines. Moral.

TM 819 Intendinge now somwhat to say.
L: Add. 33974, c 1550, ff. 14v–6. (Francis Stacy), "Of peanance the salve for synne." 132: aa4*. Rel. instruction.

TM 820 Intendynge of covytus men to wryghte.
L: Add. 33974, c 1550, ff. 64–5. (Francis Stacy), "Of <covytous rytche men>." 108: 27 x 4 abab4*. Rel., against usury.

TM 821 In tyl ane garth wndir ane reid roseir.
E2: Laing 149, 1/4 16, f. 87. [Robert Henryson, "Praise of Age."] 32: 4 x 8 MT5*. BR 1598, comp. a 1500; TP 948.7. Chanson d'aventure, moral, Scots.

TM 822 In to this world, this day dide com.
O17: Balliol 354, 1505–36, f. 229v. 18: 2 burd. (aa) + 4 x 4 aaab4* (burd. I pray you be mery and synge with me). BR (1601). Rel., carol, nativity.

Inure the with them that byn wyse. Last verses (84–85) of TM 221.

TM 823 Is it not suer a dedly Payne.
L11: PRO SP 1/246, mid 16, f. 27r–v. With music. 7: RR4*. BR (1620.5). Song, love.

TM 824 Ys yt possyble.
L: Add. 17492, 1532–39, f. 14. "Wyatt." 30: 6 x 5 ab5b8b10A5 (ref. Is it possible). Love.

TM 825 Is now the tyme is this the dulfull daye.
D: TCD 160, 1535–48, f. 116. 24: 6 x 4 abab10. Moral, satire, England.

TM 826 Is tell yw my mynd, anes tayliur dame.
L: Add. 14997, early 16, f. 39v. [in Welsh verse forms: Englyn unodl union, Englyn proest] 8: abba abbb5*. L: Harley 3725, early 16, f. 32. Lines 5–8 only, begins "ffrend an we ar ffer In det." BR (1608). Song, convivial.

TM 827 Is ther any good man here.
O17: Balliol 354, 1505–36, f. 251v. [One line missing in stanza 1.] 50: 3 burd. (aab) + 6 x 8 aaa4b3ccc2b3* (burd. Bon jowre bon jowre a vous). BR (1609). Carol, convivial, minstrel's greeting.

Ys thys a fayre avaunte ys thys honor. Extract from TM 339.

TM 828 Iste liber pertinet (and bere it well in minde) | de me Johanni Terry (soe curtise and soe kinde).
C: Ptd. book Oates #2117, early 16, sig. ?. Ownership verse of Johannes Terry. 2: aa6*. C: Ptd. book Oates #4059, early 16, sig. ?. Appears twice, once copied by Johannes D. (4 lines), and once by Thomas P. (2 lines). 4: aaba6*. C: Ptd. book Oates #3234, early 16, sig. ?. Ownership verse of Thomas Feckynham. 2: aa6*. C: Ptd. book Oates #4178, early 16, sig. ?. Ownership verse of Joannes Melsham. 2: aa6*.

TM 829 Yt be fell on sent andrewes daye.
L: Ptd. book C.18.e.1.(48), mid 16, s.sh. Copied on the verso of an indulgence. 6: aa4*. Bawdy.

TM 830 Yt fell a bowght the Lamasse tyde.
L: Cott. Cleopatra C.4, early–mid 16, ff. 64–8v. "The battel of Otterburn" 280: 70 x 4 a4b3a4b3*. BR (1620). Hist., nar.

TM 831 Yt hath beene oft both sayde and soonge.
L: Add. 15233, 1554–58, f. 63. "master Knyght." 42: 7 x 6 aaaabB4* (ref. No parte compareth to a faythfull harte). Moral, song.

TM 832 It is A thinge of passinge fame.
L: Royal 17.A.21, 1551, ff. 66–7v. William Forreste, tr. Ps 92 Bonam est confiteri. 74: 19 x 4 a8b6a8b6. Rel.

TM 833 Yt ys folly a man a thyng to begynne | Wyche to perfform his wyttes be butt theynn.
G: Hunt. 230, early 16, f. 247. Second of nine proverbs entered by Rychard Wylloughbe. 2: aa4*. Moral.

TM 834 Yt is folly to byene a begare yff it be wyell boyght | Whan it is provyd that he have ryghtt noghtt.
G: Hunt. 230, early 16, f. 247. First of nine proverbs entered by Rychard Wylloughbe. 2: aa5*. BR (1628.8). Moral.

TM 835 It is no Right alle other lustes to lese.
L: Harley 7578, early 16, f. 15r–v. 21: 3 x 7 RR10 (ref. This holde I bette thenne laboures as a reve.). BR 1635, comp. a 1456. Bawdy.

TM 836 Hit is so praty in every degre.
L: Add. 5465, 1501–04, ff. 93v–6. With music by Rychard Davy. 20: 2 + 2 burd aa + 4 x 4 aaaa4* (burd. Ihone is sike & ill at ease; ref. Alak good Ihoane what may you please | I shal bere the cost be swete sent denys). NY: Drexel 4180, 2/4 16, f. 1v. With music. 18 lines. BR (1636.5). Carol, love

TM 837 It is the properte of a gentilman | To say the beste that he can.
O: Rawl. C.86, early 16, f. 31. 2: aa4*. BR (1636.8). Moral, proverb.

TM 838 It is to me a ryght gret Joy.
L: Add. 31922, 1513+, f. 61. Incipit only, with music by "The Kynge H. viii." BR (1637.2). Song, love.

It is to me the Joy the esperance. Single line, not verse, before TM 1098.

TM 839 Hit is true I do you tell | an evell tonge seldome seth well.
O: Ashmole 1486, early 16, f. 49. 2: aa4*. Moral.

TM 840 It is well fownde a passyng grete damage.
L: Arundel 26, early 16, f. 32. 21: 3 x 7 RR5*. BR (1637.8). Moral advice.

TM 841 It is yet but a whyle.
C7: Corpus Christi 106, 1540–58, pp. 312–14. Poem on enclosures. 96: skeltonics. Social criticism, satire.

TM 842 It may be good like it who list.
L: Egerton 2711, bef. 1542, f. 17. [Wyatt.] 21: 3 x 7 RR8 (ref. For dred to fall I stond not fast.). D: TCD 160, 1535–48, f. 98. TP 973. Love.

TM 843 It was my choyse yt was no chaunce.
L: Add. 17492, 1532–39, f. 30v. A 13-line fragment also transcribed ff. 24–25, begins "It was my choyse I was my chaunce." 35: 5 x 7 ababcb8c4. Love.

TM 844 Yth was twe meusis.
COP: Gl. kgl. Saml. 1551, 1520–35, f. 62v. With music (transcribed 1520–35 by Paulus Helie (c 1480–1535) of Univ. of Copenhagen). 6: aa2b3cc2d3*. Song, fable, Scots.

Ytt were greate Ruythe. See TM 417.

TM 845 Yt will scant sincke into mans brayne.
L: Add. 60577, 1549–58, f. 223. 4: mono8. Rel. instruction.

TM 846 Iwysse I am to weake a clarke.
Y: Osborn music 13, 1553+, f. 23v. With music, subscribed "F.s." 30: 5 x 6 abacb8c2. Song.

Jesu. Alphabetized under Jesus.

Jhesu called Alpha and O. See TM 1132.

TM 847 [Jhesu crist al this worldes red].
["The Proverbs of Hendyng," BR 1669, comp. c. 1250.] L: Harley 3835, mid 16, f. 125v. Extract, stanza 2 or 41, beginning "If thow art young then mary not ekit." 4: aabb4*. Women, marriage (against).

TM 848 Jhesus Christ his Charter great.
L: Sloane 3292, early 16, f. 2. Unique introductory verses to the "Short Charter of Christ," TM 1999 (BR 4184). 6: 3 x 2 aa4*. Rel., Christ, title verse, prologue.

TM 849 Jhesu cryste I beseche the for the clennes of thyn Incarnacion.
C10: Magdalene F.4.13, 1528, f. 28. 6: mono5*. BR (1679). Rel., prayer.

TM 850 Jesu for thy demies of thy incarnacyon.
O: Ptd. book Arch. G.e.39, early 16, flyleaf. 10: mono3*. Rel., image of pity.

TM 851 Jesu for Thy Holy Name.
L: Sloane 747, bef. 1506, f. 46v. 4: abab4*. L: Arundel 285, c 1540, f. 178. "Ane uthir orisoun To the name of Jesu." 6: ababcc4*. BR 1703, comp. c 1475. TP 989. Rel., prayer, Scots.

TM 852 Jesu for thy preciose blud.
O: e Musaeo 160, 1520+, ff. 136v–9. "XV Articuli Passionis Jesum

Christum," including BR 934, the Creed. 132: 15 x 8 MT4* + 3 x 4 abab4*. BR (1709). Rel.

TM 853 Jhesu for thy wondes ffyfe.
L: Add. 5665, bef. 1511, f. 44v–5. With music. 8: 2 burd aa + 1 x 6 abab4cc2* (burd. Jhesu for thy mercy endelesse; ref. Blessed Jesu). BR 1710, comp. a 1500. Political carol, prayer for peace.

TM 854 Jhesus have mercy uppon us and this Inglishe nacyon | Which hath bene of Christs flock an habitacion.
DUR5: Cosin V.iii.9, c 1555, f. 94v. 2: aa4*. BR (1717.3). Rel., prayer, England.

TM 855 Jesu Lord that maid me.
L: Arundel 285, c 1540, ff. 177–8. "Ane orisoun to the pain of Jesu Crist" (Richard de Caistre's Hymn). 48: 12 x 4 abab4*. O: Lat. misc. c.66, c 1500, f. 106. "A prayer to Jhesus" (vv. 15–48 of Richard de Caistre's Hymn). 32 lines. BR 1727, comp. c 1400?; TP 991.7. Rel., prayer, Scots.

TM 856 Jhu lord welcom tho be.
C: Ii.6.2, c 1536, f. 109v. 10: aa4*. BR 1729, comp. c 1400. Rel., prayer.

TM 857 Jhesu of a mayde thow woldest be born.
L: Add. 5665, bef. 1511, ff. 43v–4. "De nativitate," with music by Smert. Ten-line version transcribed on ff. 29v–30. 22: 2 burd aa + 5 x 4 aabB4* (burd. Jhesu fili virginis; ref. Miserere nobis). BR (1738). Rel., carol, nativity.

TM 858 Jesu swete now wyll I syng.
HN: EL 34.B.7, early 16, ff. 83v–5v. "Carmen Christo Jhesu." 124: 31 x 4 aaaa4*. BR 3238, comp. c 1390. Rel., prayer.

TM 859 Jesu that ys most of myght.
O: Rawl. C.813, 1520–35, ff. 3–4. 56: 14 x 4 abab4*. BR (1768). Love, epistle.

TM 860 Jhesu the sonne of mare mylde.
L: Harley 4012, c 1505, ff. 106–8v. 140: 20 x 7 RR4*. BR (1779). Rel., Christ.

TM 861 Job in a donghill laye.
HN: HM 58, early 16, f. 19v. "For wormis in children." 8: aa3–6*. Medical.

John Atkynson Boke | he that stelyth he shall be hangid one a hooke. See TM 552.

TM 862 John bracke owns this booke.
O: Lyell 16, mid 16, f. i. 4: abcc4*. Ownership verse.

John Twychener ys booke. See TM 552.

TM 863 Joye in god whoes grace is beste.
C: Ii.6.2, c 1536, f. 100v. Exhortations copied by E. Robert. 8: 2 x 4 abab4*. BR (1806). Moral.

TM 864 Yoye of this wreckyd worlde is a short ffeste.
O: Ashmole 1524, pt. 6, early 16, last leaf. 29: aa5*. Rel., vanity of the world.

TM 865 Judg as ye list. say what ye cann.
L11: PRO SP 1/246, mid 16, f. 17. With music. 4: abab4*. Rel., song.

TM 866 Judge me lorde and discerne my nede.
L: Add. 30981, 1522–29, ff. 29v–30. John Croke, tr. Judica me deus [Ps. 43]. 24: 6 x 4 abab4*. Rel.

TM 867 Judge me (O lorde) for I have gone.
L: Royal 17.A.21, 1551, ff. 35v–6v. William Forreste, tr. Ps 24 Judica me. 52: 13 x 4 a8b6a8b6. Rel.

Juge noo man In noo wise. Line 33–36 of TM 219.

Justice loke th[o]u stedfast be. See TM 1426.

TM 868 Kepe and save and ye schalt have.
L: Harley 116, early 16, f. 170v. 3: aab4*. BR 3088, comp. a 1450. Moral.

Kepe not thi tresure aye Closyd in mew. Lines 27–28 of TM 221.

TM 869 Kepe well X & fflee from vii | spende well V & com to hevyn.
L: Harley 2252, 1517–38, f. 166. With the device and signature of John Colyn. 2: aa4*. C: Ee.4.35, early 16, f. 5v. Begins "Keep well x Be war off vii." C: Ee.4.37, early 16, f. v verso. Repeated on last leaf in same hand. O17: Balliol 354, 1505–36, f. 213v. BR 1817, comp. a 1500. Moral, lucky numbers.

Kyndnesse shewe wher kyndnesse ys. Lines 37–40 of TM 219.

TM 870 Kyng Edward a pure mayden shall be troubled in mynd.
O: Arch. Seld. B.8, mid 16, ff. 278–9. 61: aa5* + irreg. Prophecy.

TM 871 Kynge of grace & full of pittie.
O: Ashmole 1416, early 16, f. 124r–v. [The Fifteen Signs before the Day of Judgment, vv. 1–36 only.] 36: aa4*. O: Tanner 407, 1/4 16, ff. 45–47v. "Explicunt quinquedecim Signa," vv. 132–267 only (Day 11); begins "The

eleventh day shal com thounder lyth." 136: aa4*. BR 1823, comp. c 1450. Rel., judgment day.

TM 872 Kyt she wept I axyde why soo.
L: Royal App. 58, 1507+, ff. 6v–7. 30: 10 burd aababacbac + 5 x 4 a4b3a4b3* (burd. Kytt hathe lost hur key hur key). BR (1824.8). Carol, love, bawdy.

TM 873 Knel a down man for schame.
L: Add. 60577, 1549–58, f. 91v. 4: aabb4*. BR 1825, comp. a 1500. Rel. instruction.

TM 874 Know or thow knytte and then mayst thow slake | yf ye knette or ye knowe yt ys to late.
L: Sloane 1207, mid 16, f. 12. 2: aa4*. O17: Balliol 354, 1503–04, f. 160. [Perhaps copied from STC 17030 (?1477). DUR5: Cosin V.iii.9, c 1555, ff. 16, 36. Copied also on f. 85v. BR 1829.2, comp. c 1477; TP 1008.7. Moral, proverb.

TM 875 Labur in youth qwlyst helthe wyll last | To rest in age qwen strengh is past.
G: Hunt. 230, early 16, f. 248v. Seventh of nine proverbs entered by Rychard Wylloughbe. 2: aa4*. Proverb, moral.

TM 876 Layde in my quiet bed in study as hit were.
L: Cott. Titus A.24, 1550's, f. 83. [by Surrey, vv. 1–12 only.] 12: poulters. TP 1010. Moral.

TM 877 Lament my losse my labor and my payne.
L: Add. 17492, 1532–39, f. 76v. 32: 4 x 8 abababcc10. Love, complaint.

TM 878 Late on a nyght as I lay slepyng.
O: Rawl. C.813, 1520–35, f. 48. (Cf. TM 751.) 20: 5 x 4 aaBB4* (ref. ...But when I waked she was awey). BR (1841.5). Love, dream.

TM 879 Lawd honour praysyngis thankis Infynyte.
E2: Dk.7.49, 1515–20, ff. 2–367v. Gavin Douglas, Thirteen prologues, contents, and concluding poems to his tr. of Vergil, "Eneados" (TM 1497). 2,465: RR5*, MT5*, aa5*. LONG: Longleat 252A, 1547, ff. 2v–188v. E2: Dc.1.43, 1515–20, ff. 2–300v. C2: TCC O.3.12 (1184), 1513, ff. 1–329v. L2: Lambeth 117, 1545, ff. 11–end. BR (1842.5); TP 1016. Prologues, Virgil, poetry, moral, Scots.

TM 880 Lerne this lesson in welthe and woo.
L: Cott. Vespasian A.25, c 1555, ff.39v–40v. 54: 2 aa4* + 13 x 4 aabb4*. Moral.

TM 881 Leve thus to slaunder love.
L: Egerton 2711, bef. 1542, f. 60v–1. Answer to TM 919; answered by TM 1947. 40: 5 x 8 aabbabba6. D: TCD 160, 1535–48, ff. 117v–8. Love.

TM 882 Let be wanton your Busynes.
O: Ashmole 176, pt. 3, 2/4 16, f. 98v. 4: abab4*. BR (1863.3). Love.

TM 883 Let love to love go kyndly unsought.
L: Add. 18752, 1530's, f. 85. 24: 6 x 4 aaaa4*. BR 1864.5, comp. a1500. Love.

Let never thi wyll thi wytt over lede. Lines 39–42 of TM 221.

TM 884 Lett no man cum in to this hall.
O17: Balliol 354, 1505–36, f. 223v. 14: 2 burd. (aa) + 3 x 4 aaaB4* (burd. Make we mery bothe more and lasse; ref. For now ys the tyme of christmas). BR (1866). Rel., carol, nativity.

TM 885 Lett not the sluggish sleepe.
L: Add. 15233, 1554–58, ff. 39v–40. [Attributed to Gascoigne by Arthur Brown, Malone Soc. 87 (1951), p. ix; vv. 25–38 of "Gascoygnes Good-night" (ed. Cunliffe, 1 (1907) pp. 58–9) seem modelled on stanzas 4–9 of this poem.] 36: 9 x 4 a8b6a8b6. Death, moral.

Lett not <thy tongue clack> as mylle. See TM 789.

TM 886 Let not us that yongmen be.
L: Add. 31922, 1513+, ff. 87v–8. With music. 12: 2 x 6 aabbcc4*. BR (1866.5). Song, love, pleasure.

TM 887 Lett serch yor myndis ye of hie consideracion.
L: Add. 5465, 1501–04, f. 11. On the birth of prince Arthur (1486) or Prince Henry (1491), with music by Hamshere. 7: RR5*. BR 1866.8. Song, hist.

TM 888 Let the hethen whyche trust not in the Lorde.
D: TCD 160, 1537–48, f. 124r–v. "B. G." (George Blage), elegy on Jane Seymour, 1537. 42: 7 x 6 ababcc10. Elegy, hist.

Let us be merye | all thys long daye. Last line of acephalous TM 989.

TM 889 Lex is leyd a down. Amor is ful smal.
O: Tanner 407, 1/4 16, f. 18. 4: aabb3*. BR 1870, comp. c 1475. Moral.

TM 890 Lyffte up the eyeghen | of your advertence.
L: Add. 29729, 1558, ff. 151v–4. "A balade of good counsayle made by

lidgate." 192: 24 x 8 MT4* (ref. How this worlde is a thorowe fayre full of woo). L: Add. 60577, 1549–58, ff. 47–9. 120 lines. BR 1872, comp. a 1449. Moral.

TM 891 Lyft up your hartis & be glad.
O17: Balliol 354, 1505–36, f. 223v. 18: 2 burd. (aa) + 4 x 4 aaa3*B2 (burd. What cher Gud cher gud cheer gud cher; ref. What cher). BR (1873). Rel., carol, Christmas and new year.

TM 892 Lygth into the worlde now doth spryng & shyne | ffor ffelix unto Nicholas all ffuly dothe asyne.
L: Cott. Nero C.11, 1506+, f. 405. Robert Fabyan, tr. "lux ffulsit mundo," verses on Pope Felix, written in 1447–48. 2: poulters. HD: Eng 766F, bef. 1516, f. 376. TP 1038. Hist.

TM 893 Like as I found you.
Y: Osborn music 13, 1553+, ff. 22v–3. 48:6 x 8 ababcccb2*. Song, love.

TM 894 Lyke as the chayned wyghte.
L: Add. 30513, c 1550, f. 66. Incipit only, with music. Song.

TM 895 Lyke as the dolefull dove.
L: Add. 30513, c 1550, ff.109v–10. Incipit only, with music by Thomas Tallis. Song.

TM 896 Like as the pilgryme that hath a long way.
L: Egerton 2711, bef. 1542, f. 92v. Thomas Wyatt, Penitential Psalms, prologue to Ps. 51, based on Pietro Aretino. 32: 4 x 8 abababcc10. TP 1047. Rel.

TM 897 Lyk as the suanne towardis her dethe.
L: Add. 17492, 1532–39, f. 73. 20: 5 x 4 abaB8 (ref. ...you regarde it note). D: TCD 160, 1535–48, f. 122. L: Egerton 2711, bef. 1542, f. 46. "Tho[mas Wyatt]," incomplete due to MS damage. Love, complaint.

TM 898 Lyke as the wynde with raginge blaste.
L: Harley 78, mid 16, f. 27v. "T Wyat Of Love" [more probably by Surrey, variant version of TP 179]. 28: 7 x 4 abab4*. Love, complaint.

TM 899 Lyke as women have facis | to set me[n]s hartes on fyer.
L: Add. 60577, 1549–58, f. 45v. 4: abab3*. Love, bawdy.

TM 900 Like to these unmesurable montayns.
L: Egerton 2711, bef. 1542, f. 24. "Tho[mas Wyatt]", tr. Sanazzaro, "Simile a questi smisurati monti." 14: abbaabbacddcee10. TP 1050. Love.

TM 901 Lystyn lordyngis & ye shall here.
O17: Balliol 354, 1503–04, ff. 157–8. "how the wyse man taught his son." 152: 19 x 8 MT4*. BR 1891, comp. c 1450. Moral, education.

TM 902 Lystyn lordyngis both gret & small.
O17: Balliol 354, 1505–36, ff. 227v–8. 26: 2 burd. (aa) + 6 x 4 aaab4* (burd. A a a a). BR 1892, comp. a 1400?. Carol, macaronic, nar., hist., St. Thomas Becket.

TM 903 Lystenythe a while: and thenke nott longe.
L: Add. 60577, 1549–58, ff. 54–6. 158: 40 x 4 abab4*. Rel. instruction.

TM 904 [Little child sithen your tender infancy].
O17: Balliol 354, 1503–04, ff. 160–5. "a lyttle treatise called the boke of curtesy or little John"; begins "Lytell John sith your tender enfancye." [Copied from STC 3303 (c 1492)]. 532: 76 x 7 RR5*. BR 1919, comp. a 1477; TP 1052.5. Moral, courtesy.

TM 905 Lytyl children Her yow may Lere.
C: Ee.4.35, early 16, ff. 22v–3v. "Boke of Certesey" (tr. from French). 100: aa4*. O17: Balliol 354, 1503–04, ff. 142–3. "The boke of curtasie" (with interlinear French text), begins "Litill children here may ye lerne." 104 lines. BR 1920, comp. a 1500, TP 1052.7. Education, moral, children.

Lytell John sith your tender enfancye. See TM 904.

TM 906 Lyve not as a glutton styll for to eate | but feede to maintayne life by thy meate.
DUR5: Cosin V.iii.9, c 1555, f. 63v. [Nicholas Udall, tr. Socrates.] 2: aa10. BR (1923.5); TP 1054. Moral.

TM 907 Lyve thowe gladly yff so thowe may.
D: TCD 160, 1535–48, f. 123. Subscribed "T W[yatt?]". 12: 3 x 4 abab4* Moral.

TM 908 Loo he that ys all holly young soo free.
O: Rawl. C.813, 1520–35, ff. 48–9v. (Composed of diverse stanzas from Chaucer, *Troilus*: 2.1121–7, 841–7, 869–82, 4.561–7, 5.1072–8, 2.778–84, 1.708–12, 4.260–73.) See also TM 1510. 63: 9 x 7 RR5*. BR (1926.5). Love, letter.

TM 909 Lo here is a ladde lyght. Al fresch I you plyght.
O: Tanner 407, 1/4 16, ff. 43v–4. (Speech from a play.) 60: aabaab4*. BR (1927). Drama.

TM 910 Loo here is notyd, and putt in memory.
L: Cott. Nero C.11, 1506+, ff. 373–4. Robert Fabyan, tr. "Henrici misse Quinti," ordering three masses a day said for Henry V's soul, 1422. 28: 4 x 7 RR4*. HD: Eng 766F, bef. 1516, ff. 344–6. TP 1056. Hist.

TM 911 Loo here lyes gray under the grounde.
L: Sloane 1207, mid 16, ff. 9–10. Epitaph of [William] Gray, by himself. 80: 20 x 4 a4b3a4b3*. TP 1057. Hist.

TM 912 Loo here this lady that ye may see.
L: Add. 29729, 1558, ff. 140–4. Lydgate, "a desguysinge ... at london made by lidgate...of dame fortune dame prudence dame rightwysnesse and dame fortitude" (1427). 342: aa5*. BR 1928, comp. a 1449. Hist., allegory, mumming.

TM 913 Lo here two kinges parfyte and righte good.
L: Add. 48031, mid 16, f. 119r–v. "Soteltíes" at the feast for the coronation of Henry VI, 1432. 24: 3 x 8 MT5*. L: Cott. Nero C.11, 1506+, ff. 383v–4v. Quoted by Robert Fabyan, "Sotylties," lines 2–24; begins "Holy seyntes Edwarde and seynt Lowyce." HD: Eng 766F, 1504, ff. 354v–5v. Same as L: Cott. Nero C.11. L8: Guildhall 3313, c 1510, f.129v–30v. "A sotilte," same as L: Cott. Nero C.11. BR 1929, comp. 1432; TP 1059.5. Hist., pageant.

TM 914 Lo how I seke & seu to have.
L: Add. 17492, 1532–39, f. 52v. 24: 3 x 8 MT8. Love, lament.

TM 915 Lo in thy hast thow hast be gone.
L: Add. 17492, 1532–39, f. 59. 8: ababbaba8. Moral.

TM 916 Lo kyng Artour ful manly and ful wyse.
O: Tanner 407, 1/4 16, f. 32. Part of a poem on the Nine worthies. 12: aa4*. BR (1929.5).

TM 917 Lo Master Cayme what shares bryng I.
L: Add. 35290, 1558, f. 23v. Verses added to the York Cain and Abel play (BR 1273). 26: abab4* (irreg). Rel., drama.

TM 918 Loo this is a yoyfull day | Archedechyne for me and.
L: Add. 35290, 1558, f. 91v. Verses added to the York Marriage at Canas play (BR 1273). 2: ab4*. Rel., drama.

TM 919 Lo what it is to love.
L: Egerton 2711, bef. 1542, ff. 60–2. "Tho[mas Wyatt]" (answered by TM 881, and then by TM 1947). 40: 5 x 8 aabbabba6. D: TCD 160, 1535–48, f.

117r–v. Y: Osborn music 13, 1553+, f. 43v. Incipit only, with music. Love, question.

TM 920 Lo who must holde the candle now but he that wurst may.
L: Add. 15233, 1554–58, ff. 32–3. "Jhon Redforde." 58: 2 burd aa + 14 x 4 aaaB6* (burd. Of all the creatures, lesse and moe; ref. How we poore sylye boyes, abyde much woe). Carol, chorister's lament at harsh master.

TM 921 Looth to afende & glad ffor to please.
O: Douce 84, early 16, f. iii. "per me Johan Crowe." 2: aa4*. BR (1999). Moral.

TM 922 London thou art, of Townes A per se.
L: Cott. Vitellius A.16, 1509+, ff. 200–1. [William Dunbar, written] "This yere [1501] in the Cristmas Weke the maiore had to dyner." 56: 7 x 8 MT10 (ref. London thowe arte the flowre of cities all). PML: MA 717, c 1501–09, 2 lvs. "A balade mayde at London when my lorde Prince Arthur was wed [to Katherine of Aragon, 14 Nov. 1501] by a Skotte"; begins "London thow arte of townes chefe of dygnyte." L8: Guildhall 3313, 1510, ff. 292v–4. "A Scottys Balad." L: Lansd. 762, 1524–29, ff. 7v–8v. "An honour to london." O17: Balliol 354, 1505–36, f.199v–200. "Explicit the treatise of London, made at M. Shaa table when he was mayre...by a Skote." BR (1933.5). Hist., praise, Scots.

TM 923 Long Berdes hertlees | payntid berdis wytles.
L: Cott. Nero C.11, 1506+, f. 201. Verses made by the Scots in despite of Englishmen in 1327, quoted by Robert Fabyan citing "Guydo." 4: mono2*. HD: Eng 766F, bef. 1516, f. 172. BR 1934, comp. 1327; TP 1060.5. Hist., Scotland, satire.

TM 924 Long have I bene a singyng man.
L: Add. 15233, 1554–58, ff. 42v–3v. "Jhon Redford." 48: 8 x 6 ababcC8 (ref. Above all pertes the most to excell). Moral.

TM 925 Longe was I ladye lucke your servynge man.
L: Royal 17.D.14, mid 16, f. 453. (Sir Thomas More), "Davy the diser." 7: RR5*. TP 1063. Fortune, moral.

TM 926 lengre to muse.
L: Add. 17492, 1532–39, f. 80. 47: 6 x 8 aaa4b6ccc4b6. Love.

TM 927 Longer to troo ye.
D: TCD 160, 1535–48, f. 119r–v. 40: 5 x 8 ababbcbC2* (ref. Who cold have thowght soo). Love.

TM 928 Looke before the how thi lyfe wastyth.
C10: Magdalene F.4.13, 1528, f. 2. 6: aa4*. BR (1937). Moral.

TM 929 Loke on thys boke | and tell me woes yt ys | torne over and loke.
HN: HM 136, early 16, f. 120. "Dorothe Helbartun." (cf. TM 687 and TM 1940). 3: aba3*. Ownership rhyme.

TM 930 Loke on this wrytyng man for thi devocion.
O17: Balliol 354, 1505–36, f. 205r–v. 91: 13 x 7 RR5* (ref. Wher god in form of bred his body doth present). BR (1941). Rel. instruction, mass, Roman Catholic.

TM 931 Loke such as we ar such shall ye be.
GRAN: Grantham Church, funeral monument for an unnamed person, c. 1520. 12: aa4* and irreg. Epitaph.

TM 932 <loo>kyng for her trew love long or that yt was day.
NY: Drexel 4185, 2/4 16, f. 1v. Fragment of four lines, with music. BR (1944.5). Song, love.

TM 933 Lord here my prayre | and let my crye passe.
L: Egerton 2711, bef. 1542, ff. 95–6. Thomas Wyatt, Penitential Psalms, Ps 102. 91: terza rima10. TP 1074. Rel.

TM 934 Lorde, heare ye nowe my ryghtiousnes.
L: Royal 17.A.21, 1551, f. 21–4. William Forreste, tr. Ps 16 Exaudi domine. 76: 19 x 4 a8b6a8b6. Rel.

TM 935 Lorde holde thy hande yn thy great rage.
L: Add. 30981, 1522–29, ff. 3–4v. John Croke, tr. Ps 6, Domine ne in furore. 40: 10 x 4 abab4*. Rel.

TM 936 Lord, how shall I me complayn.
O17: Balliol 354, 1505–36, f. 252. 64: 8 x 8 MT4* (ref. That when I slepe I can not wake). BR 1957, comp. a 1475. Love, humorous complaint.

TM 937 Lorde in thye furyous passion.
L: Royal 17.A.21, 1551, ff. 6v–7v. William Forreste, tr. Ps 6 Domine ne. 44: 11 x 4 a8b6a8b6. Rel.

TM 938 Lorde, in thye name, | save me from shame.
L: Royal 17.A.21, 1551, ff. 49–50v. William Forreste, tr. Ps 53 Deus in nomine. 46: 4 + 7 x 6 aa4b6cc4b6. Rel.

TM 939 Lorde, in thy power shall the kinge | have delectation.
L: Royal 17.A.21, 1551, ff. 31v–3. William Forrest, tr. Ps 20 Deus in. 56: 14 x 4 a8b6a8b6. Rel.

TM 940 Lorde yn thy rage for myne offense.
L: Add. 30981, 1522–29, ff. 7v–11. John Croke, tr. Domine ne [Ps 38]. 92: 23 x 4 abab4*. Rel.

TM 941 Lorde in thye Tabernacle, hye | whoe shall have abydinge.
L: Royal 17.A.21, 1551, ff. 19–20. William Forrest, tr. Ps 14, Domine quis. 32: 8 x 4 a8b6a8b6. Rel.

TM 942 Lord Jhesu Cryst goddes sone on lyve | Have mercy on us for thy woundes fyve.
O: Tanner 407, 1/4 16, f. 17v. 2: aa4*. BR (1961.5). Rel., prayer.

TM 943 Lorde thou havest proved what I am.
L: Add. 30981, 1522–29, ff. 31–4v. John Croke, tr. [Ps. 139] Domine probasti me 92: 23 x 4 abab4*. Rel.

TM 944 Lorde wherto ys this worlde soo gaye.
L: Add. 60577, 1549–58, f. 53r–v. 40: 10 x 4 aaaa4*. Moral, ubi sunt.

TM 945 Lordynges I warne yow al beforne.
L: Harley 2252, 1525, f. 154v. 90: aa4*. BR 1989, comp. a 1500. Prognostications, weather.

TM 946 Lost is my love farewell adewe.
O: Ashmole 176, 2/4 16, f. 99. 4: mono4*. Love, lament.

TM 947 Love and fortune and my mynde remembre.
L: Egerton 2711, bef. 1542, f. 23. "[Thomas] Wyat[t]," tr. Petrarch, *Rime* 124. 14: abbaabbacddcee10. TP 1092. Love, adversity, age.

TM 948 Love doth againe.
L: Add. 17492, 1532–39, f. 80v. 60: 10 x 6 aa4b6aa4b6. D: TCD 160, 1535–48, f. 120r–v. Begins "Love hathe agayn." Love.

TM 949 Love fayne wold I | yff I coude spye.
L: Add. 5465, 1501–04, f. 11v. With music, possibly incomplete. 8: aaabcccb2*. BR (1999.5). Song, love.

TM 950 Love god above all thyngs, and thy nyghbouer as thy selffe.
L: Harley 424, bef. 1558, f. 9. Edwarde Underhyll, lament for the times. 16: 4 x 4 abab6*. Rel., complaint.

Love hathe agayn. See TM 948.

TM 951 Love iff that the powre yt ys with pyn.
L: Cott. Vitellius C.13, early 16, f. 310. Possibly incomplete. 7: aa5*. Love.

TM 952 Love ys a lady of the ffemynyne kynd.
L: Add. 18752, 1530's, f. 84v. 4: mono4*. Love, definition.

TM 953 Love ys hade whyll sylver dothe laste.
O: Ptd. book Douce BB.200, 1519+, sig. F4v. 3: aab4*. Love, money.

TM 954 Love is naturall to every wyght.
L: Add. 5465, 1501–04, ff. 111v–5. With music. 19: 4 burd abbc + 3 x 5 ababc4* (burd. Smale pathes to the grene woode). BR (2007.5). Love, carol.

TM 955 ...< > love shuld com | On every side.
NY: Drexel 4184, 2/4 16, f. 1v. Fragment, with music. 12: 2 x 6 aa2b3cc2b3*. BR (2012.3). Song, love.

TM 956 Love that is powre it is with pyne.
PML: Ptd. book 775, 1/2 16, last page. 8: aa4*. BR (2013). Love.

TM 957 Love thou hast which thou dost lacke.
L: Harley 78, mid 16, f. 29v. "Aunswer" to TM 1834. 6: ababcc4*. Love.

Love thy lorde and kinge celestiall. Lines 41–42 of TM 219.

TM 958 Love to be constant they may hit.
L: Royal App. 58, 1547+, f. 51. Incipit only, with music. Song, love.

TM 959 Love to gyve law unto his subject hartes.
L: Egerton 2711, bef. 1542, ff. 86–7. Wyatt, prologue to Penitential Psalms, tr. from Aretino. 72: 9 x 8 abababcc10. TP 1096. Rel.

TM 960 Love who so wyll whyt Bread I best do love browne.
D: TCD 160, 1535–48, f. 121. Answered by TM 112. 14: 2 x 7 RR5*. Love, question.

TM 961 Luf wil [I] with variance.
O: Ashmole 191, pt. 4, early 16, ff. 195v–6. With music. 6: mono3*. BR (2016). Song, love.

TM 962 Love with unkindenesse is cause of hevines.
L: Add. 17492, 1532–39, ff. 75v–6. 51: 2 burd (aa) + 7 x 7 RR4* (burd. Payne of all payne the most grevous). Carol, love.

TM 963 Loley to syng and sey as here.
L: Harley 1317, early 16, f. 94v. Incipit only of a song.

TM 964 Lusti yough shuld us ensue.
L: Add. 31922, 1513+, ff. 94v–7. With music by "The Kynge H. VIII." 36: 9 x 4 aabb8. BR (2025.5). Song, youth, pleasure vs. virtue.

TM 965 Ma dame damours | all tymes or ours.
L: Add. 31922, 1513+, ff. 73v–4. With music. 16:2 x 8 aaabaaab4. BR (2028.5). Song, love.

TM 966 Madam defrayne | ye me retayne.
L: Add. 5465, 1501–04, ff. 35v–8. With music by (?) R. Fayrfax. 24: 3 x 8 aaabaaab4. BR (2028.8). Song, love.

TM 967 Madame for youre newe fangelnesse.
L: Harley 7578, early 16, f. 17v. "Against women Inconstant" [perhaps by Chaucer]. 21: 3 x 7 RR8 (ref. In stede of blewe this may ye were al grene). BR 2029, comp. a 1400. Women.

TM 968 Madame I you requyer.
D: TCD 160, 1535–48, f. 127. Answered by TM 2040. 16: 4 x 4 abaB3* (ref. And geve me that I lak). Love, question.

TM 969 Madam withouten many wordes.
L: Egerton 2711, bef. 1542, f. 24v. "Tho[mas Wyatt]," tr. D. Bonifaco, "Madonna non so dir tante parole." 12: 3 x 4 abab8. D: TCD 160, 1535–48, f. 128. Begins "Mestres what nedis many wordis"; answered by TM 1268. TP 1102. Love, question.

TM 970 Made that bentley | beynge in the parys[h] of cheveley.
L: Stowe 38, early 16, f. 159. A satire on one Bentley. 16: mono3*.

Mayden mari mylde amen. Last line of acephalous TM 151.

TM 971 Maydyns of England, sore may ye mourn.
L: Cott. Nero C.11, 1506+, f. 178v. Verses made by the Scots at the Battle of Bannockburn, 1314, quoted by Robert Fabyan. 6: aabccb4*. HD: Eng 766F, bef. 1516, f. 149v. BR 2039.3, comp. 1314; TP 1102.5. Hist., satire, Scotland.

TM 972 Man for thyne yll lyfe formerly.
L: Add. 15233, 1554–58, f. 40r–v. "Jhon Heywood." 48: 6 x 8 mono8 in –ly. Rel., moral.

TM 973 [Man frome myschefe thou the amende].
C: Ee.4.35, early 16, ff. 1–2v. The Adulterous Falmouth Squire, acephalous beginning "The elder to hell take the way." 126: abab4*. BR 2052, comp. c 1450. Rel. instruction, nar.

TM 974 [Man have in mind].
L: Add. 5665, bef. 1511, ff. 42v–3. With music. Variant first line "In synne yf thou thi lyffe have ledde." 20: 4 burd aaaa + 4 x 4 aaa4R2* (burd. Man asay and axe mercy, while thou may; ref. Asay asay). BR 2053, comp. a 1500. Rel., carol, repentance.

TM 975 Man hef in mynd & mend the myss.
E2: Laing 149, 1/4 16, f. 87. (Cf. BR 2055.) 48: 6 x 8 ababbcbC4* (ref. Memor esto nouissima). BR 2057, comp. a 1500. Rel. instruction, Scots.

TM 976 Man, have in mynd how here beforn.
O17: Balliol 354, 1505–36, f. 220v. 30: 2 burd. (aa) + 7 x 4 aaaR4* (burd. Man asay asay asay; ref. Aske thou mercy whill thou may). BR 2053, comp. c 1450. Rel., carol, penitence.

TM 977 Man yff thou a wyseman arte.
O17: Balliol 354, 1503–04, f. 147v. (Cf. BR 685, but really two poems.) 6: aabaab2*. BR 2060, comp. a 1456. Practical, against leaving goods for executors.

TM 978 Man in the churche not Idyll thow stande.
O: Tanner 407, 1/4 16, f. 48v. 20: aa4*. BR (2065). Rel. instruction, use of the rosary.

TM 979 Man loyke and see.
O: Lat. theol. d.15, 1551–55, f. 133. Anon., "The saynge of a deyde man," copied by Robert Parkin. 16: 2 x 8 aaabaaab2*. TP 1106 (less final two lines). Death.

TM 980 Man on the molde have this in mynde.
G: Hunt. 230, early 16, f. 248v. Eighth of nine proverbs entered by Rychard Wylloughbe. 4: aa4*. L: Add. 60577, 1549–58, f. 92. Variant beginning "Where for in thi lyvyng have this in mynde"; follows TM 1876. BR 2056, comp. a 1500. Proverb, moral.

TM 981 Man remembre thy end | and thou shalt never be shende.
L: Harley 4294, early 16, f. 82. 2: aa3*. BR (2072.4). Rel., memento mori.

Man remembre whens thou com and wher thou shalt. Recorded as BR 2072.6, but not verse.

Man sobyrly thi howse begyn. Lines 31–34 of TM 221.

TM 982 Man that in erth abydys here.
O17: Balliol 354, 1505–36, f. 223. 14: 2 burd. (aa) + 3 x 4 aaab3* (burd. Mirabile misterium). BR (2076). Rel., carol, eucharist.

Man unkynde | have thow in mynde. See TM 1199.

TM 983 Many a man blamys his wyffe parde.
O17: Balliol 354, 1505–36, f. 241. 58: 2 burd. (aa) + 14 x 4 aaa4B1* (burd. In villa, in villa; ref. In villa). BR 2090, comp. a 1500. Carol, women, marriage.

TM 984 Many a man wyll go bare.
L: Lansd. 210, 1553–58, f. 80v. 8: aaa3b2ccc3b2*. Moral, marriage.

TM 985 Many man makes Ryme and lokes to no Reason.
O: Digby 145, 1532–34, ff. 160v–1v. Proverbs transcribed by Sir Adrian Fortescue, 1532–34. 64: end of one line rhymes with middle of the next. Moral.

TM 986 Many ther be that of theyr gentyll blood.
L8: Guildhall 3313, c 1510, f. 328. Tr. [by Robert Fabyan?] of Horosius, "sunt aliqui qui se." 14: 2 x 7 RR10. Moral.

TM 987 Margaret meke | whom I now seke.
L: Add. 5465, 1501–04, ff. 89v–93. With music by Browne. 32: 4 x 8 aaabCCCB2* (ref. ...So curtesly | So prately | She delis allway). BR (3270.5). Song, love.

TM 988 Marye golde ys an herbe full gracyouse.
L: Add. 60577, 1549–58, f. 119r–v. [Included in BR 2627.] 40: aa4*. Practical, herbs.

TM 989 ...Marye Tom such poyntes god send him mani.
L: Add. 15233, 1554–58, f. 28. "Jhon Redford," concluding 10 vv. of an interlude. 10: aa4*. Drama, moral.

TM 990 Marvell must I why deth is hated.
L11: PRO SP 1/246, mid 16, ff. 26v–7. With music. 6: ababcc4*. Song, death.

TM 991 Marvaill no more al tho.
L: Egerton 2711, bef. 1542, f. 35r–v. "Tho[mas Wyatt.]" 32: 4 x 8 ababacac6. L: Add. 17492, 1532–39, f. 16v. "Th[om]as Wyatt." TP 1117. Love, complaint.

TM 992 Mary, flowr of flowers all.
O17: Balliol 354, 1505–36, f. 221. 30: 2 burd. (aa) + 7 x 4 aaaB4* (burd. Now syng we wyth joy and blys; ref. Puer natus est nobis). BR (2097). Rel., carol, macaronic, Virgin Mary.

TM 993 Mary, for the love of the.
O17: Balliol 354, 1505–36, f. 223v. 26: 2 burd. (aa) + 6 x 4 aaab4* (burd. Ay ay ay ay). BR 2098, comp. a 1500. Rel., carol, macaronic, Virgin Mary.

TM 994 May not thys hate from ye estarte.
L: Add. 17492, 1532–39, f. 10v. "Anthony Lee." 20: 5 x 4 abaB8 (ref. ... not yett). Love.

TM 995 Me list no more to sing.
L: Add. 17492, 1532–39, f. 74v. 44: 9 x 5 (1 v. lacking) aaabb3*. Love, complaint, farewell to love poetry.

Me Rewis one mary my modyr. Last two stanzas of TM 523.

Memorandum that I Thomas lynsey ys the Ryght owner... Variant of TM 552.

TM 996 Men be mery I the rede.
L: Add. 5665, bef. 1511, ff. 11v–2. "In die nativitatis," with music. 14: 2 burd aa + 3 x 4 abab3* (burd. Man be joyfull and myrth thou make; ref. And he ys made man for thy sake). BR (2044). Rel., carol, nativity.

TM 997 Men may fynde in olde bokes.
L: Sloane 2232, 1502, ff. 10–117. *Sydrac and Boctus*, abridged, copied by "Robertus Wakefield...1502." 1,604: aa4*. BR 2147, comp. a 1500; TP 1122.5. Dialogue, moral, science, tr. French.

TM 998 Men most desyre, as most men most tymes see.
L: Add. 15233, 1554–58, f. 58v. 18: aa5*. Moral, song.

TM 999 Mercifull he is and full of pitie the Lorde.
L: Royal 17.A.17, 1551+, f. 2r–v. Sir Thomas Smith, tr. "Out of Psalme 102" [103.8–18]. 22: aa4*. Rel.

TM 1000 Mercifull lorde my prayer heare.
L: Add. 30981, 1522–29, ff. 15–19v. John Croke, tr. Domine exaudi [Ps 102]. 116: 29 x 4 abab4*. Rel.

TM 1001 Mercy and grace for my trespasse.
O: Ptd. book Mason H 169, mid 16, f. ii. 4: abcb4*. Rel., prayer.

TM 1002 Myght I as well within my songe belaye.
D: TCD 160, 1535–48, f. 129. 25: 5 x 5 aabcC5* (ref. Causles by cause that I have ssuffred smart). L: Add. 17492, 1532–39, f. 65v. 4: aabb10. Love, complaint.

TM 1003 Myne cuckoo co.
L: Royal App. 56, 1508+, f. 29v. Incipit only, with organ music. Song.

Myne high estate power & auctoryte. Part of TM 205.

TM 1004 [Myne olde dere enmy my frowerd mister].
L: Egerton 2711, bef. 1542, ff. 8–10v. [Wyatt, tr. Petrarch, *Rime* 360], vv. 22–147 only, begins "O small honey..." 126: 18 x 7 RR5*. TP 1133. Love, allegory, debate.

TM 1005 My nowne John poyntz sins ye delight to know.
L: Add. 17492, 1532–39, ff. 85v–7. [Wyatt, paraphrased from Luigi Alamanni's tenth satire 'Io ui diro.'] 103: terza rima5*. L: Egerton 2711, bef. 1542, f. 49r–v. Acephalous due to MS damage, beginning at line 52, "Praise him for councill that is dronck of ale." TP 1135. Letter, satire.

TM 1006 Myn unhappy chaunce to home shall I playn.
L: Add. 17492, 1532–39, f. 60v. "C anseles" [Christopher Lassells]. 21: 3 x 7 RR10. Love.

TM 1007 Miseremini mei ye that ben my ffryndys.
L: Harley 4011, mid 16, ff.169v–70v. The Lament of the Soul of Edward IV, d.1483 [doubtfully attributed to Skelton]. 96: 8 x 12 ababbcbccdcD5* (ref. Quia ecce nunc in pulvere dormio). L: Add. 29729, 1558, ff. 8–9. "the Epitaphy of kynge Edward the fowrthe compyld by Skelton" (an attribution to Lydgate is cancelled). YORK: York Minster, funeral monument. Lines 1–3, 5 beneath Latin epitaph of Thomas Dalby, Archdeacon of Richmond, d. 26 Jan. 1525/6. BR 2192, comp. a 1500; TP 1138.5. Hist., elegy, epitaph.

TM 1008 Masteres anne | I ame your man.
C2: TCC R.3.17 (597), 1501–25, flyleaf. 30: 5 x 6 aa2b3cc2B3* (ref. I am your man). BR (2195). Love.

TM 1009 Mystres Anne this Boke and my hartte ys all yours.
HN: HM 1087, early 16, f. 146v. A. W., presentation of a New Year gift, a 15th-century Book of Hours. 4: aabb5*.

TM 1010 Mystrys Barnarde gave her thys boke | God sende her well hevyn to loke.

HN: HM 136, early 16, ff. 85–6. Entered by Dorothy Helbartun 2: aa4*. Ownership rhyme.

TM 1011 Mystrys dorethe god bouth save and se | and graunte enow that she may know the verete.
HN: HM 136, early 16, f. 75. Entered by Dorothy Helbartun 2: aa5*. Rel., prayer.

TM 1012 Mystrys Dorethe, this is your boke; Who woyll you deny, | Cavle me to recorde | I wyll saye | ly.
HN: HM 136, early 16, f. 9. Ownership rhyme of Dorothy Helbartun. 2: aa5*.

Mestres what nedis many wordis. See TM 969.

Moaning my hart doth sore oppresse. See TM 1027.

TM 1013 Most clere of colour & rote of stedfastness.
L: Add. 5465, 1501–04, ff. 26v–8. With music by Robard Fayrfax. 7: RR4*. BR (2200.3). Song, praise of lady.

TM 1014 Moste excellente quene, and bounteous ladie.
L: Royal 18.A.64, 1533, ff. 8–14. Nicholas Vuedale [Udall], "Verses... unto...Quene Anne [Boleyn] at her...Coronacion at...Westmynster" [31 May 1533]. 207: 15 x 7 RR5*, 15 x 6 ababcc, 7 x 2 aa. Pageant, hist.

TM 1015 Moost hooly prophet, And Baptyst swete seynt John.
L8: Guildhall 3313, c 1510, f.330v–32v. "Ad divinum Baptistam" (prayer to St. John to protect merchants against John Baptist Grimaldis, an extortioner). 77: 11 x 7 RR4*. Satire.

TM 1016 Moste mighty lord Jubyter the gret.
L: Add. 29729, 1558, ff. 132v–4. "a balad by...lydgat brought by a pursyvaunt in wyse of momers dysguysed to fore the mayre of london estfeld vpon the twelffth nyght," comp. between 1430 and 1438. 105: 15 x 7 RR5*. BR 2210, comp. a 1449. Pageant, mumming, myth.

TM 1017 Most noble prince of cristen prences alle | flowryng in youthe.
L: Add. 29729, 1558, ff. 84–6. "a tretis of the Kynges coronacion henry the .vi. made by...lidgatt anno 1430 the 6 of november." 144: 18 x 8 MT5*. BR 2211. Hist., political advice.

TM 1018 Most noble prince of cristen prences alle | to your highnes.
L: Add. 29729, 1558, ff. 144–5v. "deuyse...to fore the kynge henry the

sixte...[at] wyndsore...by lidgate." 98: 14 x 7 RR5*. BR 2212, comp. c 1430. Rel., pageant, hist., St Clotilda.

TM 1019 Most noble prynce with support of yor grace.
L: Add. 29729, 1558, ff. 137–40. "supplycation put to the Kinge [at] hartford...deuysed by lidgate." 254: aa5*. BR 2213, comp. a 1426. Christmas disguising, moral, women.

TM 1020 Most soveren lady, comfort of care.
O: Lat. misc. c66, c 1500, f. 93v. (Humfrey Newton.) 8: 2 x 4 abab4*. BR (2217). Love.

TM 1021 Moost souveraine lord o blessith crist Jhesus.
L: Harley 7578, early 16, f. 19r–v. [Lydgate's prayer for Henry VI et al.] 84: 12 x 7 RR5* (ref. The kynge the quene the peeple and the londe; 2d ref. Him and his moder the peeple and thy londe.). BR 2218, comp. a 1450. Hist., rel., prayer.

TM 1022 Most wretched hart most myserable.
L: Egerton 2711, bef. 1542, ff. 63v–4v. "Tho[mas Wyatt]." 48 :12 x 4 abab8 (ref. most wretchid haste why arte thou nott dede; 2nd ref: ...he is wretchid that wens hym so). Love, complaint.

TM 1023 Morne and lament Chrystyans all.
L: Add. 33974, c 1550, ff. 18v–20. (Francis Stacy), "A remembrance to Chrystyans." 134: aa4*. Rel.

TM 1024 Morne wythe me good chrystyans all.
L: Add. 33974, c 1550, ff. 50–1. (Francis Stacy), "Of heretykes." 88: aa4*. Rel., heresy.

TM 1025 Mornyng mornyng now may I syng adue my Joye and <plesure>.
L: Egerton 3537, c 1553–54, f. 1. Copied twice in different hands. 8: aa7*. Love, song.

TM 1026 Mornyng mornyng thus may I syng adue my Joye and <plesure>.
L: Harley 2252, 1525, f. 140. Imperfect at the end. 45: 8 x 6 aa4b6cc4b6. BR (2224). Love, song, inconstancy.

TM 1027 Mornyng my hart doth sore opres.
D: TCD 160, 1535–48, f. 126. 16: 4 x 4 abaB4* (ref. Alas I cannot be lovyd againe). L: Add. 18752, 1530's, f. 89r–v. Begins "Moaning my hart doth sore oppresse." 28 lines. BR (2224.5). Love.

Meved of courage by vertew of the season. See TM 475.

Moche fustian and also [linen] cloth. See TM 1605.

TM 1028 Muche mischefe shalbe wrought in ye Latter end of maij.
L: Harley 559, 1554, f. 13. 4: mono4*. Prophecy.

Mukke of thys worlde is nott to truste. Lines 45–48 of TM 219.

TM 1029 Mysyng gretly yn my mynde.
L: Add. 18752, 1530's, f. 80v. 12: 3 x 4 aaaR4* (ref. And dayly comyth downe downe). Moral, ubi sunt, Adam & Eve, Methuselah, Herod.

TM 1030 Musyng uppon the mutabilitie.
O: Rawl. C.813, 1520–35, ff. 11–12v. On the deaths of Eleanor Cobham, Cardinal Beaufort, and Humphrey, Duke of Gloucester. 65: 7 x 8 MT4* + 9 ababaacaa . BR 2228, comp. c 1446. Moral, hist., fall of princes, elegy.

Myne auctoure Bochas writeth no lenger processe. Extract from TM 556 in *The Proverbs of Lydgate*.

TM 1031 My dere chyld fyrst thy self inabel.
O17: Balliol 354, 1503–04, ff. 158v–9. [Lydgate, Stans puer ad mensam.] 98: 14 x 7 RR5*. BR 2233, comp. a 1449; TP 1154.5. Moral.

TM 1032 My dutye considered, moste noble Quene.
L: Harley 3444, 1553+, ff. 2–24. Myles huggard, "Marie hath brought home christe agayne," with dedication "To the moste highe and myghtye Prynces Mary," preface to the reader, and main text. 921: aa4*, RR4*, abab6 (ref. Marie hath brought hom christe agayne). TP 1155. Rel. controversy.

TM 1033 My fance fanned onne me somwhat of ye to say.
L: Cott. Titus A.24, 1553+, f. 83v. "R[ichard] E[dwardes]," praise of eight ladies of Queen Mary's court (Hawarde, Dacars, Baynam, Arundell, Dormor, Mancell, Coke, Briges). 20: poulters. Hist., praise of women.

TM 1034 My ferefull hope from me is fledd.
L: Add. 17492, 1532–39, f. 7v. "finis qd nobody"; answered by TM 2039. 28: 7 x 4 abab8. Love, question.

TM 1035 My frynd the lyf I lead at all.
O: Ashmole 48, bef. 1558, ff. 25v–6v. Answer to TM 1550. 60: aa8. Moral, answer.

TM 1036 My frende the thinges that do attayne.
L: Cott. Titus A.24, 1550's, f. 80. [Surrey, tr. Martial, Epig. X.47.] 16: 4 x 4 abab8. L: Add. 30513, c 1550, f. 65v. Incipit only, with music. L11: PRO SP 1/246, mid 16, f. 22v. Incipit only, with music. TP 1116. Moral.

TM 1037 My galy charged with forgetfulnes.
L: Egerton 2711, bef. 1542, f. 21v. "Wyat[t]," tr. Petrarch, *Rime* 189. 14: abbaabbacddcee10. TP 1157. Love.

TM 1038 My grace to the suffysyth sayth god unto seynt powle.
L: Add. 15233, 1554–58, f. 31v. "Jhon Heywoode." 18: 2 burd aa + 4 x 4 aabb6* (burd. I desyre no number of manye thynges). Rel., carol.

TM 1039 My hert I gave the not to do it payn.
L: Egerton 2711, bef. 1542, f. 13v. Wyatt, tr. Serafino, "El cor ti diedi non che el tormentassi." 14: abbaabbacddcee10. L: Add. 17492, 1532–39, ff. 3, 75v. Text on f. 3 omits vv. 10–11, text on f. 75 omits v. 11. TP 1162. Love.

TM 1040 My herte ys yn grete mornyng.
L: Add. 5665, bef. 1511, ff. 135v–6. With music. 16:4 x 4 aaBB4* (ref. My lady hath forsakyn me). BR (2244.6). Song, love complaint.

TM 1041 My hearte ys Leied on the londe.
L: Stowe 389, c 1558, f. 120. Incipit only, with lute tablature. Song.

TM 1042 My hart ys set not to remove.
L: Add. 17492, 1532–39, f. 65. 12: 3 x 4 abab8. Love.

TM 1043 My harte ys sore, but yett noo forse.
O: Rawl. C.813, 1520–35, ff. 57v–8v. 52: 13 x 4 abab4*. BR (2245.1). Love, epistle of a woman.

TM 1044 My hart ys yours now kyp het fast.
L: Add. 18752, 1530's, f. 59. 20: 5 x 4 aaa8B4 (ref. I promys you). BR (2245.3). Love.

TM 1045 My hart my mynde & my hole poure | my servyce trew wyth all my myght.
L: Add. 18752, 1530's, f. 72r–v. Incomplete. 2: [RR5*]. BR (2245.6); TP 1163. Love.

TM 1046 My hope Alas hath me abused.
L: Egerton 2711, bef. 1542, f. 41r–v. "Tho[mas Wyatt]." 35: 5 x 7 RR8 (ref. And I remain all comfortles). L: Add. 17492, 1532–39, f. 74v. Love.

TM 1047 My hope was faire of hewe.
Y: Osborn music 13, 1553+, f. 21r–v. With music. 30: 5 x 6 abacb6c4. Song, love.

TM 1048 My Jornay lat as I dyd take.
O: Ashmole 48, bef 1558, ff. 60–2. "harry sponare." 119: 17 x 7 aaaa8b4cB8 (ref. No will quothe she alocke good Johan). Dialogue, complaint about wife.

TM 1049 My joye it is ffrome here to hyre.
L: Add. 18752, 1530's, f. 139. 20: 5 x 4 abaB4* (ref. For I love here and she loveth me). L: Harley 3362, mid 16, f. 90. BR (2249). Love.

TM 1050 My ladye hathe forsaken me.
O: Ashmole 176, pt. 3, 2/4 16, f. 98. 48: 6 x 8 abab4ccDD3* (ref. Lusty and full of strength | in labor good at length). BR (2250.3). Love.

TM 1051 My lady hath me in that grace.
L: Add. 31922, 1513+, ff. 107v–8. With music. 14: 4 burd abca + 2 x 5 a4b3a4b3R2* (burd. Why shall not I why shall not I to my la; ref. I why shall not I). BR (2250.5). Carol, love.

TM 1052 My Lady ys such one to whome our Lord hath lent.
D: TCD 160, 1535–48, f. 127v. 10: ababcdcdee12. Love.

My lady ys Unkynd perday. Second stanza of TM 85.

TM 1053 My lytell fole ys gon to play.
L: Royal App. 58, 1507+, ff. 55v–6v. With music. 8: 2 x 4 aaaB4* (ref. Hey how frisca Joly under ye grene wood tre). BR (2255.3). Song, love.

My litle pretie Nightingale. See TM 1573

TM 1054 My lytell prety one my prety bony one.
L: Add. 18752, 1530's, f. 76v. 20: 4 x 5 ab6aa4b6*. BR (2255.6). Love.

TM 1055 My lord I pray you to remember me | your true humbell wyfe and ever wyl be.
C14: Fitzwilliam 56, bef. 1542, f. 1v. Signed "Margaret Sussex" (second wife of Robert Ratcliffe, died 1542). 2: aa5*. Marriage.

TM 1056 My love ys lyke unto theternall fyre.
L: Add. 17492, 1532–39, f. 53. 9: ababcccdd10. Love.

TM 1057 My love she morneth ffor me.
L: Add. 31922, 1513+, ff. 30v–1. With music by [William] Cornysh. 66: 11 x

6 aa2b3cc2B3* (ref. Morne ye no more for me for me). BR (2261.4). Song, love.

TM 1058 My love so swyte | Jhesu kype.
L: Sloane 3501, 1530's, f. 52v. 30: 5 x 6 aa2b3cc2b3*. BR (2261.6). Love, song.

TM 1059 My love toke skorne my servise to retaine.
L: Add. 17492, 1532–39, f. 79v. [Wyatt.] 14: abbaabbacddcee10. TP 1167. Love.

TM 1060 My loving frende amorous bune.
O: Rawl. C.813, 1520–35, ff. 6v–7v. "A lettre sende by on yonge woman to a-noder whiche aforetyme were felowes togeder." 46: aa4*. BR (2261.8). Epistle, scatalogical.

TM 1061 My lute awake perfourme the last.
L: Egerton 2711, bef. 1542, ff. 43v–4. "Tho[mas Wyatt]." 40: 8 x 5 aabaB8 (ref. ...I have done). D: TCD 160, 1535–48, f. 125. L: Add. 17492, 1532–39, ff. 14v–5. TP 1168. Song, love.

TM 1062 My mynde to love ys tewrly bent.
Y: Osborn music 13, 1553+, ff. 44v–5. With music, subscribed "T. W." (composer). 48: 12 x 4 abab8. Song, love.

My mode is changyd in every wyse. See TM 79.

TM 1063 My mothers maydes when they did sow & spyn.
L: Egerton 2711, bef. 1542, ff. 50v–2v. [Wyatt.] 112: terza rima10. L: Add. 17492, 1532–39, f. 87v. Lines 1–19 only. TP 1171. Nar., fable, moral, letter.

TM 1064 Mi Mornynge M greves me sore.
O: Lat. misc. c.66, c 1500, f. 94v. (Humfrey Newton.) 16:4 x 4 abaB4* (ref. Forsothe I wold ye knew my payn). BR (2263). Love.

TM 1065 My Name ys Parett a Byrde of paradyse.
L: Harley 2252, 1517–38, ff. 134–40. [John Skelton, *Speke Parrot*, vv. 1–57, 238–513 in Robert Kinsman ed. (1969); vv. 1–57, 225–518 in John Scattergood ed. (1983); only 290 vv. in English.] 350: skeltonics, RR5*, abab2*, aa5*. BR (2263.5); TP 1172. Satire, parody.

TM 1066 My owne dere hart I grete you well.
L: Harley 4011, early 16, f. 163v. 32: 8 x 4 abab4*. Love, address.

TM 1067 My pen take payn a lytyll space.
L: Add. 17492, 1532–39, f. 3v. 30: 6 x 5 aabaB4* (ref. My pen I pray thee write no more). TP 1173. Love.

TM 1068 <My> saded yeares and tracke of tyme doth learne me this to knowe.
D: TCD 160, 1535–48, f. 95v. 36: aa14. Moral.

TM 1069 My sowle the lorde dothe magnyfye.
L: Royal 17.A.21, 1551, ff. 81v–2v. William Forreste, tr. Magnificat. 40: 10 x 4 a8b6a8b6. Rel.

TM 1070 My soverayne lorde for my poure sake.
L: Add. 31922, 1513+, ff. 54v–5. With music by W Cornysh. 20: 2 burd aa + 3 x 6 aaabb4R2* (burd. Whilles lyve or breth is in my breast; ref. My soverayne lord). BR (2271.2). Carol, love.

TM 1071 My swet alas fforget me not.
D: TCD 160, 1535–48, f. 130. 28: 4 x 7 ababab4A2* (ref. Fforget me not). Love.

TM 1072 My swetharte & my lyllye floure.
O: Rawl.C.813, 1520–35, f. 4r–v. 32: 8 x 4 abab8. BR (2271.6). Love, epistle.

TM 1073 My thoght ys full hevy.
L: Royal App. 58, 1507+, ff. 23–4. With music. 39: 3 burd aba + 3 x 12 ababcdcdEFEF2* (burd. Now marcy Jhesu I wyll amend; ref. ...unjust ...lust). BR (2272). Rel., carol, penitence.

TM 1074 My thought oppressed | my mynd in trouble.
L: Add. 31922, 1513+, f. 116v. With music 21: 3 x 7 RR4*. BR (2272.5). Song, love lament.

TM 1075 My wofull hart In paynfull weryness.
L: Add. 5465, 1501–04, ff. 7v–9. Petition to the king (Henry VII) with music by Sheryngam. 7: RR4*. BR (2277). Song, hist.

TM 1076 My wofull hert of all gladnesse bareyne.
L: Add. 5665, bef. 1511, ff. 65v–6. With music. 16: 2 x 8 MT5*. BR (2277.5). Song, love.

TM 1077 My worshipfful and reverent lady dere.
O: Lat. misc. c.66, c 1500, f. 92v. (Humfrey Newton.) 68: 17 x 4 abab4*. BR 2881, comp. a 1400. Love.

TM 1078 My yeris be yong even as ye see.
L: Add. 17492, 1532–39, f. 78. 32: 2 burd aa + 6 x 5 aaaa4R2* (burd. Grudge on who liste this ys my lott; ref. If yt were not). BR (2281.5). Carol, love.

TM 1079 My youthefful days ar past.
L: Add. 17492, 1532–39, f. 68r–v. 40: 5 x 8 ababcdcd3*. TP 1187. Love.

TM 1080 Nat dremyd I in the mount of pernaso.
L: Add. 29729, 1558, f. 6r–v. "per...[Benedict] burgh ad Joannem lidgate." 56: 8 x 7 RR5*. BR 2284, comp. a 1440. Praise of Lydgate.

TM 1081 Nature that gave the bee so feet a grase.
L: Egerton 2711, bef 1542, f. 45. "Tho[mas Wyatt]." 8: abababcc5*. L: Add. 17492, 1532–39, f. 71v. L: Harley 78, mid 16, f. 27. "Sir Tho[mas] W[yatt]." D: TCD 160, 1535–48, f. 129v. TP 1189. Love.

TM 1082 Never was I lesse alone then beyng alone.
O: Ashmole 48, bef. 1558, f. 9v. "Henry [Parker] Lord Morley to his posteritye...Wrytten over a chambar door wher he was wont to ly at Hollenbyrry." 16: aa5*. Moral.

TM 1083 Nixt at a tornament was tryit.
E: Asloan, 1513–42, ff. 210–11v. "quod Dunbar, The Justis betwix the talyeour & the sowtar." 108: 18 x 6 aa8b6cc8b6. BR (2289.8). Nar., humor, Scots.

TM 1084 No catell no care letitia.
L: Sloane 2232, early 16, f. 9v. Variant of BR 3209. 4: aaaa4*. Money.

TM 1085 No kinde of Labore is a thing of shame | but idlenesse ever more worthy blame.
DUR5: Cosin V.iii.9, c 1555, f. 60, 69v. [Nicholas Udall, tr. Hesiod.] 2: aa4*. BR (2291.5); TP 1204. Moral.

TM 1086 No wondre thow I murnyng make.
L11: PRO E/163/22/1, c 1530, s. sh. With music. 30: 2 burd aa + 7 x 4 aaaB3* (burd. Alone I lyve alone; ref. alone I lyve alone). BR (2293.5). Love, carol.

TM 1087 Nobles Report zour matinnis in this buke.
E: Asloan, 1513–42, f. 92v. [Andrew Cadiou, tr.], Alain Chartier, epilogue to prose "Porteous of Nobleness," copied from STC 5060.5 (1508). 5: ababb5*. BR (2293.6); TP 1209. Rel., envoy, Scots.

TM 1088 Noddy hoddy doddy | Se the apish [busi?] bodie.
HN: Stowe 36, 1541–55, f. 82. 2: aa3*. Humor.

TM 1089 Non sigheth so sore | as the gloton that mai no more.
O17: Balliol 354, 1505–36, f. 191v. 2: aa3*. BR (2293.8). Proverb.

TM 1090 Not long agoo.
L: Add. 17492, 1532–39, ff. 43, 77r–v. (53 line text on ff. 77r–v.) 60: 4 burd abba + 9 x 6 aa4b6cc4b6 (burd. How shold I | be so plesent). Carol, chanson d'aventure, love complaint.

TM 1091 Noghte to lyke thow me to lake.
PML: Glazier MS 39, c 1500. Colophon verses on a prayer roll by the scribe "Percevall," canon of Coverham Abbey, Yorkshire, c. 1500. 20: aa4*. BR (2300.3). Envoy.

TM 1092 Now.
L: Add. 31922, 1513+, f. 98. Incipit only, with music. Song.

TM 1093 Now all of chaunge.
L: Add. 17492, 1532–39, f. 81r–v. 48: 8 x 6 ab4c8ab4c8. Love.

TM 1094 Now beyng in preson am I not abyll.
L: Harley 2252, 1517–38, ff. 33v–4. "The complaynte of [Edward] Northe to the cardinall Wolsey" (1516); see also TM 606. 70: 10 x 7 RR5*. Hist.

TM 1095 Now deth is at myn hede.
L: Sloane 1313, early 16, f. 134r–v. 32: 8 x 4 abab3*. BR (2307). Dialogue, death.

TM 1096 Now Deathe thow arte wellcome to me.
L: Add. 33974, c 1550, f. 48. (Francis Stacy), "A Joyfull receyvinge of Deathe." 34: aa4*. Rel., death.

TM 1097 Now fayre fayrest off every fayre.
L: Royal App. 58, 1507+, ff. 17v–8. With music (welcome of Queen Margaret to Edinburgh, 1503). 16: 4 x 4 abbB4* (ref. ...queen). BR (2308.5). Hist., Scotland.

Nowe fare well love and thye lawes forever. See TM 402.

TM 1098 Now fayre wele my Joye my comfort and solace.
O: Bodl. 120, early 16, f. 95r–v. 7: RR4*. BR (766). Love.

TM 1099 Now god that Deathe thy messenger hath tak me by the hande.
L: Add. 33974, c 1550, f. 48v. (Francis Stacy), "A prayer before our ende." 14: aa7*. Rel., prayer, death.

Now good swete harte and my none god mestrys mercy. Extract from TM 1368; see also TM 1221.

TM 1100 Nowe harke nowe here my hart my dere.
Y: Osborn music 13, 1553+, ff. 26–7. 84: 6 x 14 abcdbceefgfghh8. Song, love.

Now herkynnis wordis wunder gude. See TM 523.

TM 1101 Now helpe fortune of thy godenesse.
L: Add. 5665, bef. 1511, ff. 71v–2. With music. 4: abba4*. BR (2323.8). Song, fortune, complaint.

TM 1102 Now I do know your chaungyd thought.
L: Add. 18752, 1530's, f. 77v,139v. Copied twice, version on f. 139 has variant first line "Now I perceve you chaungyd thought." 24: 6 x 4 abab4*. Dispraise of women.

Now I perceve you chaungyd thought. See TM 1102.

TM 1103 Now yn this medow fayre and grene.
L: Add. 31922, 1513+, ff. 124v–8. With music. 22:6 burd aabbcc + 4 x 4 aabb4* (burd. Hey troly loly lo mayde whether go you). BR (2034.5). Carol, love, seduction.

TM 1104 Now is Englond perisshed in sighs.
C: Hh.2.6, early 16, f. 58. 28:7 x 4 abab4*. BR 2335, comp. a 1500. Political.

Now is the lawe lede by clere conscience. See TM 1117.

TM 1105 Now ys Yole comyn with gentyll chere.
L: Add. 14997, early 16, f. 44v. Subscribed "In die dominica prima post festum sancti Michaelis archangeli anno regis henrici septimi post conquestum anglie sextodecimo [4 Oct. 1500] illa res erat scripta primo." 22: 2 burd aa + 5 x 4 aaab3* (burd. Hay ay hay ay). BR 2343. Rel., carol, nativity.

TM 1106 Now joy be to the trynyte.
O17: Balliol 354, 1505–36, f. 230. 22: 2 burd. (aa) + 5 x 4 abab3* (burd. Wassaill, wassayll, wassaill syng we). BR (2346). Rel., carol, nativity.

TM 1107 Nowe let the servaunte, lorde of light.
L: Royal 17.A.21, 1551, ff. 82v–3. William Forreste, tr. Nunc dimittis. 20: 5 x 4 a8b6a8b6. Rel., death.

TM 1108 Now lat us all | ga lof the lord.
BO: f. Med. 94, mid 16, f. 76. 8: rondeau ABaAabAB2* (ref. Now let us all; 2d ref. ga lof the lord). Rel. instruction, Scots.

TM 1109 Now master doctor how saye.
O: Rawl. C. 813, 1520–35, ff. 42v–3v. [Skelton,] epilogue to TM 417. 34: skeltonics. Moral.

TM 1110 Now may I morne as one off late.
L: Add. 17492, 1532–39, f. 26. Perhaps by Thomas Howard (d. Oct. 1537). 20: 5 x 4 abab8. Death.

TM 1111 Now may we myrthis make.
L: Add. 5665, bef. 1511, ff. 36v–7. "De nativitate," with music. 14:2 burd aa + 3 x 4 aaab4* (burd. Alleluya | Alleluya). BR 2377, comp. c 1450. Rel. carol, nativity.

TM 1112 Now must I lerne to lyve at rest.
L: Add. 17492, 1532–39, f. 54. 28: 7 x 4 a8b6a8b6. Love complaint.

TM 1113 Now of this matter to you most clere.
O: Ashmole 759, early 16, ff.128v–9v. "here folowith the exposicion of erth of erth." 68: aa3*. Alchemy.

TM 1114 Now that ye be assembled heer.
L: Add. 17492, 1532–39, f. 88. [perhaps by Lady Margaret Douglas.] 24: 3 x 8 MT8. Testament.

TM 1115 Now the cherfull daye da.
G: Hunt Mus 232, early 16, f. 98. Fragment, one line only, tr. Iam lucis orto sidere. 1: [aabb4* trochaic]. TP 1243. Rel., hymn.

TM 1116 Now the Father and the Sune and the Holy Goste.
D: TCD 652, pt. 6, c 1546, ff. 338–56. R. C. (scribe?), "The Play of the Conversyon of Ser Jonathas the Jewe by Myracle of the Blyssed Sacrament" (Croxton Play of the Sacrament). 1,007: 126 x 8 MT4*. BR 2363, comp. a 1500. Rel. drama, miracle.

TM 1117 Now the law is led be clere conciens.
L: Add. 5465, 1501–04, f. 12. With music by Rycardus Davy. 8: MT5*. L:

Harley 2250, early 16, f. 84v. L: Harley 78, mid 16, f. 30. "The truthe at on tyme affirmed." C2: TCC B.15.31 (366), bef. 1541, f. 1a. C: Hh.2.6, early 16, f. 58. BR 2364, comp. a 1500. Punctuation poem, moral.

TM 1118 Now to do well how shalt thou do.
L: Add. 5665, bef. 1511, ff. 35v–6. With music. 10: 2 burd aa + 2 x 4 abab4* (burd. Do well and drede no man). BR (2370). Carol, moral.

TM 1119 Now to speke I will noght spare.
LINC: Lincoln 105, early 16, f. 119v. 8: abababab4*. BR 2371, comp. a 1500. Moral, value of speech.

TM 1120 Now wursheppful soveryns that syttyn here in syth.
O:Tanner 407, 1/4 16, f. 44v. Epilogue to a miracle play. 28: abab4*. BR (2380). Rel. drama.

TM 1121 Now wold I ffayn | In wordis playn.
L: Cott. Nero C.11, 1506+, ff. 30v–1v. Robert Fabyan, in praise of London. 96: 12 x 8 aaabcccb2*. TP 1245. Hist.

TM 1122 Now wolde y fayne sum merthis mak.
O: Ashmole 191, pt. 4, early 16, f. 191. With music. 24: 6 x 4 abab4*. BR 2381, comp. a 1500. Love, song.

TM 1123 O all the earthe, be gladde in god.
L: Royal 17.A.21, 1551, ff. 55v–7v. William Forreste, tr. Ps 65 Jubilate. 76: 19 x 4 a8b6a8b6. Rel.

TM 1124 O all yee earthelye creatures.
L: Royal 17.A.21, 1551, f. 72r–v. William Forreste, tr. Ps 100 Jubilate domino. 28: 7 x 4 a8b6a8b6. Rel.

TM 1125 O all ye gentyles, clapp your handes.
L: Royal 17.A.21, 1551, ff. 44v–5v. William Forreste, tr. Ps 46 Omnes gentes. 40: 10 x 4 a8b6a8b6. Rel.

TM 1126 O all ye Juste, and rightyous.
L: Royal 17.A.21, 1551, ff. 36v–8v. William Forreste, tr. Ps 32 Exultati iusti. 92: 23 x 4 a8b6a8b6. Rel.

TM 1127 O allmyghtie and eternall Creator I thy poore creature above all thinges.
L: Add. 33974, 1551, f. 35. (Francis Stacy), "That hope in god may be increasyde." 20: aa7*. Rel., prayer.

TM 1128 O angell dere wher ever I go.
O17: Balliol 354, 1503–04, f. 144. "To the gud angell." 20: 5 x 4 abab4*. BR (2385). Rel., prayer.

TM 1129 O blesse god in trinitie.
L: Add. 5665, bef. 1511, ff. 25v–7. "De nativitate domine," with music. 18: 3 burd (abc) + 3 x 5 abab4R3* (burd. Te deum laudamus; ref. Te deum laudamus). BR (2388). Rel., carol, nativity, thanksgiving.

TM 1130 O blessed jesu hyghe hevens kynge.
HN: EL 34.B.7, early 16, ff. 80–1. "A devote prayer." 43: aa4–3* + irreg. BR 2391, comp. a 1500. Rel., prayer.

TM 1131 O blessed lord how may this be.
L: Add. 5665, bef. 1511, ff. 69v–70. With music. 5: abbcc4*. BR (2393.5). Song, love, complaint.

TM 1132 O blissid lord my lorde O crist Ih[es]u.
L: Add. 29729, 1558, ff. 11–16, 287–88. "the .xv. oes compiled by John lydgat...Here wryten owt of master stantons boke by John stow"; also 96-line fragment (stanzas 31–42) on ff. 287–88, beginning "Jhesu called alpha and O." 336: 42 x 8 MT5*. BR 2394, comp. a 1449. Rel., prayer, Jesus.

TM 1133 O blessed lord of hevyn celestiall.
L: Add. 5465, 1501–04, ff. 104v–8. Music by Edmund Turges (carol on a journey of Prince Arthur, 1501 or 1502). 32: 2 burd aa + 3 x 10 abab5cccc2dd2* (burd. From stormy wyndis and grevous wethir; ref. Wherefore now syng we). BR (2394.5). Hist. carol.

TM 1134 O catife corps that long hast felt | the present panges of death.
L: Cott. Titus A.24, 1550's, f. 91v. "in Wylson ... finis per me R[ichard]. E[dwardes]." 18: aa14. Love.

TM 1135 O christe thou hast restorede my soule.
COP: Old College 3500, mid 16, ft. flyleaf. 4: a8b6a8b6. BR (2403.3). Rel., prayer.

TM 1136 O Chryste who haste lente me thys lyfe heare in thys worlde to lyve.
L: Add. 33974, c 1550, f. 45r–v. (Francis Stacy), "Physycke for a syke man to dye well." 28: aa7*. Rel., death.

O cruell causer of undeserved chaynge. Fragment of TM 108.

TM 1137 O crewell hart wher ys thy ffaythe.
D: TCD 160, 1535–48, f. 139r–v. 52: 13 x 4 abab8. Love.

TM 1138 O david thou nobell key.
L: Add. 5665, bef. 1511, ff. 20v–2. "In die nativitatis"; Jhon Troulouffe written after 2nd stanza; music by Ric[hard] Smert. 22: 7 burd ababccb + 3 x 5 ababb3*, irreg. (burd. O clavis david inclita). BR (2409). Rel., carol, advent.

TM 1139 O dere God beholde this worlde so transytorye.
O: Rawl. C.813, 1521+, ff.49v–50v. "The lamentatyon of Edward [Stafford] late Duke of Buckyngham" (d. 1521). 63: 9 x 7 RR5*. BR (2409.5). Hist., elegy.

TM 1140 O dere god pereless prince of pece.
O17: Balliol 354, 1503–04, ff. 144–5. (Cf. BR 2573 and 3774.) 88: 11 x 8 MT4* (ref. Miserere mei deus). BR (2410). Rel., prayer.

TM 1141 O dethe whylum dysplesant to nature.
C15: Pembroke 307, mid 16, f. 198v. 7: RR4*. BR 2412, comp. a 1500. Love.

TM 1142 O excelent suffereigne most semely to see.
O: Rawl. C.813, 1520–35, ff. 50v–1v. 72: 6 x 12 ababbcc4d1eeed2*. BR (2421). Love, epistle.

O fayer, fayrest off every fayre. See TM 1097.

TM 1143 O faythfull hart plunged in distres.
D: TCD 160, 1535–48, f. 140. (Incomplete, damaged leaf.) 7: RR4*. Love.

TM 1144 O father deare so opulente.
O: Ashmole 48, bef. 1558, ff. 71–2. "a grace aftare dynnare," subscribed "sponare." 56: 14 x 4 a8b6a8b6. Rel., grace.

TM 1145 O gentyll & most gentyll Jesu you save.
O: Rawl. C.813, 1520–35, f. 71. 14: 2 x 7 RR4* (ref. ...in payne for your sake onlye). BR (2439.5). Love, epistle.

TM 1146 O gloryus god oure governer glad in all thys gesttyng.
L: Harley 78, early 16, ff. 74–7v. [Anon.,] The Tale of the Prioress and her Three Suitors, incorrectly attributed to Lydgate by John Stow (reference to White Rose of York puts comp. after 1461). 243: 27 x 9 aaaa5b2ccc4b2*. BR 2441, comp. a 1500. Nar., love.

TM 1147 O Glorious Lady And Vergyn Imaculatt.
L: Sloane 1584, bef. 1550, ff. 14v–15v. 56: 7 x 8 MT4* (ref. A peste succurre nobis). BR (2444). Rel., Virgin Mary.

TM 1148 O glorious mothar and mayd off pety.
L: Sloane 1584, bef. 1550, ff. 15v–16v. 42: 6 x 7 RR4* (ref. Vita et spes nostra salve). BR (2446). Rel., Virgin Mary.

TM 1149 O god be thowe, my Judge as nowe.
L: Royal 17.A.21, 1551, ff. 42v–3. William Forreste, tr. Ps 42 Judica me deus. 32: 8 x 4 a8b6a8b6. Rel.

TM 1150 O god, geve to the kinge thye soone.
L: Royal 17.A.21, 1551, ff. 59v–61v. William Forreste, tr. Ps 71 Deus iudicium. 84: 21 x 4 a8b6a8b6. Rel.

TM 1151 O god of goddes and kyng of kynges.
O: Ashmole 48, bef. 1558, ff. 69v–70v. "a grace befor dynner." 56: 14 x 4 a8b6a8b6. Rel., grace.

TM 1152 O god of my salvation.
L: Royal 17.A.21, 1551, ff. 64v–6. William Forreste, tr. Ps 87. 80: 20 x 4 a8b6a8b6. Rel.

TM 1153 O god, on me have thowe mercye.
L: Royal 17.A.21, 1551, ff. 47v–9. William Forreste, tr. Psalm 50. 84: 21 x 4 a8b6a8b6. Rel.

TM 1154 O god that art my ryghtuusnes.
Y: Osborn music 13, 1553+, f. 9. Incipit only, with lute tablature [possibly Sternhold, tr. Ps 4, TP 1277]. Rel.

TM 1155 O god: to helpe me in my neede.
L: Royal 17.A.21, 1551, ff. 58v–9v. William Forreste, tr. Ps 69. 32: 8 x 4 a8b6a8b6. Rel.

TM 1156 O god: we praise, and honour thee.
L: Royal 17.A.21, 1551, ff. 77v–80. William Forreste, tr. Te deum laudamus. 100: 25 x 4 a8b6a8b6. Rel., hymn.

TM 1157 O god we pr[a]y to the in specyall.
L: Add. 5665, bef. 1511, ff. 51v–2. "In fine nativitatis," with music. 14: 2 burd aa + 3 x 4 aaaR4* (burd. For all cristen saulys pray we; ref. Et lux perpetua luceat eis). BR (2453). Rel., carol, purgatory.

TM 1158 O goodely hand.
L: Egerton 2711, bef. 1542, f. 59v. "Tho[mas Wyatt]." 30: 5 x 6 aa4b6cc4b6.
L: Harley 78, mid 16, f. 28. "T. W[yatt]." Love, praise of mistress, blason.

TM 1159 Oh happy ar they that have forgiffnes gott.
L: Egerton 2711, bef. 1542, ff. 89–90v. Wyatt (autograph), Penitential Psalms, tr. Ps.32. 76: terza rima10. TP 1287. Rel.

TM 1160 O happy dames that may embrayce.
L: Add. 17492, 1532–39, f. 55r–v. [Henry Howard, Earl of Surrey.] 42: 6 x 7 a8b6a8b6cc8c10. L11: PRO SP 1/246, mid 16, ff. 28v–9. Lines 1–7, with music. L: Add. 30513, c 1550, f. 107. Incipit only, with music. L: Harley 78, mid 16, f. 30v. Lines 1–7 only. TP 1288. Love, complaint, song.

TM 1161 O heapid hed.
L11: PRO SP 1/246, mid 16, f. 16. Incipit only, with music. Song.

TM 1162 O hie empryss and quene celestiale.
E: Asloan, 1513–42, f. 292r–v. "Ane ballat of our lady" (incomplete). 40: 5 x 8 MT4*. BR 2461, comp. a 1500. Rel., prayer, Virgin Mary.

O hygh Incomparabyl and gloryus majeste. See TM 577.

TM 1163 O holly gode of dreydfulle majestie.
O: Lat. theol. d.15, 1551, f. 119. Thomas More, tr., prayer of Pico della Mirandola, copied by Robert Parkyn. 84: 12 x 7 RR5*. TP 1296. Rel., prayer.

TM 1164 O howe holsum and glad is the memorie.
L: Royal 18.D.2, c 1520, ff. 1v–5. "the testamente of John Lydgate" (parts 2–5 only, vv. 241–897; omits the Prologue and begins "The yere passed of my tender youthe"). 657: 47 x 7 RR5*, 41 x 8 MT5* (ref. ...shrift housell repentence; 2d ref. Was lyke a lambe offred in sacryfice).L: Add. 29729, 1558, ff.179v–83. "...the prologe of John Lydgattes testament | which I [John Stowe] fownd in Mr stantons boke." 240: 30 x 8 MT5*. L: Arundel 285, c 1540, ff. 170–4v. "Ane Devoit Remembrance of the passioun of Crist," partial text of the "Testament" beginning "Behald man lift up thy ene and see." 144: 18 x 8 MT5* (ref. Wes like ane lambe offerit in sacrafice). BR 2464, comp. a 1449; TP 1299. Rel., personal, testament, nar., Christ.

TM 1165 O jesu lett me never forgett thy bytter passion.
HN: EL 34.B.7, early 16, f. 82. "A goode praier." 8: aa5*. BR 2471, comp. a 1500. Rel., prayer, Jesus.

TM 1166 O jhesu mercy what world is thys.
O: Tanner 407, 1/4 16, f. 38v. 8: 2 x 4 abab4*. BR (2472). Rel., Jesus.

TM 1167 O jesu to all thy true lovers.
HN: EL 34.B.7, early 16, ff. 81v–2. "A devoute prayer." 30: abccddbeefggg, etc., irreg. BR 2474, comp. a 1500. Rel., prayer.

TM 1168 O Jesu who dydste me create.
L: Add. 33974, c 1550, f. 20v. (Francis Stacy), "<A Devoute prayer to our> Savyour Jesus." 34: aa4*. Rel., prayer.

TM 1169 O Jesu who haste us create.
L: Add. 33974, c 1550, f. 76r–v. (Francis Stacy), untitled (line wanting after 37). 47: aa4*. Rel., prayer.

TM 1170 O Jowe geve eare unto my cry.
D: TCD 160, 1535–48, f. 94. 36: 9 x 4 abab8. Rel., complaint.

TM 1171 O kindly creatur of beute perley.
O: Ashmole 191, pt. 4, early 16, ff. 191v–2. With music. 4: abab4*. BR (2475). Love, song.

TM 1172 O ladye deere be ye so neere to be knowne.
L: Add. 15233, 1554–58, f. 45. "The thyrd Song" [by John Redford] in *Wit and Science*. 30: 5 x 6 aabaab2*. Song, moral.

TM 1173 O Lady I schall me dress with besy cure.
O: Arch. Selden B.24, mid 16, ff. 231, 230. 32: 4 x 8 ababbcbC5* (ref. Haf piete of me cative bound and thrall). BR (2478). Love, complaint, Scots.

TM 1174 O Lady Venus what aylyth the.
L: Add. 18752, 1530's, f. 91r–v. 42: 6 x 7 aaaabB4R2* (ref. that wyll I truste relesse my smart As is my hope). Love.

TM 1175 O lamentable world wherin is grown dyversytie of faythes before not knowne.
L: Add. 33974, c 1550, ff. 32v–4. (Francis Stacy), "Certeyne notes how to know the Catholyeke churche." 60: aa8*. Rel. instruction, controversy.

TM 1176 O Lobbe Lobe on thy sowle God have mercye.
O: Rawl. C. 813, 1520–35, ff. 27v–8. "The epytaphye of Lobe the Kynges [Henry VIII] foole." 49: 7 x 7 RR5* (ref. Many fools thouse whou be gone). BR (2482.5). Epitaph, humorous, Welshman.

TM 1177 O lord as I the have both prayd & pray.
L: Egerton 2711, bef. 1542, ff. 91–2. Wyatt, Penitential Psalms, tr. Ps. 38 (autograph). 70: terza rima10. TP 1304. Rel.

TM 1178 O Lord God O Jesu Crist [should be "Crist Jesu"].
L: Arundel 285, c 1540, ff. 163–4v. "An devoit orisoun to be said in the honour of the 7 wordis that our Salviour spak apoun the croce." 66: 8 x 8 aaabcccb4* and variants. BR (2486). Rel., prayer, Scots.

TM 1179 O lorde yn the is all my trust.
L: Add. 30981, 1522–29, f. 38r–v. John Croke, tr. In te domine speravi [Ps 31]. 24: abab4*. Rel.

TM 1180 O lorde (my god) in thee truste I.
L: Royal 17.A.21, 1551, ff. 8–9v. William Forreste, tr. Ps 7 Domine Deus. 72: 18 x 4 a8b6a8b6. Rel.

TM 1181 O lorde (my strenght) thee love will I.
L: Royal 17.A.21, 1551, ff. 24–9. William Forreste tr., Ps 17 Diligente. 220: 55 x 4 a8b6a8b6. Rel.

TM 1182 O lorde our lorde how marvellous.
L: Royal App. 74–76, c 1548, ff. 15v–17, 12v–14v, 20v–22v. With music, tr. Ps 8. 66: 11 x 6 ababcc8 (ref. ...name most glorious). Rel.

TM 1183 O lorde (owre lorde moste specyall).
L: Royal 17.A.21, 1551, ff. 9v–11. William Forreste, tr. Ps 8, Domine deus. 44: 11 x 4 a8b6a8b6. Rel.

TM 1184 O lord sins in my mowght thy myghty name.
L: Egerton 2711, bef. 1542, ff. 87–8v. Wyatt, Penitential Psalms, tr. Ps 6; one leaf (vv. 28–81) missing. 57: terza rima10. TP 1330. Rel.

TM 1185 O lord so swett ser John dothe kys.
HN: EL 34.B.60, c 1532, ff. 11v, 73v. 22: 2 burd (aa) + 5 x 4 abaB4* (burd. Hey noyney | I wyll love our ser John and; ref. I have no powre to say hym nay). BR (2494). Carol, love, bawdy.

TM 1186 O lorde that ruleste bothe lande and seae even by thy hevenly poure.
L: Cott. Titus A.24, 1550's, ff. 85v–7v. "finis R[ichard]. E[dwardes]." 52: aa14. Rel., prayer.

TM 1187 O lorde turne not awaye.
L: Add. 30513, c 1550, f. 105. Incipit only, with music. Rel., prayer.

TM 1188 O lord what chance what thyng ys thys.
D: TCD 160, 1535–48, f. 136r–v. 54: aa8. Fortune, allegory.

TM 1189 O lord what ys such a worlde as this.
Y: Osborn music 13, 1553+, f. 37v. Elegy on Edward VI, d. 1552, with music. 32: 8 x 4 abab4*. Song.

TM 1190 [O] lorde what ys thys worldes wele.
L: Add. 60577, 1549–58, ff. 65v–6v. 88: 22 x 4 abab4*. Moral.

TM 1191 O lord whych art in hevyn on hye.
L: Add. 15233, 1554–58, ff. 57v–8. Subscribed "myles huggarde" [probably not by Hogarde because it is Protestant in sentiment and the meter is perfectly regular]. 45: 9 x 5 ababB8 (ref. O here me lord and graunt mercye). Rel., prayer.

TM 1192 O lord whom wilt thou count worthie.
L: Royal App. 74–76, c 1548, ff. 20, 18v– 20, 26v–8. With music, tr. Ps 15 (partial version (lines 1–6) in Royal App. 74.) 54: 9 x 6 ababcc4*. Rel.

TM 1193 O lord with all my hart & mynd.
L11: PRO SP 1/246, mid 16, ff. 24v–5. 7: 2 burd aa + 5 ababR8 (burd. Benedicam Domino in omni tempore; ref. Therfor semper laus eius in ore meo). Rel., carol, macaronic.

TM 1194 O love most dere o love most nere my harte.
O: Rawl. C.813, 1520–35, ff. 24v–7v. (Vv. 8–126 are composed of lines from Hawes, "The Comfort of Lovers," 610–924, c 1515, TP 1734.) 168: 24 x 7 RR5*. BR (2496). Love, complaint.

TM 1195 O lovesome Rosse most Redolente.
L: Harley 424, mid 16, ff. 58–9v. "1553 the 10 of october ad mariam quen." 128: 32 x 4 a8b6a8b6. Rel. controversy, Queen Mary, Protestant.

TM 1196 O lustye lyllye the lantorne of all gentylnes.
O: Rawl. C.813, 1520–35, f. 52. First line probably missing. 15: 1 x 7 + 8 MT4* (ref. Amonge your new lovers remembre your olde). BR (2498). Love.

TM 1197 O man more then madde what ys thi mynde.
O: Rawl. C.813, 1520–35, ff. 69v–71. 56: 8 x 7 RR5*. BR (2500.5). Moral, against women.

TM 1198 O man recorde.
L2: Lambeth 159, c 1525, ff. 268v–71. [Thomas Langdon], "A lytle treatyse confowndyng the great hereses that raygne now a dayes, & repynyng agaynst the order of holy church: anymatyng good people to contynew in the constancy of fayth." 276: 46 x 6 aabccb3*. TP 1347. Rel. controversy, anti-Lutheran.

TM 1199 O man unkynde | have thow in mynde.
C2: TCC O.2.53 (1157), early 16, f. 69. 6: aabaab4. O: Tanner 407, 1/4 16, f.

52v. Variant, begins "Man unkynde..." 6: aa2*. BR 2507, comp. a 1450; TP 1348.5. Rel., monologue of Christ.

O marble herte and yet more harde perde. Excerpt of TM 517.

TM 1200 O mercyfull God maker of all mankynde.
O17: Balliol 354, 1505–36, f. 210. 8:2 burd. (aa) + 6 aabaab3* (burd. To dy to dy what have I). BR (2511). Rel., carol, death.

TM 1201 O mercyfull god, what a prynce was this.
HD: Eng 766F, bef. 1516, f. ?. Robert Fabyan, "Lenvoy" (in praise of Henry V). 28: 4 x 7 RR4*. TP 1350. Hist.

O mercyfull Jhesu behold my tremeling cher. See TM 1202.

TM 1202 O mercyfull Jhesu graunt us thi grace.
O5: Ptd. book, ø.c.1.1.1, bef. 1558, sig. M6v. With a revision of the first line to "O mercyfull Jhesu behold my trembling cher." 7: RR4*. Rel., prayer.

TM 1203 [O] myghtie mars that marre mony a wight.
L: Add. 24663, 1550's, ff. 16–17v. 98: 14 x 7 ababacc5*. L11: PRO SP 1/232, 1520, f. 219. Excerpt, begins "The Blacke shall bleed." 8: aa4*. C: Kk.6.16, c 1500, ff. 8v–10. 76: four rhymes only, aa5* + irreg. L: Cott. Cleopatra C.4, early–mid 16, f. 123v. Extract, begins "The blak schal blede & the blewe schal fare..." 12: aa4*. L: Harley 559, 1554, f. 39. Extract, begins "The blak schal blede..." 12: aa4*. L: Lansd. 762, 1524–29, ff. 96, 97. Extract, vv. 28, 31–5, beginning "The black shall bleed," copied twice 6: aa4*. C2: TCC O.2.53 (1157), early 16, f. 41. Excerpt, begins "The blak shall blede the blew schall have his hed." 6: ababcc5*. BR (2515), includes BR 3308.5. Prophecy.

TM 1204 O myshchevous M, Fyrst syllable of thy name.
L8: Guildhall 3313, c 1510, f.320v–23v. "A Balade of Empson" [attributed to William Cornysh, 1504.] 140: 20 x 7 RR4*. Hist., satire.

TM 1205 O myserable sorow withouten cure.
L: Add. 17492, 1532–39, f. 58v. 7: RR10. Love.

TM 1206 O mestres whye | owte caste am I.
L: Harley 2252, 1525, f. 84. 32: 4 x 8 aaabaaab4. BR (2518). Love.

TM 1207 O mortall creatures sealing in the waves of miserye.
D: TCD 537, 2/4 16, p. 81. 10: ababcdcdee5*. TP 1354. Rel. instruction.

TM 1208 O mortall man blynde in pompe and pryde.
NOR3: Norwich ANW 1/1, 1548, ff. 132v–3. (Addition on a record of 1548

to Norwich archdeaconery visitation book.) 49: RR5* (ref. Remember the [o] man thou art þut wormes mete). Rel., sins.

TM 1209 O Mortall man By grete exaltacion.
L: Harley 2252, 1517–38, ff. 157, 160. Eight stanzas only on f. 157; full text on f. 160. 84: 12 x 7 RR4*. BR (2521). Rel. instruction.

TM 1210 O Mortall man call to Remembraunce.
L: Harley 2252, 1517–38, f. 23. Contains tr. Ps. 130 and liturgical passages Kyrie eleison, Inclina aures, et al. 132: 11 x 12 abababab bCbC4* (ref. Hys blody wondes; 2d ref. Psalme de profundes). BR (2522). Rel.

TM 1211 O mortall man in this lyffe transitore.
Y: Beinecke 337, c 1527, ff. 105v–6v. Anthony Askham, "The Complaynt off Sanct Cipriane the Grett Nigromancer Mayd after that He Was Convertid off the Virgyne Justyne" (based on some Latin version of "The Confession of Saint Cyprian"). 91: 13 x 7 RR4*. Rel., first-person nar.

TM 1212 O mortall man masyd with pompe and pride.
L: Add. 29729, 1558, ff. 7–8. 56:8 x 7 RR5* (ref. Remember man thou art but wormes mete). BR 2523, comp. a 1450. Rel., death.

TM 1213 O mortall man remember thys.
L: Add. 33974, c 1550, ff. 71v–2v. (Francis Stacy), "Consilium domini in eternum manet" [Ps. 32:11]. 126: aa4*. Rel. instruction.

O most blessid Fader omnipotent. See TM 467.

TM 1214 O mothir of God involat virgin Mary.
L: Arundel 285, c 1540, ff.174v–5v. "Off the Resurrectioun of Crist." 40: 5 x 8 MT5* (ref. Quhois blyssit uprissing glades every wycht). BR (2528). Rel., hymn, Virgin Mary, Scots.

TM 1215 O my dere harte the lanterne of lyght.
O: Rawl. C.813, 1520–35, f. 46r–v. (Lines 8–14 borrowed from Lydgate, *Temple of Glass*.) 39: 5 x 7RR4*, 2 x 2 aa4*. BR (2529). Love, epistle.

TM 1216 O my desyre what eylyth the.
L: Add. 5465, 1501–04, f. 10r–v. Music by William Newark. 16: 2 x 8 MT4* (ref. O my desyre what eylyth the). BR (2530.5). Song, love.

TM 1217 O my good brother.
C: Ff.6.31, early 16, f. iv verso. "Quod the devill to the frier." 6: aabccb3*. BR (2531). Rel. satire, anti-clerical.

TM 1218 O my hart & o my hart.
L: Add. 31922, 1513+, ff. 22v–3. With music by "The Kyng H.viij." 4: a4b3a4b3*. HN: Ptd. book 69798, early 16, sig. gg4v. BR (2531.5). Song, love.

TM 1219 O my lady dere bothe regarde and see.
O: Rawl. C. 813, 1520–35, ff. 14v–18. (Vv. 148–54 based on passages from Hawes, *Comfort of Lovers*, TP 1734; also includes extracts from Hawes, *The Pastime of Pleasure*, TM 1368.) 168: 24 x 7 RR5*. BR (2532). Love, epistle.

TM 1220 O my lady dure.
L: Royal App. 58, 1507+, f. 16v. "Quod parker monke of Stratforde," with music. 5: mono2*. BR (2532.3). Love, song.

TM 1221 O my swet lady and exelente goddas.
O: Rawl. C. 813, 1520–35, ff. 18–21v. (Incorporates 67 lines from Hawes, *The Pastime of Pleasure*, TM 1368.) 175: 25 x 7 RR5*. BR (2532.5). Love.

O o rote of trouth o princess to my pay. See TM 1232.

TM 1222 O of jesse thow holy rote.
L: Add. 5665, bef. 1511, ff. 19–20. "In die nativitatis," with music. 16: 4 burd abab + 3 x 4 abab4* (burd. O radix jesse supplices). BR (2533). Rel., carol, nativity.

TM 1223 O penful harte that lyes in travvail | And in tene luk up merely for sone it schall.
G: Hunt. 230, early 16, f. 246v. Couplet preceding TM 1368, written in a different hand. 2: aa5*. BR (2536). Love.

TM 1224 O pa[r]tyng ys a pynchyn pane.
L: Sloane 3501, 1530's, f. 2v. Incipit only, no music. Song, love.

TM 1225 O pereles prynce of peace.
PML: Ptd. book PML Checklist 1787, c 1540, flyleaf. 48: 12 x 4 abab3*. BR (2536.5). Rel., complaint, satire, deadly sins.

TM 1226 O prayse the lorde, hierusalem.
L: Royal 17.A.21, 1551, ff. 74v–5v. William Forreste, tr. Ps 148 Lauda hierusalem. 40: 10 x 4 a8b6a8b6. Rel.

TM 1227 O prayse the lorde | with true conchorde.
L: Royal 17.A.21, 1551, ff. 75v–6v. William Forreste, tr. Ps 150 Laudate dominum. 46: 4 + 7 x 6 aa4b6cc4b6. Rel.

TM 1228 O Quam mirabilia, good lord thy werkes been.
L: Cott. Nero C.11, 1506+, f. 61r–v. Robert Fabyan, tr. anon. verses on the oppression of the church by Otto IV, Philip of France, and John of England. 21: 3 x 7 RR5*. HD: Eng 766F, bef. 1516, f. 32r–v. BR (2541.5); TP 1368. Rel., hist.

O quene of heven that syttest in se. See TM 263.

TM 1229 O resplendent floure prynte this yn your mynde.
O: Rawl. C.813, 1520–35, ff. 53v–4. (Lines 15–22 are from Lydgate, *The Chorl and the Bird.*) 22: 4 x 4 abab5* + 6 aa5*. BR (2547). Love, epistle.

O restfull place renewer of my smert. See TM 1586.

TM 1230 O Rex Regum in thy realme celestialle.
L: Harley 2252, 1513+, ff. 45v–8v. "Explicyt Bellum de Brampton per ffraunces dyngley de (?) manitone," narrative of the Stanley family at the Battle of Flodden Field, comp. after 1513; ptd. STC 13445, *The Mirror for Magistrates* (1587). 182: 26 x 7 RR4* (ref. So thy helpe O Lorde preservde King Henryes right). BR (2547.3). Hist., nar.

TM 1231 O rightful rule and lyghte of lyghtes.
L: Cott. Titus A.24, 1553+, f. 79r–v. "Qd Pig," prayer for safety of Queen Mary. 32: 8 x 4 a8b6a8b6. Rel., prayer, hist.

TM 1232 O rote of trouth o princess to my pay.
L: Add. 5465, 1501–04, ff. 38v–40. With music by Tutor. 5: abbcc4*. L: Add. 60577, 1549–58, f. 116v. BR (2547.5). Song, love, praise of woman.

TM 1233 O Schotland thow was flowryng in prosperus welthe.
L: Add. 45102, 1513–20, s.sh. Lament by the ghost of James IV after defeat at Flodden Field, 9 Sept. 1513. 42: 6 x 7 RR5*. BR (2549.5); Hist., Scotland.

TM 1234 O synfull man thir ar the xl dayis.
L: Arundel 285, c 1540, ff. 161–2v. Dunbar, "The maner of passyng to confessioun." 70: 10 x 7 RR10. BR (2551.5). Rel., confession, Scots.

O small hony: much aloes, & gall. Lines 22–147 of TM 1004.

TM 1235 O sothefast son of all bryghtnes.
L: Add. 29729, 1558, ff.126v–7v. "...verses...whiche the kynge henry the .v....used in his chappell at hyse masses...translatid by...Lydegat..." (paraphrase of the Eight Verses of St. Bernard, Version II). 88: 11 x 8 MT4*. BR 2553, comp. a 1422. Rel., prayer.

TM 1236 O soorowe of all sorowes my harte doeth cleve.
O: Rawl. C.813, 1520–35, ff. 29v–30. "The lamentatyon of the Ladye Gryffythe [ap Rhys]." 21: 3 x 7 RR4*. BR (2552.5). Lament, memorial, Welsh.

TM 1237 O splendent spectakyll moste comlyeste of hewe.
L: Add. 60577, 1549–58, f. 108. 16: abab4*. Love, letter.

TM 1238 O sterne so brycht that gyfys lycht.
E2: Laing 149, 1/4 16, f. 3v. 26: 2 burd (ab) + 4 x 6 a8b6a8b6cc8 (burd. O farest lady o swetast lady). BR 2557, comp. a 1500. Rel., carol, Virgin Mary, prayer.

TM 1239 O swete angell to me soo deere.
HN: EL 34.B.7, early 16, f. 81. "A praier to the goode Angell." 20: 2 aa4* + 3 x 6 aabccb4*. BR 2560, comp. a 1500. Rel., prayer.

TM 1240 O swete harte dere & most best belovyd.
O: Rawl. C.813, 1520–35, ff. 55–6. 68: MT5*, abababacaC5*, aabb5*, ababcdcD5* (ref. your bewtye makethe my harte to blede). BR (2560.5). Love, epistle.

TM 1241 O that fface that ffragraunt fface.
L: Add. 18752, 1530's, ff. 86–7. 70: 14 x 5 aaaa4B2* (ref. O that swete face). Love, description of mistress.

TM 1242 O The syllye man.
L: Add. 30513, c 1550, ff. 77v–8. Incipit only, with music by Richard Edwardes. Song.

TM 1243 O this grete hevynese and payn.
O: e Musaeo 160, c 1520, ff. 156v–72. "Her Begynnes His [Christ's] Resurrection on Pas[c]he Daye" (included in BR 95; probably composed by and in the hand of a Carthusian monk of Kingston upon Hull, Yorks., c 1520). 766 RR, aa4b3cc4b3*, and irreg. Rel., nar., Christ.

TM 1244 O thou astroloper of prese moste worthy.
NLW: 3567B, 1551, back cover. Praise of Chaucer, appended to the *Treatise on the Astrolabe*, by "John Edw[ards]...possesor huius [libris] 1551." 4: aabb4*.

O thou fers god of armes the Rede. See TM 1684.

TM 1245 O thou hygh sonne of the hygh ffather.
L2: Lambeth 159, 1534+, f. 264. Thomas Langdon [professed as a Benedictine, 1534]. 150: 30 x 5 aabb4a2*. Rel., prayer.

TM 1246 O thowe moste myghtye lorde, and duke.
L: Royal 17.A.21, 1551, ff. 40–2v. William Forreste, tr. Ps 37 Domine ne in furore. 102: 26 x 4 a8b6a8b6. Rel.

TM 1247 O thow pore boke unworthy and < >.
O: Rawl. D.913, 2/4 16, f. 5. Two stanzas, partly effaced, of a dedication to [Henry Howard] earl of surrey. 14: 2 x 7 RR10.

O thoughtfull herte, plonged in distresse. See TM 2005.

O very lord o sone o god alas. Extracts from TM 1510.

TM 1248 O what a treasure ys love certeyne.
O: Ashmole 176, pt. 3, 2/4 16, f. 100. 4: aabb4*. BR (2579.3). Love.

TM 1249 O what undeservyd crewltye.
D: TCD 160, 1535–48, f. 137. 20: 5 x 4 abaB4* (ref. Itornyd to me contrarye). Love, fortune.

TM 1250 O wofull man why dust thow now forgett godes lent to the.
L: Add. 33974, c 1550, ff.11v–12v. (Francis Stacy), "Of the love of Chry<ste to man>." 118: aa7*. Rel., Jesus.

TM 1251 O wome[n] thys dothe note behowve youe.
O: Ashmole 48, bef 1558, f. 50r–v. "finis TSP" (in a different hand). 28: aa4*. Women, dispraise.

O worthe the lenttone.... See TM 2016.

TM 1252 O worthy Lord & most of myght.
O17: Balliol 354, 1505–36, f. 223. 18: 2 burd. (aa) + 4 x 4 abab8 (burd. Into this world now ye cum). BR (2586). Rel., carol, macaronic, Jesus.

TM 1253 O wretched synner what so ever thow be.
L: Add. 29729, 1558, ff. 129v–130. [On the Image of Pity,] subscribed "finis lidgat." 40: 5 x 8MT65*. BR 2588, comp. a 1449. Rel. instruction.

O ye folkis all which have devocion. Variant first line of TM 2023.

TM 1254 O ye my emperice I your servaunt this to you I say.
O: Lat. misc. c.66, c 1500, f. 94. (Humfrey Newton.) 48: 12 x 4 abab4*. BR (2597). Love, letter.

TM 1255 O ye my lordes whan ye be holde.
L: Add. 29729, 1558, ff. 177v–9. "Kalundare of John shirley which he sett in

the beginninge of his booke." 144: aa4*. BR 2598, comp. a 1456. Table of contents.

TM 1256 O ye tender babes.
L: Add. 30513, c 1550, f. 81r–v. Incipit only, with music by Tallys. Song.

TM 1257 O you that putt youre trust & convydence.
L: Sloane 1825, early 16, ff. 88v–9v. [Thomas More, elegy on death of Queen Elizabeth, d. 1503.] 84: 12 x 7 RR5* (ref. Your quene but late and lo now here I dy). O17: Balliol 354, 1505–36, ff. 175–6. [Thomas More], "The Lamy[n]tacion off Quene Elyzabeth," with variant first line "Ye that put your trust..." BR (4263.3); TP 1392. Hist., elegy.

TM 1258 O ye verteous soverayns spirituall and temporall.
C7: Corpus Christi 298, early 16, ff. 1–56v. Laurence Wade, "The lyff of Seynt Thomas off Canterbury," tr. "owt off Herbert Bosham [comp. 1184–86]...and John [Grandison] Bysshopp of Exceter [d.1369]." 2,303: 329 x 7 RR4*. BR 2601, comp. 1497. Rel., nar.

Othes my childe loke thou none swere. Vv. 53–56 of TM 219

Of a Cronyque in dayes gon. See TM 1279.

Off all chaunces six ys moste at the dyce. Variant of TM 387.

TM 1259 Of all good thinges the world brought forth | A faithefull frende ys thinge moste worthe.
DUR5: Cosin V.iii.9, c 1555, f. 47. 2: aa8. BR (2607.5). Moral, friendship.

TM 1260 Of all the mervels of Merlion howe he makes his men.
O: Rawl. C.813, c 1535, ff. 88v–9v. "Prophecia Johannis Merlyon," followed by four-line version on f. 89v. 52: 13 x 4 abab5*. L11: PRO SP 1/232, 1520, f. 219. Extract, vv. 25–36, 41–52; begins "Flaunders and England..." 24 lines. BR 2613.5, comp. a 1500? Prophecy.

TM 1261 Of bewty yet she passith all.
L: Add. 18752, 1530's, f. 33r–v. 32: 8 x 4 aaaR4* (ref. What wold she more what wold she more). BR (2619.5). Love.

TM 1262 Off cartage he that worthie warier.
L: Egerton 2711, bef. 1542, f. 54v. "Tho[mas Wyatt]," composed 1537, based on Petrarch, *Rime* 103. 8: abababcc10. TP 1403. Moral.

TM 1263 Off diepe secretes yet david here did sing.
L: Egerton 2711, bef. 1542, ff. 94v, 188. Wyatt, Penitential Psalms, prologue to Ps. 102, tr. Aretino. 32: 4 x 8 abababcc10. TP 1405. Rel.

TM 1264 Of Inglysh kynges, here lyeth the bewtevous floure.
L: Cott. Nero C.11, 1506+, f. 255v. Robert Fabyan, tr. "hic decus anglorum...," epitaph on the tomb of Edward III (d. 1377) at Westminster. 7: RR4*. HD: Eng 766F, bef. 1516, f. 226v. TP 1406. Epitaph, hist.

TM 1265 Of Inglish men the scourge of walsh the protector.
L: Cott. Nero C.11, 1506+, f. 140. Robert Fabyan, tr. "Hic iacet Anglorum tortor," epitaph of Lewellyn of Wales, d. 3 Dec. 1273; answered by TM 583. 7: RR4*. HD: Eng 766F, bef. 1516, f. 111v. TP 1407. Epitaph, hist., Wales.

TM 1266 Of ever or never folke ever conjecter.
L: Add. 15233, 1554–58, f. 29v. 24: 6 x 4 aaaa4*. Moral.

TM 1267 Of fastynge fyrste lett us knowe thys that we faste from all yll.
L: Add. 33974, c 1550, f. 62. (Francis Stacy), "Of fastynge." 20: aa7*. Rel. instruction.

TM 1268 Of ffewe wordes sir ye syme to be.
D: TCD 160, 1535–48, f. 128. Answer to TM 969. 12: 3 x 4 abab8. Love.

TM 1269 Of gretter cause may no wight him compleyne.
L: Harley 7578, early 16, ff. 15v–16. "complaint to my lodesterre" [sometimes attributed to Chaucer]. 49: 7 x 7 RR10. BR 2626, comp. a 1500? Love.

TM 1270 Of late as I layd me.
O: Ashmole 48, bef. 1558, ff.49v–51v. Subscribed "h. s." [Henry Spooner]. 120: 15 x 8 MT5* (ref. They may seke longe ynoughe that lystithe not to fynde). Rel., vision, moral instruction.

TM 1271 Of life and deth nowe chuse the.
L: Lansd. 762, 1524–29, f. 91v. 4: abab4*. BR (2633). Moral, women.

TM 1272 Of lyghtnes moste unsade, whiche many women shewe.
O: Ashmole 48, bef. 1558, ff. 50v–1v. "qothe henry sponare." 124: 31 x 4 abab12. Virtues of women.

TM 1273 Of mantua am I beget and boir.
E2: Dc.1.43, 1515–20, f. 300v. Gavin Douglas, tr. "Mantua me," epitaph on Virgil's tomb, preserved in Suetonius. 6: aa5*. C2: TCC O.3.12 (1184), 1513, f. 330. Scots.

TM 1274 Of mary criste was bore.
L: Add. 5665, bef. 1511, ff. 17–18. "In die nativitatis," with music. 14: 2 burd

aa + 3 x 4 aaa4R2* (burd. Have mercy of me kyng of blisse; ref. Of kyng of all kynges). BR (2636). Rel., carol, nativity.

TM 1275 Of purpos love chase first for to be blynd.
L: Egerton 2711, bef. 1542, f. 69. [Wyatt, autograph]. 8: abababcc10. TP 1417. Love.

Off quarell piking I the Forbede. Vv. 61–64 of TM 219.

TM 1276 Of Sacrilege I have to you symplie rehersed.
L: Add. 57335, early 16, ff.73v–83v. "Incipient septem sacramentes"; one of three additions to Peter Idley's *Instructions to his Son*, TM 789. 693: 99 x 7 RR5*. BR 2649.5+, comp. c 1450. Rel. instruction.

TM 1277 Off servyng men I will begyne.
L: Sloane 1584, c 1550, f. 45v. With music. 36: 4 burd abab + 8 x 4 a3B2a3B2* (burd. So well ys me be gone; ref. Troly loly). BR 2654, comp. a 1500. Carol, love.

TM 1278 Of spayne take the clere light.
O: Ashmole 1416, early 16, f.148v–50v. On preparing the Philosopher's stone [attributed to Richard Carpenter]. 96: aa4*. O: Bodley Rolls 1, early 16. Extract in an alchemical scroll, by an illustrator who did not know English; recopied in right margin in the late 16th century; begins "I shall you tell without leyssinge." 138: abab4*, aa4*. O: Ashmole 1486, early 16, f. 18v. 8: aa4*. O: Ashmole 759, early 16, ff. 125–6v. Last 12 vv. added in another hand. 108: aa4*. O: e Musaeo 63, 1550's, ff. 67–9v. 253: aa4*. BR 2656, comp. a 1500. Alchemy.

Off the mervellis off merlion howe he makis his mone. Four-line text of TM 1260.

TM 1279 [Of hem that writen us tofore].
O17: Balliol 354, 1503–04, ff. 55–96, 171v–5. John Gower, *Confessio Amantis*, 12 stories, beginning "Of a cronyqye in dayes gon." 4,850: aa4*. M2: Chetham 6696, c 1540, ff. 1–126v. Acephalous, begins at v. 193, "To thinke Apon the daies olde." 33,724 lines. BR 2662, comp. 1393; TP 1421.5. Nar., moral, love.

TM 1280 Off thy counssell yff thou have doute.
L: Sloane 1207, mid 16, f. 12v. 4: abab4*. Moral advice.

TM 1281 Of thie lyff Thomas this compas well marke.
L: Harley 78, mid 16, f. 29. Subscribed "H. B." [Surrey, tr. of Horace, Carmina 2.10 "Rectius vives"]. 20: 5 x 4 abab5*. TP 1422. Moral.

TM 1282 Of titan magnasia take the clere lyght.
L: Harley 2407, early 16, ff. 91–3. 98: aa4*. Alchemy.

TM 1283 Of wyne awey the molis maye ye wasshe.
L: Lansd. 762, 1524–29, f. 24. 7: RR5*. BR 2668, comp. a 1500. Practical.

TM 1284 Of wise heades.
L: Add. 30513, c 1550, f. 76v. Incipit only, with music. Song.

TM 1285 Oft hathe this songe bene put in ure.
L: Add. 15233, 1554–58, ff. 49v–52. "Jhon Redford." 141: 9 burd (aaaaaaabb) + 22 x 6 aaaabB8 (burd. Now will you be merrye; ref. ...merye than). BR (2668.8). Rel. instruction.

TM 1286 Oftymes the wrappinge, and unfoldinge to vue.
L: Royal 17.A.21, 1551, ff. 1–3. William Forreste, "To...Edwarde Duke of Somerset," dedication of his translations of the Psalms. 84: 12 x 7 RR4*. Rel., dedication.

Oh (exclamation). Alphabetized as O.

TM 1287 Old men sayen in wordis few.
L: Sloane 1825, early 16, f. 1v. 6: aa3*. BR (2674). Proverb, love.

TM 1288 [O]mnipotentem semper adorant.
L: Add. 60577, 1549–58, ff. 63–4. Aureate song in praise of the Lord. 72: 9 x 8 MT4* (ref. Et benedicunt omne per euum). BR 2676, comp. a 1500. Rel., praise, macaronic.

TM 1289 On a dere day by a dale so depe.
O17: Balliol 354, 1503–04, ff.170v–1v. [Cf. BR 1453.] 120: 10 x 12 ababababbcbC4* (ref. Fortis ut mors dileccio). BR (2678). Rel. instruction, moral, allegory of birds.

TM 1290 On Cristis day, I understond.
O17: Balliol 354, 1505–36, f. 228v. 22: 2 burd. (aa) + 5 x 4 aaab4* (burd. A blessid byrd as I you say). BR (2681). Rel., carol, mass.

TM 1291 On clife that castell so knetered.
O: Lat. misc. c.66, c 1500, ff. 106v–7. 53: abab3*, alliterative. BR (2682). Calendar, seasons.

TM 1292 On days when I am callit to the schole.
L: Add. 14997, early 16, f. 44v. 22: 2 burd aa + 5 x 4 abab4* (burd. Fulgens

scola disc[ipu]lus est mercator pessimus). L: Add. 60577, 1549–58, f. 93. Variant beginning "A mornynges when I am callide to scole." 22 lines (burd. Frangens scola disc[ip]ulus...). BR (2683). Carol, schoolboy's complaint, humorous, macaronic.

TM 1293 One fuyt suld be all scottis weir.
E COL: Columba House, bef. 1509, f. 157. Scots rendering of Latin verses "Scotia fit guerra peditis" in Fordun, *Scotichronicon*, marked "Testamentum Regis R. Brois." 14: aa4*. BR 2685.8, comp. a 1500. War, Scots.

TM 1294 On holly hylles whyche beeth of gret renoun.
L: Add. 29729, 1558, ff.146v–9v. "...translacyoun out of the latine...of gloriosa dicta [Ps. 87] &c...by lidgate...at thynstaunce of the bushepe of excestre..." 232: 29 x 8 MT5* (ref. gloryous thynges bene sayde and songe of the). BR 2688, comp. a 1449. Rel., Virgin Mary, praise.

TM 1295 On the rode I was put for the.
C10: Magdalene F.4.13, 1528, f. 2. Paraphrase of "In cruce sum pro te," subscribed "J ffyllol." 4: mono4*. BR (2689). Rel., monologue of Christ.

TM 1296 Ons as me thought fortune me kyst.
L: Egerton 2711, bef. 1542, f. 42v. "Tho[mas Wyatt]." 28: 7 x 4 abab8. L: Add. 17492, 1532–39, ff. 71, 73v–4. Begins "Ons me thought..."; eight-line version copied on f. 71v. TP 1429. Love.

TM 1297 Ons in your grace I knowe I was.
D: TCD 160, 1535–48, f. 138. 35: 7 x 5 abab4A2* (ref. Yet ons I was). Love.

Ons me thought ffortune me kyst. See TM 1296.

TM 1298 One god only thow shalt love and worshop perfytelie.
PML: Ptd. book 698, early 16, sig. b2v. "The ten commandementes" [by Robert Copland, tr. from French "Ung seul dieu"], added by Thomas Archer, parson of Houghton Conquest in Bedf[ord]shire. 10: mono5*. BR (2695.5); TP 1433. Rel.

Only the elect on the Sabathe doth praye. See TM 380

Or... See Ere

TM 1299 Orpheus with thy muskye and all thy pryde.
L: Royal 18.A.15, bef. 1547, f. 9v. Henry Parcare [Parker] knight Lorde Morley, tr. "Carmina Maphei Vegetij Laudensis de utilitate psalmorum...In an Italian Ryme called Soneto." 15: abbaabbacddc5c3ee5*. Rel.

TM 1300 Oure god is our refuge, and steye.
L: Royal 17.A.21, 1551, ff. 43v–4v. William Forreste tr. Ps 45 Deus no[ste]r refugium. 48: 12 x 4 a8b6a8b6. Rel.

TM 1301 Oure [heaven] thys figure callid ys.
C: Ff.2.23, 1545, f. 32. Georgius Ripla [Ripley]. Verses attached to a diagram in *The Compend of Alchemy*, transcribed by Thomas Knyvet. 7: RR4*. Alchemy.

TM 1302 Oute of the chaffe was pured this corne.
L: Add. 5665, bef. 1511, ff. 41v–2. "Sancto Thome," with music. 16: 4 burd abab + 2 x 6 aaa8BBB5 (burd. Clangat tuba martir thoma; ref. O martir thoma). BR (2731). Rel., St. Thomas a Becket, carol, macaronic.

TM 1303 Owte of the deepe, O lorde, have I.
L: Royal 17.A.21, 1551, ff. 73v–4v. William Forreste, tr. Ps 129 De Profundis. 36: 9 x 4 a8b6a8b6. Rel.

TM 1304 Owt of the est a starre shon bright.
O17: Balliol 354, 1503–04, f. 165v. 34: 2 burd. (aa) + 8 x 4 aaab4* (burd. Be mery all that be present). BR (2732). Rel., carol, epiphany.

TM 1305 Out of thre mares and eke a well.
L: Lansd. 762, 1524–29, f. 88. 4: aabb4*. Prophecy.

TM 1306 Out of your sleep arise & wake.
C: Ll.1.11, early 16, ff. 32, 33v. 13: burd 1 + 3 x 4 aaab4* (burd. Nowell). BR 2733, comp. c 1450. Rel., carol, Christmas.

Over thi hed loke thowe never hewe | povertie hathe but frendis fewe. Lines 21–22 of TM 221.

TM 1307 Parce mihi o lord moste excellent.
L: Add. 18752, 1530's, f. 77. 16: 2 x 8 MT4*. BR (2736.6). Rel., macaronic, prayer.

TM 1308 Pardon alas why saye I so.
L: Add. 18752, 1530's, f. 149. 16: 4 x 4 aba4C3* (ref. ffarewell my love and my dere). BR (2736.8). Death, love, farewell.

TM 1309 Parting parting | I may well synge | hath caused all my payne.
O: Ashmole 176, pt. 3, 2/4 16, f. 100. 24: 4 x 6 aa4b6cc4b6. BR (13.3). Love.

TM 1310 Pas fourthe my wountyd cries.
D: TCD 160, 1535–48, f. 148. [Wyatt.] 32: 4 x 8 ababcdcd6. TP 1459. Love.

TM 1311 Passe forthe pilgryme and bridle well thy beaste.
L: Add. 29729, 1558, ff. 6v–7. "Reason [or "Lesson"?] to kepe well the tongue out of Mr hanlays boke...Explicit to kepe the tonge well per magistrum benedictus burgh" [but ascribed to Gower in O: Ashmole 59]. 35: 5 x 7 RR5*. BR 2737, comp. a 1456. Moral.

TM 1312 Passe tyme with good cumpanye.
L: Add. 5665, bef. 1511, ff. 136v–7, 141v–2. "The Kynges [Henry VIII] Balade," with music. 30: 3 x 10 aaaa4bbcddc2*. L: Add. 31922, 1513+, ff. 14v–15. "The Kynge H.viij," with music. L: Royal App. 58, 1547+, f. 56. Incipit only, with lute tablature. BR (2737.5). Song, conviviality.

TM 1313 Patiens for I have wrong.
L: Add. 17492, 1532–39, f. 82v. 6: ababcc6. Love.

TM 1314 Paciens for my devise.
L: Egerton 2711, bef. 1542, f. 28v. Wyatt, answer to TM 1316. 24: 4 x 6 ababcc6. L: Add. 17492, 1532–39, f. 71. D: TCD 160, 1535–48, f. 147. Love, answer.

Patiens off all my blame. See TM 1316.

TM 1315 Pacyence of all my smart.
L: Add. 17492, 1532–39, f. 21. 48:8 x 6 ababcc6. Love

TM 1316 Patience thought I have not.
L: Egerton 2711, bef. 1542, f. 28. "Tho[mas Wyatt]," answered by TM 1314. 24: 4 x 6 ababcc6. L: Add. 17492, 1532–39, f. 13v. D: TCD 160, 1535–48, f. 146. Variant, begins at stanza 3, "Patience of all my blame." 12: 2 x 6 ababcc3*. Love.

TM 1317 Pease shall passe & warre begyn.
L: Harley 559, 1554, ff. 33v–4. 40: 10 x 4 abab4*. Prophecy.

TM 1318 Pepe I see ye | I am glad I have spyd ye.
HN: HM 3, 1546–58, f. 32. John Bale, song by Sedicyon in *King John*. 2: aa3*. Song, political.

TM 1319 Per me Johannem bracke bere it well in minde.
O: Lyell 16, mid 16, f. i. Ownership rhyme of John Bracke. 4: aabb5*.

TM 1320 Paraventure hit may hapen.
L: Add. 18752, 1530's, f. 92r–v. (Each line begins "Paraventure...") 42: 6 x 7 RR4*. Moral, love.

TM 1321 Percye and Browne, the malot and Bewchampe.
L: Harley 293, mid 16, f. 31r–v. "The names of normanns and frenche, that ca<me> in withe Kinge William the Conqueror." 49: 7 x 7 RR4*. Hist., England.

TM 1322 Perdye I saide yt not.
L: Add. 17492, 1532–39, ff. 70v–71. [Wyatt, tr. Petrarch, *Rime* 206.] 48: 6 x 8 ababacac6. D: TCD 160, 1535–48, f. 145r–v. Y: Osborn music 13, 1553+, f. 31v. Incipit only, "Perdy I said not so," with lute tablature. TP 1462. Love.

TM 1323 Parfyght and prudent Rycharde by ryght the seconde.
HD: Eng 766F, bef. 1516, f. 321v. Robert Fabyan, tr. "Prudens et mundus Richardus," epitaph on the tomb of Richard II (d.1400) in Westminster. 14: 2 x 7 RR5*. L: Cott. Nero C.11, 1506+, f. 350v. TP 1463. Hist., epitaph.

Peter apostle & doctor poule I pray. Portion of TM 467.

TM 1324 Persyd wyth payne wounded full nygh the hart.
L: Add. 18752, 1530's, f. 90v. 7: RR5*. BR (2753.5). Complaint, fortune.

TM 1325 Petyously | constraynyd am I.
L: Royal App. 58, 1507+, ff. 19v–21. With music by Cooper. 40: 5 x 8 aaabaaab4. PN: Ptd. book Taylor Coll. Inc. B.71, 2/4 16, MS leaves bound in. Variant first line reads "Petevelly constranyd am i." 24 lines. BR 2755.5, comp. a 1500? Song, love.

Petevelly constranyd am i. See TM 1325.

TM 1326 Pitee that I have sought so yoore [ago].
L: Harley 7578, early 16, ff. 13v–4v. [Chaucer, "Complaint unto Pitee".] 119: 17 x 7 RR5*. LONG: Longleat 258, 1500+, ff. 55–7v. "the exclamacion of the dethe of pite." BR 2756, comp. a 1400; TP 1467.7. Love, complaint.

TM 1327 Please ytt your grace dere harte to gyffe audyence.
O: Rawl. C.813, 1520–35, f. 1. Lines 1–7 are vv. 2052–8 from Hawes, *The Pastime of Pleasure*, TM 1368. 28: 4 x 7 RR5*. BR (2757.3). Love, complaint.

TM 1328 Plenty maketh pryde. pryde maketh playe.
O: Ptd. book 8° C 70 Th. Seld., 1540+, sig. 2L8v. 4: aabb4*. Moral.

TM 1329 Plonged yn thoughts with sighes depe.
L: Add. 30981, 1522–29, ff. 20–1. John Croke, tr. De Profundis [Ps 130]. 32: 8 x 4 abab4*. Rel.

TM 1330 Poites writen by derke parables.
O: Lat. misc. c.66, c 1500, f. 93v. (Humfrey Newton.) 21: 3 x 7 RR4*. BR (2760). Calendar, zodiac.

Praise him for counceill that is droncke of ale. Aceph. text of TM 1005.

Preyse nott thy Selffe nor be nott proude. Vv. 57–60 of TM 219.

TM 1331 Praise the Lord oh my soule and sprite.
L: Royal 17.A.17, 1551+, ff. 17v–18v. Sir Thomas Smith, tr. "Psalme 145" [146]. 36: 9 x 4 a4b3a4b3*. Rel.

TM 1332 Praise ye the lorde his woorkes all.
L: Royal App. 74–76, c 1548; 74–75, f.7v–9; 76, ff. 16v–18. With music. 36: 6 x 6 ababcc4*. Rel., hymn, Benedicite.

TM 1333 Praisid be thalmightie lorde the god of Israel.
L: Royal App. 74–76, c 1548, ff. 14–15, 9v–11, 18v–20. With music. 60: 10 x 6 ababcc4*. Rel., hymn, Benedicite.

TM 1334 Pray for bowlay that owghe this booke.
C2: TCC R.14.41 (913), early 16, f. 110v. 6: aa3*. BR (2766.2). Ownership rhyme.

TM 1335 Pray we to god that all may gyde.
L: Add. 31922, 1511–13, f. 103–6. With music by "the Kynge H.VIII." 6: aabbcc4*. BR (2766.8). Rel., song, prayer, hist.

TM 1336 Preserve me (Lorde) in thee truste I.
L: Royal 17.A.21, 1551, ff. 20–1. William Forreste, tr. Ps 1 Conserva me. 48: 12 x 4 a8b6a8b6. Rel.

TM 1337 Pryde is owt, & pride ys yn.
O17: Balliol 354, 1505–36, f. 249v. 14: 2 burd. (aa) + 3 x 4 aaab4* (burd. Man be ware or thou be wo). BR 2771, comp. c 1450. Rel., carol, moral.

TM 1338 Problemes of olde lyknes and fygures.
O17: Balliol 354, 1503–04, ff.166–69v. [Lydgate, *The chorle and the byrde* (lacks stanzas 49–50); probably copied from STC 17008 (1477?)] 372: 52 x 7 RR5* + 1 x 8 MT4*. LONG: Longleat 258, 1500+, ff. 137–47. "the Chorle and the bridde" (stanzas 49–50 wanting, stanzas 46–48 in a later hand). 364 lines. BR 2784, comp. a 1410?; TP 1491.5. Nar.

TM 1339 Processe of tyme worketh such wounder.
L: Egerton 2711, bef. 1542, f. 55. "Tho[mas Wyatt.]" 24: 6 x 4 abab4*. Love.

TM 1340 Prove wythr I do chainge my dere.
L: Egerton 2711, bef. 1542, f. 66. A fragment, erased and written over. 4: aba?. Love.

TM 1341 Punyshe moderatly and dyscretly correcte.
L: Royal 18.D.2, c 1520, f. 209. "The counsell of Aristotill whiche he gayfe to Alexandre kynge of Massydony whiche ar writyn in the syde of the utter chamber above of the house in the gardynge at Wresyll [Wressel, Yorks.]" 38: aa4*. BR (2785). Moral, proverbs.

TM 1342 Put not in this world to much trust | The riches whereof wil turne to dust.
L: Harley 2321, early 16, f. 149. 2: aa4*. BR (2785.5). Moral, proverb.

TM 1343 Putrefacion most destroy & deface.
E2: Laing III.164, early 16, p. 229. 10: aa4*. Alchemy.

TM 1344 Quene of hevyn, blessyd mot thou be.
O17: Balliol 354, 1505–36, f. 249v. 14: 2 burd. (aa) + 3 x 4 aaaB3* (burd. Virgo rosa virginum; ref. Gloria tibi domine). BR 236, comp. c 1450. Rel., carol, Virgin Mary.

TM 1345 Qwene of hevene of helle eeke Empresse.
O: Tanner 110, early 16, f. 241r–v. [Lydgate, Prayer to the Virgin, vv. 1–54 only; also ff. 244r–v, 1–84 only.] 84: MT5*, RR5* (ref. To thy v Joyes that have Devocion). BR 2791, comp. a 1449. Rel., Virgin Mary, prayer.

TM 1346 Quondam was I in my ladys grace.
D: TCD 160, 1535–48, f. 150. 20: 4 x 5 abab4R2* (ref. ...that quondam was I). Love.

TM 1347 Rasyd is my mynde.
L: Royal App. 58, 1507+, f. 17. With music. 5: ababa2*. BR (2794.4). Song.

TM 1348 Rather then gould | will I unfould.
Y: Osborn music 13, 1553+, f. 321v. Fragment, with music. 7: aa4b6ccdd4. Love, song.

TM 1349 Ravyshed was I that well was me.
O: Ashmole 176, pt. 3, 2/4 16, f. 100v. (Song on Henry VIII dancing with his daughter Mary, composed between 1516 and 1527.) 24: 6 x 4 a4b3a4b3*. L: Cott. Titus D.11, early 16, f. 56v. Incipit only, with music. BR (2794.2). Song, hist.

TM 1350 Rede dystynctlye | pray devoutelye.
L: Harley 2252, 1525, f. 166. "A specyall glase to loke in daylye." 27: mono2*. L30: Univ. of London MS 278, 1516, flyleaf. "A spesiall glasse," added 14 Sept 1516 on verso of 2nd flyleaf. 34 lines (4 unrhymed). F: X.d.532, 1534+, [unfol.]. Lines 108–16 of a vellum strip; "A spirituall glasse dayly to loke on (at the end of a prose prayer, or four prayers, attributed to Thomas More [verses were copied from a 1531? or later edition of STC 23961, where they are anonymous or edited by Richard Whitford]). 21 lines. BR (2794.8); TP 1500. Rel. instruction.

TM 1351 Recomptinge the brute of your worthy fame.
L: Add. 34791, 1543–47, ff. 1–116v. William Forrest, "Josephe the chaiste," dedicated to William [Parr] Earle of Eastsex," comp. 1543–47. Argument, Invocation, Chapters 1–23, Excusation. 6,694: 18 x 7 RR4*, 22 aa4*, 932 x 7 RR4*. Rel., nar.

TM 1352 <...> red rosse fayre and sote off sent trew off < > good lord graunt both of that dysposiccion.
NY: Drexel 4180, 2/4 16, f. 1v. Fragment of a song celebrating alliance of England and Scotland, perhaps on the occasion of the marriage of Princess Margaret to James IV in 1503. 10: ?. BR (2797.5). Song, hist.

TM 1353 Remember good Chrystyanes all.
L: Add. 33974, c 1550, ff. 26–7v. (Francis Stacy), "A fearfull remembraunce of godes Just Judggemente." 146: aa4*. Rel. instruction.

TM 1354 Remember man the paines and smarte.
LINC: Lincoln 129, early 16, f. 87v. 8: 2 x 4 abab4*. BR (2806). Rel., passion.

TM 1355 Remember man the payne and smart.
L: Harley 4826, early 16, f. 146v. 20: 2 x 10 ababcc4d2ee4D2* (ref. Come to me frinde). BR (2806.5). Rel., monologue of Christ.

TM 1356 Remember man thy frayle estate: Repent thy folles past.
O; Ashmole 48, bef. 1558, ff. 35v–7. "quothe Rychard Sheale." 94: aa14. Moral.

TM 1357 Remember that there be in hell.
L: Add. 60577, 1549–58, f. 51v. Subscribed "W. W" [William Way, an owner of the MS]. 4: aabb8. Rel. instruction.

TM 1358 Remembrance.
L: Add. 15233, 1554–58, f. 27v. "Jhon Redford," incipit of last song in *Wit and Science*.

TM 1359 Remons[tranc]es nowe be fell I live.
L: Sloane 2578, c 1557, f. 89v. 16: 4 x 4 abab4*. Prophecy.

TM 1360 Remorde thyne ey inwordly.
L: Royal 18.D.2, c 1520, ff. 210–11v. "The proverbis in the syde of thutter chamber above the hous in the gardyng at Wresyll [Wressel, Yorks.]" 135: aa4*. BR (2811). Moral, proverbs.

TM 1361 Repentance ransom of each offence.
D: TCD 160, 1535–48, f. 174. [Rough draft heavily revised, uncertain rhyme scheme.] 14: 4 x 4 abab4* + irreg. Moral.

TM 1362 Resound my voyse ye woodes that here me plain.
L: Egerton 2711, bef. 1542, f. 17v. Wyatt, tr. Serafino "Laer che sente el mesto e gran clamore." 21: 3 x 7 RR10. L: Add. 17492, 1532–39, f. 72. TP 1520. Love, complaint.

TM 1363 Returne my hart homewart agayne.
Y: Osborn music 13, 1553+, ff. 45v–6. With music. 48: 12 x 4 abab8. Song, love, lament.

TM 1364 Rex glorie kyng omnipotent.
O: Digby 133, c 1515–25, ff. 37–50v. "Finis convercionis sancti pauli." 662: 95 x 7 RR4*. BR 2814, comp. a 1500? Rel. drama.

TM 1365 Riches are gotten with labor holden with feare | And lost with greyfe and excessive care.
L: Harley 2321, early 16, f. 148. 2: aa4*. BR (2818.3). Moral, proverb.

TM 1366 Ryd of bondage free from kaer seven yeiers space and more.
D: TCD 160, 1535–48, f. 152r–v. "G[eorge]. B[lage]." 40: aa7*. Love.

TM 1367 Right best beloved & most in assurance.
O: Rawl. C.813, 1520–35, ff. 71–2v. 63: 9 x 7 RR5*. BR (2821). Love, epistle.

Ryght gentyll harte of greane flouryng age. Extract from TM 1368.

TM 1368 [Ryght myghty prynce and redoubted soverayne].
[Stephen Hawes, *The Pastime of Pleasure*, comp. 1505–06.] O: Rawl. C.813, 1520–35, ff. 21v–24. Extract, vv. 3951–4076, including (vv. 50–56) one other stanza; begins "Ryght gentyll harte of greane flouryng age." Listed separately as BR 2822. Shares verses with TM 1838. 133: 19 x 7 RR5*. G: Hunt. 230, early 16, f. 246v. Extract, vv. 2542–8, begins "Now good swet harte and my none god" (preceded by TM 1223). Listed separately as BR 2318. 7 lines. BR (4004); TP 1531. Love, epistle.

TM 1369 [R]yghte noble and blessede fader, to whom of excellence.
L: Add. 60577, 1549–58, ff. 22v–4. (Autobiographical poem addressed to William Waynflete, Bishop of Winchester, comp. c 1451.) 128: 16 x 8 MT5*. BR 2825.5+, comp. c 1451. Nar, allegory, hist.

TM 1370 Right true it is and said full yore agoo.
L: Egerton 2711, bef. 1542, f. 33. "Tho[mas Wyatt]." 7: ababbbb10. TP 1534. Moral, friendship.

TM 1371 Right welbeloved prentise.
O: Rawl. C.813, 1520–35, f. 8r–v. "A letter send by R. W. to A. C[hatwyn]." 54: aa4*. BR (2827.5). Epistle, humorous.

TM 1372 Ryght worshupfulle Mustres I pray.
O: Ptd. book Gough Miss. 145, 1520+, sig. C8. Love note by "franc louuyll," answered by TM 1474. 4: aa6*, fragmentary. Love, question.

TM 1373 Robbers me beyte and made me bonde.
L: Add. 60577, 1549–58, ff. 76v–7. Tr. "Ex vespilionibus". 4: aabb4*. Mnenomic.

Robert Welburne This boke. Variant of TM 552.

TM 1374 Royss mary most of Vertu Virginall.
E2: Laing 149, 1/4 16, f. 183v. [Ane Ballat of Our Lady]. 40: 5 x 8 MT5* (ref. O mater Jesu salve maria). E: Asloan, 1513–42, f. 301r–v. "Heir followis diverss ballatis of our ladye." 48: 6 x 8 MT5* (ref. O mater Jhesu salve maria). BR (2381.8). Rel., Virgin Mary, Scots.

TM 1375 Rowe the bote Norman | Rowe to thy lemman.
HD: Eng 766F, bef 1516, f.?. Song by the Thames waterman at the installation of John Norman as Lord Mayor of London in 1454, quoted by Robert Fabyan. 2: aa2*. BR 2832.5, comp. 1454; TP 1537.5. Hist., song, humorous.

TM 1376 Rew on me lord for thy goodnes and grace.
L: Egerton 2711, bef. 1542, ff. 93–4. Wyatt, Penitential Psalms, tr. Ps 51, autograph. 82: terza rima10. TP 1540. Rel.

TM 1377 Rule they tong in every place.
L: Sloane 1207, mid 16, f. 13. Incomplete. 3: abb? Moral, proverb.

Rule thy tonge by good reason. Vv. 65–68 of TM 219.

TM 1378 Rutterkyn is com unto oure towne.
L: Add. 5465, 1501–04, ff. 101v–4. With music by William Cornyssh the Younger. 18: 2 burd ab + 4 x 4 aaa4B2* (burd. Hoyda hoyda Joly rutterkyn; ref. Like a rutter). BR (2832.2). Carol, humor, Dutchmen.

TM 1379 Seint Patrik thorow god all myght.
L: Harley 4012, c 1505, ff. 40–51v. "The lif of Sent Patrick et extractum suum purgatorij" [based directly on the South English Legendary, c 1300]; incomplete. 570: abab4*. BR (3038). Rel., nar., saint's life.

TM 1380 Saynt valentyne of custome yeare by yeare.
L: Add. 29729, 1558, ff. 155–7. "...balade made of the reverence of our lady by lidgate in wyse of chousinge loves at sainte valentynes daye." 140: 20 x 7 RR5*. BR 3065, comp. c 1425. Rel., Virgin Mary.

TM 1381 Salvator mundi domine.
O: Tanner 110, early 16, ff. 238–40. 112: 14 x 8 ababcdcD4* (ref. I lefte my myght and toke Mercy). BR 3071, comp. a 1500. Rel., dialogue, Homo et Deus.

TM 1382 Salue with obeysance to god in humblesse.
O17: Balliol 354, 1503–04, f. 159v. 40: 5 x 8 MT5*. BR 3074. comp. 1477; TP 1542. Rel., hymn, macaronic.

TM 1383 Sauns remedye | endure must I.
O: Ashmole 176, pt. 3, 2/4 16, f. 99v. 48: 6 x 8 aaabcccb2*. BR (3074.6). Love, lament.

TM 1384 Save me (O lorde) & mend this wronge.
L: Royal 17.A.21, 1551, ff. 16–17. William Forreste, tr. Ps 11, Saluum me. 40: 10 x 4 a8b6a8b6. Rel.

TM 1385 Say well ys a worthy thyng.
L6: Dyce 45, 2/4 16, ff. 42v–4. 38: 2 burd aa + 4 x 9 aabb4* (burd. Sayewell & do well they are thynge twain). BR (3079.7). Carol, moral.

TM 1386 Sayk[?] had at all tymes to god mayk the redy | for trust assurd[l]y that d[e]athe wyll not tary.
L: Royal 7.C.9, 2/4 16, f. 192. 2: aa4*. Rel., death.

Sed libera nos a malo amen. Last line of acephalous TM 781.

TM 1387 See myche say lyttell & lerne to soffar in tyme.
L: Add. 29729, 1558, f. 130r–v. Subscribed "Explicit lidgat," but ascribed

elsewhere to R. Stokys. 35: 5 x 7 RR5*. BR 3083, comp. a 1500. Moral, proverbs.

TM 1388 Seynge owr lyfe uncertayne ys.
L: Add. 33974, c 1550, ff. 55v–6. (Francis Stacy), "What < > uncerteynte of Deathe." 48: 12 x 4 abab4*. Rel., death.

TM 1389 [Seeing the manifolde inconvenience].
[*The Remedy of Love*, printed as Chaucer's in STC 5068 (1532).] L: Add. 17492, 1532–39, f. 90. Extract, vv. 239–45, begins "Yff all the earthe were parchment scrybable." 7: RR5*. BR (3084); TP 1549. Love, praise of women.

TM 1390 Selde dyeth the oxe | that wepeth for the cok.
O17: Balliol 354, 1505–36, f. 200v. Tr. of "Bos moritur rara..." 2: aa3*. Proverb.

TM 1391 Send forth thy ugly syghtes.
O: Ashmole 1479, c 1550, f. i. Fragmentary song, with music. 7: ? Love.

TM 1392 Serve God truly.
O17: Balliol 354, 1505–36, f. 213v. (Cf. TM 1393 and TM 739.) 8: aaabaaab3*. Rel. instruction.

Serve god well and have no drede. Vv. 64–5 of TM 221; 15–16 of TM 219.

TM 1393 Serve thi God trewly.
O: Tanner 407, 1/4 16, f. 17v. (Cf. TM 1392 and TM 739.) 8: mono3*. BR 3087, comp. c 1450. Rel. instruction.

TM 1394 Shall I dispaire thus sodeynly.
L11: PRO SP 1/246, mid 16, f. 20. With music. 7: aabbcbc4*. Song, love.

TM 1395 Shale I rejoyce or fayn gladnesse that swalowed am in sorow.
L2: Lambeth 159, 1556+, f. 276v. "Wordes that John Hartgyll [murdered in 1556] spoke before his death". 60: aa14. Hist.

TM 1396 Shall she never out of mynde.
L: Add. 18752, 1530's, f. 87v. Complaint of a silent lover. 20: 5 x 4 abab4*. TP 1558. Love, complaint.

TM 1397 ...Shall we three joyne in unitie.
L: Add. 15233, 1554–58, f. 38. Fragment of an interlude, probably by John Redford; speakers are Corage, Kyndnes, [Concupiscence], Clenness. Last

line: "Ther is concupiscence gone quighte." 8: abaccded8. Moral interlude, drama.

She beseithe her in every estate. Single line preceding acephalous TM 1398.

TM 1398 She is A covetyse excyssive.
L: Harley 7332, c 1500, f. 214r–v. Acephalous fragment; parts of ten RR stanzas, preceded by single line: "She besiethe her in every estate." 60: RR4*. Against women.

TM 1399 She parfytt of the more.
L: Royal App. 58, 1547+, f. 51. With music. 4: abab3*. Song, love.

TM 1400 She sat and sowde that hathe done me the wrong.
L: Egerton 2711, bef. 1542, f. 37. "Tho[mas Wyatt]." 8: abababcc10. L: Add. 17492, 1532–39, f. 73. TP 1565. Love.

TM 1401 She that hathe a wantan eye.
O: Rawl. C.813, 1520–35, f. 31v. (Cf. STC 6807 (1560?), *a dialogue betwene the comen secretary and Jalowsye.*) 64: 16 x 4 aabb4*. BR (3098.3). Against women.

TM 1402 Sche that shuld most percevyth lest.
D: TCD 160, 1535–48, f. 155. (Leaf damaged). 21: 3 x 7 RR4* (ref. ...I cam to late). Love.

TM 1403 Sickness [?] speches of many akyd thyng.
L: Harley 559, 1554, ff. 45–7v. "Prophetia Joannes Hermite" (transcription of first word uncertain; possibly "hekhnes"). 147: aa4*. Rel., prophecy.

TM 1404 Syghes ar my foode drynke are my teares.
L: Harley 78, mid 16, f. 27. "Th. W[yatt] to [Sir Francis] Bryan." 8: abababcc5*. TP 1569. Prisoner's complaint, hist.

Since. See also Sith.

TM 1405 Sence David the prophet and Kinge of Jury and Israell.
L: Royal 7.F.14, bef. 1547, ff. 53v–5. Edwarde Leibourne prest, "A declaracion of the xx [21st] psalme of David resembling our most gracious king Henry [VIII]." 147: 21 x 7 RR5*. Rel., hist.

TM 1406 Syns Love ys founde wythe parfytnes.
D: TCD 160, 1535–48, f. 162. Subscribed "A A." 28: 4 x 7 RR8 (ref. Mon cuer aves pense de moy). Love.

TM 1407 Syns love is suche that as ye wott.
L: Add. 17492, 1532–39, ff. 51v–2. 40: 5 x 8 ababbabab8. Love.

TM 1408 Since of a womans breastes I was fostered.
DUR5: Cosin V.iii.9, c 1555, f. 56. "quod [Thomas] carter." 4: abab4*. BR (3135.5). Love.

TM 1409 Syns so ye please to here me playn.
L: Add. 17492, 1532–39, f. 53. 12: 3 x 4 abab8. Love.

TM 1410 Sens that my Language without eloquence.
D: TCD 160, 1535–48, f. 87. 24: 3 x 8 MT4*. Love.

TM 1411 Syne the tyme I knew yow fryst.
L: Royal App. 58, 1507+, f. 6. With music. 15: 3 burd abb + 6 x 2 aa4* (burd. Why soo unkende Alas). BR (3144.5). Carol, love.

TM 1412 Synce thow arte false to me.
L: Add. 30513, c 1550, f. 106v. Incipit only, with music. Song.

TM 1413 Syns ye delite to knowe.
L: Egerton 2711, bef. 1542, f. 47r–v. "Tho[mas Wyatt]" (cf. TM 1414). 35: 5 x 7 aa6bb4aaB6 (ref. For to content your cruelnes). L: Add. 17492, 1532–39, f. 72v. Love.

TM 1414 Sens ye delight to knowe.
D: TCD 160, 1535–48, f. 156. (Cf. TM 1413.) 24: 4 x 6 aabaab6 (ref. For to content your cruelnes). Love.

TM 1415 Sins you will nedes that I shall sing.
L: Add. 17492, 1532–39, f. 73v. 30: 5 x 6 abacb8c4. Love.

TM 1416 Synge to the lorde, a newe set songe.
L: Royal 17.A.21, 1551, ff. 70v–2. William Forreste, tr. Ps 97 Cantate. 44: 11 x 4 a8b6a8b6. Rel.

TM 1417 Singular shepperde gardeyn of cristis folde.
O: Tanner 110, early 16, ff. 245r–v. [Lydgate,] Prayer to St. Thomas of Canterbury, stanzas 1–10 only; stanzas 4–10 also copied on f. 242. 80: 10 x 8 MT5*. BR 3115, comp. a 1449. Rel., prayer.

TM 1418 [Sir John Mandevelle and Sir Marc of Veneese].
O: e Musaeo 160, c 1520, ff. 109–13v, 15. "The commonyng of sir John Mandevell and the gret souden," extract from Mandeville's Travels,

beginning "Opon a time when Ser Iohn Mandevelle." 313: 39 x 8 MT5*. BR (3117.6). Nar., romance

TM 1419 Sir patrik barclay of tollere.
L: Royal 17.D.20, mid 16, f. 262v. Ownership note, preceded by TM 1648. 16: aa4*. Scots.

TM 1420 Serys a merakly or to I schal you tell.
O: Tanner 407, 1/4 16, ff. 29v–32. Two miracles of the Virgin. 134: aa5*. BR (3119). Rel., Virgin Mary, nar.

...Syster loke that ye be not forlorn. Part of TM 1802.

TM 1421 <...si>t amonges the knyghtes all.
L: Harley 4294, early 16, f. 81v. Text badly defaced at left margin. 26: 2 burd aa + 6 x 4 aaaR4* (burd. He hath myne hart every dele; ref. Whatsoever ye thynk avyse ye wele). BR (3119.5)*. Moral, carol.

Sith. See also Since.

TM 1422 Sythe I my selffe dysplease the.
D: TCD 160, 1535–48, f. 160r–v. 44: ababccdcd6, ababccdd6, ababccddd6. Love.

TM 1423 Sith it concludid was in the Trinitie.
L: Add. 5465, 1501–04, ff. 58v–63. With music. 32: 4 burd abab + 4 x 7 aaabbCC4* (burd. Affraid alas and whi so sadenly; ref. Now blessid lady wepe no more). BR (3131). Rel., carol, Virgin Mary.

TM 1424 Syethe yt ys so that I am thus refusyd.
D: TCD 160, 1535–48, f. 158. 24: 3 x 8 MT5* (ref. Yt wold not be but ffals nuffanglydnes). Love.

TM 1425 Sythe profounde sorow my harte ys sore grevyd.
L: Harley 2252, 1517–20, ff. 25–8. "here begynnyth the Sorowfull complaynte for the Ruyn of a Realme." 259: 37 x 7 RR5*. Rel., satire, hist., Henry VIII, complaint.

TM 1426 [Sitting on this se[g]e].
L: Lansd. 210, 1553–58, f. 70. [Lines 2–8, beginning "Justice loke th[o]u stedfast be," of John Trevisa, tr. "Sede sedens ista iudex...," as quoted by Ranulf Higden, *Polycronycon* 3.8.] 7: aa4*. BR 3156.5+, comp. 1387; TP 1596.5. Hist., Cambyses.

TM 1427 vi is com v is goon wyth thris ten be ware a men.
L11: PRO SP 1/121, 1537, f. 238. 6: aa5*. Prophecy.

Syse is evermore the best caste of the dyse. See TM 387.

TM 1428 Skelton, tis pitty that thy bookes should rust | <Whyle> they doe live, thoughe thow art turnd to dus<t>.
HN: Ptd. book 69485, mid 16, sig. D8v. George Stawrton, commendation of Skelton in his copy of *Why come ye not to court*. 2: aa5*.

Slain have I by unfaithfulnes. Last line of acephalous TM 292.

TM 1429 Smised [?] in the myddes in [sic] marked A. P.
L: Add. 24663, 1550's, ff. 14v–16. "Incipit alia prophecia." 88: allit. BR 2834.3, comp. a 1500. Prophecy.

TM 1430 So blessid a sight it was to see.
O17: Balliol 354, 1505–36, f. 226. 36: 2 burd. (aa) + 7 x 4 aaaB4* + 6 ababaa4* (burd. Lulley Jhesu lulley lulley; ref. My owne dere moder syng lulley). BR (3161). Rel., carol, Virgin Mary, lullaby.

TM 1431 So fer I trow from remedy.
L: Add. 5465, 1501–04, ff. 6v–7. Music by William Newark. 7: RR4*. BR (3162.5). Complaint.

TM 1432 So feble is the threde that doth the burden stay.
L: Egerton 2711, bef. 1542, ff. 67–8v. [Wyatt], "In Spayne," tr. Petrarch, *Rime* 37. 100: poulters. L: Add. 17492, 1532–39, ff. 49–50v. TP 1599. Love.

TM 1433 So hight my leman | rede her yf you can.
O17: Balliol 354, 1505–36, f. 219. Riddle [answer = "Lucy"; included in BR 597.5]. 2: aa2*.

TM 1434 So longe may a droppe fall.
L: Cott. Vespasian A.25, c 1555, f. 40v. 40: 10 x 4 abab3*. Rel., truth and God's mercy.

TM 1435 So noble medesyne ne so sovereyne.
L: Add. 29729, 1558, ff. 4v–5. "how the plage was sesyd in rome John lidgat"; subscribed "Explicit John lidgate" (each ascription in a different hand). 43: 1 x 8 MT4* + 5 x 7 RR4*. BR 3168, comp. a 1500. Rel., nar., miracle of St. Sebastian.

TM 1436 So propre cappes.
L: Sloane 747, bef. 1506, ff. 88v–9. 120:30 x 4 aaaB2* (ref. Saw I never). BR (3168.2). Satire.

TM 1437 So put yn fere I dare not speke.
L: Add. 5665, bef. 1511, ff.137v–40. With music. 21: 3 x 7 RR4*. BR (3168.4). Song, love.

TM 1438 So put in fere I dare not speke.
L: Add. 60577, 1549–58, f. 116v. With music. 5: abbcc4*. Song, love.

TM 1439 So unwarily was never no man cawght.
L: Add. 17492, 1532–39, f. 32. "W[yatt]." 24: 6 x 4 aba10b8. TP 2078. Love.

TM 1440 Sum be mery, & sum be sade.
O17: Balliol 354, 1505–36, f. 250. 44: 2 burd. (aa) + 6 x 7 aaa4BCCB3* (burd. Women women love of women; ref. ...and sum be shrewed | Go shrew wheresoever ye go). BR 3171, comp. a 1500. Carol, women.

TM 1441 Some desarve or they desyre.
DUR5: Cosin V.iii.9, c 1555, f. 55v. "quod [Thomas] carter." 4: aabb8. BR (3171.5). Moral

TM 1442 Som do entende.
L: Harley 2252, 1517–38, f. 84. 20: 5 x 4 aaab2*. BR (3172). Marriage, practical.

TM 1443 Sum festynnys fast for fifti yer that <l>ests noth for ten.
BO: f. Med. 94, mid 16, f. i. 6: aa7* Moral, Scots.

TM 1444 Som fowles ther be that have so parfaict sight.
L: Egerton 2711, bef. 1542, f. 19v. "Wyat[t]," tr. Petrarch, *Rime* 19. 14: abbaabbacddcee10. TP 1610. Love.

Som men thynke that ye. See TM 1813.

TM 1445 Some men wold thynke of Right to have.
D: TCD 160, 1535–48, f. 154. 28: 4 x 7 RR4*. TP 1615. Love.

TM 1446 Som say I love sum say I moke.
L: Add. 17492, 1532–39, f. 58v. 6: abab4cc5*. Love.

TM 1447 Some tyme I fled the fyre that me brent.
L: Egerton 2711, bef. 1542, f. 40. "Tho[mas Wyatt]." 8: abababcc10. L: Add. 17492, 1532–39, f. 38v. "Wiatt." L: Harley 78, mid 16, f. 27. "Tho. W[yatt]." TP 1621. Love.

TM 1448 Sum tyme I have you seyn.
L: Add. 18752, 1530's, f. 85v. 32: 8 x 4 abab4*. Moral.

TM 1449 Sum tyme I syghe sumtyme I syng.
L: Add. 17492, 1532–39, f. 20v. 20: 5 x 4 aaaa8. Love.

TM 1450 Some tyme I was a persone here.
WADDE: Waddesdon Church, Bucks. Verses on the tomb of Hugh Brystowe, 1548. 16: abab4*. Epitaph.

TM 1451 Somme tyme worlde was stedfast and stable.
L: Harley 7578, early 16, f. 17r–v. [Chaucer, "Lak of Steadfastnesse."] 28: 4 x 7 RR10 (same rhymes) (ref. That alle is loste for lake of steadfastnesse). BR 3190, comp. a 1400; TP 1623.5. Moral.

Sum wemen wepyn of peure feminite. See TM 429.

TM 1452 Sum what musyng | And more morenyng
L: Add. 5465, 1501–04, ff. 33v–5. With music by Robard ffayfax [poem attributed to Anthony Woodville, Lord Rivers, written before his execution, 1483]. 40: 5 x 8 aaabaaab2*. NY: Drexel 4183, 2/4 16, f. 1v. Fragmentary, vv. 1, 3–6, 8, 13–19, with music. 13: [2 x 8 aaabcccb2*]. C14: Fitzwilliam Music 784, early 16, recto. Fragmentary text, lines 1–9, with the setting by Fayrfax. L: Add. 31922, 1513+, ff. 120v–2. With the setting by Fayrfax. 40 lines. BR 3193.5, comp. 1483. Song, complaint, fortune, death.

Sonne be nott covetous I the Forbede. Lines 43–44 of TM 219.

Son yf thou wyste whate thynge hyt were. Lines 48–51 of TM 221.

TM 1453 Sone efter the tyme that ald saturnus.
E: Asloan, 1513–42, ff. 41–76v. "Heir begynnis The buke of the chess," tr. from the Latin of Jacobus de Cessolis. 2,191: aa5*. Chess, Scots.

TM 1454 Son crokith the tre | that crokid will be.
O17: Balliol 354, 1505–36, f. 191v. 2: aa2*. BR (3199.3). Proverb.

TM 1455 Sore this dere stryken ys.
L: Add. 31922, 1513+, ff. 39v–40. With music by W. Cornysh. 31: 3 burd aab6* + 7 x 4 a4b3a4b3* (burd. Blow the horne & blow the horne on hye). L: Royal App. 58, 1507+, f. 5v. Burden only, with music, begins "Blow thy horn hunter cum blow thy horne" (three lines written as six). BR (3199.8). Carol, love, bawdy.

TM 1456 Sowters have a nyse pryde.
L: Add. 60577, 1549–58, f. 76. Tr. "Sutores utuntur quadam pompa." 6: aa4b2cc4b2*. Moral, on shoemakers.

TM 1457 Soverayn lord In erth most excellent.
L: Add. 5465, 1501–04, ff. 115v–18. With music by Edmond Turges. 16: 2 burd aa + 2 x 7 RR4* (burd. Enforce your selfe as goddis knyght). BR (3206.5). Carol, hist., commons, Henry VII or VIII.

TM 1458 Sovereynys and serys yf it be your wylle.
O: Tanner 407, c 1500, f. 21. The Life of St Anne. 460: 115 x 4 abab4*. L: Harley 4012, c 1500, ff130v–39v. "The lif of Sent Anne"; variant first line "Soveraignes and frendes..." 453 lines. BR (3207). Rel., nar.

Spend no manus good in vayne. Lines 13–14 of TM 221.

TM 1459 Spight hathe no powre to make me sadde.
L: Add. 17492, 1532–39, f. 78. 32: 4 x 8 ababbaba8. Love.

TM 1460 Spytt off ther spytt shiche ys in vayn.
D: TCD 160, 1535–48, f. 157. 30: 5 x 6 ababcC4* (ref. My ffancy ys to hard to torne). Love.

TM 1461 Stay gentel frend that passest bye.
L: Cott. Titus A.24, 1551+, f. 79v. "finis norton" (monologue of a corpse speaking on Henry Williams, d. 1551). 20: 5 x 4 abab8. TP 1633. Elegy, hist.

TM 1462 Stedes ther stumbelyd in that stownde.
L: Cott. Cleopatra C.4, early–mid 16, ff. 25v–6v. On the Battle of Agincourt [1415]. 64: 8 x 8 MT4* (ref. Thorow myght of god omnipotent). BR 3213, comp. c 1450. Hist.

Stephen George cristofer and clement. Portion of TM 467.

Strive not with thy better lest thou have worse. Vv. 69–72 of TM 219.

TM 1463 Studying as I stode I was moved yn my mynde.
Y: Osborn music 13, 1553+, ff. 49v–50. 48: 6 x 8 ababcdcd5*. Song, allegory of music.

TM 1464 Suche happe as I ame happed in.
L: Egerton 2711, bef. 1542, ff. 25v–6. "Tho[mas Wyatt]." 35: 5 x 7 ababcb8c4. Love.

Such Joy as long may rejoyse them all best. Last line of acephalous TM 1620.

TM 1465 Suche vayn thought as wonted to myslede me.
L: Egerton 2711, bef. 1542, f. 38. "Wyat[t]," tr. Petrarch, *Rime* 169. 14: abbaabbacddcee10. L: Add. 17492, 1532–39, f. 31. TP 1640. Love.

TM 1466 Suche wayward ways hathe love.
D: TCD 160, 1535–48, ff. 177–8v. "H. S." [Henry Howard, Earl of Surrey]. 50: poulters. TP 1641. Love.

Sodeyne departynge oute of felicite. Extract from TM 556 in *The Proverbs of Lydgate*.

TM 1467 Sodeynly me thought I hard a sound.
L11: PRO SP 1/246, mid 16, f. 24. Incipit only, with music. Song.

TM 1468 Suffryng in sorow in hope to attayn.
L: Add. 17492, 1532–39, ff. 6v–7. (With acrostic: [Mary] "Sheltvn."] 35: 7 x 5 aabaB10 (ref. ...suffer styll I must). D: TCD 160, 1535–48, f. 159. 30 lines. Love, letter.

TM 1469 Sunday pryme fayre wether and drye.
PML: Ptd. book 776, 1549, f. 10v. MS leaves bound in at the end. 8: aa4*. Weather prognostications, calendar.

TM 1470 Sustine, abstine kepe well in yowr mynde.
O23: Allestree Frags, c 1555, s. sh. 35: 5 x 7 RR4* (ref. ...ye of all other shalbe moste happy). D: TCD 160, 1535–48, f. 161r–v. (ref. Among all other for the moost happy). BR (3226); TP 1650. Moral.

TM 1471 Swere not Lye not nor fylthyly talke | fyrme not owery not but Ryghtfully walke.
O: Douce 54, early 16, f. 64, 71. Copied twice by the same hand. 2: aa4*. Moral.

TM 1472 Swete harte be trewe | Change [not] for newe.
L6: Dyce 45, 2/4 16, ff. 21v–2. 42: 7 x 6 aabccB2* (ref. And delyver the owte of payne). BR (3228.3). Rel., monologue of Christ.

TM 1473 Swetharte I love yow more fervent then my fader.
O: Rawl. C.813, 1520–35, f. 63. 15: 8 MT4* + 7 RR4*. BR (3228.5). Love, lament, epistle.

TM 1474 Swett harte when ye call for grace.
O: Ptd. book Gough Miss. 145, 1520+, sig. C8v–a1. Love note by "Coosyn Brews," answer to TM 1372. 3: aba4*. Love, answer.

Swete Jhesu now wol I synge. See TM 858

TM 1475 Swet lady mary myld thou me defend & thou me shilde.
LONG: Longleat 29, mid 16, f. 57. 32: aa4*. Rel., prayer, Virgin Mary.

TM 1476 Sweit lord I thank the as I can.
L: Arundel 285, c 1540, ff. 93–4v. Includes verse title "Quhen ze have said thir ois to an end | Than say this orisoun till a commend." 51: aa4*. BR (3243). Rel., prayer, Scots.

Sylvester leo benedicte and [ ]tyne. Portion of TM 467.

TM 1477 Tagus fare well that westeard with thy stremes.
L: Egerton 2711, bef. 1542, f. 69. [Wyatt,] "Spayn." 8: abababcc10. TP 1653. Personal, patriotic.

TM 1478 Take earth of earth, earthes brother.
D: TCD 389, c 1550, ff. 101–3v. Verses on the Elixir [ascribed elsewhere to Pearce the Black Monk]. 196: aa4*. O: Ashmole 759, early 16, ff. 127–8. 72 lines. O: Ashmole 1486, early 16, f. 18v. 4 lines. BR 3249, comp. a 1500. Alchemy.

TM 1479 Take hede be tyme leste ye be spyede.
L: Add. 17492, 1532–39, f. 2. 20: 5 x 4 aaa8R4 (ref. Therefore take hede). Love.

TM 1480 Take hede In tyme whylste yowthe dothe rem< >.
O: Ashmole 48, bef. 1558, ff. 19–21v. (Perhaps a parody of TM 1479.) 68: 17 x 4 aaa8R4 (ref. Therefor take hede). Moral, parody.

TM 1481 [Take Mercury from Mercury which is his wyfe].
L: Harley 2407, early 16, f. 2v. Acephalous, begins "And thou wed mercury..." 4: mono4*. BR 3253, comp. a 1500. Alchemy.

TM 1482 Take thou this treatise thi time therin to use.
HN: EL 26.C.9, c 1555+, f. ii. [Quatrain from Thomas Paulfreyman, Prologue to William Baldwin, *A Treatise of Moral Philosophy*, added to the Ellesmere MS of Chaucer, *Canterbury Tales*.] 4: abab5*. BR (3256.1); TP 1657. Commendation, moral.

TM 1483 Tanglid I was yn loves snare.
L: Add. 17492, 1532–39, ff. 79v–80. 36: 6 x 6 aaabbB8 (ref. For I am not at libertye). Love.

TM 1484 That a dogge shall di a-for his praye.
L11: PRO SP 1/246, 1546, f. 37. 35: aa4* and irreg. Prophecy.

TM 1485 That every man in his degree.
L: Add. 29729, 1558, f. 2. "out of Mr blomfelds boke a pece of the battayl of the psalms" (imperfect). 31: aa4*. BR (3269). Rel., Bible.

That goodly las when she me bas. See TM 987.

TM 1486 That hart my hart hath in such grace.
CANT: Christ Church Letters 2, a 1550, No. 174. 26: 2 burd + 6 x 4 abaR4* (burd. For [weal or woe] I will not fle; ref. To love that hart that lovyth me). BR (3271). Carol, love.

TM 1487 That I can I can.
L: Add. 18752, 1530's, f. 84r–v. "The p< >ars & singgers of pype...can not dow away your gestinge of I wolle & canne." 48: 12 x 4 aabb2*. Moral.

TM 1488 That mony hardie Knycht of gret renoun.
L: Add. 40732, early 16, ff. 1–282. [Gilbert Hay], "The buike of King allexander the conqueroure." 18,000: aa5*. BR (3287.5). Hist., romance, Scots.

TM 1489 That peticion may Justly be denyed | Whiche at no tyme to reason is applyed.
L: Add. 20059, early 16, f. 2. Second of five moral couplets. 2: aa4*. Proverb.

TM 1490 That the hasty or tymly sowyng Som tyme yt fayleth | But to late sowyng Seldom or never wyll provyth.
L: Lansd. 210, 1553–58, f. 80v. 2: aa5*. Proverb, practical, farming.

TM 1491 That tyme that myrthe dyd stere my shypp.
L: Add. 17492, 1532–39, f. 17v. Last stanza lacks one verse. 34: 5 x 7 RR8 (ref. ...lyff doth dure). D: TCD 160, 1535–48, f. 175r–v. Love.

TM 1492 That was my Joy is now my woo & payne.
L: Add. 5465, 1501–04, ff. 31v–3. With music. 14: RR5* (ref. That hath byn your fayre lady and mastress). BR (3297.3). Song, love.

TM 1493 That was my woo is nowe my most gladness.
L: Add. 5465, 1501–04, ff. 12v–13. With music by R. ffayrfax. 7: RR5*. L: Add. 60577, 1549–58, f. 116v. BR (3297.5). Song, love.

TM 1494 That worthy david whiche that sloughe golie.
L: Add. 29729, 1558, ff.134–7v. "made by Jon lidgat for a momynge whiche the gold smythes of london shewyd before Eestfyld mayr on candylmas day...presented by an harold called fortune." 98: 14 x 7 RR5*. BR 3301, comp. a 1440. Rel., mumming.

TM 1495 [The ancient writers with wisdom decorate].
[Alexander Barclay, dedication to his *Life of St. George*, TP 1678.] L: Sloane

4031, early 16, f. 2. Extract, lines 1261–1323, beginning "Ye that ar comons obey your kynge and lorde." 70: 10 x 7 RR5*. BR (4257); TP 1678. Political.

TM 1496 Thanswere that ye made to me my dere.
L: Egerton 2711, bef. 1542, f. 63r–v. "T[homas]. W[yatt]." 22: 2 x 5 ababb10 + 2ab10 + 10 ababb, ababb10. TP 1679. Love.

TM 1497 The battles and the man I wil discrive.
E2: Dk.7.49, 1515–20, ff. 2–367v. Gavin Douglas, tr. Vergil, *Aeneid*, including the 13th book added by Mapheus Vegius; prologues, preliminary and concluding verses indexed as TM 879. 22,098: aa5*. C2: TCC O.3.12 (1184), 1513, ff. 9–329v. "Virgyll... Eneados." E2: Dc.1.43, 1515–20?, ff. 2–300v. E2: Laing II.655, 1/2 16, ff. 1–3. Fragment of three leaves; begins "With ceptour in hand ther muyd to meyss and still." 198: aa5*. L2: Lambeth 117, 1545 ff. 3–end. Copied "by...thomas Bellenden 1545." LONG: Longleat 252A, 1547, ff.2v–188v. Copied by Henry Aytoun, notary public, 1547. TP 1681. Nar., epic, Scots.

TM 1498 The beare all boldly to hys deth shall goo.
O: Arch. Seld. B.8, mid 16, f. 293v. 26: aa4*. Prophecy.

TM 1499 The best tre yf ye take entent.
O17: Balliol 354, 1503–04, f. 101r–v. "A treatise of wyne." 92: abab3*. BR 3307, comp. a 1500. Macaronic, wine, practical.

The beste wysdom that I Can. Lines 9–10 of TM 221.

TM 1500 The bitter swete that straynes my yeldid hart.
L11: PRO SP 1/246, mid 16, f. 29r–v. With music. 6: ababcc10. L: Add. 30513, c 1550, f. 109. Incipit only, with music. Song, love.

The blak schal blede and the blewe... Extract of TM 1203 (listed separately as BR 3308.5).

TM 1501 The blynd I thynk my lady dere.
L: Add. 18752, 1530's, f. 90r–v. 32: 4 x 8 ababacaC8 (ref. Why caws you thys my hart to brek). Love, complaint.

TM 1502 The boris hed in hondis I brynge.
O17: Balliol 354, 1505–36, f. 228. A boar's head carol. 14: 2 burd. (aa) + 3 x 4 aaab4* (burd. Caput apri refero). BR (3313). TP 1693. Carol, macaronic, Christmas.

TM 1503 The borys hede that we bryng here.
L: Add. 5665, bef. 1511, ff. 7v–8. A boar's head carol with music by Smert;

cf. TP 1693. 16: 4 burd aaaa + 3 x 4 aaa4B2* (burd. Nowell, nowell nowell nowell; ref. Nowell nowell). BR (3315). Carol, Christmas.

TM 1504 The boke of marchalsie here shall begyn.
O17: Balliol 354, 1503–04, f. 7. Prologue to a prose treatise on horses. 14: aa5*. BR 3318, comp. a 1400. Table of contents.

TM 1505 The borne hys the world blynde.
C3: Emmanuel 4.3.31 (263), early 16, f. i–ii verso. [Religious parody of a secular song.]. 94: 3 burd. aaa + 13 x 7 aaa2b1cc2B3* (burd. Come over the burne Besse; ref. Cum over the borne to me). L: Add. 5665, bef. 1511, ff. 143v–4. With music. 9: 3 burd aaa + 6 aabccB3* (ref. Cum over the borne besse to me). O: Ashmole 176, pt. 3, bef. 1551, f. 100. 8: 1 burd + 7 aaa2b1cc2B3*. C2: TCC O.2.53 (1157), early 16, ff. 55–6. 84: 1 burd + 12 x 7 aaa6b2ccB6. BR (3318.4). Rel., carol, allegory, monologue of Christ.

TM 1506 The brwett of evill tonges what women can eschew | Or who can lett a fowle to wrytt the thinge that is untrewe.
DUR5: Cosin V.iii.9, c 1555, f. 56. "quod [Thomas] carter." 2: poulters. BR (3318.3). Women, moral.

TM 1507 The Catt the Ratt, and lovell owr Dogge | Rulyth all England, undyr the hogge.
L: Cott. Nero C.11, 1506+, f. 461v. Rhyme against Richard III and his advisors by William Collingbourn (executed 1485), quoted by Robert Fabyan. 2: aa4*. HD: Eng 766F, bef. 1516, f. 435v. BR 3318.7, comp. 1485; TP 1695.5. Hist., political satire.

TM 1508 The cawse of joy or of dispayer.
O: e Musaeo 63, mid 16, flyleaf verso. 7: RR4*. Riddle.

TM 1509 The cocke of the northe shalbe fayne to fflee.
L: Add. 24663, 1550's, f. 5v. Written as prose. 5: ababb4*. Prophecy.

The diepe secrets that David here did syng. See TM 1263.

TM 1510 [The double sorwe of Troilus to tellen].
[Chaucer, *Troilus and Criseyde*, comp. 1385–86.] L: Add. 17492, 1532–39, ff. 29v–30, 59v, 91–92. Extracts on love from 4. 13–14, 288–315, 323–29, copied from STC 5068 (1532). Extracts begin: "Also wicked tongues...," "Yf it be so that ye so creuel be...," "And now my pen...," "And who that sayeth...," "For love is yet...," "O very lord o son o god alas." 65: aa5*, RR5*. C: Gg.4.12, early 16, f. 105v. Extract, 1. 400–06 (based on Petrarch, *Rime* 132), begins "If love be not o Lord what fele I so." 7: RR5*. BR 3327, TP 1702.5 (see also TM 908). Love.

TM 1511 The earthe, and all that thearin is.
L: Royal 17.A.21, 1551, ff. 34–5. William Forreste, tr. Ps 23 Domini est terra. 44: 11 x 4 a8b6a8b6. Rel.

The elder to hell take the wey. Acephalous text of TM 973.

The xi–th day schal come thounder lyth. See TM 871.

TM 1512 Thenmy of liff decayer of all kynde.
L: Egerton 2711, bef. 1542, f. 42v. "Tho[mas Wyatt]." 8: abababcc10. TP 1707. Love.

TM 1513 The eye doeth fynde.
O: Ptd. book Douce L.645, 1529+, ff. 2v–3. 4: aabb2*.

TM 1514 The farther I go the more be hynde.
L: Add. 5465, 1501–04, ff. 2v–3. With music by William Newark (cf. TM 1568). 7: ababaca5*. Song, complaint.

TM 1515 The ffathers preceptes he that abservythe | In full gret surety hym self conservythe.
L: Add. 20059, early 16, f. 2. Third of five moral couplets. 2: aa4*. Proverb.

TM 1516 The fierce & wanton Colt.
L11: PRO SP 1/246, mid 16, f. 22. Incipit only, with music. Song.

TM 1517 The furst day of the mone Adam.
L: Harley 3725, early 16, ff. 66–81v. [Pseudo-Aristotle, Course of the Moon, tr. from French, without prologue.] 672: aa4*. BR 3341, comp. a 1500; TP 499.5. Astronomy.

TM 1518 The first strooke [*sic* for stok] fader of gentlenesse.
L: Harley 7578, early 16, f. 17. [Chaucer, "Gentilesse."] 21: 3 x 7 RR5* (ref. All were he myter corowne or dyademe). BR 3348, comp. a 1400; TP 1719.5. Moral.

TM 1519 The flowr ys fresshe & fayer the hewe.
O17: Balliol 354, 1505–36, f. 220. 46: 4 burd. (aabb) + 7 x 6 aaaa4bb2* (burd. Ther ys a flowr sprung of a tre). BR 3603, comp. c 1426. Rel., carol, Virgin Mary.

TM 1520 The foolysche carnall man dothe saye.
L: Royal 17.A.21, 1551, ff. 17v–19. William Forreste, tr. Ps 13 Dixit inspiriens. 52: 13 x 4 a8b6a8b6. Rel.

TM 1521 The fox with his long tayle full bushy shall barke.
O: Arch. Seld. B.8, mid 16, f. 272v. 22: aa4*. Prophecy.

TM 1522 The ffrende of pyte, and al almesse dede.
L: Cott. Nero C.11, 1506+, f. 117. Robert Fabyan, tr. "Tercius henricus jacet...," epitaph on the tomb of Henry III, d. 1273. 7: RR4*. HD: Eng 766F, bef. 1516, f. 88. TP 1727. Hist., epitaph.

TM 1523 The fructe of all the servise that I serve.
L: Add. 17492, 1532–39, f. 72. 8: abababcc10. Love.

TM 1524 [The fruytfyll sentence and the noble werkes].
[Stephen Hawes, *The Convercyon of Swerers*," 1509, BR (3354.5), TP 1730.] L: Harley 4294, early 16, f. 80. Two extracts from vv. 234–89, headed "Ricardus Spery," beginning "<Wo> worth your hartes so plantyd in pryde" and "Blessed be..."; listed separately as BR 4216. 56: 8 x 7 RR5*. Moral.

TM 1525 The furyous gonne in his raging yre.
L: Egerton 2711, bef. 1542, f. 40v. "'Tho[mas Wyatt]," tr. Serafino, "Se una bombarda e dal gran foco mossa"; first line revised from "Like as the cannon..." 8: abababcc10. TP 1731. Epigram, love.

TM 1526 The god that giveth lyfe and light.
C3: Emmanuel 4.1.17 (260), mid 16, ff. 255–60. "An other letter to a certayne Christian beyng imprisoned for Christs gosple sake," subscribed "R. S." 154: aa14. Rel. instruction.

TM 1527 The godes off love sytts a bove.
Y: Osborn music 13, 1553+, ff. 55v–6. With music [related to a ballad by William Elderton; cf. Shakespeare, *Much Ado About Nothing*, V.ii.26–29.] 70: 5 x 14 abcdacdefgfghh8. Love, song.

TM 1528 The good or evell fortune of all a mans lyffe | Ys in the good or evell chousinge of his frend or his wiffe.
DUR5: Cosin V.iii.9, c 1555, f. 66. 2: aa5*. BR (3361.6). Moral, friendship, marriage.

TM 1529 The governoure that gydeth with vertue and grace | Shulde never be changed lest woorse have his place.
L: Add. 20059, early 16, f. 2. First of five moral couplets. 2: aa11, anapest. BR (3364). Moral.

TM 1530 The greatnes of trewe cha[r]ytie god hathe sett in his wyll.
L: Add. 33974, c 1550, f. 61r–v. (Francis Stacy), "Of <...charytye>." 22: aa7*. Rel. instruction.

TM 1531 The hare & the hound shall fyrst agre.
Y: Osborn music 13, 1553+, f. 37. With music, subscribed "Arthur Blanchinden" (prob. composer). 24: 4 x 6 abab8. Love, song.

TM 1532 The hart & servys to you profferd.
L: Add. 17492, 1532–39, f. 11v. 24: 6 x 4 abab8. Love.

TM 1533 The heavyns, goddes glorye dothe declare.
L: Royal 17.A.21, 1551, ff. 29–30v. William Forreste, tr. Ps 18 Coeli enarrant. 68: 17 x 4 a8b6a8b6. Rel.

TM 1534 The hevens in ther excellence, O god they utter thy glory.
L: Royal App. 74–76, c 1548, ff. 17v–19, 16v–18, 24v–6. Tr. Ps 19, with music. 56: 8 x 7 RR5*. Rel.

TM 1535 The hedge hoge will the cookcok fede.
L: Lansd. 762, 1524–29, ff. 59–60v. 140: 12 x 12 ababababab cC4*, irreg. (ref. When cockowe cometh ofte so sone). BR (3375). Prophecy.

TM 1536 The hye desire that y have ffor to se.
L: Add. 5665, bef. 1511, ff. 68v–9. With music. 6: aabaab5*. BR (3376.5). Song, love.

TM 1537 The hye divine eternall majestie.
L: Harley 838, early 16, ff. 67–91v. Anthony Babington, tr. Christine de Pisan "Epistle of Othea"; Proheme and Epistle, with prose Glose and Moralite. 973: 139 x 7 RR5*. BR (3377). Moral, epistle.

TM 1538 The hyer men clemmeth the sorer ys the falle.
L: Add. 5665, bef. 1511, f. 14v. With music. 16: 4 burd aaaa + 3 x 4 abaB4* (burd. In every state in every degre; ref. The mene ys best as semeth me). BR (3382). Carol, moral.

TM 1539 The hinde shall hunte the harte to deathe | Tyll he him selfe hath lost his breathe.
L: Cott. Vespasian E.7, early 16, f. 133. 2: aa8. Prophecy.

TM 1540 The holy danyell telle the playne.
L: Sloane 2578, c 1557, f. 110v. 40: aa8, written as prose. Prophecy.

TM 1541 The house of Justyce where it standes.
L: Add. 33974, c 1550, ff. 23v–4. (Francis Stacy), "<...> Amonste the Juste to be | lett this way the dyrecte | herin sett downe to the." 52: aa4*. Moral.

TM 1542 The hunt ys up.
L: Add. 15233, 1554–58, ff. 32–4v. "Jhon thorne," on the creation, fall, and redemption, a religious parody of a secular song. 104: 2 burd aa + 17 x 6 aa4b6cc4B6 (burd. Nolo mortem peccatoris; ref. Nolo mortem peccatoris). Rel., carol, parody, nar.

TM 1543 The joye so short alas the paine so nere.
L: Add. 17492, 1532–39, f. 75v. 21: 3 x 7 RR10. Love.

TM 1544 The Kyng of Kynges, that lord, that Rulyth all.
L: Cott. Nero C.11, 1506+, f. 52. Robert Fabyan, tr. "Destruet hoc regnum...," verses capping the contest between a knight and master Moris. 7: RR4*. HD: Eng 766F, bef. 1516, f. ?. TP 1762. Hist., capping verse.

TM 1545 The knyght knokett at the castell gate.
L: Add. 31922, 1513+, ff. 45v–6. With music by Cornysh for the burden only. 20: 4 burd abaa + 8 x 2 aa4* (burd. You and I and amyas). BR (3405.5). Carol, love.

TM 1546 The knot which fyrst my hart did strayn.
L: Add. 17492, 1532–39, f. 23r–v, 33r–v, and a four-line fragment on f. 22v subscribed "quod John." 42: 6 x 7 ababab8a4. D: TCD 160, 1535–48, f. 173r–v. Love.

TM 1547 The knowledge of god passith comparyson.
L: Royal 18 D.2, c 1520, ff. 163–4. William Cornysshe, "A Treatis bitwene Trowthe and enformacon," dated July, 19 Henry VII [1504]. 140: 20 x 7 RR4* (ref. ...wrong). L: Harley 43, early 16, ff. 88–91v. (Imperfect, stanza 3 damaged.) 133: 19 x 7 RR4*. BR (3405.8). Moral, music.

TM 1548 The laborous & ye most mervelus werkes.
L: Add. 29729, 1558, ff.87–121v. "the court of sapyence compylyd by dan Iohn lydgate...[copied by] Iohn Stowe" [not by Lydgate]. 2,310: 330 x 7 RR5*. BR 3406, comp. c 1475; TP 1766. Nar., allegory, dream vision, moral.

TM 1549 The laughynge tymes, with theyr Crymes spent.
HD: Eng 766F, bef. 1516, ff.437v–8v. Robert Fabyan, tr. of "Sunt tua criminibus," verses on Daniel, a Fleming, favorite of King Lowys. 42: 6 x 7 RR4*. TP 1767. Hist., satire.

The legend of Baptyst here Afftyr ensuyth. Rhymed title to TM 383.

TM 1550 The lyf ys long that lothsumlye dothe last.
O: Ashmole 48, bef. 1558, ff. 24v–5. Answered by TM 1035. 42: 7 x 6 ababcc10. TP 1768. Moral, question.

TM 1551 The lif so short the craft so long to lere.
LONG: Longleat 258, 1500+, ff. 85–101. Chaucer, "the parlement of foules." 699: 100 x 7 RR5*. BR 3412, comp. a 1400; TP 1768.5. Nar., dream, debate, parliament, allegory.

TM 1552 The lighte of clere grace that never endeth.
L: Add. 57335, early 16, ff. 83v–91. "Sequitur de Confessione," one of three additions to Peter Idley, *Instructions to his Son*, TM 789. 512: 73 x 7 RR4*. BR 3412.2+, comp. c 1450. Rel. instruction.

TM 1553 The lylie that faire flowre.
L: Lansd. 762, 1524–29, f. 52. "Declaracio signorum." 18: aa4*. BR (3412.3). Political, allegory.

TM 1554 The lyvely sperkes that issue from those Iyes.
L: Egerton 2711, bef. 1542, f. 23v. "Tho[mas Wyatt]," tr. Petrarch, *Rime* 258. 14: abbaabbacddcee10. L: Add. 17492, 1532–39, f. 36v. TP 1770. Love.

TM 1555 The longe love, that in my thought doeth harbar.
L: Egerton 2711, bef. 1542, f. 5r–v. [Wyatt,] tr. Petrarch, *Rime* 140. 14: abbaabbacddcee10. TP 1771. Love.

TM 1556 The lorde, and god, of Israell.
L: Royal 17.A.21, 1551, ff. 80–1v. William Forreste, tr. Benedictus. 52: 13 x 4 a8b6a8b6. Rel., hymn.

TM 1557 The lorde dothe reigne, the earthe: let joye.
L: Royal 17.A.21, 1551, ff. 69–70v. William Forreste, tr. Ps 96 Deus regnavit. 56: 14 x 4 a8b6a8b6. Rel.

TM 1558 The lorde heare thee in the streyte daye.
L: Royal 17.A.21, 1551, ff. 30v–1v. William Forreste, tr. Ps 19 Exaudiat te. 44: 11 x 4 a8b6a8b6. Rel.

TM 1559 The lorde (hym self) dothe governe mee.
L: Royal 17.A.21, 1551, ff. 33–4. William Forreste, tr. Ps 22 Deus regit me. 40: 10 x 4 a8b6a8b6. Rel.

TM 1560 The lorde ys at hande and wyll come shortly.
L: Add. 33974, c 1550, ff. 68v–71. (Francis Stacy), "Comyng of <...> Chryste come." 212: 53 x 4 abab5*. Rel., Christ.

TM 1561 The losse is small to lese such on.
L: Add. 17492, 1532–39, f. 77v. 4: abab8. Love.

TM 1562 The majestie of god above.
L: Add. 30981, 1522–29, ff. 25–7v. John Croke, tr. Celi enarrant [Ps 19]. 76: 19 x 4 abab4*. Rel.

The maker of this legend... Title verse to TM 1619.

TM 1563 The man is bleste.
L: Add. 30513, c 1550, f. 80v. [Perhaps Thomas Sternhold, tr. Ps. 41, TP 1786,] incipit only, with music. Rel.

TM 1564 The masse is of so high dignytee.
O17: Balliol 354, 1505–36, f. 229v–30. 26: 2 burd. (aa) + 6 x 4 aaaa3* (burd. I counsell you both more & lesse). BR 3424, comp. a 1500. Rel., carol, mass.

TM 1565 The mas it hath bene usyd.
G: Hunt. 232, 1/2 16, f. 98v. Lines 1–6 repeated f. 103v. 11: aabccbddefg3*. Rel., mass.

TM 1566 The mercye of god etc.
PFOR: MS 40A, 1553+, f. 380. [Nicholas Udall?], incipit of a song by Pax, Justitia, Veritas, Misericordia, and Respublica at the end of V.iv (after line 1430) of *Respublica*. Rel., song

TM 1567 The mil gothe and let hir go | So merely goth the mila.
L: Add. 60577, 1549–58, f. 222. Drinking song with music for four voices, repeated. 2: ab4*. Song, convivial.

TM 1568 The more I goo: the ferther I am behynde.
L: Add. 29729, 1558, ff. 131v–2. Between the first and second stanza is written "le dis de lydgate" [incorrect attribution; see TM 1514]. 21: 3 x 7 RR4* (ref. Though I go lowse I tyed am with a lyne). L: Harley 7578, early 16, f. 20. First stanza only. 7: RR4*. L: Add. 60577, 1549–58, f. 92r–v. Variant first line "Ever the ferther I goo the ferther I am behynde." 42 lines. BR 3437, comp. a 1500. Moral.

TM 1569 The morow ffolowyng, Tiburce and Valerian.
L: Cott. Nero C.11, 1506+, f. 147v. Robert Fabyan, tr. "Crastino Tiburci...," on snow and wind, 24 May 1294. 8: 2 x 4 abab4*. HD: Eng 766F, bef. 1516, f. 118v. TP 1804. Hist.

TM 1570 The moder full manerly and mekely as a mayd.
L: Add. 31922, 1513+, ff. 112v–5v. With music by Pygott. 16: 4 burd abab + 3 x 4 mono4* (burd. Quid petis o fily). BR (3438.3). Rel., carol, nativity, macaronic.

TM 1571 The mother full of sorow stode even by the cross whenas.
L: Add. 33974, c 1550, f. 21. (Francis Stacy), "< >Lady the virgine Mary." 38: aa7*. Rel., Virgin Mary.

TM 1572 The mowse goth abrode | wher the cat is not lorde.
O17: Balliol 354, 1505–36, f. 200v. Tr. "Mus deuagatur..." 2: aa2*. BR (3438.6). Proverb.

TM 1573 The nyghyngale sat one abrere.
L: Royal App. 58, 1507+, ff. 8v, 9v. With music to burden only. 20: 4 burden abab + 4 x 4 abaB4* (burd. The lytyll prety nyghtyngale; ref. But yet ye wot not whom I mean). BR (3413.3). Carol, love.

TM 1574 The nobilness and gret magnificence.
E: Asloan, 1513–42, ff.247–56v. [Robert Henryson], "The tale of Orpheus and Erudices his quene," based on Nicholas Trivet's commentary on Boethius; probably copied from STC 13166 (1508?). 578: 19 x 7 RR5*, 5 x 9 aabaabbcC10, 33 x 7 RR5*, 164 aa5* (ref. Quhair art thou gone my luve euridices). BR 3442, comp. a 1500; TP 1809.5. Nar., allegory, myth, Scots.

TM 1575 Thr nobylnes of thys vayne worlde wherein men do delyghte.
L: Add. 33974, c 1550, f. 59. (Francis Stacy), "Of trewe nobylytie." 20: aa7*. Rel. instruction.

TM 1576 The old dog the old dog.
L: Add. 60577, 1549–58, f. 221v. Drinking song with music. 6: ab4c2ab4C2*. Song, convivial.

TM 1577 The olde kyng Arthure and all the bonde ryall.
O: Arch. Seld. B.8, mid 16, f. 295v. 34: abab4*, irreg. Prophecy.

TM 1578 The Perse owt of Northombarlonde and a vowe to god mayd he.
O: Ashmole 48, bef. 1558, ff. 15–18. [Chevy Chase,] "quoth Rychard sheale." 282: aa7*, a4b3a4b3*. BR (3445.5). Hist., Scotland, ballad, nar.

TM 1579 The perverse heretyke, thouth that he doo brenne.
L: Cott. Nero C.11, 1506+, f. 357. Robert Fabyan, tr. "hereticus credat...," on John Bodby, burned 1410. 7: RR4*. HD: Eng 766F, bef. 1516, f?. TP 1814. Hist.

TM 1580 The pleasaunt beayt of swet delyte dothe blynd.
L: Add. 17492, 1532–39, f. 66. 6: ababcc10. Moral.

TM 1581 The plowman plucked upp his plowe.
TEX: Ptd. book Stark +6451, 1532+, f. 1 of MS quire bound in. "The

plowmanys Prologue" (to TM 40). 52: abababab4*, abab4*. BR 3448; TP 1818. Rel. controversy, nar.

TM 1582 The prophetez sage we rede in storys and comment.
L37: Coll. of Arms, 1st M.13, 1503, ff. 45v–6. Verses recited at the marriage of Katherine of Aragon and Prince Arthur, 1501 (lacks one line). 48: 7 x 7 RR5*. Hist., pageant.

TM 1583 The proverbes of Salmon do playnly declare.
HN: HM 183, 2/4 16, ff. 7–9. "[Sir Francis] Bryan." 184: 23 x 8 ababab cc5*. Proverbs, moral.

TM 1584 The rar and grettyst gyfte of all.
O: Ashmole 48, bef. 1558, ff.29v–30v. 56: 7 x 8 ababccdd8. Rel. instruction, Solomon's request.

TM 1585 The Reconisaunce of all fleshely luste.
F: V.a.198, early 16, s. sh. 35: 5 x 7 RR4*. Rel. instruction.

TM 1586 The restfull place Revyver of my smarte.
L: Add. 17492, 1532–39, f. 18. "ffynys qd Wyatt" (based on Petrarch, *Rime* 234). 21: 3 x 7 RR10. L: Egerton 2711, c 1549, f. 7v. "Too hiz bedde," vv. 1–8 only, beginning "O restfull place..."; copied by Nicholas Grimald. TP 1825. Love.

TM 1587 The rote of wysdom is god to drede.
O: Tanner 407, 1/4 16, f. 32. 4: mono4*. BR (3456). Rel. instruction.

TM 1588 The rose both white and rede.
L11: PRO E 36/228, 1509, ff. 7–8. John Skelton, "A Lawde and Prayse made for our Sovreigne Lord the Kyng [Henry VIII, on his accession, 1509]," subscribed "per me laurigerum britonum skeltonida Vatem" (autograph). 56: 8 x 7 RR6. BR (3456.5). Hist., praise.

TM 1589 The Rose female shall dolefullye dye.
L: Harley 559, 1554, f. 7v. Also vv. 1–2 only on f. 34. 8: aabcbcbc4*. Prophecy, hist., Thomas Becket.

TM 1590 The Roose in his reigne shall have battelis ffyve.
O: Rawl. C.813, c 1535, f. 90r–v. 28: aa4*, abab4*, and irreg. Prophecy.

TM 1591 The Scottes shall ryse and make ado.
L: Sloane 2578, c 1557, f. 68r–v. 50: 13 x 4 abab8. Prophecy.

TM 1592 The sheperd upon a hill he satt.
O17: Balliol 354, 1505–36, f. 224r–v. 63: 2 burd. (aa)+ 7 aaaab4b2B4* + 9 x 6 aaaa4b2B4* (burd. Can I not syng but hoy; ref. For in hys pype he made so mych joy.). BR (3460). Rel., carol, nativity.

The sylle man. See TM 1242.

TM 1593 The son of Richard Duke of Normandy.
D: TCD 484, c 1531, ff. 8–11. (Cf. BR 3632.) 160: 20 x 8 MT10. Hist., kings of England.

TM 1594 The Son of the Fader of hevyn blys.
O17: Balliol 354, 1505–36, f. 221v. 18: 2 burd. (aa) + 4 x 4 aaaB4* (burd. Verbum patris hodie; ref. processit ex virgine). BR (3473). Rel., carol, nativity, macaronic.

TM 1595 The sueden chance ded mak me mues.
L: Add. 17492, 1532–39, f. 67v. 9: ababccdcd8. Love.

TM 1596 The sermountynge pleasure who can expresse.
L: Royal 18.D.2, c 1520, ff.195v–7v. "The proverbis of the garett over the bayne at Lekingfelde" [Leconfield]; dialogue between the "part sensitive" and the "part intellect" on the vanity of human delights. 150: aa4*. BR (3482). Dialogue, moral.

TM 1597 The tender love that dredethe losse.
Y: Osborn music 13, 1553+, f. 1. Incipit only, with lute tablature. Song, love.

TM 1598 The thynge good lorde that I pray for | Gyve me thy grace to labor for.
F: X.d.532, 1535+, [unfol.]. Vv. 105–6 (at the end of prose) of a vellum strip headed "Oratio devotissima Thomae More..." [probably not by More]. 2: aa8. TP 1844.5. Rel., prayer.

TM 1599 The thowgts within my brest.
L: Add. 31922, 1513+, ff. 29v–30. With music by "The Kynge H viii." 4: abab3*. BR (3486.5). Love, song.

TM 1600 The thre crowns doo hoont after the harte lyffe.
L11: PRO SP 1/244, 1543, f. 194. "The seditious ryme" reported to the Lord Chamberlain in an examination dated 1543. 16: aa4*. Prophecy.

TM 1601 The tyme approched of necessite.
L: Harley 7578, early 16, ff. 3v–13. [Sayings of Old Philosophers.] 854: 122 x 7 RR4*. BR 3487, comp. c 1475. Moral.

TM 1602 The tyme of youthe is to be spent.
L: Add. 31922, 1513+, ff. 28v–9. With music by "The king Henry viii." 12: aa4*. BR (3487.5). Song, conviviality.

TM 1603 The tyme shall come as true as the crede.
O: Arch. Seld. B.8, mid 16, f. 272r–v. "Thys was found within an alter in Suffolke at the pullyng downe of the alters in the tyme of Kyng Edward the Syxte." 54: aa4*. Prophecy.

TM 1604 The tyme will comme as true as I reade.
L: Sloane 2578, c 1557, ff. 109–10. 58: aa4*. Prophecy.

TM 1605 [The trewe processe of Englysch polycye].
L: Harley 78, mid 16, ff. 54–69. [*The Libel of English Policy*, vv. 76–1156, omitting 856, 985–6, and adding a new line after 857; begins: "Moche fustian and also [linen] cloth."] 1,078: aa5*, MT5*. M: Rylands 955, mid 16, ff. 4–5, 8–27. Acephalous text, begins at v. 44, "Whiche hathe nobles much like to ours," omitting 57, 135, 140–231, 430–1, 931–51. 970 lines. BR 3491, comp. 1436. Political, economic, practical.

TM 1606 The twelf giftes of goddes grace.
L: Add. 57335, early 16, ff. 91–4v. "The xii giftes of Goddes grace," incomplete (ends after six gifts, probably four leaves containing 30-odd stanzas lacking); one of three additions to Peter Idley, *Instructions to his Son*, TM 789. 259: 37 x 7 RR4*. BR 3492.4+, comp. a 1500. Rel. instruction.

The unsure gladnes the Joye transytory. Extract from TM 556 in *The Proverbs of Lydgate*.

TM 1607 The Wandering [gadlyng] in the somer tyde.
L: Egerton 2711, bef. 1542, f. 32. "Tho[mas Wyatt]." 8: abababcc10. L: Add. 17492, 1532–39, f. 35v. TP 1854. Love.

The Western Wynde. Title to music in L: Add. 17802–05, no text. Cf. TM 1811.

TM 1608 The whele of fortune who can hold.
L: Royal App. 58, 1507+, f. 50r–v. With music. 21: 3 x 7 RR4* (ref. ...borne). BR (3498.5). Song, fortune.

TM 1609 The wycked, in hym self (prowdelye).
L: Royal 17.A.21, 1551, ff. 39–40. William Forreste, tr. Ps 35 Dixit iniustus. 56: 14 x 4 a8b6a8b6. Rel.

TM 1610 The winter withe his ougly storms [no lenger dare abyde].
L: Cott. Titus A.24, mid 16, ff. 81v–2v. Tr. Horace, Carm. 4.7. 30: aa14. TP 1858. Moral.

TM 1611 The wourkes of God be greate, and also straunge.
C: Dd.9.31, 1550–58, p. 25. "When the Duke of Somersett was set at his libertie upone newe yeares day [1 Jan. 1550/51]... [William] Gray his servaunte gave these sayeings unto the sayde Duke his master." 110: aa10. L: Sloane 1207, 1550+, ff. 7–8v, 38–39v (two copies). Subscribed "gray"; preceded by title verses "Helthe onor and vertue longe tyme and spase ..." 107 lines. Moral, hist.

TM 1612 The worlde so wide the eyre so remuable.
L: Harley 7578, early 16, f. 20. 7: RR4*. BR 3504, comp. c 1450. Mutability.

TM 1613 The worthynes of holly lyfe olde fathers doe commende.
L: Add. 33974, c 1550, f. 63r–v. (Francis Stacy), "Of a holly lyfe." 24: aa7*. Rel. instruction.

TM 1614 The wretched wandringe Prince of troye.
L: Add. 30513, c 1550, f. 87v. Incipit only, with music. Song.

TM 1615 The yere of our lorde M CCCC lxxxiii.
L: Lansd. 762, 1524–29, ff. 63v–5. 134: aa4*, abab4*. BR 3510, comp. 1484. Prophecy.

The yeres passed of my tender youthe. See TM 1164.

TM 1616 Thee o Lord will I magnifie.
L: Royal 17.A.17, 1551+, ff. 14v–17. Sir Thomas Smith, "Psalmes of Thanksgiving... [tr. Ps] 144" [145]. 84: 21 x 4 a4b3a4b3*. Rel.

TM 1617 Then all bestis and fowles shall maike thaym gaie.
C17: Sidney Sussex 39, 1500–25, ff. 1–69v. 2000: ? BR (3514). Prophecy.

TM 1618 Then all your doyngs schold here in earthe.
C2: TCC O.7.31 (1359), c 1500, f. 202v–4. Three transcripts with variants. 26: 2 burd. aa + 6x4 aaaa4* (burd. Be mery all with one accorde). BR (3515). Carol, moral.

TM 1619 Than Fyrst to begyn, At his tender Age.
L8: Guildhall 3313, c 1510, ff. 332v–38. "Legenda, sed non Aurea, hic inscribitur Johannis spurcissimi qui sic vocabitur," satire on John Baptist de Grimaldis, extortionist, with title verse beginning "The maker of this

legend...," giving the author's name "Tom a dale." 287: 41 x 7 RR4*. Nar., hist., satire.

TM 1620 ...Then in rembrance of reson hold yee.
L: Add. 15233, 1554–58, ff. 11–27v. Acephalous, "the play of Wyt & science made by master Ihon Redford," comp. between 1554 and 1558. Last line: "Such joy as long may rejoyse them all best." 1,123: aa4*, abab4*, RR4*. Moral, interlude, drama.

Then quater shall a-Ryse. See TM 1884.

TM 1621 Ther bien fowr thyngs causyng gret folye.
L: Add. 29729, 1558, f. 132. "yet of the same" (follows TM 1623). 7: RR5*. BR 3521, comp. a 1500. Moral.

TM 1622 Ther ben iiii thynges full harde for to knowe | Whych way that they will draw.
L: Ptd. book IB 49437, early 16, f. 1. Rhymed title to prose; probably copied from STC 3309, *The bokys of haukyng and huntyng* (1496); (cf. prose version in L: Lansd. 762, f. 16v). 2: aa3*. BR 3521.5, comp. a 1486; TP 1875.5. Moral.

TM 1623 Ther be fowr thyngs that makyth man a fool.
L: Add. 29729, 1558, f. 132. "A seyng of dan lydgate" [speculative attribution]. 6: ababcc5*. BR 3523, comp. a 1449. Moral.

TM 1624 Ther ben iii poyntis of myscheff that are confusion to many man.
O: Tanner 407, 1/4 16, ff. 18v–19. 52: aa7*. BR (3522). Moral.

TM 1625 Ther beth iii thynges that be moche of prys.
O: Tanner 407, 1/4 16, f. 18. 4: mono4*. BR (3524). Moral, proverb.

TM 1626 Ther ys a blossum sprong of a thorn.
O17: Balliol 354, 1505–36, f. 222v. (Cf BR 2730.) 38: 2 burd. (aa) + 9 x 4 aaaB4* (burd. Alleluya, alleluia; ref. Deus Patri sit gloria). BR 3527, comp. c 1450. Rel., carol, epiphany, macaronic.

TM 1627 Ther ys a bodi of a bodi.
L: Harley 2407, early 16, f. 90v. (Also vv. 1–3 only on f .67v, copied in the later 15th century.) 11: abbccddddee4*. BR 3528, comp. a 1500. Alchemy.

TM 1628 Ther ys a chyld borne of a may.
O17: Balliol 354, 1505–36, f. 221v. [By John Audelay.] 18: 2 burd. (aa) + 4 x 4 abab4* (burd. Conditor alme siderum). BR 20, comp. c 1450. Rel., carol, epiphany, macaronic.

TM 1629 Ther ys a saying bothe olde & trewe.
L6: Dyce 45, 2/4 16, ff. 15v–16. Song in praise of mirth. 36: 6 x 6 aaaaBB4* (burd. Nowe will ye be mery & can ye be mery; ref. So shall yow please bothe god & man). BR (3530.5). Carol, conviviality.

Ther is concuposcence gone quighte. Last line of acephalous TM 1397.

TM 1630 Ther is full lytell sikerness.
L: Add. 29729, 1558, ff.127v–9v. "a balade wyche Iohn lydgate...made at the commaundment of the quene Kateryne." 136:17 x 8 MT4* (ref. That nowe is haye som tyme was grasse). BR 3531, comp. a 1437. Moral.

TM 1631 Ther ys leythe reythe And meythe.
C: Ee.4.35, early 16, f. 21. 4: mono3*. BR (3532). Moral.

TM 1632 Ther ys no cure ffor care of mynd.
L: Add. 17492, 1532–39, f. 41. 8: MT4*. Moral.

TM 1633 Ther is no man so myghty but som man may hym dere.
C2: TCC O.2.53 (1157), early 16, f. 29v. 4: aabb5*. BR 3538, comp. c 1475. Moral.

TM 1634 Ther ys sur guy the brybar.
O: Ashmole 1438, early 16, f. 143. "resydants In numarket," written as prose. 6: mono3*. Humor.

TM 1635 There shalbe a whyte bore in England.
O: Arch. Seld. B.8, mid 16, f. 283v. 30: aa4*. Prophecy.

TM 1636 There was never file half so well filed.
L: Egerton 2711, bef. 1542, f. 14v. "Tho[mas Wyatt]," based on Petrarch, *Rime* 258. 14: abbaabbacddcee10. D: TCD 160, 1535–48, f. 174. L: Add. 17492, 1532–39, f. 19v. Variant first line "Was never yet fyle half so well fyled." TP 2094. Love.

TM 1637 There was never nothing more me payned.
L: Egerton 2711, bef. 1542, f. 27r–v. "Tho[mas Wyatt]." 30: 6 x 5 a8b6a8b6C4 (ref. Alas the while). Love.

TM 1638 Ther was the deyn and ye offycyall.
ETON: Eton 98, early 16, lst flyleaf. [Scrap from an English version of Walter Mapes, *Apocalypsis Goliae*]. 5: aa4*. BR (3551). Satire.

TM 1639 Ther wer iii lowely on pyllgrymag wolld goo a.
F: V.a.354, 1/4 16, ff. 111v–2. 4: abbC6* (ref. ... maria). Rel., song, Virgin Mary, Mary Magdalene, Mary of Egypt.

TM 1640 ...Therefor be thyn own frend.
O17: Balliol 354, 1503–04, f. 156v. Acephalous, last line: "And know thy self wysely I rede." 44: 6 x 8 MT4* (ref. And know thy self wysely I rede). BR (3553.5). Moral.

Thes maydyns all, both great & small. See TM 1643.

TM 1641 This prowde Galantis thriftles.
C2: TCC O.2.53 (1157), early 16, f. 27. "Tempore R[ex] E[wardus] iiijth made by prestes agenst Galantes"; answered by TM 2028. 5: aabab3*. BR 4255, comp. c 1475. Rel., satire.

TM 1642 These Scaterand Scottys.
L: Cott. Nero C.11, 1506+, f. 153. Verses by "Inglyshmen In Reprocch of the Scottes" at the siege of Dunbar in 1296, quoted by Robert Fabyan. 6: aabccb2*. HD: Eng 766F, bef. 1516, f. ?. BR 3558.5, comp. 1296; TP 1889.5. Hist., Scotland, satire.

TM 1643 These women all | bothe great and small.
F: V.b.135, mid 16, s. sh. 42: 7 x 6 aa4b6cc4B6 (ref. But I will not say so). Y: Osborn music 13, 1553+, f. 39v. With music; variant first line "Thes maydyns all..." 36 lines. BR (3559.8). Love, complaint, dispraise of women.

TM 1644 They fle from me that sometyme did me seke.
L: Egerton 2711, bef. 1542, f. 26v. "Tho[mas Wyatt.]" 21: 3 x 7 RR10. L: Add. 17492, 1532–39, ff.69v–70v. TP 1894. Love.

TM 1645 Thirti dayes hath novembir.
L: Harley 2341, early 16, f. 3. 4: aabb4*. BR (3571). TP 1905. Mnenomic, calendar, tr. French.

TM 1646 This babe to us now is born.
O17: Balliol 354, 1505–36, f. 227v. 30: 2 burd. (aa) + 4 x 7 ababccC4* (burd. Now syng we right as it is; ref. He asketh nothyng but that is his). BR 3574, comp. a 1450. Rel., carol, nativity.

TM 1647 Thys blessyd babe that thou hast born.
O17: Balliol 354, 1505–36, f. 223. 22: 2 burd. (aa) + 5 x 4 aaaa4* (burd. Mary moder cum and se). BR (3575). Rel., carol, Jesus.

Thys Boke byth whon thing. See TM 1649.

TM 1648 This buik dois perteine.
L: Royal 17 D.20, early 16, ff. 262v–3. Ownership verse by George Barclay, followed by TM 1419. 8: aa4*. BR (3577). Scots.

TM 1649 Thys booke is own thyng and gods curys is another | he that stelys the own thyng I pray god send hem the other.
L: Harley 2320, early 16, f. 72v. 2: aa5*. HN: HM 140, early 16, f. 170v. Variant, begins "Thys Boke byth whon thing". BR 3580, comp. a 1500. Ownership rhyme, moral.

TM 1650 This brevit buke of sober quantite.
L: Arundel 285, c 1540, ff. 47–84. "The contemplacioun of synnars compilit be frer William of Touris," tr. from scriptural and liturgical passages interpersed with Latin prose. 1,560: 195 x 8 MT5*. E: Asloan, 1513–42, ff. 263–90. "Heire ffollowis the contemplaciouns of synnaris applaind for everilk day of the oulk and first for mounday of the blyndand blunder and viciouss wanyte of this warld." 1,552 lines. L: Harley 6919, c 1550, ff. 2–49v. With six illustrations from the printing in STC 5643 (1499). 1,559 lines. BR 3584, comp. 1497–99. Rel. instruction, Scots.

TM 1651 Thys enders nyght | I herd a wyght.
L: Royal App. 58, 1507+, f. 10v. With music. 7: aabccbb2*. BR (3595.6). Rel., complaint of Christ.

TM 1652 This endurs nyght | I sawe a syght.
L: Add. 5465, 1501–04, ff. 50v–53. With music. 40: 4 burd abcb + 6 x 6 aabccb2* (burd. A my dere a my dere son sayd mary). BR 3597, comp. a 1500? Rel., carol, nativity.

TM 1653 Thys enders nyte When staernes shone bryte.
L6: Dyce 45, 2/4 16, ff. 16–19. 12: 2 x 6 aabccb3*. BR (3598.5). Rel., mercy of Christ.

TM 1654 This hardy foole bryd victoryous.
L: Add. 29729, 1558, ff.145v–6v. "given to the King henry [VI] and to his moder the quene Kateryne...vpon the yeares day in the castell of hartford made by lidgate," c 1425. 77: 11 x 7 RR5* (ref. Honour of knighthode conquest and victorye; 2d ref. Helth and welfare Joye and prosperyte). BR 3604, comp. c 1425. Political, hist., presentation verses.

TM 1655 This hidde ston is but on thyng therfore calcyon and putrefie.
O: Ashmole 759, early 16, ff.35v, 68v, 77. 3: abb5*. BR (3605). Alchemy.

TM 1656 This hye feste now for to magnefye.
L: Add. 29729, 1558, ff. 166–8v. "a preseseyon of the feste of corpus cristie made in london by...lydegate." 224: 28 x 8 MT5*. BR 3606, comp. a 1449. Rel., Christ, pageant.

TM 1657 This idlenes in sum of us.
L: Add. 15233, 1554–58, f. 42r–v. "Finis qd John Heywood" 44: 2 burd aa + 6 x 7 RR4* (burd. What hart can thynk or toong expres). Moral, carol.

Thys ys Dorethe Helbartun Boke | And she wyll a pon ym loke. Variant of TM 1659.

This is dorethe helbartun boke | I pray god she may have loyng Apon ym to l[o]ke. Variant of TM 1659.

TM 1658 Thys ys John Hancock ys boke ho so ever saye naye | The devyll of hell bere Thomas carter awaye.
DUR5: Cosin V.iii.9, c 1555, f. 36. Rhyme by Thomas Carter attesting to John Hancock's ownership of the book. 2: aa12. BR (3612.5).

Thys ys meyster wyllyam Bromwelles boke. Variant of TM 552.

TM 1659 Thys ys my mystrys boke, | w[h]o woll A pon yw loke.
HN: HM 136, early 16, f. 52. Ownership rhymes of Dorothy Helbartun. 2: aa4*. Variants in the same MS: "I saye this is my mystrys boke..." (f. 117); "Thys ys Dorethe Helbartun Boke | And she will..." (f. 50); "This is dorothe helbartun boke | I pray god..." (f. 114).

TM 1660 This is the boke off william tucke.
L: Add. 10336, early 16, f. 3v. 4: aa4*. BR (3615). Ownership verse.

TM 1661 Thys [is] the parlament of byrdys.
L: Lansd. 210, 1553–58, ff. 74–8v. "The parlament of byrdes." 304: 76 x 4 aabb4*. BR (3642.5); TP 1908. Debate, parliament, political, nar., allegory.

This is William Patrike book. Variant of TM 552.

[This lovely lady sat and sang]. Variant of TM 24.

TM 1662 Thys myghty wyllyam duke of normandy.
L: Lansd. 762, 1524–29, ff. 10–12. [Lydgate, Kings of England, plus additional stanzas through Henry VII.] 133: 19 x 7 RR5*. L: Lansd. 210, 1553–58, ff. 27–42v. [From William I to Henry VI.] 105 lines. BR 3632, comp. c 1449; TP 1911.5. Nar, hist.

TM 1663 Thys myserable world Indede, this day for to be holde.
O: Ashmole 48, bef. 1558, ff. 51v–4v. Subscribed "q S[pooner]." 64: 16 x 4 abab6*. Moral, evils of the times.

TM 1664 Thys my mystrys boke.
HN: HM 136, early 16, f. 80. Ownership rhyme of "Dorothe Helbartun." 4: abab3*.

TM 1665 This nyght ther is a child born.
O17: Balliol 354, 1505–36, f. 231. 18: 2 burd. (aa) + 4 x 4 aaaB3* (burd. All this tyme this songe is best; ref. Verbum caro factum est). BR 3635, comp. a 1500. Rel., carol, nativity.

TM 1666 This other day | I hard a may.
L: Add. 31922, 1513+, f. 36. With music. 56:2 burd aa + 9 x 6 aa4b6aa4b6 (burd. Hey nony nony nony nony no). BR (3635.5). Carol, nar., love, dialogue, chanson d'aventure.

TM 1667 This picture presentythe to yore rememberance.
SHIP: Shipton-under-Wychwood Church. Verses on a cadaver tomb, memorial to Elizabeth Thame, 1548. 12: ababccddefef5*. Epitaph.

TM 1668 This rotyd gresse will not but growe.
L: Add. 17492, 1532–39, f. 47. Subscribed "T[homas]. H[oward]." (d.Oct 1537). 4: abab8. Complaint.

TM 1669 This silver plate and riche araye.
DUR5: Cosin V.iii.9, c 1555, f. 60. [Nicholas Udall, tr. anon. Greek verses.] 4: abab4*. BR (3639.5); TP 1915. Moral.

TM 1670 This solenne fest to be had in remembraunce.
O: Digby 133, c 1515–25, ff. 146–57. "Candlemesday and the kyllynge of the children of Israelle"; in a later hand "Jhon Parfre ded wryte thys booke." 567: MT4*, RR4*, and irreg. BR 3642, comp. a 1500? Rel. drama, Holy Innocents.

TM 1671 This song endid david did stint his voyce.
L: Egerton 2711, bef. 1542, ff. 90v–91. Wyatt, Penitential Psalms, prologue to Ps 38, tr. from Aretino. 32: 4 x 8 abababcc5*. TP 1916. Rel.

TM 1672 This Sorowfull Deth, which bryngith grete full lowe.
L: Cott. Nero C.11, 1506+, ff. 162–4. Robert Fabyan, tr. "Balade Royall...Nullus In orbe fuit," on the death of Edward I, 1307. 42: 6 RR4*. HD: Eng 766F, bef. 1516, ff. 133–4. TP 1917. Hist., elegy.

This tragedye doth naturally complayn. Extract from TM 556 in *The Proverbs of Lydgate*.

This tragedye gyveth a gret warnynge. Excerpt from TM 556.

TM 1673 Thys vyrgyn clere wythowtyn pere.
L: Royal App. 58, 1547+, ff. 52v–4v. With music, evidently based on TM 24. 66: 6 burd aabccb + 6 x 10 a8b6a8b6cc4b6dd4B6 (burd. Thys enders nyght | I saw a syghth; ref. Baby baby lullay). Rel., lullaby, carol, Virgin Mary.

TM 1674 Thys wynde be reson ys callyd temptacyon.
O: Ashmole 1379, early 16, pp. 32–4. 44: 4 burd (abxb) + 10 x 4 abaB3* (burd. There blows a colde wynde todaye todaye; ref. To kype ye colde wynde a waye). BR (3525). Rel., carol, Jesus.

TM 1675 This word redeme that in his mowght did sownd.
L: Egerton 2711, bef. 1542, f. 97v. Wyatt, Penitential Psalms, prologue to Ps 143, tr. Aretino. 32: 4 x 8 abababcc10. TP 1923. Rel.

TM 1676 This worlde ys but a vanite.
L: Add. 5665, bef. 1511, ff. 49v–50. 18: 2 burd aa + 4 x 4 aaaR4* (burd. O blessed lord full of pete; ref. Mane nobiscum Domine). BR (3652). Carol, mortality.

TM 1677 This world is full of stabellnes.
L: Add. 29729, 1558, ff. 154–5. "a balad made...[by] lidgate...translated out of frenche ['Le monde va en amendaunt']." 56: 7 x 8 MT4*. BR 3655, comp. a 1449. Satire.

TM 1678 This worlde is false [*sic*, for "full"] of variaunce.
L: Harley 7578, early 16, ff.17v–18v. [Lydgate, "Doublenesse."] 103: 7 RR5* + 12 x 8 MT5* (ref. Yet ay be ware of doblenesse). BR 3656, comp. a 1449. Moral.

TM 1679 This world is mutable so seyth sage | Therfor gader in tyme or thou fall to age.
O17: Balliol 354, 1503–04, f. 160. [Printed in STC 17030 (1477?); also appears as vv. 25–26 of TM 221.] 2: aa4*. BR 3656.3+, comp. c 1477; TP 1924.3. Moral, proverb.

TM 1680 This wredched worlde is transmutacion.
O: Arch. Seld. B 10, c 1520, ff. 200v–1v. "paupertas conqueritur super fortunam" [Chaucer, "Fortune" without envoy], included in *The Proverbs of Lydgate* (see TM 556). 72: 9 x 8 MT5* (ref. For fynally fortune I defye; 2d. ref. And eke thou hast thy best frende alyve; 3d ref. In generall this rule may not fayle). BR 3661, comp. c 1390; TP 1924.5. Rel. instruction.

TM 1681 Thomas Beech is my name.
L: Harley 3118, early 16, f. ?. Ownership verse and pen practice. 4:2 x 2 aa4*.

TM 1682 Thomas thomas all hayle sythe.
L: Harley 2252, 1528–38, ff. 158–9v. Satire on Cardinal Wolsey, 1528. 282: 47 x 6 aa4b3cc4b3*. Hist.

TM 1683 Thow dereste disciple of Jhesu Criste.
O17: Balliol 354, 1505–36, ff. 228v–9. (Cf. BR 2443.) 22: 2 burd. (ab) + 5 x 4 aaa4b3* (burd. Pray for us to the Trinite). BR (3669). Rel., carol, St. John Evangelist.

TM 1684 [Thou fers god of armes the Rede].
LONG: Longleat 258, 1500+, ff. 76–84. [Chaucer,] "the complaint of Annelada the quene ayent fals Arcite the Theban knyght"; variant first line "O thou fers god..." 357: 30 x 7 RR5*, 5 x 9 aabaabbab5*. L: Add. 17492, 1532–39, f. 91. Extract on the fickleness of men, vv. 308–18, copied from STC 5068 (1532), begins "For though I had you tomorrow agayne." 9 lines. BR 3670, comp. a 1400; TP 1940.5. Nar., classical, love, complaint.

TM 1685 Thow gracious lord graunt me memory.
C2: TCC O.2.53 (1157), early 16, f. 70. 7: RR4*. BR (3672). Rel., prayer.

TM 1686 Thou hast no faith of him that hath none.
L: Egerton 2711, bef. 1542, f. 16. "Tho[mas Wyatt]." 15: aabbaaab10-C4aabba10C4 (ref. Thou hast no faith). L: Add. 17492, 1532–39, f. 69v. Love.

TM 1687 Thowe haste (O god) repelled us.
L: Royal 17 A.21, 1551, ff. 53v–4v. William Forreste, tr. Ps 59 Deus repulisti. 52: 13 x 4 a8b6a8b6. Rel.

TM 1688 Thou hidd and secret deitye I worshipp and adore.
HN: HM 183, mid 16, f. 11v. Tr. St. Thomas Aquinas, "Confession and honor to the B[lessed] Sacrament," copied on the verso of an inventory dated 1552. 32: aa14. Rel.

TM 1689 Thow man enured with temptacion.
L: Add. 5665, bef. 1511, ff. 70v–1. With music. 6: abbcbc4*. BR (3677.5). Rel. instruction, death.

TM 1690 Thow martiall buke pas to the nobill prince.
PML: M527, 1531–36, ff. 310–13. Johanne Bellantyme [Bellenden] Channon of Ross, "The translator sayis to his buke"; dedication to James V of his

translation of Hector Boece, *Cronikillis of Scotland.* 200: 25 x 8 MT10. C2: TCC O.3.21 (1193), early 16, ff. 24v–7v. "Ane ballate" prefaced to Hector Boece's Chronicle. 208 lines. LONG: Longleat 96, bef. 1544, ff. 29–31v. TP 1945. Hist., prologue, Scots.

TM 1691 Thow schalt haffe on god & ne mo.
C: Ee.4.35, early 16, f. 6. "The x commandements" (plus the creed, etc.). 24: aa4*. L: Sloane 1313, early 16, f. 127r–v. 25 lines. BR 3685, comp. a 1500. Rel. instruction.

TM 1692 Thou slepest ffast & I with woffull hart.
D: TCD 160, 1535–48, f. 167. Leaf damaged. 8: abababcc10. Love.

TM 1693 Thow that in prayeris hes bene lent.
L: Arundel 285, c. 1540, ff.175v–6v. "Off the Resurrectioun." 40: 5 x 8 MT4* (ref. The Lord is rissin fra deth to life). BR (3695). Rel., hymn, Scots.

TM 1694 Thow achylles in batayl me slow.
O: Tanner 407, 1/4 16, f. 32v. "ix Wurthy." 18: aa3*. BR (3666). Hist., nine worthies.

TM 1695 Thoghe dyverse men be of that mynde.
L: Add. 33974, c 1550, ff. 56v–7. (Francis Stacy), "Of virgynyte and chastytie." 52: 13 x 4 abab4*. Rel. instruction.

TM 1696 Thowcht fenyeit fables of auld poetry.
E2: Laing 149 , 1/4 16, ii verso to iii. [Robert Henryson, *Fables*, Prologue and first fable, "The Cock and the Jewel"; see also TM 70.] 161: 23 x 7 RR10. BR 3703, comp. a 1500. Nar., moral, Scots.

TM 1697 Thoghe first of faythe we learne to feare what force this feare dothe bring.
L: Add. 33974, c 1550, ff. 6v–7. (Francis Stacy), "Of the <feare of god>." 32: aa7*. Rel. instruction.

TM 1698 Thowghe I Be Bonde yette am I ffree.
L: Harley 2252, 1517–38, f. 133*. 24: 6 x 4 abab8. BR (3703.3). Love, riddle.

TM 1699 Tho I be woe yt ys no wonder.
Y: Osborn music 13, 1553+, ff. 46v–7. With music. 54: 9 x 6 aaabab9. Love, lament, song.

TM 1700 Tho I cannot yor crueltie constrain.
L: Egerton 2711, bef. 1542, f. 38v. "Tho[mas Wyatt]." 20: 4 x 5 aa10bb8A6 (ref. Rew upon my pain). L: Add. 17492, 1532–39, f. 37v. Love.

TM 1701 Thofe I doo syng my hert dothe wepe.
L: Royal App. 58, 1507+, ff. 18v–19. With music. 14: 2 x 7 RR8. BR (3703.5). Song, love.

TM 1702 Though I me self be bridilled of my mynde.
L: Egerton 2711, bef. 1542, f. 21. "Tho[mas Wyatt]," tr. Petrarch, *Rime* 98. 14: abbaabbacddcee10. Love.

TM 1703 Tho i seyme ded unto the daslynge Iy.
D: TCD 160, 1535–48, f. 177. "B. G." [George Blage], "A remembrance of the dethe of...Quene Kateryne [Parr]," d. 1548. 28: 7 x 4 abab5*. Hist., elegy.

TM 1704 Tho of the sort ther be that ffayne.
D: TCD 160, 1535–48, f. 169. 28: 4 x 7 ababcc8R4 (ref. Then have I wronge). Moral, complaint.

TM 1705 Thought peper be blake | It hathe a gud smake.
L: Egerton 3537, c 1554, f. 58v. Tr. of "Tametsi peper nigri coloris sit bun sapit." 2: aa3*. O17: Balliol 354, 1505–36, f.191v, 200. Tr. "Est piper nigrum..." (copied twice). 2: aa2*. BR 3706.2, comp. a 1500. Proverb.

TM 1706 Tho some do grodge to se me Joye.
D: TCD 160, 1535–48, f. 168. 32: 4 x 8 ababccdd8. Love.

TM 1707 Though sum saith that youngh rulyth me.
L: Add. 31922, 1513+, ff. 71v–3. With music (attributed to Henry VIII). 38: 8 x 5 a4b3a4b3A4* (ref. Thow sum say that yough rulyth me). BR (3706.5). Song, youth.

TM 1708 Thow that men do call it dotage.
L: Add. 31922, 1513+, ff. 55v–6. With music by "The Kyng h.VIII." 20: aa4*. BR (3706.7). Song, love.

TM 1709 Though that she can not redresse.
L: Royal App. 58, 1507+, f. 1v. With music. 24: 6 x 4 a4b3a4b3*. BR (3706.8). Song, love.

TM 1710 [Though that thy power stretcheth bothe ferre and large].
L: Royal 9 C.ii, 1531+, f. 124v. [Vv.13–14 of Sir Thomas Elyot, tr. Claudian, De IV cons. Hon., 257–302] copied by Thomas Lower; begins "If Luste or anger de thy mynde assayle." 2: [RR4*]. BR (1421); TP 1974. Moral.

TM 1711 Though this thye port and I thy servaunt true.
L: Egerton 2711, bef. 1542, ff. 53v–4. [Wyatt.] 28: 4 x 7 RR10 (ref. ...en vogant la galere). D: TCD 160, 1535–48, f. 171. Love.

Though thou depart now thus me fro. Stanza 2 of TM 403.

TM 1712 Though thow take much payne.
C7: Corpus Christi 106, 1540–58, pp. 315–18. "Jack of the North, beyond the stile." 56: 7 x 8 aaabcccb3*. Social criticism, satire, enclosures.

TM 1713 Thoughe weddynge go be destenye.
O: Ashmole 48, bef. 1558, ff. 47v–9. Subscribed "T. S. P." 188: aa4*. Women, praise of a lady.

TM 1714 Though ye my love were a ladye fayr.
O: Ashmole 176, pt. 3, 2/4 16, f. 99. 16: 4 burd (aaaa) + 3 x 4 abaB8 (burd. Lost ys my love farewell adewe; ref. Nay my love nay farewell adewe). BR (3707.3). Love, carol.

TM 1715 Thrice fifti ances [aves?] make or ladi psalter | at every tenth one a pater noster.
L: Ptd. book C.35.a.4, mid 16, sig. A8v. 2: aa5*. Rel. instruction.

TM 1716 Throughe a forest as I can ryde.
O: Rawl. C.813, 1520–35, ff. 56v–7v. 68: abaB4*, ababcdcD4*, ababbcbC4* (ref. therfore the crowe shall byte yow; 2d ref. for now the pye hath pechyd yow). BR (3713.5). Love, pastourelle.

TM 1717 Thorow a forest that was so longe.
O17: Balliol 354, 1505–36, f. 231. 26: 2 burd. (aa) + 6 x 4 abaB4* (burd. Man be ware & wise in dede; ref. Assay a frend or thou have nede). BR 3820, comp. a 1500. Carol, moral, friendship.

TM 1718 Thorugh glad aspectis of the god cupyde.
L: Add. 29729, 1558, ff. 157v–60. "a balade by lydgate...at the reuerence of my lady of holand and my lord of glousester to fore the daye of there maryage." 197: 27 x 7 RR4* + 8 MT4*. BR 3718, comp. a 1449. Hist.

TM 1719 Thorow owt a pales as I can passe.
O17: Balliol 354, 1503–04, ff. 169v–70v. "The lamentacion of the duches of Glossester," c 1440. 104: 13 x 8 MT4* (ref. All women may beware by me). BR 3720, comp. a 1500. Hist. 1440's, lament.

TM 1720 <...> thus hath mayd my payne | have the moved thoghe I do complayne.
NY: Drexel 4181, 2/4 16, f. 1. Fragment, last two lines only, with music. 2: aa4*. BR (3721.5). Song, love.

TM 1721 Thus y compleyne my grevous hevynesse.
O: Ashmole 191, pt. 4, early 16, ff. 193v–4. With music. 6: ababcc4*. BR (3722). Love, song.

TM 1722 Thus lyvethe the deade that whilome lived here.
L: Harley 78, mid 16, f. 15. "Sir Antonie Sentlenger [St. Leger] of Sir T. W[yatt]." 7: RR10. TP 1055. Elegy.

TM 1723 Thus me to cummande | to wryght wyth my left hande.
F: V.a.354, 1/4 16, ff. 98v, 114v. Written backwards 2: aa3*. Pen practice.

TM 1724 Thus musyng In my mynde gretly marvelyng.
L: Add. 5465, 1501–04, ff. 24v–6. With music by William Newark. 8: MT4*. C14: Fitzwilliam Music 784, early 16, s. sh. verso. Acephalous text beginning "Hope to fynd a specyll remedy," with setting by Newark, 2 vv. only. NY: Drexel 4183, 2/4 16, f. 1v. Acephalous fragment, with music, last two lines only, beginning "As solen as so pretty." BR (3724.5). Song, love, women.

TM 1725 Thy promese was to love me best.
L: Add. 17492, 1532–39, f. 40. 24: 6 x 4 aaaB8 (ref. Thy promese was thy promese was). Love.

TM 1726 Tydyngis trewe, ther be com newe.
O17: Balliol 354, 1505–36, f. 229v. 30: 2 burd. (aa) + 7 x 4 aaaa6* (burd. Nowell nowell). BR 3736, comp. c 1475. Rel., carol, annunciation.

TM 1727 Tydynges trew tolde ther ys trewe.
L: Add. 5665, bef. 1511, ff. 33v–4. With music. 11: 3 burd (aaa) + 2 x 4 aaa4A3* (burd. Tydynges trew ther buthe come new; ref. Blessed be Jesu). BR (3737). Rel., carol, nativity.

TM 1728 To all folkys vertuowse.
L: Add. 29729, 1558, ff. 184–286v. Lydgate, *Reason and Sensuality*. 7,042: aa4*. BR 3746, comp. a 1449. Nar., vision, allegory, chess.

TM 1729 To calle theim Whiche have no suffisance.
L: Harley 7578, early 16, ff. 2–3v. [Prologue to the *Summum Sapientie*]. 126: 18 x 7 RR4*. BR (3749). Moral instruction.

TM 1730 To Calvery he bare his cross with doullfull payne.
L: Add. 5465, 1501–04, ff. 77v–82. subscribed "Gilbert Banastir"; with music. 46: 2 burd aa + 4 x 11 aaaa6bbb3acca4* (burd. Me thought a maydynly childe causeless). BR (3750). Rel., carol, crucifixion.

TM 1731 To cause accord or to aggre.
L: Egerton 2711, bef. 1542, f. 53. "Tho[mas Wyatt]." 25: 5 x 5 aaaa8B6 (ref. It is impossible). L: Add. 17492, 1532–39, f. 69. Love.

TM 1732 To chaunge councell and promys alsso.
L: Sloane 1207, mid 16, f. 12v. 3: mono4*. Moral.

To Crystis own derlyng. See TM 1753.

TM 1733 To complayne me alas why shulde I so.
L: Add. 5465, 1501–04, ff. 15v–17. With music by T. Fairfax. 7: RR4*. BR (3751.3). Song, love.

TM 1734 To countarffete a mery mode.
L: Add. 17492, 1532–39, f. 65v. 7: abaacac8. Moral.

TM 1735 To declare the powres and the strenght [rev. their force] to enlarge.
HN: HM 3, 1538, 1546–58, ff. 1–35. [John Bale], *Kyng Johan.* 1,814 lines (c 1538) revised to 2,691 (in 1558–60). 2,691: aa4–6*, RR5*. Drama, hist., allegory, rel. controversy.

TM 1736 To doo good for good is found in every place.
O: Ptd. book Mason H 169, mid 16, f. i verso. 4: aa5*. Moral.

TM 1737 To God For all his Benefites who render thankes eche one.
CU: Plimpton 276, 1554, f. 17v. William Somers. 2: poulters. Rel., prayer.

TM 1738 To hym and of his foolish tendirnesse | Why maketh thou all this wo and hevynes.
DUR5: Cosin V.iii.9, c 1555, f. 84. 2: aa5*. Moral.

To hys lady he cam full courteyslye. Stanzas 25–96 of TM 517.

TM 1739 To joye in payne my will.
L: Add. 17492, 1532–39, f. 44v. 20: 4 burd abab + 4 x 4 abab3*, irreg. (burd. Althought my payne be greater). Love, carol.

To Judge the trewthe as befor it hath been. Rhymed title of TM 43.

TM 1740 To loughe to smyll to sporte to play.
L: Add. 18752, 1530's, f. 76. 24: 6 x 4 aaa4b2*. Love, praise of mistress.

TM 1741 To let a scape be it no blame | for Lords and Ladies doe the same.
L: Ptd. book 6190.a18, 1538+, sig.?. Signed "James Colbrond." 2: aa8. Moral.

TM 1742 To Luf allone | comfort is non.
L: Royal App. 58, 1507+, f. 10. With music. 30: 5 x 6 aa2b3cc2b3*. BR (3758.5). Song, love.

TM 1743 To make an ende of all this strif.
L: Add. 17492, 1532–39, f. 83r–v. 35: 5 x 7 ababcb8c4. Love.

TM 1744 To men that knows ye not.
L: Add. 17492, 1532–39, f. 60. [Attributed elsewhere to Edmund Knevet.] 24: 3 x 8 ababcdcd6. Love.

TM 1745 To my meshap alas y ffynd.
L: Add. 17492, 1532–39, f. 42r–v. 35: 5 x 7 abababab8C4 (ref. So oftyn warned.). D: TCD 160, 1535–48, f. 172. TP 2028. Moral.

TM 1746 To ples or dysples suer I am.
L: Royal 7.C.ix, 2/4 16, f. 192. Signed "Io Symond goldsmith." 4: aa4*. TP 2031. Moral.

TM 1747 To prove & passe the panges of love.
Y: Osborn music 13, 1553+, ff. 38v–9. With music, subscribed "T. C." (probably composer). 56: 7 x 8 abaabcd8D6 (ref. To love so fervently). Song, love, lament.

TM 1748 To rayle or geste ye kno I use yt not.
L: Add. 17492, 1532–39, f. 75r–v. 14: abbaabbacddcee10. Love.

TM 1749 To seke eche where: where man doth lyve.
L: Egerton 2711, bef. 1542, f. 59. "Tho[mas Wyatt]." 24: 4 x 6 aaba8bB10 (ref. dare I well say than that I gyve to yere). Love.

TM 1750 To seek the way all parties to pleas.
L: Royal 12.E.xvi, mid 16, f. 42. 4: a4b3a4b3*. BR (3767.5). Rel. instruction.

TM 1751 To the blak draw thy knyf | With the brown led thy lyf.
L: Harley 3362, early 16, f. 17. Tr. "Cum fusco stabis cum nigro tela parabis." 2: aa2*. BR (3769.5). Proverb.

TM 1752 To the honour of god oon, in persones thre.
O: e Musaeo 63, early 16, ff. 2–40. "Prohemium liber T[homas]. N[orton]. qui intitulatur ordinale secretorum (*The Ordinal of Alchemy*, prologue and seven chapters). 2,600: aa5*. L: Sloane 1873, 2/4 16, ff. 4–84. 2,994: aa5*. E2: Laing III.164, early 16, pp. 129–35. Partial text. 178: aa5*. BR 3772, comp. c 1477. Alchemy.

TM 1753 To the now crists derlyng.
L: Add. 5665, bef. 1511, ff. 37v–8, also 48v. With music. 18: 2 burd (aa) + 4 x 4 aaaB4* (burd. Pray for us thow prince of pesse; ref. Amice Christi Johannes). L: Harley 4294, early 16, f. 81v. Begins "I shall you tell of Cristes derlyng." (burd. Pray we all to the Prynce of Pece). O17: Balliol 354, 1505–36, f. 222. Begins "To Crystis own derlyng." (burd. Pray for us to the prince of peace). BR 3776, comp. a 1450. Rel., carol, St. John Evangelist.

TM 1754 To thee o Lorde I crie and call and my voice I do exalte.
L: Royal 17.A.17, 1551+, ff. 2v–3v. Sir Thomas Smith, tr. "Psalme 152" [142]. 36 lines as 18: a4b3a4b3*. Rel.

TM 1755 To thee (O lorde) I will geeve thanks.
L: Royal 17.A.21, 1551, ff. 9v–11. William Forreste, tr. Ps 8 Domine dominus. 172: 43 x 4 a8b6a8b6. Rel.

TM 1756 To thee O lorde I will geeve thankes.
L: Royal 17.A.21, 1551, ff. 11–15. William Forreste, tr. Ps 9 Confitibar. 170: 42 x 4 a8b6a8b6. Rel.

TM 1757 To the O marcifull salviour myn Jesus.
L: Arundel 285, c 1540, ff. 1–4v. "The tabill of confessioun compilit be Mr William Dunbar." 168: 21 MT4* (ref. I cry the marcy and laser to repent). BR (3776.5). Rel., confession, Scots.

TM 1758 To thame that luffis the in cleynnes.
L: Arundel 285, c 1540, ff. 85–93. "OIS" [The Fifteen O's]. 326: aa4*. BR (3777.5). Rel., prayer, Scots.

To thinke Apon the daies olde. See TM 1279.

TM 1759 To thy frende thowe lovest moste.
L: Lansd. 762, 1524–29, f. 92. 6: aa7b5aa7b5. BR (3780). Moral.

TM 1760 To onpreyse women yt were a shame.
L: Harley 4294, early 16, f. 81. 14: 2 burd (aa) + 3 x 4 aaaB4* (burd. I am as lyght as any roe; ref. and yet she hath but care and woo). BR (3782). Carol, defense of women.

To veri god & to alle trewe in Crist. C: Ff.6.2, ff. 71–80. *Jack Upland*, BR 3782.5, but not verse.

TM 1761 To wette your Iye withouten teare.
L: Add. 17492, 1532–39, f. 5. 16: 2 x 8 abababcc8. D: TCD 160, 1535–48, f. 170. Love.

TM 1762 To wisshe and want and not obtain.
L: Egerton 2711, bef. 1542, f. 39r–v. "Tho[mas Wyatt]." 36: 9 x 4 aaa8B6 (ref. What may it availl me). L: Add. 17492, 1532–39, f. 71v. Love.

TM 1763 To Whyshe the best and fere the worst are to pointes of the Wyse | To suffer then Whatt happen shall That man is happe thryese.
F: book, STC 12721, 1551, sig. R8. Entered by Mary Sidney. 2: aa7*. Moral.

TM 1764 To yow mastres whyche have belonge.
O: Rawl. C.813, 1520–35, f. 62r–v. 56: 7 x 8 MT8 (ref. Wher many dogges be att on bone). BR (3785.5). Love, epistle.

TM 1765 To yowr gentyll letters an answere to resyte.
L: Add. 17492, 1532–39, f. 29. Subscribed "T. H." (?Thomas Howard, d. Oct. 1537). 28: 4 x 7 RR4*. Love, letter.

TM 1766 Tonge breketh bon | wher bon he hathe non.
O17: Balliol 354, 1505–36, f. 200v. Tr. "Ossa terit glossa..." 2: aa2*. BR 3792.5, comp. a 1500?; TP 2053. Proverb.

To aventurous to amerous me anger the not to moche. Variant of TM 1767.

TM 1767 To amerous to avunterus.
O: Lat. misc. c.66, c 1500, f. 26v. [The ABC of Aristotle]. 42: allit. L: Add. 60577, 1549–58, f. 56v. Preceded by TM 312 as a title verse. 23: allit. C2: TCC O.2.53 (1157), early 16, f. 69v. Variant beginning "To aventurous to amerous me anger the not to moche." 22: aa5*. BR 3793, comp. c 1450. Moral, ABC, proverbs.

TM 1768 To dere is bowght the doblenes.
L: Add. 17492, 1532–39, f. 59v. 8: MT8. Love.

TM 1769 To[o] derely had I bought my grene and yowthfull yeres.
Y: Osborn music 13, 1553+, f. 36. [Henry Howard, Earl of Surrey] with music. 16: poulters. TP 2054. Love.

TM 1770 To hasty of sentence.
O: Rawl. C. 813, 1520–35, f. 36. [Skelton, a carol prefaced to TM 417.] 24: 2 burd aa + 22 skeltonics (burd. All noble men of this take hede.). BR (194.5); TP 2055. Moral, carol.

TM 1771 Tote abowt and take good Hede.
L11: PRO SP 1/220, 1546, f. 64. Richard Laynam, 9 June 1546, confessed "he hathe redde or seen" this poem. 22: aa4* + 14 Latin vv. Prophecy.

TM 1772 Towarde the ende of ffrosty Ianvarye.
O: Arch. Seld. B.10, c 1520, ff. 206v–9v. "Lenvoy" to "The prouerbes of Lydgate" (see TM 556), transcribed from STC 17026 [1510?]. 216: 27 x 8 MT5* (ref. Lok in thi myrrour and deme non other wight). BR 3798, comp. a 1449; TP 2056.3. Moral.

TM 1773 Towarde the ende off wyndy Februarie.
L: Cott. Cleopatra C.4, early to mid 16, f. 38. Verses by Lydgate for King Henry VI's entry into London (1432). 533: 75 x 7 RR5* + 8 MT5*. LONG: Longleat 53, early 16, ff. 83–5v. "The Ordenaunces made in the Cittee of London Agaynste the Commyng of the kyng [Henry VI] ffrom his Cronacion oute of ffraunce" (incomplete). 156 lines. L8: Guildhall 3313, c 1510, ff.132v–42. "The ordenaunces made in the Cite of London a yenst the comyng of the kyng from his coronacion oute of Fraunce." 532 lines. L: Cott. Nero C.11, 1506+, ff. 386v–9v. Extracts (TP 2056.5) quoted by Robert Fabyan, beginning "All thoo that been Enemyes to the Kyng." 98 lines. HD: Eng 766F, 1504, ff. 357v–60v. Extracts (TP 2056.5) quoted by Robert Fabyan, beginning "All thoo that been Enemyes to the Kyng." 110: 14 x 7 RR5*, 12 abbaabaabbaa5*. BR 3799, comp. 1432; TP 2056.5. Hist., pageant.

TM 1774 Trolly lolly loly lo.
L: Add. 31922, 1513+, ff. 43v–4. With music by William Cornyshe. 5: aabaa4*. BR (3800.5). Song, love.

TM 1775 Trew love to me yn harte soo dere.
O: Rawl. C. 813, 1520–35, f. 33. 12: 3 x 4 abab8. BR (3804). Love, epistle.

TM 1776 Trusty seldom to their ffrendys unjust.
C15: Pembroke 307, mid 16, f. 197v. 7: RR4*. BR (3809). Punctuation poem, satire against clergy.

TM 1777 Truthe withe the towchestonne triethe eche thinge we dayly see.
L: Cott. Titus A.24, mid 16, ff. 83v–5. "finis R[ichard]. E[dwardes]." 32: poulters. Defense of women.

TM 1778 Twoe men came riding over Hackney hay.
L: Cott. Titus D.12, mid 16, f. 93v. Prophecy of dissolution of Reves Abbey in Yorkshire. 4: mono4*. BR (3815.8).

TM 1779 Too wyffes in one howse.
L: Ptd. book IB.49437, early 16, f. 1. 4: aa2*. C7: Corpus Christi 379, 1534+, f. 17v. Variant, begins "ii Wyfes and one howse." L: Lansd. 762, 1524–29, f. 16v. Variant, begins "Two women in one house." BR 3818, comp. a 1489; TP 2069.5. Moral, women, proverb.

Two wymen in one howse. Variant of TM 1779.

TM 1780 Under this stone ther lyethe at rest.
L: Harley 78, mid 16, f. 28v. "An Epitaphe of Sir Thomas Grauener [i.e., Grosvener] knyght" (d. c 1550). 18: 3 x 4 abab4* + 6 ababcc4*. Epitaph.

TM 1781 Under nethe a lovere.
L: Add. 60577, 1549–58, f. 76v. Tr. "Sub lodio plumabam..." 6: aaaabb3*. Love, proverb.

TM 1782 Unkynd man take hede of mee.
L: Harley 4012, c 1505, f. 94r–v. 14: aa4*. BR 3827, comp. a 1500. Rel., monologue of Christ.

TM 1783 Unstable dreme according to the place.
L: Egerton 2711, bef. 1542, f. 54. [Wyatt, tr. of Filosseno, "Pareami in questa nocte."] 14: abbaabbacddcee10. TP 2076. Love, lament.

TM 1784 Unto the lorde, wheare he dothe sytt.
L: Royal 17.A.21, 1551, ff. 68–9. William Forreste, tr. Ps 95 Cantate domino. 56: 14 x 4 a8b6a8b6. Rel.

TM 1785 Up y Arose in verno tempore.
L: Add. 5665, bef. 1511, ff. 145v–6. With music. 16: 4 x 4 aaaa4*. O: Ashmole 176, pt. 3, 2/4 16, f. 98v. BR (3832.5). Song, nar., love, macaronic.

TM 1786 Upon a lady fayre & bright.
O17: Balliol 354, 1503–04, f. 178. 18: 2 burd. (aa) + 4 x 4 abaB4* (burd. Newell newell newell newell; ref. ...I thynk and say right nowght). BR (3835). Rel., carol, Virgin Mary.

TM 1787 Apon a mornyng of May.
L: Harley 1317, early 16, f. 94v. With music. 22: 4 burd (abab) + 3 x 6 aa2b3cc2b3* (burd. Wep no more for me swet hart). BR (3836.5). Carol, love, chanson d'aventure.

Opon a tyme when Ser John Mandevelle. See TM 1418.

TM 1788 Upon the crosse nayled I was for the.
L: Add. 29729, 1558, f. 131r–v. "By lydgate"; cf. TM 1789. 40: 5 x 8 MT5*. BR 3845, comp. a 1449. Rel., monologue of Christ.

TM 1789 Upon the cross nailed I was for the.
L: Add. 5465, 1501–04, ff. 67v–73. Based on TM 1788, music (and possibly

burden) by Sheryngam. 50: 10 burd (abbccdddda) + 5 x 8 MT5* (burd. A gentill Jhesu; ref. Whi art thou froward syth I am mercyable). Rel., carol, monologue of Christ.

TM 1790 Opon the good daye have thou in mind | The unware woe that may Come behind.
F: Ptd. book STC 12721, 1551, sig. 3K7v. Entered by Henry Sidney. 2: aa4*. Moral.

TM 1791 Upon <the hipocrysye?> of the Cruell C[ler]gy.
L: Lansd. 794, 1533+, ff. 2–155. "Thus endith this boke called the Image of ypocresye." [comp. 1533]. 2,576: skeltonics + 8 x 4 abab3*. Rel. controversy, protestant.

TM 1792 Utter thy language wyth good avisement.
O: Rawl. C.86, early 16, f. 31. 7: RR4*. BR (3847). Moral.

TM 1793 Vayne is the fleting welth.
L11: PRO SP 1/246, mid 16, ff. 18v–9. With music by W. persons. 20: poulters. TP 2085. Song, moral.

TM 1794 Venemus thornes that ar so sharp & kene.
L: Egerton 2711, bef. 1542, f. 50. "Tho[mas Wyatt]," tr. Serafino, "Ogni pungente et venenosa spina." 8: abababcc10. L: Add. 17492, 1532–39, f. 72v. L: Harley 78, mid 16, f. 27. "Sir T. W." TP 2086. Moral.

TM 1795 Venus in sport to plese ther with her dere.
D: TCD 160, 1535–48, f. 184. 8: abababcc10. Love, bawdy, myth.

TM 1796 Vices be wyld & vertues lame.
O17: Balliol 354, 1505–36, f. 227. 26: 2 burd. (aa) + 6 x 4 aaab8 (burd. God that sitteth in trinite). BR 3852. comp. a 1500. Carol, moral.

Vertue of vertues O noble pacience. Extract from TM 556 in *The Proverbs of Lydgate*.

TM 1797 Vulcan begatt me, menerva me taughte.
L: Harley 78, mid 16, f. 29v. "A Ridell. Tho. W[yatt]....latine ex Pandulpho." [Answer = gun.] 8: abababcc10. TP 2090.

TM 1798 Walkyng alone Ryhgt secretly.
L: Add. 15233, 1554–58, ff. 52v–3v. "Jhon Redforde." 81: 18 aa4* + 9 x 7 RR4* (ref. Why thankes not me thy maker than). L11: PRO SP 1/246, mid 16, f. 23. Incipit only, with music. Rel., song, monologue of Christ.

TM 1799 Was I never yet, of yor love greved.
L: Egerton 2711, bef. 1542, f. 11. Wyatt, tr. Petrarch, *Rime* 82. 14: abbaabbacddcee10. TP 2335. Love.

Was never yet file half wo well filed. See TM 1636.

TM 1800 Water ffrosen Caymes brother | so hight my leman and no other.
O17: Balliol 354, 1505–36, f. 219. 2: aa4*. Riddle (answer = Isabel); cf. BR 597.5.

TM 1801 Wavering & wandering ar womens witts.
L11: PRO SP 1/246, mid 16, ff. 27v–8. With music. 4: abab4*. Song, women.

TM 1802 We be maydins fayr and fre.
NY: Drexel 4184, 2/4 16, f. 1 (Quintus), Drexel 4185, 2/4 16, f. 1r–v (Sextus). Fragment reconstructed from TP 2095.5. 18: 2 burd (aa) + 4 x 4 aaa4b3* (burd. The bella the bella). BR (3863.5); TP 2095.5. Love, carol, bawdy.

TM 1803 We can have no more of the fox but the skyne | and the fox thynketh that too moughe we wyne.
L: Harley 1304, early 16, f. 103. [John Heywood, Epig. 3.19] 2: aa4*. TP 2098. Epigram, humorous.

TM 1804 We Englisshemen beholde lorde.
L2: Lambeth 159, c 1520, ff. 261–3v. "Now a Dayes." 280: 35 x 8 aaabcccb6. Satire, social criticism, ballad.

TM 1805 We nede so Bloudy Sacryfyce Christ once ffor all was slayne.
CU: Plimpton 276, c 1554, ff. 4, 5. 16: poulters. Rel. controversy, against the Real Presence.

TM 1806 Wee will geve thankys to thee (O lorde).
L: Royal 17 A.21, 1551, ff. 61v–2v. William Forreste, tr. Ps 74 Confitebimus. 40: 10 x 4 a8b6a8b6. Rel.

TM 1807 Wedde me Robyn and brynge me home | have I owght have I nowght thain I am a dame.
L: Add. 60577, 1549–58, f. 76. Tr. "Tibi nubam Roberte ut me ducas domum..." 2: aa4*. Epigram, marriage.

TM 1808 Welcum ffortune wellcum agayne.
L: Add. 18752, 1530's, f. 88. 24: 6 x 4 abab4*. BR (3880.6). Love.

TM 1809 Well ys the man that Dothe bestowe.
L: Add. 15233, 1554–58, f. 55r–v. "John Thorne." 42: 2 burd aa + 7 x 6 ababcc8 (burd. In Wordlye Welthe for mans releafe). Carol, moral.

TM 1810 Well on my way as I forth wente.
L: Lansd. 762, 1524–29, ff. 75–88. "Explicias proficiae venerabilis bede Marlionis Thome Asslaydon [i.e., Erceldoune] et al." 590: 74 x 8 abababab4*, irreg. O: Rawl. C.813, c 1535, ff. 72v–88. "A prophesye." 615 lines. BR (3889.5). Prophecy, hist., Henry VIII.

TM 1811 Westron wynde when wyll thow blow.
L: Royal App. 58, 1507+, f. 3. With music. 4: a4b3c4b3*. BR (3899.3). [Title "The Western wind" appears with music, but no text, in L: Add. 17802–5, ff. 25v–46.] Song, love.

TM 1812 Quhat aylt ye men to ved a vyf.
E: Gaelic 37, early 16, p. 48. 8: aa8. Lament, sorrows of marriage, Scots.

TM 1813 Whate can hyt avayle | To dryve forth a snayle.
L: Harley 2252, 1519–38, ff. 147–53. "Sceltonyus lawreatus" (John Skelton, *Colin Clout*, comp. 1522–23; lacks vv. 431–58, 479–556 in John Scattergood ed. (1983), but includes Latin epilogue not in TP 2114). 1,160: skeltonics. L: Lansd. 762, 1524–29, f. 71. "The profecy of Skelton," extract, vv. 462–80, begins "Some men thynke that ye." 17 lines. BR (3903.5), TP 2114. Satire, moral.

TM 1814 What causyth me wofull thoughtis to thynk.
L: Add. 5465, 1501–04, ff. 4v–6. With music by William Newark. 7: RR4*. BR (3903.8). Song, complaint.

TM 1815 What dames by faythe and love have wone.
D: TCD 160, 1535–48, f. 94v. 8: aa14. Praise of women.

TM 1816 What deth is worse then this.
L: Egerton 2711, bef. 1542, f. 42. "Tho[mas Wyatt]." 24: 4 x 6 a6b4a6bb4a6. L: Add. 17492, 1532–39, ff. 39v, 74v. Love, lament.

TM 1817 Quhat dollour persit our Ladyis hert.
L: Arundel 285, c 1540, ff. 141v–2. "The houris of oure Ladyis dollouris." 36: 9 x 4 abab4*. BR (3904). Rel., nar., crucifixion, Scots.

TM 1818 What happynes here can any procure.
L: Add. 33974, c 1550, f. 11. (Francis Stacy), "No happynes in this lyfe." 22: aa4*. Rel. instruction.

TM 1819 What helpythe hope of happy hape.
L: Add. 17492, 1532–39, ff. 46v–7. 42: 6 x 7 RR8. Love.

TM 1820 What helpith it man to be unstable.
C2: TCC O.2.53 (1157), early 16, f. 73v. 7: RR4*. BR (3905). Moral.

TM 1821 What man thou servyst all wey hym drede.
O: Rawl. C. 86, early 16, f. 31. 4: abab4*. Moral.

TM 1822 What manere of Ivell thou be.
L: Sloane 747, bef. 1506, f. 57. A charm against fever. 18: aa4*. BR (3911). Medical.

TM 1823 What meane thei thus to fret and fume.
L: Royal 17.A.17, 1551+, f. 24r–v. Sir Thomas Smith, tr. "Collectes or Prayers" (liturgical passages). 24: 6 x 4 a4b3a4b3*. Rel., prayer.

TM 1824 What menythe thys when I lye alone.
L: Add. 17492, 1532–39, ff. 12v–13. "Wyatt." 32: 8 x 4 aaa8B4 (ref. What menys thys). Love, lament.

TM 1825 What more poyson than ys venome.
L: Harley 43, early 16, f. 92r–v. "A balade of trouthe" (incomplete at end). 42: 6 x 7 RR4*. Moral.

TM 1826 What natures woork ys this in one wyghtes co<rpse to hide>.
D: TCD 160, 1535–48, f. 186. "J[ohn]. C[heke]." 30: blank12. Praise of a poet.

TM 1827 What nedythe lyff when I requyer.
L: Add. 17492, 1532–39, ff. 43v–4. 36: 6 x 6 ababcc8. Love.

TM 1828 What nedeth these threning wordes & wasted wynde.
L: Egerton 2711, bef. 1542, f. 33. "Tho[mas Wyatt]," tr. Serafino, "A che minacci." 8: abababcc10. TP 2126. Love.

TM 1829 What no perdy ye may be sure.
L: Egerton 2711, bef. 1542, f. 31v. "Tho[mas Wyatt]." 15: aabb-aaab10C4aabba10C4 (ref. What no perdy). L: Add. 17492, 1532–39, f. 19. Love.

Whate prophytis plente and grete tresure. Lines 29–30 of TM 221.

TM 1830 What rage is this what furour of <excesse> what kynd.
L: Egerton 2711, bef. 1542, f. 69v. Wyatt (autograph). 20: 5 x 4 aaa10b6. TP 2131. Love.

TM 1831 What shulde I saye.
L: Add. 17492, 1532–39, f. 77. 28: 4 x 7 RR4. Love.

TM 1832 What schulde physyke but yf sikenes were.
L: Add. 60577, 1549–58, ff. 44v–5. 14: 2 x 7 RR4*. Moral.

TM 1833 What shulde these clothes thus many folde.
L: Harley 7578, early 16, f. 20. Chaucer [first of his Riddles]. 8: 2 x 4 abab8. BR 3914, comp. a 1500.

TM 1834 What thynge is that that I bothe have and lacke.
L: Harley 78, mid 16, f. 29v. "Ridle" (answered by TM 957). 7: RR10. TP 2136. Riddle, love.

TM 1835 What thing restethe not now and then amonge | but still travailleth cannot endure longe.
DUR5: Cosin V.iii.9, c 1555, f. 57v. [Nicholas Udall, tr. Ovid "Quod caret alterna," as quoted by Erasmus, *Apophthegms*.] 2: aa5*. BR (3917.5); TP 2137. Moral.

TM 1836 What thyng shold cawse me to be sad.
L: Add. 17492, 1532–39, f. 27. [?by Lord Thomas Howard, d. Oct. 1537]. 28: 4 x 7 RR8. Love.

TM 1837 Whatt tyme appelles lernyd hand.
Y: Osborn music 13, 1553+, ff. 56v–7. On the Venus of Appelles, with music. 30: 5 x 6 ababcc8. Song, love.

TM 1838 Whatt tyme as Parys son of Kyng Priame.
O: Rawl. C.813, 1520–35, ff. 64–9v. "A lettre of love in the prease of the bewtye of his love with the description of her qualities." (Vv. 64ff. incorporate passages from TM 1368 and a tr. of Tibullus III.3.11–14.) 273: 39 x 7 RR5*. BR (3917.8). Love, letter, praise, description.

TM 1839 What tyme the famos towen of troye, by grecians gate the soyle.
D: TCD 537, 2/4 16, pp. 12–25. "Here begineth the history of brute" 400: aa14. Hist., kings of England.

TM 1840 What vailith trouth? or, by it, too take payne.
L: Egerton 2711, bef. 1542, f. 4r–v. [Wyatt.] 15: aabbaaab10C4aabba10C4 (ref. What vaileth trouth). TP 2143. Love.

TM 1841 What wenys Kyng Edward, with his long shankis.
L: Cott. Nero C.11, 1506+, f. 152r–v. Scots verses on King Edward I at the

siege of Berwick, 1296, quoted by Robert Fabyan. 5: aa4b2c4b2*. HD: Eng 766F, bef. 1516, f. ?. BR 3918.5, comp. 1296; TP 2143.5. Hist., Scotland, satire.

TM 1842 What women be in dede, why shold nott all men know | ffyckell to there ffrende, and spytfull to ther foo.
C2: O.1.13 (1037), pt. 5, early 16, f. 205v. "Robert Jernegan." 2: aa12. BR (3919.5). Dispraise of women.

TM 1843 What wourde is that that chaungeth not.
L: Egerton 2711, bef. 1542, f. 33v. "Tho[mas Wyatt]." 7: RR8. TP 2145. Riddle, love.

TM 1844 What wolde ye mor of me your slav Requyer.
D: TCD 160, 1535–48, f. 182. 25: 5 x 5 aabCC5* (ref. That without cause causes that sufferth smart). Love.

TM 1845 When a sondaye goeth by b & c.
L: Harley 559, 1554, f. 34. 8: 2 x 4 abab4*. O: Rawl. C.813, c 1535, f. 89v. Variant, "When sondey goys by C and d and prime by i and ii and iii..." 4: mono8. BR 4018, comp. a 1500. Prophecy.

TM 1846 When a M ccccc to gyther be knett.
L: Lansd. 762, 1524–29, ff. 52–3. "The prophecy of Merlyon." 52: aa4*. BR (3945). Prophecy.

TM 1847 When Ace takithe uppe Sece.
L: Harley 559, 1554, f. 34v. "Prophetia 10 April 1554" (cf. TM 387.) 4: aa3*. Prophecy.

TM 1848 Whan Adam delffid and Eve span | who was than a gentilman.
O17: Balliol 354, 1505–36, f. 200v. Tr. of "Cum vanga quadam..." 2: aa4*. BR 3922, comp. a 1500; TP 2149.5. Proverb.

TM 1849 Whan all this ssowghte that may be fownde.
L: Cott. Vespasian A.25, c. 1555, f. 39v. 14: aa4*. Moral, the grounds of pleasure.

TM 1850 When Audleye had Rone owte his Rase and ended were his dayes.
L: Add. 23971, 1553+, ff. 37v–9. Subscribed "C" [?Thomas Churchyard], "An Epitaphe upon the dethe of Master Thomas Awdeley" [soldier, fl. 1546–54]. 46: aa14. TP 2152. Epitaph, praise.

TM 1851 Whan brighte phebus passid was the Ram.
L: Add. 29729, 1558, ff. 17–83. "the sege of worthy thebes by John

lydgatt...wretyn by John Stowe" (incomplete). 4,500: aa5*. L: Add. 5140, 1501–03, ff. 358–423. Imperfect at end. 4,503 lines. BR 3928, comp. a 1449. Nar., hist.

TM 1852 Whan Chryste on earthe a mongste men was.
L: Add. 33974, c 1550, f. 44r–v. (Francis Stacy), "And forgyve us our trespasses as we forgyve them that trewspas agenst us a hardy condycyone." 64: 16 x 4 abab8. Rel., prayer.

TM 1853 When Cressyde wente from troye.
L: Add. 30513, c 1550, f. 88. Incipit only, with music. Song.

TM 1854 When david had perceyvid in his brest.
L: Egerton 2711, bef. 1542, f. 96v. Wyatt, Penitential Psalms, Prologue to Ps. 130, tr. Aretino. 32: 4 x 8 abababcc10. TP 2158. Rel.

TM 1855 When Dido festid first the wandryng troian knyght.
L: Egerton 2711, bef. 1542, ff. 100–01. "Iopas Song" (unfinished, based on Vergil, *Aeneid*, 1.740ff.) 77: poulters. TP 2159. Astronomy, time reckoning.

TM 1856 Quhen fair flora the goddas of al flowirs.
E2: Laing 149, 1/4 16, f. 181v. [Robert Henryson, "The Ressoning betwixt Aige and Yowtht."] 40: 5 x 8 MT10. BR (3942). Moral, debate, Scots.

TM 1857 When faithe faylethe in priestes sawes.
L: Sloane 2578, c 1557, f. 100. "St. Thomas and Marlion, and John of bridlington and other saye." 6: aa4*. L: Add. 24663, 1550's, f. 1. "Wrytten by Jefferae chawser." O: Lat. misc. c.66, c 1500, f. 104. BR 3943, comp. a 1477; TP 2160.5. Rel., prophecy.

TM 1858 When father blythe the beggar canne saye ii Credes.
L: Harley 559, 1554, f. 11r–v. "Prophetia: wrytten by one brydlington and Dated ...vC + vi and found in an old Nunnes sell at Syon"; repeated on f. 34v with the heading "Prophetia 10 April 1554." 20: 5 x 4 abab4* and 28: 7 x 4 abab4*. O: Arch. Seld. B.8, mid 16, f. 268. "Thys was found in an olde sell at Syon with thys date of Anno domine 906." 28: 7 x 4 abab4*. Prophecy.

TM 1859 When fishes in the water leve their swymmyng.
C: Gg.4.12, early 16, f. 105v. "Didiscere flere feminam mendacium est." 4: mono10. BR (3946). Againt women.

TM 1860 When fflora the Quene of pleasaunce.
L: Add. 10303, 1550+, f. 1v–9. "The death of Blaunche the Dutchesse of Lancaster ffyrst wief to Jo of Gaunte...written by...Geoffrey Chaucer" [i.e.,

Anon., *The Isle of Ladies*; prologue, text, and envoy]. 2,237: 2,210 aa4*, 6 aa5*, 3 x 7 RR4* (ref. Geve the the blisse that thou desyers ofte). LONG: Longleat 256, c 1550, ff. 2–24v. Spurious title added in later hand: "The Temple of Glass by Geffrey Chaucer"; same hand added a couplet to the envoy. BR (3947), includes BR 923 and 755.2. Nar., romance, love, allegory.

TM 1861 When fortune had me avaunsyd.
L: Royal App. 58, 1507+, ff. 19v–20v. With music. 14: 2 x 7 RR3* (ref. ...payne). BR (3947.6). Song, love.

TM 1862 When freendys lyke freendes, do frendlye showe.
L: Add. 15233, 1554–58, ff. 59v–60. "Jhon Haywood." 56: 2 burd ab + 8 x 7 aaaa8b4cC8 (burd. Ye be welcum ye be welcum; ref. Yet wellcum is the best dysh). Carol, moral.

TM 1863 When goostely unkyndenes in the wyll ys wrought.
O: Arch. Seld. B.8, mid 16, ff. 287v–8v. "Alium vaticinum de Merlyn of Saladon." 95: 7 x 4 abab4* + 33 aa4* + irreg. Prophecy.

TM 1863.5 When god of the earthe dyd Adam fyrste create.
L: Add. 33974, c 1550, f. 39r–v. (Francis Stacy), "Of the lyfe of man." 52: 13 x 4 abab5*. Rel. instruction.

TM 1864 When god was born of mary ffre.
L: Add. 5665, bef. 1511, ff. 23v–4. "De innocentibus," with music, lacking lines 10–11. 14: 4 burd (aaaa) + 2 x 6 aaabbb4* (burd. Psallite gaudentes). BR (3950). Rel., carol, macaronic, Holy Innocents.

TM 1865 When grypinge griefes.
L: Add. 30513, c 1550, f. 108v. Incipit only, with music. Song.

TM 1866 When I bethynk my wonted ways.
L: Add. 17492, 1532–39, ff. 58, 59. 8: abababab8. Moral, age.

TM 1867 When I considre what is man, O Lorde I knowe of right.
C: Dd.9.31, 1550–58, p. 10. "quod Collyns." 20: aa14. Rel. instruction.

TM 1868 When I do cawll to mynd.
O: Ashmole 48, bef. 1558, ff. 27–9v. 132: 11 x 12 ababababcdcd6. Rel., moral instruction.

TM 1869 <When> I have plesyd my lady now and than.
NY: Drexel 4184, 2/4 16, f. 1v. Acephelous fragment, with music. 13: 1 burd + 3 x 4 aaaa4* (burd. For all a grene wyllo ys <my garl>and). Love, carol, lament.

TM 1870 When I lent I was a frend | When I asked I was unkind.
L: Harley 2321, early 16, f. 147. Also appears as part of TP 402. 2: aa4*. BR 3960.5, comp. a 1500; TP 402. Moral, money.

TM 1871 When I revolve yn my remembrance.
O: Rawl. C.813, c 1521+, f. 28v–9v. "The Epytaphye of Sir Gryffyth ap Ryse" (d. 1521?). 63: 9 x 7 RR4*. BR (3962.5). Epitaph.

TM 1872 Whan I thynk on thyngis thre.
O17: Balliol 354, 1505–36, f. 213v. Tr. "sunt tria que..." 10: aa4*. BR 3969, comp. a 1300. Rel., moral, tr Lat.

TM 1873 When I was in trouble on the Lorde I called.
L: Royal 17.A.17, 1551+, f. 5. Sir Thomas Smith, tr. "Psalme 119" [120]. 24: 6 x 4 a4b3a4b3*. Rel.

TM 1874 Whan I wold fayne begynne to playne.
L: Add. 60577, 1549–58, f. 115v. 8: abababab4*. Love, complaint.

When it is tyme of coste and greate expens. See TM 429.

TM 1875 When Jhesus criste baptyzed was.
L: Add. 5665, bef. 1511, f. 40v–1. "Epiphanie," with music. 20: 4 burd (aaaa) + 4 x 4 aaaB4* (burd. Jhesus autem hodie; ref. Hic est filius meus [dilectus] Ipsum audite). O17: Balliol 354, 1503–04, f. 178. Two-line burden. BR (3975). Rel., carol, epiphany, macaronic.

TM 1876 When lyffe ys most loffyt and dethe ys most hattyt | Dethe dravse hys draght and makys men full nakyt.
L2: Lambeth 223, bef. 1558, f. 296. "quod Petrus Ravenscroft." 2: aa4*. E: Adv. 19.1.11, pt. 3, 1/2 16, f. 176v. Written twice. L: Add. 60577, 1549–58, f. 92. Introductory couplet to BR 2056. BR 3985, comp. c 1400. Proverb, death, moral.

TM 1877 When lordechype ys loste & lusti lekyng with all.
L: Add. 5665, bef. 1511, ff. 30v–31. With music. 11: 2 burd (aa) + 3 x 3 aaa5* (burd. Spes mea in deo est). BR (3988). Rel. instruction, carol.

TM 1878 When many dayis and nyghtes in grefe were paste.
D: TCD 160, 1535–48, f. 180r–v. Headed "T." 30: 5 x 6 ababcc5*. Love, dream.

TM 1879 When may.
L11: PRO SP 1/246, mid 16, f. 21v. Incipit only, with music. Song.

TM 1880 Whan netillis in wynter bare rosis rede.
O17: Balliol 354, 1505–36, f. 250. 28: 4 x 7 RR5* (ref. Than put in a woman your trust and confidens). L: Ptd. book. IB 55242, early 16, ff.477v–8v. Variant first line "When Netylles in wynter: bryngthith forth Rooses reed"; 26 lines. BR 3999, comp. a 1500. Song, against women.

TM 1881 When 1 is up, and 6 is under.
L: Sloane 2578, c 1557, ff. 45v–6. (1 and 6 drawn with dots, as on dice.) 8: aabbcdcd4*, as prose. Prophecy.

TM 1882 When MCCCCC and XXti to gether are bent.
O: Arch. Seld. B.8, mid 16, f. 296r–v. 52: aa5*, irreg. Prophecy.

TM 1883 Whan phebus in the crabbe had nere his cours ronne.
L: Royal 18 D.2, c1520, ff.167–80v. [*Reason and Sensuality* (or *The Assembly of Gods*), comp. 1478–83; copied from STC 17007 (1500?); first edition incorrectly attributed to Lydgate.] 2,107: 301 x 7 RR5*. BR 4005; TP 2180.5. Nar., allegory, classical myth.

TM 1884 [When] quater shall a-Ryse.
L11: PRO SP 1/232, 1520, f. 219. [Included in BR 4018.] 11: aa4*. Prophecy.

TM 1885 When qwene Anne was crownyd.
L22: Hale 73, 1533, f. 26. Epitaph of John Digby, 1533. 4: aabb4*.

TM 1886 When Ragyng dethe doth drawe his dart.
O: Ashmole 48, bef. 1558, ff. 64–6. "sponer." 112: 16 x 7 RR8. Death.

TM 1887 Whane raginge love.
Y: Osborn music 13, 1553+, f. 40v. [Henry Howard, Earl of Surrey], incipit only, with music . [ababcc8.] TP 2184. Song, love.

TM 1888 When Rome is Removyd into Ingland.
L: Harley 559, 1554, f. 10. (A text.) 7: aa3*, irreg. L: Cott. Cleopatra C.4, early–mid 16, f. 86v. [The Second Scottish Prophecy (C text)]. 14: aa3*. L: Sloane 2578, c 1557, f. 67. (A text.) 4: aa3*, written as prose. L11: PRO SP 1/232, 1520, f. 219. Variant first line "When that Rome Remeveth into England." 15: aa3*. BR 4008, comp. a 1500. Prophecy.

TM 1889 Whan seynt Stevyn was at Jerusalem.
O17: Balliol 354, 1505–36, f. 228. 22: 2 burd. (aa) + 5 x 4 aaaR4* (burd. Nowe syng we both all and sum; ref. ...lapidaverunt Staphanum). BR (4012). Rel., carol, St. Stephen.

TM 1890 Whan satorn, wyth his cold Isy fface.
L: Cott. Nero C.11, 1506+, f. 191v. Robert Fabyan, tr. "Dampnum michi contulit tempore brumali," verses made by Edward II when he was imprisoned at Berkeley in 1327. 58: 28 aa5*, 8 aaa2b3ccc2b3*, 7 aaaaabb5*, 8 MT5*. HD: Eng 766F, bef. 1516, ff.162v–3v. TP 2185. Hist.

TM 1891 When shall my sorowfull sythyng slake | When shall my wofull waylyng....
L: Royal App. 74, c 1548, ff. 35v–6. With music (not in either of the other two partbooks; 2d line incomplete). 2: aa4*. L: Add. 30513, c 1550, f. 83v. Incipit only, with music. Song, love.

TM 1892 Whan shall relyfe reles my wo.
L: Royal 9.C.ii, 1525, f. 44v. Copied by Thomas Lower. 4: abab4*. BR (4013). Death.

TM 1893 When shall thie cruell scornes be past.
L: Harley 78, mid 16, f. 30. "A preti conceate" (first words of each line form an acrostic: "When shall I meddle with the"; answered by TM 1895). 6: ababcc8. D: TCD 160, 1535–48, f. 58. Love, question.

When <six> is the best cast of the dyse. See TM 387.

TM 1894 When sol is in aries and phebus shynyth bright.
O: Ashmole 759, early 16, f.106v–13v. [George Ripley, *Mystery of Alchemists*.] 448: 112 x 4 abab3–4*. BR 4017, comp. a 1490. Alchemy.

TM 1895 When stormes be past then caumes be nexte.
L: Harley 78, mid 16, f. 20. "Answere" to TM 1893; first words form an acrostic: "When tyme dothe serve you shall." 6: ababcc8. D: TCD 160, 1535–48, f. 58. Damaged text, but the acrostic is legible. Love, answer.

TM 1896 When somer comethe efte sones yett.
L: Sloane 2578, c 1557, f. 89. Followed by prose continuation. 11: abababab bcb4*. Prophecy.

TM 1897 Whan that Aprylle wyth hys showres soote.
L: Add. 5140, 1501–3, ff. 2–357v. Geoffrey Chaucer, *The Canterbury Tales*, in the order A B1 D E F C B2 G H I. 18,000: aa5*, RR5*, MT5*, 6 ababca5*, 6 aa8b6aa8b6. BR 4019, comp. a 1400; TP 2188.5. Nar., fabliau, fable, moral, humor, etc.

TM 1898 When that Aurora illumynath lyght.
L: Add. 18752, 1530's, ff. 30v–3. (On the execution of Ann Boleyn; cf. TM

748). 130: 26 x 5 aaaa4R2* (ref. ...good fortune). Hist., nar., allegory, dream vision, elegy.

TM 1899 When that brydes be brought to rest.
O: Rawl. C.813, 1520–35, f. 60r–v. 32: 4 x 8 ababcdcD4* (ref. Your bryde shall never hoppe yn my cage). BR (4020.3). Love, debate.

TM 1900 When that I call to memori what lerned men do shoo.
L: Cott. Titus A.24, 1550's, ff. 95v–6. 44: aa14. Love, women.

TM 1901 When that I call unto my mynde.
L: Add. 17492, 1532–39, ff. 82v–3. 35: 5 x 7 RR8. Love.

TM 1902 Whan that my swete son was XXXti wynter old.
O17: Balliol 354, 1505–36, f. 230. 22: 2 burd. (aa) + 5 x 4 aaaa5* (burd. O my harte is woo mary she sayd so). BR (4023). Rel., carol, Virgin Mary.

TM 1903 Whan that phebus beemes schynyng as golde.
L: Cott. Cleopatra C.4, c 1550, ff. 69–70. 96: 12 x 8 MT5* (ref. Trust not the ontrustye for hys promysse ys not sure). BR 4025, comp. a 1450. Chanson d'aventure, trust.

TM 1904 Whenne that the yere beginneth recomforte.
L: Harley 7578, early 16, f. 16. 14: 2 x 7 RR10. Love.

TM 1905 Whan that this cokk, loo here doth synge | Than shall this newe ffond kyng, his hoost in brynge.
L: Cott. Nero C.11, 1506+, f. 257. Robert Fabyan, tr. "Quant ce quoc...," verses by Flemings in derision of Philip de Valois, 1328. 2: aa4*. HD: Eng 766F, bef. 1516, f ?. TP 2189. Hist., satire.

TM 1906 When the beare ys musselyd and cann nott byte.
L: Cott. Vespasian E.7, early 16, f. 133. 4: aabb4*. Prophecy.

TM 1907 When the coke of the northe hathe builded his nest.
L: Add. 24663, 1550's, ff. 13v–4v. 84: 21 x 4 abab4* allit. L: Harley 559, 1554, ff. 43v–4v. "Verba Thome writ mibitis in hora mortis sue," 12 Apr. 1554. 78 lines. L: Harley 1717, early 16, ff. 249v–50. First line "Quen the kokke in the north bygges his nest." 72 lines. L: Lansd. 762, 1524–29, ff. 62–3. Headed "Brydlyngton." 81 lines. L: Sloane 2578, c 1557, ff. 15v–17. 72 lines. L: Sloane 4031, early 16, f. 189v. 80 lines. BR 4029, comp. a 1500. Prophecy, Scotland.

TM 1908 When the crabbe in hys cowntrye on hys comons shall call.
O: Arch. Seld. B.8, mid 16, ff. 291v–3. "A prophecye of ffysshes...Explicit p[a]ter Roberti scriba bridlington." 105: abab4* + irreg. Prophecy.

TM 1909 When the philosophers Putagoras and Tuball.
L: Royal 18.D.2, c 1520, ff. 198–9v. "The proverbis in the garet at the new lodge in the parke of Lekingfelde [Leconfield]." 132: 30 x 4 aabb5*, 2 x 6 aabbcc5*. BR (4039). Music.

TM 1910 When the prime fallythe uppon sonday.
L: Harley 2252, 1517–38, f. 159. 36: irreg. BR (4040). Weather, prognostication.

TM 1911 When the stede ys shakeled and can not stryke.
O: Arch. Seld. B.8, mid 16, f. 277v. "A proph[ecy]." 4: aa4*. Prophecy.

TM 1912 Whan the whelpe gameth | the old dogge grenneth.
O17: Balliol 354, 1505–36, f. 200v. Tr. of "Dum ludit catulus..." 2: aa2*. BR (4044.3). Proverb.

When thyn head shaketh memento. See TM 1917.

TM 1913 Whan thou art at Rome.
O17: Balliol 354, 1505–36, f. 200. Tr. of "Cum fueris Roma..." 4: aa4*. BR 4049.2, comp. a 1500. Proverb.

TM 1914 When thou hast gathered all that thou may | Thou shalt departe and knowest not what day.
L: Harley 2321, early 16, f. 148. 2: aa4*. BR (4049.5). Moral, death.

TM 1915 Whan thow haste made thy quaderangyll round | ther is all the secret found.
E2: Laing III.164, early 16, p. 112. Fragment. 2: aa4*. Alchemy.

TM 1916 When thou leste wenythe.
L: Add. 60577, 1549–58, f. 52r–v. (Cf. BR 4049.6.) 76: 19 x 4 a3b4a3b4*. Rel., moral, macaronic.

TM 1917 Whan thy hed quakes memento.
C: Ee.4.35, early 16, f. 24. 16: aa3*, irreg. O: Tanner 407, 1/4 16, f. 35v. 8: mono3*. L: Royal 8.C.12, early 16, f. 1v. 8: aa4*. C2: TCC O.2.53 (1157), early 16, f. 72. Begins "When thyn head shaketh memento." 8: aa3*. BR 4035, comp. a 1400. Signs of death, macaronic.

TM 1918 When travelles grete in matters thycke.
L: Add. 15233, 1554–58, f. 44. (John Redford), "The fyrst song" in the play *Wit and Science*. 26: 2 burd aa + 6 x 4 aaaa8 (burd. Gyve place gyve place to honest recreacion). Carol, moral.

TM 1919 When wemen firste dame nature wrowghte.
L: Cott. Titus A.24, 1550's, ff. 85–7v. "R[ichard]. E[dwards]." 40: 5 x 8 aabbccdD8 (ref. I praye you aske them if I do lye). Women, satire.

TM 1920 When words of witt not prevaile.
L: Cott. Titus A.24, mid 16, f. 96. 6: ababcc8. Moral.

Quhen ze have said thir ois to an end. Rhymed title to TM 1476.

When you se the sonne a mysse and ii monkes heades. Extract from TM 754.

TM 1921 When zepheres eeke with his fresshe tarage.
O: Lat. misc. c.66, c 1500, f. 93. (Humfrey Newton.) 40: 10 x 4 abab4*. BR (4057). Love.

TM 1922 Where fairres do boldly presse or bost.
D: TCD 160, 1535–48, f. 96. (Probably incomplete). 4: abab5*. Love.

TM 1923 NOT USED.

TM 1924 Where power with wyll can not agree.
L: Add. 15233, 1554–58, f. 45v. "Jhon Redford." 21: 3 RR8. Moral.

TM 1925 Wher Ryghtwysnes doth say.
L: Add. 15233, 1554–58, f. 54r–v. "Master [John] Redforde." 64: 8 x 8 ababcdcd6. Rel., repentence.

TM 1926 Where shall I have at myn owne will.
L: Egerton 2711, bef. 1542, f. 36r–v. "Tho[mas Wyatt]," subscribed, "Podra esse che no [sic] es." (tr. Giustio de Conti, "Chi dara a gliocchi miei..."). 28: 7 x 4 abab8. TP 2212. Love.

TM 1927 Where shall my hote syghes find refuge.
D: TCD 160, 1535–48, f. 111v. 32: abab5*, RR5*. Love.

TM 1928 Qwhereas Adam cawsed be synne.
L: Lansd. 379, early 16, f. 38. 20: 2 burd (aa) + 3 x 6 abab4C2C4* (burd. Tydynges tydynges that be trwe; ref. And that ys trwe). BR (4065). Rel., carol, nativity.

Where for in thi lyvyng have this in mynde. Variant of TM 980.

TM 1929 Wherfor shuld I hang up my bow | upon the grenewood bough.
L: Add. 31922, 1513+, ff. 69v–71. With music; reply to TM 643. 22: 6 burd

(aabcbb) + 4 x 4 a8b6a8b6 (burd. I am a Joly foster). BR (4068.6). Carol, love, bawdy.

TM 1930 Where ssom ever thys Boke be com | yt ys Wyllyam Barbors off newe Bokenham.
C: Ii.6.4, 1/4 16, f. 1v. 2: aa4*. Ownership rhyme.

TM 1931 Wher to shuld I expresse.
L: Add. 31922, 1513+, ff. 51v–2. With music by "The Kynge H. VIII." 20: 5 x 4 abab3*. BR (4070.5). Song, love.

Where ever thou be in bowur or hall. Lines 54–55 of TM 221.

Whiche hathe nobles much like to ours. See TM 1605.

TM 1932 While fortune the favorthe frendes thow hast plentye.
DUR5: Cosin V.iii.9, c 1555, f. 64v. [Thomas Elyot, tr.] "Ovidius de Ponto" [Trist. 1.9.5–10]. 6: RR4*. L: Royal 9.C.ii, 1525+, f. 45. Vv. 1–3 only. BR (4073.3); TP 2222. Moral, friendship, fortune.

TM 1933 While y was yong & hadde carage.
L: Add. 5665, bef. 1511, ff. 45v–46. With music. 16: 4 burd (aaaa) + 3 x 4 aaab4* (burd. The beste song as hit semeth me). BR (4077). Carol, mortality.

TM 1934 Whyle lyvyd this kyng.
L: Cott. Nero C.11, 1506+, f. 161v. Robert Fabyan, tr. "Dum vivit Rex...," on death of Edward I (1307). 6: aabccb2*. HD: Eng 766F, bef. 1516, f. 132v. TP 2221. Hist. epitaph.

TM 1935 While the fote warmith | the sho harmith.
O17: Balliol 354, 1505–36, f. 191v. 2: aa2*. BR 4079.3, comp. a 1500. Proverb.

TM 1936 While the gresse growith | the hors stervith.
O17: Balliol 354, 1505–36, f.191v200v. Tr. of "Dum gramen cressit..." 2: aa2*. BR 4079.6, comp. a 1500. Proverb.

TM 1937 Who hath herd of suche crueltye before.
L: Egerton 2711, bef. 1542, f. 29v. [Wyatt], "crueltye" revised from "tyranny." 8: abababcc10. L: Add. 17492, 1532–39, f. 73. TP 2123. Love.

TM 1938 Who hath more cause for to complayne.
L: Add. 17492, 1532–39, f. 28. [?by Lord Thomas Howard, d. Oct. 1537.] 16: 4 x 4 aaaa4*. Love.

TM 1939 Ho ys my love | butt good above.
HN: Ptd. book 69798, early 16, sig. gg4v. (First two lines of a song printed in STC 22924 (1530).) 2: aa2*. BR (4094.3); TP 2229. Rel., carol.

TM 1940 Who is the onor of thy boke | maye torne over the leafe and loke.
HN: HM 136, early 16, f. 100. "Dorothe Helbartun" (cf. TM 687 and 929). 2: aa4*. Ownership rhyme.

TM 1941 Who justely may rejoyce in owghte under the skye.
L: Cott. Titus A.24, mid 16, f. 80r–v. [John Harington the Elder,] "to Devers where he lyeth," on Richard Devereux, d. 1547. 24: poulters. TP 2232. Epitaph.

TM 1942 Who lyst his welth and eas Retayne.
D: TCD 160, 1535–48, f. 183. Headed "V. Innocencia | Veritas Viat [Wyatt] fides | Circumderunt me inimici mei." 25: 5 x 5 aabaB8 (ref. For sure circa Regna tonat). Moral.

TM 1943 Who list to here this song.
L11: PRO SP 1/246, mid 16, f. 20v. Incipit only, with music. Song.

TM 1944 Who list to lerne to thrive.
L11: PRO SP 1/246, mid 16, f. 21. Incipit only, with music. Song.

TM 1945 Who liste to live uprighte and holde himselfe content.
L: Cott. Titus A.24, mid 16, f. 81r–v. 16: poulters. TP 2234. Moral.

TM 1946 Who lovithe to lyve In peas & merkithe every change.
O: Ashmole 48, bef. 1558, ff. 37v–9. 82: poulters. TP 2236. Moral.

TM 1947 Who most doeth slaunder love.
L: Egerton 2711, bef. 1542, ff. 61v–2. [Wyatt,] answer to TM 881 and 919. 41: 5 x 8 aabbabba6 + 1. D: TCD 160, 1535–48, f. 118r–v. Love, answer.

TM 1948 Who of thys wretchyde worlde wyll take in hande.
L: Add. 33974, c 1550, ff. 65v–8. (Francis Stacy), "Of <the mysery of this> worlde." 236: 59 x 4 abab5*. Rel. instruction.

TM 1949 Who Redith in this booke discretly.
O: Rawl. C.448, 1535–47, inside front cover. Added to a copy of Lydgate, *Fall of Princes*. 7: RR5*. Rel. controversy, anti-Catholic.

Whoe Rayneth now in blisse but venus. See TM 466.

TM 1950 Who runneth oversee ffrom place to place | Though he chaunge here his mynde is as it was.
DUR5: Cosin V.iii.9, c 1555, f. 62v. [Nicholas Udall, tr. Horace.] 2: aa4*. BR (4096.5); TP 2239. Moral.

TM 1951 Who sekethe the renoune to have.
DUR5: Cosin V.iii.9, c 1555, f. 82v. 4: abab8. BR (4098.1). Moral.

TM 1952 Who shall have my fayre lady.
L: Add. 5465, 1501–04, ff.99v–101. With music. 6: 2 x 3 aa4B3* (ref. Undir the levys grene). BR (4098.6). Song, love.

TM 1953 Who shall profoundlye way and scan.
L: Add. 15233, 1554–58, ff. 58v–9. "Mr [John] Thorne." 45: 9 x 5 aaabB4* (burd. Now mortal man behold and see; ref. All is subject to vanitee). Carol, moral, vanity.

Who so. Alphabetized as Whoso.

TM 1954 Who that buldyth his howse of sallowes.
L: Ptd. book IB 49437, early 16, f. 1. 4: mono3*. L: Lansd. 762, 1524–29, f. 16v. BR 4101, comp. a 1400 (cited by Chaucer in Wife of Bath's Prologue 655–58); TP 2242.3. Proverb, moral.

TM 1955 Who that drynketh wele mych is he the gladder.
L: Lansd. 762, 1524–29, f. 91v. Tr. "Si quis bene biberit..." 5: mono4*. BR (4103). Moral.

TM 1956 Who that makyth in Crystnmas a dooge to his lardere.
L: Ptd. book IB 49408, early 16, f. 34v. 5: aabab4*. L: Lansd. 762, 1524–29, f. 16v. 4 lines. BR 4106, comp. a 1486; TP 2242.5. Moral, proverb.

TM 1957 Who that manyth hym with his kyn.
L: book, IB 49437, early 16, f. 1. 4: abab4*. BR 4106.5, comp. a 1486; TP 2242.7. Moral, proverb.

TM 1958 Who that wyll lyve and with god Reygne.
L: Ptd. book C.15.c.7, mid 16, sig. L10. 6: aabcbc4*. Rel. advice.

TM 1959 Who the paynes of this worlde And myseryes beholde.
L: Add. 33974, c 1550, ff. 53v–4. (Francis Stacy), "The contempte of thys worlde." 30: aa7*. Rel. instruction.

TM 1960 Who wilbe hole & kepe him selfe from sicknes.
D: TCD 537, 2/4 16, pp. 83–84. ["The Governance of Health."] 24: 3 x 8

MT5* (ref. ...eschew the mystes black). BR 4112, comp. a 1449; TP 2246.5. Medical.

Hoo will be war in purchasyng. See TM 1979.

TM 1961 Quha will persew I will defend | My lyef and honor to the end.
L: Add. 40732, mid 16, f. iv. 2: aa8. Moral, Scots.

TM 1962 Who ever thow hate is good or yll.
L: Add. 15233, 1554–58, f. 62r–v. "Fynnis qd John haywoode." 51: 2 burd aa + 7 x 7 RR4* (burd. Man yf thow mynd heven to obtayne). Carol, moral.

TM 1963 Whose faytheful service.
L: Add. 30513, c 1550, f. 14v. Incipit only, with music. Song.

TM 1964 Whose thought is cumbered and is not clere.
L: Lansd. 762, 1524–29, f. 94. 4: aabb4*. BR (4118). Moral.

TM 1965 Who so desyreth the swete to assay | He most taste the bytter this is no nay.
L: Add. 20059, early 16, f. 2. Fourth of five moral couplets. 2: aa4*. Proverb.

TM 1966 Who so dothe kepe hatred < > mynde Thys fyrste he owghte to knowe.
L: Add. 33974, c 1550, f. 58v. (Francis Stacy), "Of envye and anger." 16: aa7*. Rel. instruction.

TM 1967 Whoso for grace and good thynges wyll To god by prayer call.
L: Add. 33974, c 1550, ff. 5v–6. (Francis Stacy), "A medytacyo<n how to> pray." 36: aa7*. Rel. instruction.

TM 1968 Who so hath sene the sikk in his [dolour].
L: Egerton 2711, bef. 1542, ff. 88v–9. Wyatt, Penitential Psalms, prologue to Ps 32, tr. Aretino. 32: 4 x 8 abababcc10. TP 2255. Rel.

TM 1969 Who so have sore pappys or bolnyng.
C2: TCC R.14.39 (911), early 16, f. 1v. "for sore brystys or pappys" (included in BR 1408). 6: aa4*. Medicine.

TM 1970 Who so hym bethought | Inwardely and ofte.
C10: Magdalene F.4.13, 1528, f. 2. 8: aa3*. O: Ptd. book Douce A.314, early–mid 16, flyleaf. HN: Ptd. book 61866, early 16, sig. b4v. O: Tanner 407, 1/4 16, f. 36v. Variant first line "He that hath thoughte." C2: TCC O.2.53 (1157), early 16, f. 74. Damaged text. 4 lines. BR 4129, comp. a 1325. Rel., death, hell.

TM 1971 Who soo hym lykeyth, these verses to Rede.
L: Cott. Nero C.11, 1506+, f. 31v. Robert Fabyan, apology for his "Ryme Dogerell." 14: 2 x 7 RR4*. Poetry.

Who so in youthe no vertu usith. See TM 540.

Who soo l[i]st on me to lok. See TM 1975.

TM 1972 Wo so lyst to gett them lyght.
C: Gg.4.12, early 16, f. 105v. 4: abab3*. BR (4133). Moral.

TM 1973 Who so list to hunt I know where is an hynd.
L: Egerton 2711, bef. 1542, f. 7v. [Wyatt], tr. Petrarch, *Rime* 190. 14: abbaabbacddcee5*. D: TCD 160, 1535–48, f. 185. Love.

TM 1974 Who so of welth takyth non hede.
O17: Balliol 354, 1503–04, f. 160. [Appears as vv. 23–24 of TM 221 and 79–80 of TM 219.] 2: aa4*. G: Hunt. 230, early 16, f. 248v. Sixth of nine proverbs entered by Rychard Wylloughbe; begins "He that of wast takys no hede." BR 4137, comp. a 1477; TP 2255.5. Moral, proverb.

TM 1975 Ho so on me doth loke.
C2: TCC R.3.17 (597), 1501–25, f. 123. "Thomas Stapilton." 6: aa3*. D: TCD 223, early 16, f. 38. "John Lawmlay <...> in thys hows of westderan." Variant: "Who so hon thys do loke | shalle fynde me eyn thys boke." 2: aa6. LINC: Ptd. book RR.4.20, 1534+, sig. ?. Variant: "Who so on me loke | I am Thomas Metcalfe boke | Therfor I praye you let me have yt a gane." 3: aab3*. L: Add. 22718, early 16, f. 31v. Variant: "Who soo list on me to look | this is Cristofer Trevylans book." 2: aa4*. BR 4138, comp. a 1500. Ownership rhyme.

Who so hon thys do loke. Variant of TM 1975.

TM 1976 Who so that wyll all feattes optayne.
L: Add. 31922, 1513+, ff. 38v–9. With music by "The Kynge H. viii." 14: aa4*. BR (4143.3). Song, love.

TM 1977 Who so that wyll for grace sew.
L: Add. 31922, 1513+, ff. 84v–5. With music by "The Kynge H. viii." 12: 2 x 6 aabbcc4*. BR (4143.5). Song, love.

TM 1978 Who se that wyll hymselff applye.
L: Add. 31922, 1513 +, ff. 27v–8. With music by "Rysbye." 4: mono4*. BR (4143.8). Song, invitation to a tournament.

TM 1979 Who so wilbe wise in purchasinge.
O: Douce 54, early 16, f. 64. 22: aa4*. O17: Balliol 354, 1503–04, f. 100v. Begins "Who so will beware in purchasynge." 24 lines. L: Add. 25001, 1535–58, f. 2v. Begins "Whoso will be ware of purchasing." 22 lines. L: Lansd. 762, 1524–29, f. 2v. Begins "Who wolbe ware in purchasing." 24 lines. O: Lat. misc. c.66, c 1500, f. 101v. Headed "fortescue." 20 lines. C: Hh.2.6, early 16, f. 58v. 18 lines. C2: TCC O.2.53 (1157), early 16, f. 24. 20 lines. L8: Guildhall 3035, early 16, f. 58r–v. "A treatys to purchase landes"; begins "Hoo will be war in purchasing." 28 lines. BR 4148, comp. a 1500. Practical, land purchasing.

TM 1980 Who so wyll dewly call to mynde and well consyder than.
L: Add. 33974, c 1550, ff. 17v–18. (Francis Stacy), "Of the <blessed lyfe>." 34: aa7*. Rel. instruction.

TM 1981 W[h]o so wil the caracteres gretly lok.
L: Harley 559, 1554, ff. 41v–2v. 56: aa3*. BR 4154.3, comp. c 1450. Prophecy of Bede.

TM 1982 [Who-so wilneth to be wiis...] who so wil be wise and worship desireth.
L: Harley 1304, early 16, f. 103r–v. [The ABC of Aristotle (cf. TM 1767) with allit. prologue.] 59: 10 + 49 allit. BR 4155, comp. c 1450. Moral, ABC.

TM 1983 Who so ever thys booke fynde.
C: Ii.6.4, 1/2 16, f. 2. "Wylliam Barbor of new Bokenham." 4: aabb4*. BR (4126). Ownership rhyme.

TM 1984 Why dare I not compleyn to my lady.
L: Add. 60577, 1549–58, f. 116v. 4: abba5*. Love, song.

TM 1985 Why doe ye doble my desyer.
Y: Osborn music 13, 1553+, ff. 20–1. With music. 64: 8 x 8 ababccdD8 (ref. Alas leave of & lett me dye). Love, song.

TM 1986 Why is this worlde belovyd that false is and veyne.
O: Ashmole 1524, pt. 6, early 16, f. 171. ["Cur mundus militat," lacks vv. 30–40.] 29: aa5*. BR 4160, comp. a 1450. Moral.

TM 1987 Whie shall we still in this prison abide.
L: Royal 17.A.17, 1551+, f. 26v. Sir Thomas Smith, "An-other Psalme." 60: 15 x 4 a4b3a4b3*. Lament.

TM 1988 Whye shulde man dowtefully questyons make.
L6: Dyce 45, 2/4 16, ff. 25v–7v. "The wonderfull workes & powr of god

wherein every christian maye learne to geve place unto ffaythe...quod Wynton." 116: 29 x 4 aaab4*. BR (4162.5). Rel. instruction.

TM 1989 Wyll ye se what wonderous love hathe wroughte.
L: Add. 17492, 1532–39, f. 84. 24: 6 x 4 a8b6a8b6. Love.

TM 1990 Wyll you daunce hey the gie, trimly tripin to and fro.
L: Harley 2383, mid 16, f. 93v. Incipit only. Dance, song.

TM 1991 Well yow her agod borde to make yow lawke all.
C: Ee.4.35, early 16, ff. 19v–21. "Expleycet the kyng & the Barker." 114: aa7*. BR (4168). Nar., humorous, ballad.

TM 1992 William Conqueror duke of Normandye.
O: Lat. theol. d.15, 1551, ff. 125v–32. "Here after followith certayne Englishe verses in metre Compilde furthe of the Cronicle, conteinyng the kyngs of Englande sithen the conquest...writtyn by Robert parkyn Curett of Aithewike by the streatt Anno domini 1551." 336: 42 x 8 MT5*. O: Rawl. C. 448, 1505+, ff. 182v–3v, also on f. ii verso. (Fragmentary text.) 151 lines. BR (4174.3). Hist.

TM 1993 Wilyam Rufus otherwise william the red.
C10: Pepys 2163, c 1555, ff. 1–642v. "Herdinges metrical chronicle" [from 1087 to 1547, drawing on Fabyan and John Harding], with envoy TM 2031. 43,940: aa5*, RR5*. BR (4174.5). Hist., England and France.

TM 1994 Willingly have I soughte.
L: Harley 78, 1544+, f. 19. Charles Blount, Lord Mountjoy, epitaph written in his will, 1544 [and later placed on his tomb in Aldermary Church, London, 1545; ptd. from the tomb in Stow, *Survey of London* (1598).] 8: abababab3*. Epitaph.

TM 1995 Wyly no dought ye be a wry.
L: Add. 17492, 1532–39, f. 59v. "E. Knywet." 3: abc4*. Moral.

TM 1996 Wyne of hys nature hathe properties ix.
L: Harley 2252, 1517–38, f. 2. (Part of Lydgate's and Burgh's *Secrees of Old Philosophers*.) 8: MT5*. L: Add. 29729, 1558, f. 16. "The ix properties of wyne per Johan lidgate." BR 4175, comp. a 1449. Practical.

TM 1997 Winter etith | that somer getith.
O17: Balliol 354, 1505–36, f. 191v, 200. Tr. of "Brume [tem]pestas vorat..." 2: aa2*. BR 4176.5, comp. a 1500. Proverb.

Wysdom stondyth not all be speche. Lines 35–36 of TM 221

Wysse men ar blynd. Lines 13–16 of TM 463.

TM 1998 Witte hath wonder that reason <not tell can>.
L: Harley 1587, 2/4 16, ff. 203, 213r–v. [The speech of "Antiquitie" in STC 20406, John Proctor, *The Fal of the Late Ariann* (1549); elsewhere ascribed to Reginald Pecock], copied as pen practice nine times. 4: aa4*. O17: Balliol 354, 1503–04, f. 159v. Begins "Wytt hath wonder and kynde ne can." BR 4181, comp. c 1455; TP 2292.5. Rel. instruction.

Wyt ys trechery | luff ys lechery | play ys vylany | and holyday ys glotony. Lines 5–8 of TM 463.

Wyte ye well all that be here. See TM 1999.

TM 1999 [Wyteth now all that ben here].
L: Add. 60577, 1549–58, ff. 114v–15. "Carta generis humani" [The Short Charter of Christ], variant beginning "Wyte ye well all that be here." 32: aa4*. L: Sloane 3292, early 16, f. 2. Preceded by six unique introductory verses, TM 848. BR 4184, comp. a 1400. Rel., Jesus.

TM 2000 Wyth bodylye ffode Encressyng in quantitee.
L2: Lambeth 259, early 16, f. 231v. 7: RR4*. BR (4187). Rel. instruction, Christ to a glutton.

TM 2001 With boidekynnes, was Cesar Julius.
L: Add. 48031, mid 16, f. 156. John lidgate [in his *Serpent of Division*] quoting Geffrey Chauser (conveys sense but not words of Monk's Tale 7.2674, 2703–07, 2723–4). 4: aa5*. BR 4186.5, comp. a 1450; TP 2295.5. Hist., nar., moral.

TM 2002 With greate humylyte I submytt me to your gentylnes.
O: Rawl. C.813, 1520–35, f. 63r–v. 35: 5 x 7 RR5* (ref. Remembre your promesse & bryng ytt to an ende). BR (4190). Love, epistle, presentation verse.

TM 2003 With hevy hart I call & cry.
L11: PRO SP 1/246, mid 16, f. 16v. 6: ababcc8. Rel., song.

TM 2004 Wythe hufa | Wythe huffa.
F: V.a.354, 1/4 16, f. 117. Chorus of song; marginal addition to the play of *Wisdom*. 4: aabc2*. Song, chorus.

TM 2005 With laude and prays my sowle magnifieth.
L: Add. 29729, 1558, ff. 122–3. "magnificat...[tr.] lidgate" (BR 2574, extract

from *The Life of Our Lady*, II.xxii.981–1060). 80: 10 x 8 MT5*. BR 4192.5+, comp. a 1422?; TP 2298.5. Rel., Virgin Mary.

TM 2006 With proffownde sorow my hert ys sor greved.
L: Lansd. 858, 1520's, ff. 25v–30. (Edwarde North, acrostic in stanzas 35–36). 259: 37 x 7 RR5*. Hist., complaint, Cardinal Wolsey.

TM 2007 Wyth Ropes wert thow bounde, and on the Galow hong.
L: Cott. Nero C.11, 1506+, f. 190v. Robert Fabyan, tr. "ffinis cum lignis...," on the execution of Hugh Spenser the Younger, 1316. 7: RR5*. HD: Eng 766F, bef. 1516, f. 161v. TP 2303. Hist.

With ceptour in hand thar muyd to meyss and still. See TM 1497.

TM 2008 Wyth serving still.
L: Add. 17492, 1532–39, f. 81. 20: 5 x 4 abab4. D: TCD 160, 1535–48, f. 181. Love.

TM 2009 With sorowfull syghs and grevos payne.
L: Add. 31922, 1513+, ff. 33v–4. With music by T. ffardynge. 4: a4b3a4b3*. BR (4201.3). Song, love.

TM 2010 With sorowful syghes and wondes smart.
L: Add. 17492, 1532–39, f. 26v. [? by Lord Thomas Howard, d. Oct. 1537] 20: 5 x 4 abab8. BR (4201.6). Love.

TM 2011 With woofull harte plungede yn dystresse.
O: Rawl. C.813, 1520–35, ff. 43v–4v. 77: 11 x 7 RR4*. BR (4210). Love, epistle, farewell.

Wyth wrathffull wretches be not att debate. Vv. 73–74 of TM 219.

TM 2012 With wronge or nay yf < >.
C2: TCC O.2.53 (1157), early 16, ff. 74, 74v. Damaged text. 8: ?. BR (4212). Rel. instruction.

TM 2013 Within the chamber of deepe floodde the mother harde a sowne.
L: Royal 18.C.9, 1540's, f. ?. Vergil, Georg. 4, in an English tr. of Polydore Vergil, Anglica historia, Book 1. 2: poulters. Husbandry.

TM 2014 With owt dyscord | and bothe acorde.
L: Add. 31922, 1513+, ff. 68v–9. With music by "The kynge H.viii." 24: 4 x 6 aabccb2*. BR (4213.5). Song, love.

Withoute disease or adversyte. Last line of acephalous TM 673.

TM 2015 Wo worth debate that never hath pees.
O: Ashmole 1152, early 16, f. 9v. 7: RR4*. BR 4215. comp. c 1490. Moral.

Wo worthe the fayre gemme vertulesse. See TM 1510.

TM 2016 [W]o worthe the lenttone that ever thowe waste wrought.
O: Ashmole 48, bef. 1558, ff. 8v–9, 10v–15v. 288: 36 x 8 aaa5b1ccc2b2*. Rel. controversy, lenten fast.

TM 2017 Woe worth the welthe of wyckyde worlde whereon men sett ther care.
L: Add. 33974, c. 1550, f. 46r–v. (Francis Stacy), "A caveat to covytus men." 26: aa7*. Rel. instruction.

<Wo> Worth your hartes so plantyd in pryde. Extract from TM 1524.

Womans harte unto no creweltye. Extract from TM 339.

TM 2018 Women be wytles & childer be unkynd | Executors be covetus and breke the dedes mynde.
O: Ptd. book 8° C.70.Th. Seld., 1540+, sig. 2L7v. (Cf. last two lines of TM 980.) 2: aa4*. Moral, death.

TM 2019 Wunderus thynges.
L: Sloane 3501, 1530's, f. 2v. Incipit only, no music. Song.

TM 2020 Worshipe women wine unwisely age.
L: Harley 7578, early 16, f. 20. Lydgate(?), "Four things that make a man fall from reason." 7: RR4*. BR 4230, comp. c 1450. Moral.

TM 2021 Wiat restethe here that quicke cowlde never reste.
L: Harley 78, mid 16, f. 15v. [Henry Howard, Early of Surrey], "Epitaphium Tho. Wiatt" (d. 1542). 38: 8 x 4 abab10, 6 ababcc10. TP 2319. Epitaph.

Ye be MI FA-yr LA-dye FA-yr be-FA-l youre[?] grace[?]. L: Add. 5665, f. 135. Musical rebus (uppercase letters are notes), probably not verse.

TM 2022 Yee chyldren, prayse the lorde all yee.
L: Royal 17.A.21, 1551, ff. 72v–3v. William Forreste, tr. Ps 112 Laudate pueri. 36: 9 x 4 a8b6a8b6. Rel.

TM 2023 Ye folkis all which have devocion.
O17: Balliol 354, 1503–04, ff.148–55v. [Lydgate, *Virtues of the Mass*], variant

first line "O ye folkis..." 654: 82 x 8 MT4*. BR 4246, comp. a 1449; TP 2320.3. Rel. instruction.

TM 2024 Ye grett astronemars now awake.
COV: City Record Office, 1534/5, ff. 1–17. Coventry Weavers Pageant transcribed by Robert Croo 2 March 1535 (Prophets, Purification, Disputation in the Temple), plus 2 leaves in a 15th-century hand, vv. 1–58, 182–243. 1,192: MT4*, aaa4b3ccc4b3* RR4*, abab4*, irreg. BR (4248). Rel. drama, miracle cycle.

TM 2025 Ye know my herte my ladye dere.
L: Add. 17492, 1532–39, f. 73v. [Wyatt.] 39: 3 x 13 ababbca8dede4cc8. L: Egerton 2711, bef. 1542, f. 29. Lacking vv. 1–14 owing to missing leaf; begins "All to my harme." Love.

TM 2026 Ye men that wysdome wilt lerne.
L: Harley 2252, 1517–39, f. 141. "Ezechyelys Prophete," prologue plus prognostications according to the day of the new year. 174: aa3*. BR (4253). Prognostications, calendar.

TM 2027 Ye old mule that thinck your self so fayre.
L: Egerton 2711, bef. 1542, f. 25. "Tho[mas Wyatt]." 16: aabba5c2-aab5c2aabba5c2*. Satire, women.

TM 2028 Ye pop holy pristes full of presumcion.
C2: TCC O.2.53 (1157), early 16, f. 27. "An answer [to TM 1641] by the Galantes." 14: aaaabbbccccddd4*. BR 4254.5, comp. a 1500. Rel., satire, anti-clerical.

Ye that ar comons obey your kynge and lorde. See TM 1495.

TM 2029 Yee that lengen in londe Lordes and oother.
O: Greaves 60, 1551–52, ff. iv–24v. Parts of *Alisaunder*, comp. 1340–70, copied by Nicholas Grimald. 1,247: allit. BR 4262. Hist., nar., romance.

Ye that put your trust in confydence. See TM 1257.

TM 2030 Ye that stonde in welthe and grete plesaunce.
L: Add. 60577, 1549–58, f. 91v. 7: RR10. Moral.

Ye that this balad rede shall | I praye you Kepe you from the fall. Later addition to TM 1860.

Yet excusith me besech you hertely. Last line of acephalous TM 419.

TM 2031 Yow Comydes and Tragedes me recommend.
C10: Pepys 2163, c 1555, ff. 643–4. (Herdinge), "Ane Lenvoy to his iiii volumes" [to TM 1993]. 42: RR5*. Hist, moral.

TM 2032 You Juge or you knowe and condemne or you trye.
D: TCD 160, 1535–48, f. 96. Also five-line text on f. 95. 6: ababbb5*. Moral.

TM 2033 Yow precios lovers ladis all.
Y: Osborn music 13, 1553+, ff. 52v–3. With music. 78: 13 x 6 abbacc8. Nar., love.

TM 2034 You that have redd the contentes of thys booke.
L2: Lambeth 265, mid 16, f. 107. Subscribed "TER< >," added as an epilogue to Anthony Woodville, Earl Rivers, tr. *Dictes and Sayings of Philosophers*. 14: ababcdcdefefgg10. Epilogue, moral.

TM 2035 You that in love finde lucke and habundance.
L: Egerton 2711, bef. 1542, f. 64v. "Tho[mas Wyatt]." 14: abbaabba-cdcdee10. TP 2329. Love.

TM 2036 Yong and lusty thowgh ye be.
L: Sloane 1825, early 16, f. 1v. 14: 2 x 7 RR4*. BR (4274). Against women.

TM 2037 Yower company| makes me so mery.
L: Add. 31922, 1513+, ff.110v–12. With music. 30: 6 burd (aabccb) + 4 x 6 aa2b3cc2B3* (burd. Wher be ye | my love my love | and...; ref. But you my love alone). BR (4058.3). Love, carol.

TM 2038 Yowre counturfetyng | with doubyll deylyng.
L: Add. 5465, 1501–04, ff. 22v–4. With music by William Newark. 16: 2 x 8 aaabaaab2*. BR (4281.5). Dispraise of women.

TM 2039 Yowre ferefull hope cannot prevayle.
L: Add. 17492, 1532–39, f. 8. Answer to TM 1034, subscribed "finis qd somebody." 28: 7 x 4 abab8. Love, answer.

TM 2040 Your ffolyshe fayned hast.
D: TCD 160, 1535–48, f. 127. "The answer" to TM 968. 16: 4 x 4 abaB3* (ref. Ye get not that ye lack). Love, answer.

TM 2041 Your light grevans schall not me constrayn.
L: Add. 5665, bef. 1511, ff. 38v–9. With music. 13: 1 burd + 4 x 3 aaa5* (burd. How shall y plece A creature uncerteyn). BR (4283.5). Love, carol, against fickleness.

TM 2042 Your lokes so often cast.
D: TCD 160, 1535–48, f. 104r–v. [Wyatt,] answered by TM 386. 40: 5 x 8 MT6. TP 2342. Love, question.

TM 2043 Youre servand madame | quhatever ye be go hence sir.
O: Arch. Selden B.24, mid 16, f. 230. Largely illegible. 23: ? (burd. Go fro my window go). BR (4284.3). Carol, love, dialogue, Scots.

TM 2044 Yougth luste Reches or Manhod.
C2: TCC O.2.53 (1157), early 16, ff. 57–8. 50: 2 burd aa + 12 x 4 aaaa4* (burd. When all ys don and all ys sayd). BR (4285). Carol, satire.

Ywis. See Iwis.

Indexes

BURDENS (alphabetized by first line; number of lines and stanza form in parentheses).

REFRAINS (alphabetized by last words).

VERSE FORMS AND RHYME SCHEMES

Listed in order according to number of lines in stanza, order of rhymes, and line length; capital letters indicate refrains. Almost all lines are iambic or approximations of iambic; the only other rhythms are:

ONE-LINE

TWO-LINE (476 poems, 174,612 lines)

THREE-LINE (31 poems, 1047 lines)

FOUR-LINE (555 poems, 32,131 lines)

FIVE-LINE (69 poems, 1711 lines)

SIX-LINE (169 poems, 8450 lines)

aaaa4bb2*: 1519.
aaaa4b2B4*: 1592.
aaaabB7*: 238.
aaaabB8: 1285.
aaa4b2a4b2*: 90, 625.
aaa5b2ab5*: 315.
aaa6B5a6B5: 601.
aaabaB4*: 749.
aaabab9: 1699.
aaabbb4*: 234, 1864.
aaabbB8: 1483.
aaa8BBB5: 1302.
aaabb4C2*: 684, 1070.
aaa4b2c4b2*: 523.
aabaab2*: 145, 812, 977, 1172.
aa2b3aa2b3*: 50.
aabaab3*: 1200.
aabaab4: 1199.
aabaab4*: 909.
aa4b3aa4b3*: 1897.
aa4b6aa4b6: 948, 1666.
aabaab5*: 1536.
aabaab6: 1414.
aa7b5aa7b5: 1759.
aa2B1ab2B3*: 654.
aaba8bB10: 1749.
aababb10: 108.
aabb5cc2*: 494.
aabbcC4*: 488.
aabbcc4*: 337, 886, 1335, 1977.
aabbcc5*: 1909.
aabcbc4*: 1958.
aabccB2*: 1472.
aabccb2*: 1642, 1652, 1934, 2014.
aa2b3cc2B3*: 1008, 1057, 2037.
aa2b3cc2b3*: 139, 288, 620, 661, 955, 1058, 1742, 1787.
aabccb3*: 440, 1198, 1217, 1653.
aabccb4*: 25, 71, 151, 489, 714, 971, 1239.
aa4b2cc4b2*: 1456.
aa4b3cc4b3*: 38, 1243, 1682.
aa4b6cc4B6: 1542, 1643.
aa4b6cc4b6: 66, 127, 938, 1026, 1090, 1158, 1227, 1309.
aa4b7cc4b7: 289.
aabccb6: 737.
aa8b6cc8b6: 1083.
aa2b3cc2d3*: 844.
abaa10b6b10: 742.
ababaa4*: 1430.
ababab4*: 730.
ababa8B4: 668.
ababba5*: 879.
a6b4a6bb4a6: 1816.
ababbb5*: 2032.
ababbb8: 465.
ababb8C4: 682.
ababcb10: 1897.
abab4cc2*: 853.
ababcC3*: 644.
ababcC4*: 408, 722, 1460.
ababcc4*: 36, 380, 851, 957, 990, 1192, 1332, 1333, 1721, 1780.
ababc4C3*: 295.
abab4C2C4*: 1928.
a4b3a4b3cc4*: 356.
abab4cc5*: 1446.
ababcc5*: 1014, 1623, 1878.
ababcc6: 1313, 1314, 1315, 1316.
abab6cc8: 401.
ababcC8: 924.
ababcc8: 98, 184, 333, 569, 700, 728, 734, 805, 1182, 1809, 1827, 1837, 1887, 1893, 1895, 1920, 2003.
a8b6a8b6cc8: 1238.
ababcc10: 37, 888, 1500, 1550, 1580, 2021.
abacb6c4: 1047.
abacb8c2: 846.
abacb8c4: 1415.
a8b6a8c6b8c6: 689.
abacc4D2*: 189.
abbaba5*: 409.
abbacc8: 2033.
abbba6C4: 164.
abbcbc4*: 1689.
ab2c3ab2c3*: 360.
ab4c2ab4C2*: 1576.
ab4c8ab4c8: 1093.
ab4cc2b3d1*: 110.
abccca3–4*: 320.

SEVEN-LINE (345 poems, 121,790 lines)
aaaaaBB4*: 232.
aaaaabb5*: 1890.
aaaa4bcd2*: 599.
aaaab4b2B4*: 1592.
aaaabB4C2*: 1174.
aaaabb4C2*: 750.
aaaa8b4cB8: 1048.
aaaa8b4cC8: 1862.
aaabbCC4*: 1423.
aaa2b1cc2B3*: 1505.
aaa4BCCB3*: 1440.
aaa8bccb4: 468.
aaabcc4B8: 713.
aa2b3aaa2C3*: 45.
aabaabb3*: 509.
aa6bb4aaB6: 1413.
aabbcbc4*: 1394.
aabbcbc8: 784.
aabbc5CC7*: 79.
aa14bcbcd8: 449.
aabccbb2*: 1651.
aa4b6ccdd4: 1348.
abaacac8: 1734.
abababA2*: 1071.
ababab8a4: 1546.
ababab8C4: 1745.

EIGHT-LINE (272 poems, 27,339 lines)

ENGLISH POETS

(See the main poem entry for information on whether the attribution is made in the MS text or elsewhere. A poem number followed by "x" indicates an erroneous attribution; where the "x" is followed by a name, this gives the correct author, if known. The 1,381 anonymous poems (68 %) are not separately listed here.)

COMPOSERS

The 97 poems having a musical setting and a known composer are listed here. See also under Musical Settings for the additional 188 poems (66%) whose setting is anonymous.

COPYISTS, MANUSCRIPT COMPILERS AND OWNERS

HISTORICAL PERSONS AND EVENTS

(For biblical names, see RELIGION; for fictional names, SUBJECTS AND TITLES; for authors, ENGLISH POETS; for authors translated, TRANSLATIONS AND ADAPTATIONS.)

Kings of England. 224, 452, 801, 1593, 1662, 1839, 1992.

Llewelyn ap Griffydd (d. 1282). 583, 1265.
Lob (Welshman and court fool, fl. a 1535). 1176.
London. 1121.
Louis XI (K. of France, d. 1483). 1549.
Lydgate, John (d. 1449). 1080.

Mancell, Lady (fl. c 1553). 1033.
Margaret, Princess (married K. James IV, 1503). 1352.
Margaret of Anjou (Queen of Henry VI, d. 1482). 1097.
Mary I (Queen of England, d. 1558). 1032, 1195, 1231, 1349.
Moris, Master (fl. c 1210). 1544.

Norman conquest (1066). 1321.
Norman, John (Mayor of London, 1454). 1375.
Norris, Henry (d. 1536). 778.
Northumberland. See Percy.

Orleans, Duke of. 258.
Otterburn, Battle of (1388). 830, 1578.
Otto IV (Emperor, d. 1218). 1228.

Parr, Katherine (d. 1548). 1703.
Parr, William, earl of Essex (fl. 1540's). 1351.
Percy family. 313.
Percy, Henry (Earl of Northumberland, d. 1489), 693.
Petrarch, Francis (d. 1374). 120.
Philip de Valois (d. 1328). 1905.
Philip II (K. of France, d. 1223). 1228.

Rampston, Roland (d. 1549). 479.
Richard I (K. of England, d. 1199). 308.
Richard II (K. of England, d. 1400). 258, 1323.
Richard III (K. of England, d. 1485). 1507.
Rouen, Siege of (1415). 490, 1462.
Rowlat, Margery (d. 1547). 581.

Scotland. 203, 923, 1578.
Seymour, Edward (Duke of Somerset, d. 1552). 715, 1611.
Seymour, Jane (d. 1537). 888.
Skelton, John (d. 1529). 1428.
Smeaton, Mark (d. 1536). 778.
Somerset. See Seymour, Edward.
Spenser, Hugh (d. 1316). 2007.
Stafford, Edward (Duke of Buckingham, d. 1521). 109, 1139.
Stanley family. 1230.

Thame, Elizabeth (d. 1548). 1667.
Thebes. 1851.
Thomas à Becket (Abp. of Canterbury, d. 1170). 902, 1589.
Thomas of Woodstock (Duke of Gloucester, d. 1397). 258.

Waynflete, William (Bishop, fl. 1450's). 1369.
West, Lewes (d. 1556). 770, 1556.
Weston, Francis (d. 1536). 778.
Williams, Henry (d. 1551). 1461.
Wolsey, Thomas (Cardinal, d. 1530). 295, 417, 484, 606, 1094, 1682, 2006.
Wyatt, Sir Thomas (d. 1542). 1722, 2021.

KINDS

(This index combines the grouping of poems according to present-day generic classifications and according to the 16th-century terms used in their titles and texts. See also RELIGION.)

ABC. 10, 157, 162, 1767, 1982.
Acrostic. 1468, 1893.
Address. See Greeting.
Allegory. 184, 299, 384, 426, 753, 773, 777, 785, 792, 912, 1004, 1188, 1289, 1369, 1463, 1505, 1548, 1551, 1553, 1574, 1661, 1728, 1735, 1860, 1883, 1898.
Answer. 6 (to 701), 112 (to 960), 386 (to 2042), 583 (to 1265), 881 (to 919 and answered by 1947), 957 (to 1834), 1035 (to 1550), 1268 (to 969), 1314 (to 1316), 1474 (to 1372), 1895 (to 1893), 1947 (to 881 and 919), 2039 (to 1034), 2040 (to 968).

Ballad. 92, 99, 127, 235, 252, 258, 295, 317, 331, 445, 516, 556, 605, 697, 726, 761, 769, 830, 890, 922, 1016, 1162, 1312, 1374, 1380, 1578, 1630, 1672, 1677, 1718, 1770, 1804, 1825.
Book. 904, 905.
Book motto. 495.

Capping verse. 1544.
Captions. 627.
Carol, secular (94 poems); see also Carols under RELIGION. 22, 42, 66, 76, 92, 97, 127, 134, 138, 150, 196, 210, 214, 216, 240, 288, 289, 418, 424, 462, 488, 518, 548, 578, 602, 654, 656, 660, 680, 684, 695, 704, 718, 749, 750, 764, 790, 809, 827, 836, 853, 872, 920, 954, 962, 983, 1051, 1070, 1078, 1086, 1090, 1103, 1118, 1133, 1185, 1277, 1292, 1378, 1385, 1411, 1421, 1440, 1455, 1457, 1486, 1502, 1503, 1538, 1545, 1573, 1618, 1629, 1657, 1666, 1714, 1717, 1739, 1760, 1770, 1787, 1796, 1802, 1809, 1862, 1869, 1918, 1929, 1933, 1953, 1962, 2037, 2041, 2043, 2044.
Chanson d'aventure. 591, 749, 821, 1090, 1666, 1787, 1903.
Cipher. 234.
Commendation. 271, 384, 1428, 1482.
Complaint (Lament) (76 poems). 32, 78, 139, 185, 217, 257, 259, 289, 315, 328, 329, 356, 372, 435, 466, 606, 613, 670, 699, 777, 791, 813, 877, 897, 898, 914, 920, 936, 946, 991, 995, 1002, 1007, 1022, 1040, 1074, 1090, 1094, 1112, 1131, 1139, 1160, 1173, 1194, 1233, 1236, 1257, 1269, 1326, 1327, 1362,

RELIGION (563 religious poems, 86,282 lines)

(Includes all verse primarily religious in content, biblical paraphrases, controversial divinity, religious instruction, etc.)

SUBJECTS, TITLES, FICTIONAL CHARACTERS

TRANSLATIONS AND ADAPTATIONS

FRENCH (16 poems, 18,153 lines)

GREEK (5 poems, 78 lines)

ITALIAN (48 poems, 2089 lines)

LATIN (99 poems, 34,640 lines)

1: Classical and Late Classical

2: Medieval and Renaissance.

APPENDIX

TABLE 1

Concordance of Tudor Manuscript poems (TM) with *Index of Middle English Verse* poems (BR), Tudor Print (TP) poems, and poems printed from 1476 through 1500 (EP).

TM	BR	TP	EP
1	22.0	0.0	
3	31.0	0.0	
8	0.0	11.0	
9	33.9	0.0	
10	0.1	0.0	
11	35.5	0.0	
12	37.5	0.0	
13	39.5	0.0	
14	49.0	0.0	
15	54.5	0.0	
17	0.0	23.0	
21	63.8	0.0	
22	65.0	0.0	
24	3627.0	0.0	
25	68.0	0.0	
26	0.0	30.0	
28	77.0	0.0	
29	78.0	0.0	
32	79.5	0.0	
33	81.5	0.0	
34	18.0	0.0	
38	95.0	0.0	
39	0.0	47.0	
40	95.7 +	47.5	
41	95.8	0.0	
42	98.5	0.0	
45	103.0	0.0	
47	106.5	0.0	
48	108.5	0.0	
49	112.0	0.0	
50	112.5	0.0	
57	113.5	0.0	
58	113.8	0.0	
59	0.0	61.0	
61	119.0	0.0	
63	120.4	0.0	

TM	BR	TP	EP
64	120.5	0.0	
65	120.6	0.0	
66	120.7	0.0	
69	0.0	203.0	
76	134.5	0.0	
78	0.2	0.0	
79	1.0	0.0	
81	13.0	0.0	
82	13.5	0.0	
85	13.8	0.0	
86	14.5	0.0	
88	135.5	0.0	
89	137.0	0.0	
94	146.0	0.0	
95	146.5	0.0	
97	150.0	0.0	
99	154.0	0.0	
100	155.5	0.0	
101	0.0	87.0	
102	158.2	0.0	
109	158.9	0.0	
110	159.5	0.0	
111	159.8	0.0	
113	173.0	0.0	
114	172.0	0.0	
115	186.0	0.0	
118	0.0	104.0	
121	199.0	0.0	
122	231.0	0.0	
123	232.0	0.0	
125	237.0	0.0	
126	239.0	0.0	
131	254.0	0.0	
132	2514.0	0.0	
133	0.0	126.0	
134	263.3	0.0	
135	263.5	0.0	
136	263.8	0.0	
138	266.5	0.0	
144	276.5	0.0	
146	285.5	0.0	
148	0.0	143.0	
150	294.0	0.0	

TM	BR	TP	EP	TM	BR	TP	EP
151	296.6	0.0		258	500.0	0.0	
152	301.0	0.0		261	506.5	0.0	
154	302.5	0.0		262	506.0	0.0	
159	303.3	0.0		263	507.0	0.0	
162	312.5	0.0		264	511.0	0.0	
165	285.0	156.9		267	513.0	241.5	
167	320.5	0.0		274	532.0	0.0	
168	321.0	0.0		278	548.0	0.0	
169	0.0	160.0		284	550.0	0.0	
170	324.0	160.5	Yes	285	551.0	0.0	
178	340.5	0.0		286	552.5	0.0	
179	343.0	0.0		287	553.5	0.0	
180	373.0	0.0		288	554.5	0.0	
182	346.0	0.0		291	556.0	0.0	
183	350.0	0.0		293	557.5	0.0	
185	366.8	0.0		294	558.5	0.0	
188	354.0	0.0		298	572.0	0.0	
190	375.0	170.5		299	1547.5	0.0	
191	363.0	0.0		300	576.5	0.0	
192	364.0	0.0		301	581.0	0.0	
193	365.0	0.0		302	584.0	0.0	
194	366.0	0.0		304	0.0	295.0	
195	367.0	0.0		307	608.0	0.0	
196	102.3	0.0		308	0.0	307.0	
197	368.0	0.0		309	612.0	0.0	
198	374.0	0.0		310	622.0	0.0	
199	372.0	0.0		311	1731.0	0.0	
200	3754.0	0.0		313	631.8	0.0	
201	397.0	0.0		314	633.5	310.0	
203	399.0	0.0		317	636.0	0.0	
205	2183.5	180.0		322	642.5	0.0	
207	404.5	0.0		326	648.0	0.0	
210	409.5	0.0		327	649.0	0.0	
212	410.0	0.0		328	0.0	320.0	
213	417.5	0.0		331	653.0	327.5	Yes
214	418.0	193.0		332	655.0	0.0	
215	425.0	0.0		336	663.0	332.5	
219	430.0	0.0		337	664.3	0.0	
220	430.5	0.0		338	665.0	0.0	
221	432.0	0.0		339	666.0	333.5	
223	439.0	0.0		344	675.5	0.0	
224	444.0	0.0		345	675.8	0.0	
225	0.0	201.0		349	676.5	0.0	
230	455.5	0.0		350	0.0	344.0	
232	456.5	0.0		352	680.0	0.0	
235	458.0	0.0		354	681.0	0.0	
237	465.5	0.0		355	681.5	348.0	
238	467.0	209.0		359	686.0	351.0	
239	469.0	0.0		362	687.5	0.0	
240	470.0	0.0		367	688.8	0.0	
244	474.5	0.0		368	690.0	0.0	
245	481.0	0.0		369	691.0	0.0	
246	0.0	221.0		370	0.0	356.0	
250	484.5	0.0		375	698.0	0.0	
252	490.0	0.0		376	0.0	359.0	
253	490.5	0.0		377	704.0	0.0	
254	0.0	227.0		379	717.0	0.0	
256	497.0	0.0		381	726.0	0.0	

TM	BR	TP	EP	TM	BR	TP	EP
382	729.0	0.0		474	926.0	0.0	
384	729.5	366.0		475	931.0	0.0	
385	730.0	0.0		476	933.0	0.0	
387	734.8	0.0		478	935.0	482.0	
388	0.0	374.0		480	940.0	483.0	
389	737.0	0.0		482	952.0	491.0	
390	735.0	0.0		485	960.3	0.0	
393	0.0	385.0		486	960.5	0.0	
394	753.8	0.0		488	962.0	0.0	
395	755.0	0.0		489	977.0	500.5	
396	756.0	0.0		490	979.0	0.0	
398	757.0	0.0		491	994.5	0.0	
400	761.0	389.5	Yes	493	1006.5+	0.0	
402	0.0	390.0		495	1007.0	0.0	
403	765.5	0.0		496	1009.3	0.0	
404	767.0	0.0		499	1015.0	0.0	
405	768.0	0.0		500	1017.5	0.0	
406	0.0	391.0		502	1018.0	0.0	
407	769.0	0.0		503	1018.5	0.0	
408	782.5	0.0		506	1032.0	0.0	
411	801.0	0.0		507	1035.0	0.0	
413	805.0	0.0		508	1040.0	0.0	
414	809.0	404.5	Yes	509	1044.0	0.0	
417	813.3	411.0		510	1046.0	0.0	
418	813.6	0.0		511	1051.0	0.0	
419	819.5*	0.0		512	1055.0	0.0	
420	824.0	415.5	Yes	513	1065.0	0.0	
421	825.0	0.0		514	1070.3	0.0	
422	832.0	0.0		515	1077.0	0.0	
424	835.5	0.0		516	1082.5	0.0	
426	851.0	434.5		517	1086.0	529.0	
427	851.3	0.0		518	1303.5	0.0	
429	854.0	428.5	Yes	520	1088.5	0.0	
430	855.0	0.0		521	3721.0	0.0	
432	859.5	0.0		523	1119.0	0.0	
437	860.3	435.5	Yes	524	1097.0	0.0	
441	864.5	0.0		525	1119.3	0.0	
442	0.0	438.0		530	1132.0	0.0	
444	870.5	0.0		531	1136.5	0.0	
445	869.0	0.0		532	0.0	560.0	
447	0.0	441.0		533	1139.0	0.0	
448	878.0	0.0		534	1142.5	0.0	
450	0.0	444.0		536	1148.0	0.0	
452	882.0	0.0		537	1149.0	0.0	
454	887.0	0.0		539	1149.5	0.0	
455	889.0	0.0		540	1151.0	576.5	
456	890.0	0.0		541	1151.5	0.0	
457	892.5	0.0		545	1160.0	0.0	
459	895.0	0.0		546	0.0	581.0	
460	898.0	0.0		547	1162.8	0.0	
462	903.0	0.0		548	1163.5	0.0	
463	906.0	0.0		551	1163.0	585.0	
466	913.0	466.3	Yes	552	1165.0	0.0	
467	914.0	466.5		553	0.0	587.0	
468	916.0	0.0		554	1166.5	0.0	
469	918.0	0.0		556	1168.0	588.5	Yes
471	0.0	468.0		558	1173.0	590.0	
473	925.0	0.0		561	1174.5	0.0	

TM	BR	TP	EP
565	0.0	597.0	
567	1176.5	0.0	
568	1176.8	0.0	
571	1180.0	0.0	
572	1181.0	0.0	
573	1181.5	0.0	
576	1187.0	0.0	
577	595.0	0.0	
578	1194.5	0.0	
579	1198.0	0.0	
580	1203.0	0.0	
583	0.0	613.0	
585	1206.9	0.0	
587	3848.0	0.0	
588	1212.0	0.0	
591	1214.5	0.0	
594	1214.6	0.0	
595	1214.7	0.0	
597	1218.0	0.0	
598	1218.8	620.0	
600	0.0	623.0	
601	1222.0	0.0	
602	1226.0	0.0	
604	1234.0	0.0	
605	1237.0	0.0	
610	1255.0	0.0	
615	0.0	694.0	
616	1261.0	0.0	
617	1259.0	0.0	
622	1270.1	0.0	
624	1270.2	0.0	
625	1273.0	0.0	
626	1273.3	0.0	
627	1275.0	0.0	
628	1276.0	0.0	
630	1278.0	0.0	
634	1286.0	0.0	
635	1286.5	0.0	
637	1291.0	0.0	
638	1294.0	735.5	
639	1294.3	0.0	
640	0.0	740.0	
641	1653.0	0.0	
642	1297.0	0.0	
643	1303.3	0.0	
645	1307.0	0.0	
646	1308.0	0.0	
647	1315.0	0.0	
649	1314.0	0.0	
651	1322.0	0.0	
652	1322.8	0.0	
659	0.0	762.0	
660	1327.0	0.0	
662	1328.5	0.0	
664	1328.7	0.0	
665	1328.8	0.0	
666	1329.0	0.0	
667	1329.5	0.0	
670	1333.0	0.0	
673	1339.5	0.0	
675	1343.0	0.0	
677	1344.0	0.0	
678	1349.0	0.0	
679	1349.5	0.0	
680	1350.0	0.0	
681	1354.5	0.0	
683	1356.8	0.0	
684	1362.0	0.0	
685	1363.0	0.0	
689	0.0	784.0	
691	1376.0	0.0	
692	0.0	788.0	
693	1378.0	0.0	
694	1383.0	0.0	
695	1386.0	0.0	
698	1400.0	0.0	
702	1392.0	0.0	
704	1399.0	0.0	
708	1409.1	0.0	
710	0.0	821.0	
712	0.0	825.0	
714	1411.0	0.0	
716	0.0	830.0	
717	0.0	831.0	
718	1412.0	0.0	
720	1414.5	0.0	
721	1414.8	0.0	
726	1419.0	0.0	
729	1420.5	0.0	
731	0.0	840.0	
733	0.0	846.0	
736	1426.1	853.0	
737	1429.0	0.0	
738	1436.2	862.0	
741	0.0	867.0	
744	1440.0	0.0	
745	1444.0	0.0	
746	1445.5	0.0	
749	1449.5	0.0	
750	1450.0	0.0	
751	1450.5	0.0	
752	1455.5	0.0	
753	1459.0	877.5	
754	1451.0	0.0	
759	1471.0	0.0	
762	0.0	888.0	
764	1485.0	0.0	
765	0.0	892.0	
767	1488.0	0.0	
771	1494.5	0.0	
773	1498.0	0.0	
775	1502.0	0.0	
776	1504.5	0.0	
777	1507.0	906.5	
779	1509.0	0.0	
780	3187.0	0.0	

TM	BR	TP	EP
782	1522.5+	0.0	
784	1527.0	0.0	
785	1528.0	912.5	
786	1528.5	0.0	
788	1533.0	0.0	
789	1540.0	0.0	
790	1540.5	0.0	
791	1548.0	918.0	
792	1554.0	923.5	
794	1560.0	0.0	
800	1570.5	0.0	
802	1575.0	0.0	
803	1578.0	0.0	
808	1586.0	0.0	
809	1587.0	0.0	
811	1587.8	943.5	Yes
812	1589.5	0.0	
813	0.0	944.0	
814	1593.0	0.0	
818	1597.0	948.5	
821	1598.0	948.7	
822	1601.0	0.0	
823	1620.5	0.0	
826	1608.0	0.0	
827	1609.0	0.0	
830	1620.0	0.0	
834	1628.8	0.0	
835	1635.0	0.0	
836	1636.5	0.0	
837	1636.8	0.0	
838	1637.2	0.0	
840	1637.8	0.0	
842	0.0	973.0	
847	1669.0	0.0	
849	1679.0	0.0	
851	1703.0	989.0	
852	1709.0	0.0	
853	1710.0	0.0	
854	1717.3	0.0	
855	1727.0	991.7	
856	1729.0	0.0	
857	1738.0	0.0	
858	3238.0	0.0	
859	1768.0	0.0	
860	1779.0	0.0	
863	1806.0	0.0	
868	3088.0	0.0	
869	1817.0	0.0	
871	1823.0	0.0	
872	1824.8	0.0	
873	1825.0	0.0	
874	1829.2	1008.7	Yes
876	0.0	1010.0	
878	1841.5	0.0	
879	1842.5	1016.0	
882	1863.3	0.0	
883	1864.5	0.0	
884	1866.0	0.0	
886	1866.5	0.0	
887	1866.8	0.0	
889	1870.0	0.0	
890	1872.0	0.0	
891	1873.0	0.0	
892	0.0	1038.0	
896	0.0	1047.0	
900	0.0	1050.0	
901	1891.0	0.0	
902	1892.0	0.0	
904	1919.0	1052.5	Yes
905	1920.0	1052.7	Yes
906	1923.5	1054.0	
908	1926.5	0.0	
909	1927.0	0.0	
910	0.0	1056.0	
911	0.0	1057.0	
912	1928.0	0.0	
913	1929.0	1059.5	
916	1929.5	0.0	
921	1999.0	0.0	
922	1933.5	0.0	
923	1934.0	1060.5	Yes
925	0.0	1063.0	
928	1937.0	0.0	
930	1941.0	0.0	
932	1944.5	0.0	
933	0.0	1074.0	
936	1957.0	0.0	
942	1961.5	0.0	
945	1989.0	0.0	
947	0.0	1092.0	
949	1999.5	0.0	
954	2007.5	0.0	
955	2012.3	0.0	
956	2013.0	0.0	
959	0.0	1096.0	
961	2016.0	0.0	
964	2025.5	0.0	
965	2028.5	0.0	
966	2028.8	0.0	
967	2029.0	0.0	
969	0.0	1102.0	
971	2039.3	1102.5	Yes
973	2052.0	0.0	
974	2053.0	0.0	
975	2057.0	0.0	
976	2053.0	0.0	
977	2060.0	0.0	
978	2065.0	0.0	
979	0.0	1106.0	
980	2056.0	0.0	
981	2072.4	0.0	
982	2076.0	0.0	
983	2090.0	0.0	
987	3270.5	0.0	
991	0.0	1117.0	
992	2097.0	0.0	

TM	BR	TP	EP	TM	BR	TP	EP
993	2098.0	0.0		1097	2308.5	0.0	
996	2044.0	0.0		1098	766.0	0.0	
997	2147.0	1122.5		1101	2323.8	0.0	
1004	0.0	1133.0		1103	2034.5	0.0	
1005	0.0	1135.0		1104	2335.0	0.0	
1007	2192.0	1138.5		1105	2343.0	0.0	
1008	2195.0	0.0		1106	2346.0	0.0	
1013	2200.3	0.0		1111	2377.0	0.0	
1016	2210.0	0.0		1115	0.0	1243.0	
1017	2211.0	0.0		1116	2363.0	0.0	
1018	2212.0	0.0		1117	2364.0	0.0	
1019	2213.0	0.0		1118	2370.0	0.0	
1020	2217.0	0.0		1119	2371.0	0.0	
1021	2218.0	0.0		1120	2380.0	0.0	
1026	2224.0	0.0		1121	0.0	1245.0	
1027	2224.5	0.0		1122	2381.0	0.0	
1030	2228.0	0.0		1128	2385.0	0.0	
1031	2233.0	1154.5	Yes	1129	2388.0	0.0	
1032	0.0	1155.0		1130	2391.0	0.0	
1036	0.0	1116.0		1131	2393.5	0.0	
1037	0.0	1157.0		1132	2394.0	0.0	
1039	0.0	1162.0		1133	2394.5	0.0	
1040	2244.6	0.0		1135	2403.3	0.0	
1043	2245.1	0.0		1138	2409.0	0.0	
1044	2245.3	0.0		1139	2409.5	0.0	
1045	2245.6	1163.0		1140	2410.0	0.0	
1049	2249.0	0.0		1141	2412.0	0.0	
1050	2250.3	0.0		1142	2421.0	0.0	
1051	2250.5	0.0		1145	2439.5	0.0	
1053	2255.3	0.0		1146	2441.0	0.0	
1054	2255.6	0.0		1147	2444.0	0.0	
1057	2261.4	0.0		1148	2446.0	0.0	
1058	2261.6	0.0		1154	0.0	1277.0	
1059	0.0	1167.0		1157	2453.0	0.0	
1060	2261.8	0.0		1159	0.0	1287.0	
1061	0.0	1168.0		1160	0.0	1288.0	
1063	0.0	1171.0		1162	2461.0	0.0	
1064	2263.0	0.0		1163	0.0	1296.0	
1065	2263.5	1172.0		1164	2464.0	1299.0	
1067	0.0	1173.0		1165	2471.0	0.0	
1070	2271.2	0.0		1166	2472.0	0.0	
1072	2271.6	0.0		1167	2474.0	0.0	
1073	2272.0	0.0		1171	2475.0	0.0	
1074	2272.5	0.0		1173	2478.0	0.0	
1075	2277.0	0.0		1176	2482.5	0.0	
1076	2277.5	0.0		1177	0.0	1304.0	
1077	2881.0	0.0		1178	2486.0	0.0	
1078	2281.5	0.0		1184	0.0	1330.0	
1079	0.0	1187.0		1185	2494.0	0.0	
1080	2284.0	0.0		1194	2496.0	0.0	
1081	0.0	1189.0		1196	2498.0	0.0	
1083	2289.8	0.0		1197	2500.5	0.0	
1085	2291.5	1204.0		1198	0.0	1347.0	
1086	2293.5	0.0		1199	2507.0	1348.5	
1087	2293.6	1209.0		1200	2511.0	0.0	
1089	2293.8	0.0		1201	0.0	1350.0	
1091	2300.3	0.0		1203	2515.0	0.0	
1095	2307.0	0.0		1206	2518.0	0.0	

TM	BR	TP	EP
1207	0.0	1354.0	
1209	2521.0	0.0	
1210	2522.0	0.0	
1212	2523.0	0.0	
1214	2528.0	0.0	
1215	2529.0	0.0	
1216	2530.5	0.0	
1217	2531.0	0.0	
1218	2531.5	0.0	
1219	2532.0	0.0	
1220	2532.3	0.0	
1221	2532.5	0.0	
1222	2533.0	0.0	
1223	2536.0	0.0	
1225	2536.5	0.0	
1228	2541.5	1368.0	
1229	2547.0	0.0	
1230	2547.3	0.0	
1232	2547.5	0.0	
1233	2549.5	0.0	
1234	2551.5	0.0	
1235	2553.0	0.0	
1236	2552.5	0.0	
1238	2557.0	0.0	
1239	2560.0	0.0	
1240	2560.5	0.0	
1248	2579.3	0.0	
1252	2586.0	0.0	
1253	2588.0	0.0	
1254	2597.0	0.0	
1255	2598.0	0.0	
1257	4263.3	1392.0	
1258	2601.0	0.0	
1259	2607.5	0.0	
1260	2613.5	0.0	
1261	2619.5	0.0	
1262	0.0	1403.0	
1263	0.0	1405.0	
1264	0.0	1406.0	
1265	0.0	1407.0	
1269	2626.0	0.0	
1271	2633.0	0.0	
1274	2636.0	0.0	
1275	0.0	1417.0	
1276	2649.5+	0.0	
1277	2654.0	0.0	
1278	2656.0	0.0	
1279	2662.0	1421.5	Yes
1281	0.0	1422.0	
1283	2668.0	0.0	
1285	2668.8	0.0	
1287	2674.0	0.0	
1288	2676.0	0.0	
1289	2678.0	0.0	
1290	2681.0	0.0	
1291	2682.0	0.0	
1292	2683.0	0.0	
1293	2685.8	0.0	

TM	BR	TP	EP
1294	2688.0	0.0	
1295	2689.0	0.0	
1296	0.0	1429.0	
1298	2695.5	1433.0	
1302	2731.0	0.0	
1304	2732.0	0.0	
1306	2733.0	0.0	
1307	2736.6	0.0	
1308	2736.8	0.0	
1309	13.3	0.0	
1310	0.0	1459.0	
1311	2737.0	0.0	
1312	2737.5	0.0	
1322	0.0	1462.0	
1323	0.0	1463.0	
1324	2753.5	0.0	
1325	2755.5	0.0	
1326	2756.0	1467.7	
1327	2757.3	0.0	
1330	2760.0	0.0	
1334	2766.2	0.0	
1335	2766.8	0.0	
1337	2771.0	0.0	
1338	2784.0	1491.5	Yes
1341	2785.0	0.0	
1342	2785.5	0.0	
1344	236.0	0.0	
1345	2791.0	0.0	
1347	2794.4	0.0	
1349	2794.2	0.0	
1350	2794.8	1500.0	
1352	2797.5	0.0	
1354	2806.0	0.0	
1355	2806.5	0.0	
1360	2811.0	0.0	
1362	0.0	1520.0	
1364	2814.0	0.0	
1365	2818.3	0.0	
1367	2821.0	0.0	
1368	4004.0	1531.0	
1369	2825.5+	0.0	
1370	0.0	1534.0	
1371	2827.5	0.0	
1374	2831.8	0.0	
1375	2832.5	1537.5	
1376	0.0	1540.0	
1378	2832.2	0.0	
1379	3038.0	0.0	
1380	3065.0	0.0	
1381	3071.0	0.0	
1382	3074.0	1542.0	Yes
1383	3074.6	0.0	
1385	3079.7	0.0	
1387	3083.0	0.0	
1389	3084.0	1549.0	
1393	3087.0	0.0	
1396	0.0	1558.0	
1400	0.0	1565.0	

TM	BR	TP	EP	TM	BR	TP	EP
1401	3098.3	0.0		1510	3327.0	1702.5	Yes
1404	0.0	1569.0		1512	0.0	1707.0	
1408	3135.5	0.0		1517	3341.0	499.5	
1411	3144.5	0.0		1518	3348.0	1719.5	Yes
1417	3115.0	0.0		1519	3603.0	0.0	
1418	3117.6	0.0		1522	0.0	1727.0	
1420	3119.0	0.0		1524	3354.5	1730.0	
1421	3119.5*	0.0		1525	0.0	1731.0	
1423	3131.0	0.0		1528	3361.6	0.0	
1426	3156.5+	1596.5	Yes	1529	3364.0	0.0	
1429	2834.3	0.0		1535	3375.0	0.0	
1430	3161.0	0.0		1536	3376.5	0.0	
1431	3162.5	0.0		1537	3377.0	0.0	
1432	0.0	1599.0		1538	3382.0	0.0	
1435	3168.0	0.0		1544	0.0	1762.0	
1436	3168.2	0.0		1545	3405.5	0.0	
1437	3168.4	0.0		1547	3405.8	0.0	
1439	0.0	2078.0		1548	3406.0	1766.0	Yes
1440	3171.0	0.0		1549	0.0	1767.0	
1441	3171.5	0.0		1550	0.0	1768.0	
1442	3172.0	0.0		1551	3412.0	1768.5	Yes
1444	0.0	1610.0		1552	3412.2+	0.0	
1445	0.0	1615.0		1553	3412.3	0.0	
1447	0.0	1621.0		1554	0.0	1770.0	
1451	3190.0	1623.5		1555	0.0	1771.0	
1452	3193.5	0.0		1563	0.0	1786.0	
1454	3199.3	0.0		1564	3424.0	0.0	
1455	3199.8	0.0		1568	3437.0	0.0	Yes
1457	3206.5	0.0		1569	0.0	1804.0	
1458	3207.0	0.0		1570	3438.3	0.0	
1461	0.0	1633.0		1572	3438.6	0.0	
1462	3213.0	0.0		1573	3413.3	0.0	
1465	0.0	1640.0		1574	3442.0	1809.5	
1466	0.0	1641.0		1578	3445.5	0.0	
1470	3226.0	1650.0		1579	0.0	1814.0	
1472	3228.3	0.0		1581	3448.0	1818.0	
1473	3228.5	0.0		1586	0.0	1825.0	
1476	3243.0	0.0		1587	3456.0	0.0	
1477	0.0	1653.0		1588	3456.5	0.0	
1478	3249.0	0.0		1592	3460.0	0.0	
1481	3253.0	0.0		1594	3473.0	0.0	
1482	3256.1	1657.0		1596	3482.0	0.0	
1485	3269.0	0.0		1598	0.0	1844.5	
1486	3271.0	0.0		1599	3486.5	0.0	
1488	3287.5	0.0		1601	3487.0	0.0	
1492	3297.3	0.0		1602	3487.5	0.0	
1493	3297.5	0.0		1605	3491.0	0.0	
1494	3301.0	0.0		1606	3492.4+	0.0	
1495	4257.0	1678.0		1607	0.0	1854.0	
1496	0.0	1679.0		1608	3498.5	0.0	
1497	0.0	1681.0		1610	0.0	1858.0	
1499	3307.0	0.0		1612	3504.0	0.0	Yes
1502	3313.0	1693.0		1615	3510.0	0.0	
1503	3315.0	0.0		1617	3514.0	0.0	
1504	3318.0	0.0		1618	3515.0	0.0	
1505	3318.4	0.0		1621	3521.0	0.0	
1506	3318.3	0.0		1622	3521.5	1875.5	Yes
1507	3318.7	1695.5		1623	3523.0	0.0	

TM	BR	TP	EP
1624	3522.0	0.0	
1625	3524.0	0.0	
1626	3527.0	0.0	
1627	3528.0	0.0	
1628	20.0	0.0	
1629	3530.5	0.0	
1630	3531.0	0.0	
1631	3532.0	0.0	
1633	3538.0	0.0	
1636	0.0	2094.0	
1638	3551.0	0.0	
1640	3553.5	0.0	
1641	4255.0	0.0	
1642	3558.5	1889.5	Yes
1643	3559.8	0.0	
1644	0.0	1894.0	
1645	3571.0	1905.0	
1646	3574.0	0.0	
1647	3575.0	0.0	
1648	3577.0	0.0	
1649	3580.0	0.0	
1650	3584.0	0.0	Yes
1651	3595.6	0.0	
1652	3597.0	0.0	
1653	3598.5	0.0	
1654	3604.0	0.0	
1655	3605.0	0.0	
1656	3606.0	0.0	
1658	3612.5	0.0	
1660	3615.0	0.0	
1661	3642.5	1908.0	
1662	3632.0	1911.5	
1665	3635.0	0.0	
1666	3635.5	0.0	
1669	3639.5	1915.0	
1670	3642.0	0.0	
1671	0.0	1916.0	
1672	0.0	1917.0	
1674	3525.0	0.0	
1675	0.0	1923.0	
1676	3652.0	0.0	
1677	3655.0	0.0	
1678	3656.0	0.0	
1679	3656.3+	1924.3	Yes
1680	3661.0	1924.5	Yes
1683	3669.0	0.0	
1684	3670.0	1940.5	Yes
1685	3672.0	0.0	
1689	3677.5	0.0	
1690	0.0	1945.0	
1691	3685.0	0.0	
1693	3695.0	0.0	
1694	3666.0	0.0	
1696	3703.0	0.0	
1698	3703.3	0.0	
1701	3703.5	0.0	
1705	3706.2	0.0	
1707	3706.5	0.0	

TM	BR	TP	EP
1708	3706.7	0.0	
1709	3706.8	0.0	
1710	1421.0	1974.0	
1714	3707.3	0.0	
1716	3713.5	0.0	
1717	3820.0	0.0	
1718	3718.0	0.0	
1719	3720.0	0.0	
1720	3721.5	0.0	
1721	3722.0	0.0	
1722	0.0	1055.0	
1724	3724.5	0.0	
1726	3736.0	0.0	
1727	3737.0	0.0	
1728	3746.0	0.0	
1729	3749.0	0.0	
1730	3750.0	0.0	
1733	3751.3	0.0	
1742	3758.5	0.0	
1745	0.0	2028.0	
1746	0.0	2031.0	
1750	3767.5	0.0	
1751	3769.5	0.0	
1752	3772.0	0.0	
1753	3776.0	0.0	
1757	3776.5	0.0	
1758	3777.5	0.0	
1759	3780.0	0.0	
1760	3782.0	0.0	
1764	3785.5	0.0	
1766	3792.5	2053.0	
1767	3793.0	0.0	
1769	0.0	2054.0	
1770	194.5	2055.0	
1772	3798.0	2056.3	
1773	3799.0	2056.5	
1774	3800.5	0.0	
1775	3804.0	0.0	
1776	3809.0	0.0	
1778	3815.8	0.0	
1779	3818.0	2069.5	Yes
1782	3827.0	0.0	
1783	0.0	2076.0	
1785	3832.5	0.0	
1786	3835.0	0.0	
1787	3836.5	0.0	
1788	3845.0	0.0	
1792	3847.0	0.0	
1793	0.0	2085.0	
1794	0.0	2086.0	
1796	3852.0	0.0	
1797	0.0	2090.0	
1799	0.0	2335.0	
1802	3863.5	2095.5	
1803	0.0	2098.0	
1808	3880.6	0.0	
1810	3889.5	0.0	
1811	3899.3	0.0	

TM	BR	TP	EP
1813	3903.5	2114.0	
1814	3903.8	0.0	
1817	3904.0	0.0	
1820	3905.0	0.0	
1822	3911.0	0.0	
1828	0.0	2126.0	
1830	0.0	2131.0	
1833	3914.0	0.0	
1834	0.0	2136.0	
1835	3917.5	2137.0	
1838	3917.8	0.0	
1840	0.0	2143.0	
1841	3918.5	2143.5	Yes
1842	3919.5	0.0	
1843	0.0	2145.0	
1845	4018.0	0.0	
1846	3945.0	0.0	
1848	3922.0	2149.5	
1850	0.0	2152.0	
1851	3928.0	0.0	Yes
1854	0.0	2158.0	
1855	0.0	2159.0	
1856	3942.0	0.0	
1857	3943.0	2160.5	Yes
1859	3946.0	0.0	
1860	3947.0	0.0	
1861	3947.6	0.0	
1864	3950.0	0.0	
1870	3960.5	402.0	
1871	3962.5	0.0	
1872	3969.0	0.0	
1875	3975.0	0.0	
1876	3985.0	0.0	
1877	3988.0	0.0	
1880	3999.0	0.0	
1883	4005.0	2180.5	Yes
1887	0.0	2184.0	
1888	4008.0	0.0	
1889	4012.0	0.0	
1890	0.0	2185.0	
1892	4013.0	0.0	
1894	4017.0	0.0	
1897	4019.0	2188.5	Yes
1899	4020.3	0.0	
1902	4023.0	0.0	
1903	4025.0	0.0	
1905	0.0	2189.0	
1907	4029.0	0.0	
1909	4039.0	0.0	
1910	4040.0	0.0	
1912	4044.3	0.0	
1913	4049.2	0.0	
1914	4049.5	0.0	
1917	4035.0	0.0	
1921	4057.0	0.0	
1926	0.0	2212.0	
1928	4065.0	0.0	
1929	4068.6	0.0	

TM	BR	TP	EP
1931	4070.5	0.0	
1932	4073.3	2222.0	
1933	4077.0	0.0	
1934	0.0	2221.0	
1935	4079.3	0.0	
1936	4079.6	0.0	
1937	0.0	2123.0	
1939	4094.3	2229.0	
1941	0.0	2232.0	
1945	0.0	2234.0	
1946	0.0	2236.0	
1950	4096.5	2239.0	
1951	4098.1	0.0	
1952	4098.6	0.0	
1954	4101.0	2242.3	Yes
1955	4103.0	0.0	
1956	4106.0	2242.5	Yes
1957	4106.5	2242.7	Yes
1960	4112.0	2246.5	
1964	4118.0	0.0	
1968	0.0	2255.0	
1970	4129.0	0.0	
1972	4133.0	0.0	
1974	4137.0	2255.5	Yes
1975	4138.0	0.0	
1976	4143.3	0.0	
1977	4143.5	0.0	
1978	4143.8	0.0	
1979	4148.0	0.0	
1981	4154.3	0.0	
1982	4155.0	0.0	
1983	4126.0	0.0	
1986	4160.0	0.0	
1988	4162.5	0.0	
1991	4168.0	0.0	
1992	4174.3	0.0	
1993	4174.5	0.0	
1996	4175.0	0.0	
1997	4176.5	0.0	
1998	4181.0	2292.5	Yes
1999	4184.0	0.0	
2000	4187.0	0.0	
2001	4186.5	2295.5	
2002	4190.0	0.0	
2005	4192.5+	2298.5	
2007	0.0	2303.0	
2009	4201.3	0.0	
2010	4201.6	0.0	
2011	4210.0	0.0	
2012	4212.0	0.0	
2014	4213.5	0.0	
2015	4215.0	0.0	
2020	4230.0	0.0	
2021	0.0	2319.0	
2023	4246.0	2320.3	Yes
2024	4248.0	0.0	
2026	4253.0	0.0	
2028	4254.5	0.0	

TM	BR	TP	EP
2029	4262.0	0.0	
2035	0.0	2329.0	
2036	4274.0	0.0	
2037	4058.3	0.0	
2038	4281.5	0.0	
2041	4283.5	0.0	
2042	0.0	2342.0	
2043	4284.3	0.0	
2044	4285.0	0.0	

TABLE 2

Concordance of Tudor Print poems (TP) with Tudor manuscript poems (TM), *Index of Middle English Verse* poems (BR), and poems printed from 1476 through 1500 (EP).

TP	TM	BR	EP
11.0	8	0.0	
11.5	0	33.5	Yes
18.5	0	42.5	Yes
23.0	17	0.	
30.0	26	0.	
47.0	39	0.	
47.5	40	95.7+	
50.3	0	99.0	
50.5	0	100.0	
53.0	0	107.0	
61.0	59	0.0	
87.0	101	0.0	
104.0	118	0.0	
114.5	0	223.0	
116.0	0	228.0	
126.0	133	0.0	
143.0	148	0.0	
155.0	0	306.5+	
156.3	0	311.5+	
156.7	0	316.6	Yes
156.9	165	285.0	
160.0	169	0.0	
160.5	170	324.0	Yes
170.5	190	375.0	
171.0	0	377.5	
178.5	0	399.5	Yes
180.0	205	2183.5	
193.0	214	418.0	
201.0	225	0.0	
203.0	69	0.0	
203.5	0	455.8	
209.0	238	467.0	
221.0	246	0.0	
227.0	254	0.0	
241.5	267	513.0	Yes
253.5	0	524.0	Yes
264.5	0	527.5	Yes
288.5	0	576.3+	Yes
295.0	304	0.0	
307.0	308	0.0	
307.5	0	611.5	Yes
310.0	314	633.5	
320.0	328	0.0	
327.5	331	653.0	Yes
332.5	336	663.0	
333.5	339	666.0	
339.0	0	672.4	
344.0	350	0.0	
345.5	0	679.0	
348.0	355	681.5	
348.5	0	683.0	
351.0	359	686.0	
356.0	370	0.0	
359.0	376	0.0	
362.5	0	710.0	
366.0	384	729.5	
373.5	0	736.0	
374.0	388	0.0	
378.5	0	746.5	Yes
385.0	393	0.0	
389.5	400	761.0	Yes
390.0	402	0.0	
391.0	406	0.0	
402.0	1870	3960.5	
404.5	414	809.0	Yes
405.0	0	811.5	
411.0	417	813.3	
411.0	0	813.3	
414.5	0	5.5	
415.5	420	824.0	Yes
428.5	429	854.0	Yes
434.5	426	851.0	Yes
435.5	437	860.3	Yes
438.0	442	0.0	
440.5	0	875.0	
441.0	447	0.0	
444.0	450	0.0	
454.0	0	905.5	
466.3	466	913.0	Yes
466.5	467	914.0	
466.7	0	919.0	
468.0	471	0.0	
469.3	0	920.0	Yes
470.5	0	927.5	Yes
482.0	478	935.0	
483.0	480	940.0	
488.5	0	945.8	
491.0	482	952.0	
491.0	0	952.0	
499.3	0	969.0	
499.5	1517	3341.0	
499.5	0	970.0	
500.5	489	977.0	
501.0	0	978.0	
504.3	0	983.0	
504.5	0	988.0	
506.5	0	991.0	Yes

TP	TM	BR	EP	TP	TM	BR	EP
529.0	517	1086.0		957.3	0	1618.0	Yes
545.5	0	1129.5+	Yes	957.5	0	1619.0	Yes
560.0	532	0.0		972.0	0	1637.6	Yes
576.5	540	1151.0		973.0	842	0.0	
579.0	0	1155.0		978.0	0	1641.5	
581.0	546	0.0		979.0	0	1644.0	
585.0	551	1163.0		982.5	0	1654.5	
587.0	553	0.0		989.0	851	1703.0	
588.5	556	1168.0	Yes	991.3	0	1721.0	
590.0	558	1173.0		991.5	0	1725.0	Yes
597.0	565	0.0		991.7	855	1727.0	
599.5	0	1177.0		994.5	0	1752.0	
605.5	0	1184.0		1008.5	0	1824.3+	Yes
606.0	0	1192.5		1008.7	874	1829.2	Yes
613.0	583	0.0		1010.0	876	0.0	
620.0	598	1218.8		1015.0	0	1841.0	
623.0	600	0.0		1016.0	879	1842.5	
694.0	615	0.0		1038.0	892	0.0	
735.5	638	1294.0		1047.0	896	0.0	
740.0	640	0.0		1050.0	900	0.0	
745.5	0	1306.0		1051.5	0	1894.5	
748.0	0	1309.0		1052.1	0	1895.0	
762.0	659	0.0		1052.3	0	1915.0	Yes
770.0	0	1341.8		1052.5	904	1919.0	Yes
784.0	689	0.0		1052.7	905	1920.0	Yes
788.0	692	0.0		1054.0	906	1923.5	
821.0	710	0.0		1055.0	1722	0.0	
825.0	712	0.0		1056.0	910	0.0	
830.0	716	0.0		1057.0	911	0.0	
831.0	717	0.0		1059.5	913	1929.0	
840.0	731	0.0		1060.5	923	1934.0	Yes
846.0	733	0.0		1063.0	925	0.0	
853.0	736	1426.1		1074.0	933	0.0	
857.5	0	1426.6	Yes	1085.5	0	1979.0	
858.5	0	1427.7+	Yes	1088.5	0	1993.0	Yes
862.0	738	1436.2		1089.0	0	1984.5	
867.0	741	0.0		1092.0	947	0.0	
877.3	0	1453.0		1096.0	959	0.0	
877.5	753	1459.0		1102.0	969	0.0	
879.0	0	1466.5		1102.5	971	2039.3	Yes
880.5	0	1470.5	Yes	1104.0	0	2039.5	
888.0	762	0.0		1106.0	979	0.0	
891.0	0	1486.0		1111.5	0	2092.0	
892.0	765	0.0		1116.0	1036	0.0	
894.0	0	1487.0		1117.0	991	0.0	
906.5	777	1507.0		1119.5	0	2139.0	
908.5	0	1515.0		1121.5	0	2142.0	
912.5	785	1528.0		1122.5	997	2147.0	
918.0	791	1548.0		1133.0	1004	0.0	
923.5	792	1554.0		1135.0	1005	0.0	
926.4	0	1567.0		1138.5	1007	2192.0	
937.0	0	1575.5		1143.0	0	2217.5	
943.5	811	1587.8	Yes	1146.0	0	2223.0	
944.0	813	0.0		1154.0	0	2231.5	
945.5	0	1596.5	Yes	1154.5	1031	2233.0	Yes
948.5	818	1597.0		1155.0	1032	0.0	
948.7	821	1598.0		1157.0	1037	0.0	
953.0	0	1605.5		1160.0	0	2244.0	

TP	TM	BR	EP
1162.0	1039	0.0	
1163.0	1045	2245.6	
1165.0	0	2250.9	
1167.0	1059	0.0	
1168.0	1061	0.0	
1168.5	0	2262.0	Yes
1171.0	1063	0.0	
1172.0	1065	2263.5	
1172.5	0	2264.0	Yes
1173.0	1067	0.0	
1187.0	1079	0.0	
1189.0	1081	0.0	
1204.0	1085	2291.5	
1209.0	1087	2293.6	
1227.5	0	2320.0	
1243.0	1115	0.0	
1243.5	0	2361.5	Yes
1245.0	1121	0.0	
1253.0	0	2392.5	
1277.0	1154	0.0	
1287.0	1159	0.0	
1288.0	1160	0.0	
1296.0	1163	0.0	
1299.0	1164	2464.0	
1300.5	0	2479.0	
1304.0	1177	0.0	
1330.0	1184	0.0	
1347.0	1198	0.0	
1348.5	1199	2507.0	
1350.0	1201	0.0	
1351.5	0	2516.0	
1354.0	1207	0.0	
1355.0	0	2522.5	
1359.5	0	2587.0	
1368.0	1228	2541.5	
1369.0	0	2546.0	
1379.5	0	2574.0	Yes
1381.0	0	2577.3	
1385.0	0	2579.5	
1388.3	0	2590.0	
1388.5	0	2591.0	
1392.0	1257	4263.3	
1400.0	0	2609.5	
1403.0	1262	0.0	
1405.0	1263	0.0	
1406.0	1264	0.0	
1407.0	1265	0.0	
1409.5	0	2627.3+	Yes
1417.0	1275	0.0	
1417.5	0	2652.5	
1421.5	1279	2662.0	Yes
1422.0	1281	0.0	
1426.5	0	2673.0	Yes
1429.0	1296	0.0	
1433.0	1298	2695.5	
1445.5	0	2701.0	
1450.5	0	2714.0	
1457.5	0	2736.2	Yes

TP	TM	BR	EP
1459.0	1310	0.0	
1462.0	1322	0.0	
1463.0	1323	0.0	
1467.5	0	2753.7+	Yes
1467.7	1326	2756.0	
1468.0	0	2756.5	
1471.0	0	2757.5	
1472.0	0	2759.0	
1491.5	1338	2784.0	Yes
1500.0	1350	2794.8	
1500.0	0	2794.8	
1520.0	1362	0.0	
1525.5	0	2818.8	
1527.0	0	2820.5	
1531.0	1368	4004.0	
1531.0	0	4004.0	
1534.0	1370	0.0	
1536.5	0	2831.4	Yes
1537.5	1375	2832.5	
1540.0	1376	0.0	
1542.0	1382	3074.0	Yes
1549.0	1389	3084.0	
1558.0	1396	0.0	
1565.0	1400	0.0	
1568.5	0	3099.5+	Yes
1569.0	1404	0.0	
1581.0	0	3117.8	
1592.5	0	3153.0	
1595.5	0	3146.5+	Yes
1596.5	1426	3156.5+	Yes
1599.0	1432	0.0	
1610.0	1444	0.0	
1615.0	1445	0.0	
1621.0	1447	0.0	
1622.0	0	3182.0	
1623.0	0	3183.0	
1623.3	0	3183.5	Yes
1623.5	1451	3190.0	
1633.0	1461	0.0	
1636.5	0	3218.3	Yes
1640.0	1465	0.0	
1641.0	1466	0.0	
1650.0	1470	3226.0	
1653.0	1477	0.0	
1657.0	1482	3256.1	
1661.0	0	3265.5	
1663.0	0	3302.3	
1677.0	0	3302.5	
1678.0	1495	4257.0	
1679.0	1496	0.0	
1681.0	1497	0.0	
1693.0	1502	3313.0	
1695.5	1507	3318.7	
1702.5	1510	3327.0	Yes
1707.0	1512	0.0	
1719.0	0	3347.5	
1719.5	1518	3348.0	Yes
1727.0	1522	0.0	

TP	TM	BR	EP
1730.0	1524	3354.5	
1731.0	1525	0.0	
1734.0	0	3357.5	
1736.5	0	3361.0	
1744.5	0	3372.1	Yes
1746.0	0	3372.2	
1753.5	0	3385.0	
1762.0	1544	0.0	
1766.0	1548	3406.0	Yes
1767.0	1549	0.0	
1768.0	1550	0.0	
1768.5	1551	3412.0	Yes
1770.0	1554	0.0	
1771.0	1555	0.0	
1786.0	1563	0.0	
1795.5	0	3428.0	
1804.0	1569	0.0	
1805.5	0	3437.5+	
1806.5	0	3438.8	
1809.5	1574	3442.0	
1810.0	0	3443.5	
1814.0	1579	0.0	
1818.0	1581	3448.0	
1825.0	1586	0.0	
1844.5	1598	0.0	
1846.5	0	3492.3	Yes
1854.0	1607	0.0	
1857.5	0	3496.6	Yes
1858.0	1610	0.0	
1875.5	1622	3521.5	Yes
1884.5	0	3542.0	Yes
1888.5	0	3558.0	Yes
1889.5	1642	3558.5	Yes
1894.0	1644	0.0	
1904.5	0	3563.5	
1904.7	0	3568.5	
1905.0	1645	3571.0	
1907.5	0	3602.5+	Yes
1908.0	1661	3642.5	
1910.0	0	3623.5	
1911.3	0	3625.0	
1911.5	1662	3632.0	
1912.0	0	3632.3	
1915.0	1669	3639.5	
1916.0	1671	0.0	
1917.0	1672	0.0	
1920.0	0	3645.8	
1923.0	1675	0.0	
1924.0	0	3648.5	
1924.3	1679	3656.3+	Yes
1924.5	1680	3661.0	Yes
1940.5	1684	3670.0	Yes
1945.0	1690	0.0	
1952.0	0	3689.5	
1974.0	1710	1421.0	
1976.0	0	3707.5	
1984.5	0	3721.3	Yes
2014.5	0	3748.0	

TP	TM	BR	EP
2028.0	1745	0.0	
2031.0	1746	0.0	
2050.5	0	3787.0	Yes
2051.3	0	3788.0	
2051.5	0	3747.0	Yes
2051.7	0	3795.5	Yes
2053.0	1766	3792.5	
2054.0	1769	0.0	
2055.0	1770	194.5	
2056.3	1772	3798.0	
2056.5	1773	3799.0	
2069.5	1779	3818.0	Yes
2076.0	1783	0.0	
2076.5	0	3830.5	Yes
2078.0	1439	0.0	
2081.0	0	3845.5	
2085.0	1793	0.0	
2086.0	1794	0.0	
2090.0	1797	0.0	
2094.0	1636	0.0	
2095.5	1802	3863.5	
2098.0	1803	0.0	
2106.5	0	3876.0	
2114.0	1813	3903.5	
2123.0	1937	0.0	
2126.0	1828	0.0	
2131.0	1830	0.0	
2136.0	1834	0.0	
2136.5	0	3917.3	Yes
2137.0	1835	3917.5	
2137.0	0	3917.5	
2143.0	1840	0.0	
2143.5	1841	3918.5	Yes
2145.0	1843	0.0	
2149.5	1848	3922.0	
2152.0	1850	0.0	
2158.0	1854	0.0	
2159.0	1855	0.0	
2160.5	1857	3943.0	Yes
2164.5	0	3955.0	Yes
2175.5	0	3992.0	
2178.0	0	4002.5	
2180.5	1883	4005.0	Yes
2184.0	1887	0.0	
2185.0	1890	0.0	
2188.5	1897	4019.0	Yes
2189.0	1905	0.0	
2205.5	0	4058.6+	
2212.0	1926	0.0	
2217.5	0	4064.0	Yes
2221.0	1934	0.0	
2222.0	1932	4073.3	
2229.0	1939	4094.3	
2232.0	1941	0.0	
2234.0	1945	0.0	
2236.0	1946	0.0	
2239.0	1950	4096.5	
2239.0	0	4096.5	

TP	TM	BR	EP
2242.3	1954	4101.0	Yes
2242.5	1956	4106.0	Yes
2242.7	1957	4106.5	Yes
2246.5	1960	4112.0	
2255.0	1968	0.0	
2255.5	1974	4137.0	Yes
2292.5	1998	4181.0	Yes
2295.5	2001	4186.5	
2296.5	0	4189.5	Yes
2298.5	2005	4192.5+	
2302.0	0	4198.5	
2303.0	2007	0.0	
2311.0	0	4217.3	
2319.0	2021	0.0	
2320.3	2023	4246.0	Yes
2329.0	2035	0.0	
2335.0	1799	0.0	
2342.0	2042	0.0	
2344.0	0	4284.5	

TABLE 3

Concordance of *Index of Middle English Verse* poems (BR) with Tudor manuscript poems (TM), Tudor print poems (TP), and poems printed from 1476 through 1500 (EP).

BR	TM	TP	EP
0.1	10	0.0	
0.2	78	0.0	
1.0	79	0.0	
5.5	0	414.5	
13.0	81	0.0	
13.3	1309	0.0	
13.5	82	0.0	
13.8	85	0.0	
14.5	86	0.0	
18.0	34	0.0	
20.0	1628	0.0	
22.0	1	0.0	
31.0	3	0.0	
33.0	0	0.0	Yes
33.5	0	11.5	Yes
33.9	9	0.0	
35.5	11	0.0	
37.5	12	0.0	
39.5	13	0.0	
42.5	0	18.5	Yes
49.0	14	0.0	
54.5	15	0.0	
63.8	21	0.0	
65.0	22	0.0	
68.0	25	0.0	
77.0	28	0.0	
78.0	29	0.0	
79.5	32	0.0	
81.5	33	0.0	

BR	TM	TP	EP
95.0	38	0.0	
95.7+	40	47.5	
95.8	41	0.0	
98.5	42	0.0	
99.0	0	50.3	
100.0	0	50.5	
102.3	196	0.0	
103.0	45	0.0	
106.5	47	0.0	
107.0	0	53.0	
108.5	48	0.0	
112.0	49	0.0	
112.5	50	0.0	
113.5	57	0.0	
113.8	58	0.0	
119.0	61	0.0	
120.4	63	0.0	
120.5	64	0.0	
120.6	65	0.0	
120.7	66	0.0	
134.5	76	0.0	
135.5	88	0.0	
137.0	89	0.0	
146.0	94	0.0	
146.5	95	0.0	
150.0	97	0.0	
154.0	99	0.0	
155.5	100	0.0	
158.2	102	0.0	
158.9	109	0.0	
159.5	110	0.0	
159.8	111	0.0	
172.0	114	0.0	
173.0	113	0.0	
186.0	115	0.0	
194.5	1770	2055.0	
199.0	121	0.0	
223.0	0	114.5	
228.0	0	116.0	
231.0	122	0.0	
232.0	123	0.0	
233.0	0	0.0	Yes
236.0	1344	0.0	
237.0	125	0.0	
239.0	126	0.0	
254.0	131	0.0	
263.0	0	0.0	Yes
263.3	134	0.0	
263.5	135	0.0	
263.8	136	0.0	
266.5	138	0.0	
276.5	144	0.0	
285.0	165	156.9	
285.5	146	0.0	
286.5	0	0.0	Yes
294.0	150	0.0	
296.6	151	0.0	
301.0	152	0.0	

BR	TM	TP	EP	BR	TM	TP	EP
302.5	154	0.0		497.0	256	0.0	
303.3	159	0.0		500.0	258	0.0	
306.5+	0	155.0		506.0	262	0.0	
311.5+	0	156.3		506.5	261	0.0	
312.5	162	0.0		507.0	263	0.0	
313.5+	0	0.0	Yes	511.0	264	0.0	
316.6	0	156.7	Yes	513.0	267	241.5	
320.5	167	0.0		513.0	0	241.5	Yes
321.0	168	0.0		517.7+	0	0.0	Yes
324.0	170	160.5	Yes	524.0	0	253.5	Yes
338.5+	0	0.0	Yes	527.5	0	264.5	Yes
340.5	178	0.0		532.0	274	0.0	
343.0	179	0.0		540.0	0	0.0	Yes
346.0	182	0.0		548.0	278	0.0	
350.0	183	0.0		550.0	284	0.0	
354.0	188	0.0		551.0	285	0.0	
363.0	191	0.0		552.5	286	0.0	
364.0	192	0.0		553.5	287	0.0	
365.0	193	0.0		554.3+	0	0.0	Yes
366.0	194	0.0		554.5	288	0.0	
366.8	185	0.0		556.0	291	0.0	
367.0	195	0.0		557.5	293	0.0	
368.0	197	0.0		558.5	294	0.0	
372.0	199	0.0		572.0	298	0.0	
373.0	180	0.0		576.3+	0	288.5	Yes
374.0	198	0.0		576.5	300	0.0	
375.0	190	170.5		581.0	301	0.0	
377.5	0	171.0		584.0	302	0.0	
397.0	201	0.0		595.0	577	0.0	
399.0	203	0.0		608.0	307	0.0	
399.5	0	178.5	Yes	611.5	0	307.5	Yes
404.5	207	0.0		612.0	309	0.0	
409.5	210	0.0		622.0	310	0.0	
410.0	212	0.0		631.8	313	0.0	
411.5	0	0.0	Yes	633.5	314	310.0	
417.5	213	0.0		636.0	317	0.0	
418.0	214	193.0		642.5	322	0.0	
425.0	215	0.0		648.0	326	0.0	
430.0	219	0.0		649.0	327	0.0	
430.5	220	0.0		653.0	331	327.5	Yes
432.0	221	0.0		655.0	332	0.0	
439.0	223	0.0		658.0	0	0.0	Yes
442.3+	0	0.0	Yes	663.0	336	332.5	
444.0	224	0.0		664.3	337	0.0	
448.5+	0	0.0	Yes	665.0		338	0.0
455.5	230	0.0		666.0	339	333.5	
455.8	0	203.5		672.4	0	339.0	
456.5	232	0.0		675.5	344	0.0	
458.0	235	0.0		675.8	345	0.0	
465.5	237	0.0		676.5	349	0.0	
467.0	238	209.0		679.0	0	345.5	
469.0	239	0.0		680.0	352	0.0	
470.0	240	0.0		681.0	354	0.0	
474.5	244	0.0		681.5	355	348.0	
481.0	245	0.0		683.0	0	348.5	
484.5	250	0.0		686.0	359	351.0	
490.0	252	0.0		687.5	362	0.0	
490.5	253	0.0		688.8	367	0.0	

BR	TM	TP	EP
690.0	368	0.0	
691.0	369	0.0	
698.0	375	0.0	
704.0	377	0.0	
710.0	0	362.5	
717.0	379	0.0	
726.0	381	0.0	
729.0	382	0.0	
729.5	384	366.0	
730.0	385	0.0	
731.5	0	0.0	Yes
734.8	387	0.0	
735.0	390	0.0	
736.0	0	373.5	
737.0	389	0.0	
746.5	0	378.5	Yes
753.8	394	0.0	
755.0	395	0.0	
756.0	396	0.0	
757.0	398	0.0	
761.0	400	389.5	Yes
765.5	403	0.0	
766.0	1098	0.0	
767.0	404	0.0	
768.0	405	0.0	
769.0	407	0.0	
782.5	408	0.0	
801.0	411	0.0	
805.0	413	0.0	
809.0	414	404.5	Yes
811.5	0	405.0	
813.3	417	411.0	
813.3	0	411.0	
813.6	418	0.0	
819.5*	419	0.0	
824.0	420	415.5	Yes
825.0	421	0.0	
832.0	422	0.0	
835.5	424	0.0	
851.0	426	434.5	
851.0	0	434.5	Yes
851.3	427	0.0	
854.0	429	428.5	Yes
855.0	430	0.0	
859.5	432	0.0	
860.3	437	435.5	Yes
864.5	441	0.0	
869.0	445	0.0	
870.5	444	0.0	
875.0	0	440.5	
878.0	448	0.0	
882.0	452	0.0	
887.0	454	0.0	
889.0	455	0.0	
890.0	456	0.0	
892.5	457	0.0	
895.0	459	0.0	
898.0	460	0.0	

BR	TM	TP	EP
903.0	462	0.0	
905.5	0	454.0	
906.0	463	0.0	
913.0	466	466.3	Yes
914.0	467	466.5	
916.0	468	0.0	
918.0	469	0.0	
919.0	0	466.7	
920.0	0	469.3	Yes
925.0	473	0.0	
926.0	474	0.0	
927.5	0	470.5	Yes
931.0	475	0.0	
933.0	476	0.0	
935.0	478	482.0	
940.0	480	483.0	
945.8	0	488.5	
952.0	482	491.0	
952.0	0	491.0	
960.3	485	0.0	
960.5	486	0.0	
962.0	488	0.0	
969.0	0	499.3	
970.0	0	499.5	
977.0	489	500.5	
978.0	0	501.0	
979.0	490	0.0	
983.0	0	504.3	
988.0	0	504.5	
991.0	0	506.5	Yes
994.5	491	0.0	
1006.5+	493	0.0	
1007.0	495	0.0	
1009.3	496	0.0	
1015.0	499	0.0	
1017.5	500	0.0	
1018.0	502	0.0	
1018.5	503	0.0	
1032.0	506	0.0	
1035.0	507	0.0	
1040.0	508	0.0	
1044.0	509	0.0	
1046.0	510	0.0	
1051.0	511	0.0	
1055.0	512	0.0	
1065.0	513	0.0	
1070.3	514	0.0	
1077.0	515	0.0	
1082.5	516	0.0	
1086.0	517	529.0	
1088.5	520	0.0	
1097.0	524	0.0	
1119.0	523	0.0	
1119.3	525	0.0	
1129.5+	0	545.5	Yes
1132.0	530	0.0	
1136.5	531	0.0	
1139.0	533	0.0	

BR	TM	TP	EP
1142.5	534	0.0	
1148.0	536	0.0	
1149.0	537	0.0	
1149.5	539	0.0	
1151.0	540	576.5	
1151.5	541	0.0	
1155.0	0	579.0	
1160.0	545	0.0	
1162.8	547	0.0	
1163.0	551	585.0	
1163.3+	0	0.0	Yes
1163.5	548	0.0	
1165.0	552	0.0	
1166.5	554	0.0	
1168.0	556	588.5	Yes
1173.0	558	590.0	
1174.5	561	0.0	
1176.5	567	0.0	
1176.8	568	0.0	
1177.0	0	599.5	
1180.0	571	0.0	
1181.0	572	0.0	
1181.5	573	0.0	
1184.0	0	605.5	
1187.0	576	0.0	
1192.5	0	606.0	
1194.5	578	0.0	
1198.0	579	0.0	
1203.0	580	0.0	
1206.9	585	0.0	
1212.0	588	0.0	
1214.5	591	0.0	
1214.6	594	0.0	
1214.7	595	0.0	
1218.0	597	0.0	
1218.8	598	620.0	
1222.0	601	0.0	
1226.0	602	0.0	
1234.0	604	0.0	
1237.0	605	0.0	
1242.0	0	0.0	Yes
1243.0	0	0.0	Yes
1244.0	0	0.0	Yes
1245.0	0	0.0	Yes
1246.0	0	0.0	Yes
1247.0	0	0.0	Yes
1248.0	0	0.0	Yes
1249.0	0	0.0	Yes
1255.0	610	0.0	
1259.0	617	0.0	
1261.0	616	0.0	
1270.1	622	0.0	
1270.2	624	0.0	
1273.0	625	0.0	
1273.3	626	0.0	
1275.0	627	0.0	
1276.0	628	0.0	
1278.0	630	0.0	

BR	TM	TP	EP
1286.0	634	0.0	
1286.5	635	0.0	
1291.0	637	0.0	
1294.0	638	735.5	
1294.3	639	0.0	
1296.0	0	0.0	Yes
1297.0	642	0.0	
1303.3	643	0.0	
1303.5	518	0.0	
1306.0	0	745.5	
1307.0	645	0.0	
1308.0	646	0.0	
1309.0	0	748.0	
1314.0	649	0.0	
1315.0	647	0.0	
1322.0	651	0.0	
1322.8	652	0.0	
1327.0	660	0.0	
1328.5	662	0.0	
1328.7	664	0.0	
1328.8	665	0.0	
1329.0	666	0.0	
1329.5	667	0.0	
1333.0	670	0.0	
1339.5	673	0.0	
1341.8	0	770.0	
1342.0	0	0.0	Yes
1343.0	675	0.0	
1344.0	677	0.0	
1349.0	678	0.0	
1349.5	679	0.0	
1350.0	680	0.0	
1354.5	681	0.0	
1356.8	683	0.0	
1362.0	684	0.0	
1363.0	685	0.0	
1376.0	691	0.0	
1378.0	693	0.0	
1383.0	694	0.0	
1386.0	695	0.0	
1392.0	702	0.0	
1399.0	704	0.0	
1400.0	698	0.0	
1409.1	708	0.0	
1411.0	714	0.0	
1412.0	718	0.0	
1414.5	720	0.0	
1414.8	721	0.0	
1419.0	726	0.0	
1420.5	729	0.0	
1421.0	1710	1974.0	
1426.1	736	853.0	
1426.6	0	857.5	Yes
1427.7+	0	858.5	Yes
1429.0	737	0.0	
1436.2	738	862.0	
1438.5+	0	0.0	Yes
1440.0	744	0.0	

BR	TM	TP	EP	BR	TM	TP	EP
1444.0	745	0.0		1635.0	835	0.0	
1445.5	746	0.0		1636.5	836	0.0	
1449.5	749	0.0		1636.8	837	0.0	
1450.0	750	0.0		1637.2	838	0.0	
1450.5	751	0.0		1637.6	0	972.0	Yes
1451.0	754	0.0		1637.8	840	0.0	
1453.0	0	877.3		1641.5	0	978.0	
1455.5	752	0.0		1644.0	0	979.0	
1459.0	753	877.5		1653.0	641	0.0	
1466.5	0	879.0		1654.5	0	982.5	
1470.5	0	880.5	Yes	1669.0	847	0.0	
1471.0	759	0.0		1679.0	849	0.0	
1485.0	764	0.0		1703.0	851	989.0	
1486.0	0	891.0		1709.0	852	0.0	
1487.0	0	894.0		1710.0	853	0.0	
1488.0	767	0.0		1717.3	854	0.0	
1491.0	0	0.0	Yes	1719.0	0	0.0	Yes
1494.5	771	0.0		1721.0	0	991.3	
1498.0	773	0.0		1725.0	0	991.5	Yes
1502.0	775	0.0		1727.0	855	991.7	
1504.5	776	0.0		1728.0	0	0.0	Yes
1507.0	777	906.5		1729.0	856	0.0	
1509.0	779	0.0		1731.0	311	0.0	
1515.0	0	908.5		1738.0	857	0.0	
1522.5+	782	0.0		1752.0	0	994.5	
1527.0	784	0.0		1768.0	859	0.0	
1528.0	785	912.5		1779.0	860	0.0	
1528.5	786	0.0		1806.0	863	0.0	
1533.0	788	0.0		1808.7+	0	0.0	Yes
1540.0	789	0.0		1817.0	869	0.0	
1540.5	790	0.0		1823.0	871	0.0	
1547.5	299	0.0		1824.3+	0	1008.5	Yes
1548.0	791	918.0		1824.8	872	0.0	
1554.0	792	923.5		1825.0	873	0.0	
1560.0	794	0.0		1829.2	874	1008.7	Yes
1567.0	0	926.4		1841.0	0	1015.0	
1570.5	800	0.0		1841.5	878	0.0	
1575.0	802	0.0		1842.5	879	1016.0	
1575.5	0	937.0		1863.3	882	0.0	
1578.0	803	0.0		1864.5	883	0.0	
1586.0	808	0.0		1866.0	884	0.0	
1587.0	809	0.0		1866.5	886	0.0	
1587.8	811	943.5	Yes	1866.8	887	0.0	
1589.5	812	0.0		1870.0	889	0.0	
1593.0	814	0.0		1872.0	890	0.0	
1596.5	0	945.5	Yes	1873.0	891	0.0	
1597.0	818	948.5		1891.0	901	0.0	
1598.0	821	948.7		1892.0	902	0.0	
1601.0	822	0.0		1894.5	0	1051.5	
1605.5	0	953.0		1895.0	0	1052.1	
1608.0	826	0.0		1915.0	0	1052.3	Yes
1609.0	827	0.0		1919.0	904	1052.5	Yes
1618.0	0	957.3	Yes	1920.0	905	1052.7	Yes
1619.0	0	957.5	Yes	1923.5	906	1054.0	
1620.0	830	0.0		1926.5	908	0.0	
1620.5	823	0.0		1927.0	909	0.0	
1628.8	834	0.0		1928.0	912	0.0	
1629.0	0	0.0	Yes	1929.0	913	1059.5	

BR	TM	TP	EP
1929.5	916	0.0	
1933.5	922	0.0	
1934.0	923	1060.5	Yes
1937.0	928	0.0	
1941.0	930	0.0	
1944.5	932	0.0	
1957.0	936	0.0	
1961.5	942	0.0	
1979.0	0	1085.5	
1984.5	0	1089.0	
1989.0	945	0.0	
1993.0	0	1088.5	Yes
1999.0	921	0.0	
1999.5	949	0.0	
2007.5	954	0.0	
2012.3	955	0.0	
2013.0	956	0.0	
2016.0	961	0.0	
2025.5	964	0.0	
2028.5	965	0.0	
2028.8	966	0.0	
2029.0	967	0.0	
2034.5	1103	0.0	
2039.3	971	1102.5	Yes
2039.5	0	1104.0	
2044.0	996	0.0	
2052.0	973	0.0	
2053.0	974	0.0	
2053.0	976	0.0	
2056.0	980	0.0	
2057.0	975	0.0	
2060.0	977	0.0	
2065.0	978	0.0	
2072.4	981	0.0	
2076.0	982	0.0	
2090.0	983	0.0	
2092.0	0	1111.5	
2097.0	992	0.0	
2098.0	993	0.0	
2119.0	0	0.0	Yes
2139.0	0	1119.5	
2142.0	0	1121.5	
2147.0	997	1122.5	
2167.0	0	0.0	Yes
2183.5	205	180.0	
2192.0	1007	1138.5	
2195.0	1008	0.0	
2200.3	1013	0.0	
2210.0	1016	0.0	
2211.0	1017	0.0	
2212.0	1018	0.0	
2213.0	1019	0.0	
2217.0	1020	0.0	
2217.5	0	1143.0	
2218.0	1021	0.0	
2223.0	0	1146.0	
2224.0	1026	0.0	
2224.5	1027	0.0	
2228.0	1030	0.0	
2231.5	0	1154.0	
2233.0	1031	1154.5	Yes
2233.5	0	0.0	Yes
2244.0	0	1160.0	
2244.6	1040	0.0	
2245.1	1043	0.0	
2245.3	1044	0.0	
2245.6	1045	1163.0	
2249.0	1049	0.0	
2250.3	1050	0.0	
2250.5	1051	0.0	
2250.9	0	1165.0	
2255.3	1053	0.0	
2255.6	1054	0.0	
2261.4	1057	0.0	
2261.6	1058	0.0	
2261.8	1060	0.0	
2262.0	0	1168.5	Yes
2263.0	1064	0.0	
2263.5	1065	1172.0	
2264.0	0	1172.5	Yes
2271.2	1070	0.0	
2271.6	1072	0.0	
2272.0	1073	0.0	
2272.5	1074	0.0	
2277.0	1075	0.0	
2277.5	1076	0.0	
2281.5	1078	0.0	
2284.0	1080	0.0	
2289.8	1083	0.0	
2291.5	1085	1204.0	
2293.5	1086	0.0	
2293.6	1087	1209.0	
2293.8	1089	0.0	
2300.3	1091	0.0	
2307.0	1095	0.0	
2308.5	1097	0.0	
2320.0	0	1227.5	
2323.8	1101	0.0	
2335.0	1104	0.0	
2343.0	1105	0.0	
2346.0	1106	0.0	
2361.5	0	1243.5	Yes
2363.0	1116	0.0	
2364.0	1117	0.0	
2370.0	1118	0.0	
2371.0	1119	0.0	
2377.0	1111	0.0	
2380.0	1120	0.0	
2381.0	1122	0.0	
2385.0	1128	0.0	
2388.0	1129	0.0	
2391.0	1130	0.0	
2392.5	0	1253.0	
2393.5	1131	0.0	
2394.0	1132	0.0	
2394.5	1133	0.0	

BR	TM	TP	EP	BR	TM	TP	EP
2403.3	1135	0.0		2560.5	1240	0.0	
2409.0	1138	0.0		2574.0	0	1379.5	Yes
2409.5	1139	0.0		2577.3	0	1381.0	
2410.0	1140	0.0		2579.3	1248	0.0	
2412.0	1141	0.0		2579.5	0	1385.0	
2421.0	1142	0.0		2586.0	1252	0.0	
2428.0	0	0.0	Yes	2587.0	0	1359.5	
2439.5	1145	0.0		2588.0	1253	0.0	
2441.0	1146	0.0		2590.0	0	1388.3	
2444.0	1147	0.0		2591.0	0	1388.5	
2446.0	1148	0.0		2597.0	1254	0.0	
2453.0	1157	0.0		2598.0	1255	0.0	
2461.0	1162	0.0		2601.0	1258	0.0	
2464.0	1164	1299.0		2607.5	1259	0.0	
2471.0	1165	0.0		2609.5	0	1400.0	
2472.0	1166	0.0		2613.5	1260	0.0	
2474.0	1167	0.0		2619.5	1261	0.0	
2475.0	1171	0.0		2626.0	1269	0.0	
2478.0	1173	0.0		2627.3+	0	1409.5	Yes
2479.0	0	1300.5		2633.0	1271	0.0	
2482.5	1176	0.0		2636.0	1274	0.0	
2486.0	1178	0.0		2649.5+	1276	0.0	
2494.0	1185	0.0		2652.5	0	1417.5	
2496.0	1194	0.0		2654.0	1277	0.0	
2498.0	1196	0.0		2654.5+	0	0.0	Yes
2500.5	1197	0.0		2656.0	1278	0.0	
2507.0	1199	1348.5		2662.0	1279	1421.5	Yes
2511.0	1200	0.0		2663.5	0	0.0	Yes
2514.0	132	0.0		2664.5	0	0.0	Yes
2515.0	1203	0.0		2668.0	1283	0.0	
2516.0	0	1351.5		2668.8	1285	0.0	
2518.0	1206	0.0		2673.0	0	1426.5	Yes
2521.0	1209	0.0		2674.0	1287	0.0	
2522.0	1210	0.0		2676.0	1288	0.0	
2522.5	0	1355.0		2678.0	1289	0.0	
2523.0	1212	0.0		2681.0	1290	0.0	
2528.0	1214	0.0		2682.0	1291	0.0	
2529.0	1215	0.0		2683.0	1292	0.0	
2530.5	1216	0.0		2685.8	1293	0.0	
2531.0	1217	0.0		2688.0	1294	0.0	
2531.5	1218	0.0		2689.0	1295	0.0	
2532.0	1219	0.0		2695.5	1298	1433.0	
2532.3	1220	0.0		2701.0	0	1445.5	
2532.5	1221	0.0		2714.0	0	1450.5	
2533.0	1222	0.0		2731.0	1302	0.0	
2536.0	1223	0.0		2732.0	1304	0.0	
2536.5	1225	0.0		2733.0	1306	0.0	
2541.5	1228	1368.0		2736.2	0	1457.5	Yes
2546.0	0	1369.0		2736.6	1307	0.0	
2547.0	1229	0.0		2736.8	1308	0.0	
2547.3	1230	0.0		2737.0	1311	0.0	
2547.5	1232	0.0		2737.5	1312	0.0	
2549.5	1233	0.0		2753.5	1324	0.0	
2551.5	1234	0.0		2753.7+	0	1467.5	Yes
2552.5	1236	0.0		2755.5	1325	0.0	
2553.0	1235	0.0		2756.0	1326	1467.7	
2557.0	1238	0.0		2756.5	0	1468.0	
2560.0	1239	0.0		2757.3	1327	0.0	

BR	TM	TP	EP
2757.5	0	1471.0	
2759.0	0	1472.0	
2760.0	1330	0.0	
2766.2	1334	0.0	
2766.8	1335	0.0	
2771.0	1337	0.0	
2784.0	1338	1491.5	Yes
2785.0	1341	0.0	
2785.5	1342	0.0	
2791.0	1345	0.0	
2794.2	1349	0.0	
2794.4	1347	0.0	
2794.8	1350	1500.0	
2794.8	0	1500.0	
2797.5	1352	0.0	
2806.0	1354	0.0	
2806.5	1355	0.0	
2811.0	1360	0.0	
2814.0	1364	0.0	
2818.3	1365	0.0	
2818.6	0	0.0	Yes
2818.8	0	1525.5	
2820.5	0	1527.0	
2821.0	1367	0.0	
2825.5+	1369	0.0	
2827.5	1371	0.0	
2831.4	0	1536.5	Yes
2831.8	1374	0.0	
2832.2	1378	0.0	
2832.5	1375	1537.5	
2834.3	1429	0.0	
2881.0	1077	0.0	
2910.5	0	0.0	Yes
3038.0	1379	0.0	
3065.0	1380	0.0	
3071.0	1381	0.0	
3074.0	1382	1542.0	Yes
3074.6	1383	0.0	
3074.8+	0	0.0	Yes
3079.7	1385	0.0	
3083.0	1387	0.0	
3084.0	1389	1549.0	
3087.0	1393	0.0	
3088.0	868	0.0	
3098.3	1401	0.0	
3099.5+	0	1568.5	Yes
3115.0	1417	0.0	
3117.6	1418	0.0	
3117.8	0	1581.0	
3119.0	1420	0.0	
3119.5*	1421	0.0	
3131.0	1423	0.0	
3135.5	1408	0.0	
3144.5	1411	0.0	
3146.5+	0	1595.5	Yes
3153.0	0	1592.5	
3156.5+	1426	1596.5	Yes
3161.0	1430	0.0	

BR	TM	TP	EP
3162.5	1431	0.0	
3168.0	1435	0.0	
3168.2	1436	0.0	
3168.4	1437	0.0	
3171.0	1440	0.0	
3171.5	1441	0.0	
3172.0	1442	0.0	
3182.0	0	1622.0	
3183.0	0	1623.0	
3183.5	0	1623.3	Yes
3187.0	780	0.0	
3190.0	1451	1623.5	
3193.5	1452	0.0	
3199.3	1454	0.0	
3199.8	1455	0.0	
3206.5	1457	0.0	
3207.0	1458	0.0	
3213.0	1462	0.0	
3218.3	0	1636.5	Yes
3226.0	1470	1650.0	
3228.3	1472	0.0	
3228.5	1473	0.0	
3238.0	858	0.0	
3243.0	1476	0.0	
3249.0	1478	0.0	
3253.0	1481	0.0	
3256.1	1482	1657.0	
3265.5	0	1661.0	
3269.0	1485	0.0	
3270.5	987	0.0	
3271.0	1486	0.0	
3287.5	1488	0.0	
3297.3	1492	0.0	
3297.5	1493	0.0	
3301.0	1494	0.0	
3302.3	0	1663.0	
3302.5	0	1677.0	
3307.0	1499	0.0	
3313.0	1502	1693.0	
3315.0	1503	0.0	
3318.0	1504	0.0	
3318.3	1506	0.0	
3318.4	1505	0.0	
3318.6	0	0.0	Yes
3318.7	1507	1695.5	
3327.0	1510	1702.5	Yes
3341.0	1517	499.5	
3347.5	0	1719.0	
3348.0	1518	1719.5	Yes
3354.5	1524	1730.0	
3357.5	0	1734.0	
3361.0	0	1736.5	
3361.6	1528	0.0	
3364.0	1529	0.0	
3372.1	0	1744.5	Yes
3372.2	0	1746.0	
3375.0	1535	0.0	
3376.5	1536	0.0	

BR	TM	TP	EP
3377.0	1537	0.0	
3382.0	1538	0.0	
3385.0	0	1753.5	
3405.5	1545	0.0	
3405.8	1547	0.0	
3406.0	1548	1766.0	Yes
3412.0	1551	1768.5	Yes
3412.2+	1552	0.0	
3412.3	1553	0.0	
3413.3	1573	0.0	
3424.0	1564	0.0	
3428.0	0	1795.5	
3437.0	1568	0.0	Yes
3437.5+	0	1805.5	
3438.3	1570	0.0	
3438.6	1572	0.0	
3438.8	0	1806.5	
3442.0	1574	1809.5	
3443.5	0	1810.0	
3445.5	1578	0.0	
3446.0	0	0.0	Yes
3448.0	1581	1818.0	
3456.0	1587	0.0	
3456.5	1588	0.0	
3460.0	1592	0.0	
3473.0	1594	0.0	
3482.0	1596	0.0	
3486.5	1599	0.0	
3487.0	1601	0.0	
3487.5	1602	0.0	
3491.0	1605	0.0	
3492.3	0	1846.5	Yes
3492.4+	1606	0.0	
3496.6	0	1857.5	Yes
3498.5	1608	0.0	
3504.0	1612	0.0	Yes
3510.0	1615	0.0	
3514.0	1617	0.0	
3515.0	1618	0.0	
3521.0	1621	0.0	
3521.5	1622	1875.5	Yes
3522.0	1624	0.0	
3523.0	1623	0.0	
3524.0	1625	0.0	
3525.0	1674	0.0	
3527.0	1626	0.0	
3528.0	1627	0.0	
3530.5	1629	0.0	
3531.0	1630	0.0	
3532.0	1631	0.0	
3538.0	1633	0.0	
3540.0	0	0.0	Yes
3542.0	0	1884.5	Yes
3551.0	1638	0.0	
3553.5	1640	0.0	
3558.0	0	1888.5	Yes
3558.5	1642	1889.5	Yes
3559.8	1643	0.0	
3563.5	0	1904.5	
3568.5	0	1904.7	
3571.0	1645	1905.0	
3574.0	1646	0.0	
3575.0	1647	0.0	
3577.0	1648	0.0	
3580.0	1649	0.0	
3584.0	1650	0.0	Yes
3595.6	1651	0.0	
3597.0	1652	0.0	
3598.5	1653	0.0	
3602.5+	0	1907.5	Yes
3603.0	1519	0.0	
3604.0	1654	0.0	
3605.0	1655	0.0	
3606.0	1656	0.0	
3612.5	1658	0.0	
3615.0	1660	0.0	
3623.5	0	1910.0	
3625.0	0	1911.3	
3627.0	24	0.0	
3632.0	1662	1911.5	
3632.3	0	1912.0	
3635.0	1665	0.0	
3635.5	1666	0.0	
3639.5	1669	1915.0	
3642.0	1670	0.0	
3642.5	1661	1908.0	
3645.8	0	1920.0	
3648.5	0	1924.0	
3652.0	1676	0.0	
3655.0	1677	0.0	
3656.0	1678	0.0	
3656.3+	1679	1924.3	Yes
3661.0	1680	1924.5	Yes
3666.0	1694	0.0	
3669.0	1683	0.0	
3670.0	1684	1940.5	Yes
3672.0	1685	0.0	
3677.5	1689	0.0	
3685.0	1691	0.0	
3689.5	0	1952.0	
3695.0	1693	0.0	
3703.0	1696	0.0	
3703.3	1698	0.0	
3703.5	1701	0.0	
3706.2	1705	0.0	
3706.5	1707	0.0	
3706.7	1708	0.0	
3706.8	1709	0.0	
3707.3	1714	0.0	
3707.5	0	1976.0	
3713.5	1716	0.0	
3718.0	1718	0.0	
3720.0	1719	0.0	
3721.0	521	0.0	
3721.3	0	1984.5	Yes
3721.5	1720	0.0	

BR	TM	TP	EP
3722.0	1721	0.0	
3724.5	1724	0.0	
3736.0	1726	0.0	
3737.0	1727	0.0	
3746.0	1728	0.0	
3747.0	0	2051.5	Yes
3748.0	0	2014.5	
3749.0	1729	0.0	
3750.0	1730	0.0	
3751.3	1733	0.0	
3754.0	200	0.0	
3758.5	1742	0.0	
3767.5	1750	0.0	
3769.5	1751	0.0	
3772.0	1752	0.0	
3776.0	1753	0.0	
3776.5	1757	0.0	
3777.3	0	0.0	Yes
3777.4+	0	0.0	Yes
3777.5	1758	0.0	
3780.0	1759	0.0	
3782.0	1760	0.0	
3785.5	1764	0.0	
3787.0	0	2050.5	Yes
3788.0	0	2051.3	
3792.5	1766	2053.0	
3793.0	1767	0.0	
3795.5	0	2051.7	Yes
3798.0	1772	2056.3	
3799.0	1773	2056.5	
3800.5	1774	0.0	
3804.0	1775	0.0	
3809.0	1776	0.0	
3815.8	1778	0.0	
3818.0	1779	2069.5	Yes
3820.0	1717	0.0	
3827.0	1782	0.0	
3830.5	0	2076.5	Yes
3832.5	1785	0.0	
3835.0	1786	0.0	
3836.5	1787	0.0	
3845.0	1788	0.0	
3845.5	0	2081.0	
3847.0	1792	0.0	
3848.0	587	0.0	
3852.0	1796	0.0	
3863.5	1802	2095.5	
3876.0	0	2106.5	
3880.6	1808	0.0	
3889.5	1810	0.0	
3899.3	1811	0.0	
3903.5	1813	2114.0	
3903.8	1814	0.0	
3904.0	1817	0.0	
3905.0	1820	0.0	
3911.0	1822	0.0	
3914.0	1833	0.0	
3917.3	0	2136.5	Yes
3917.5	1835	2137.0	
3917.5	0	2137.0	
3917.8	1838	0.0	
3918.5	1841	2143.5	Yes
3919.5	1842	0.0	
3922.0	1848	2149.5	
3928.0	1851	0.0	Yes
3942.0	1856	0.0	
3943.0	1857	2160.5	Yes
3945.0	1846	0.0	
3946.0	1859	0.0	
3947.0	1860	0.0	
3947.6	1861	0.0	
3950.0	1864	0.0	
3955.0	0	2164.5	Yes
3960.5	1870	402.0	
3962.5	1871	0.0	
3969.0	1872	0.0	
3975.0	1875	0.0	
3985.0	1876	0.0	
3988.0	1877	0.0	
3992.0	0	2175.5	
3999.0	1880	0.0	
4002.5	0	2178.0	
4004.0	1368	1531.0	
4004.0	0	1531.0	
4005.0	1883	2180.5	Yes
4008.0	1888	0.0	
4012.0	1889	0.0	
4013.0	1892	0.0	
4017.0	1894	0.0	
4018.0	1845	0.0	
4019.0	1897	2188.5	Yes
4020.3	1899	0.0	
4023.0	1902	0.0	
4025.0	1903	0.0	
4029.0	1907	0.0	
4035.0	1917	0.0	
4039.0	1909	0.0	
4040.0	1910	0.0	
4044.3	1912	0.0	
4049.2	1913	0.0	
4049.5	1914	0.0	
4057.0	1921	0.0	
4058.3	2037	0.0	
4058.6+	0	2205.5	
4064.0	0	2217.5	Yes
4065.0	1928	0.0	
4068.6	1929	0.0	
4070.5	1931	0.0	
4073.3	1932	2222.0	
4077.0	1933	0.0	
4079.3	1935	0.0	
4079.6	1936	0.0	
4094.3	1939	2229.0	
4096.5	1950	2239.0	
4096.5	0	2239.0	
4098.1	1951	0.0	

BR	TM	TP	EP	BR	TM	TP	EP
4098.6	1952	0.0		4186.5	2001	2295.5	
4101.0	1954	2242.3	Yes	4187.0	2000	0.0	
4103.0	1955	0.0		4187.8	0	0.0	Yes
4106.0	1956	2242.5	Yes	4189.5	0	2296.5	Yes
4106.5	1957	2242.7	Yes	4190.0	2002	0.0	
4109.5	0	0.0	Yes	4192.5+	2005	2298.5	
4112.0	1960	2246.5		4198.5	0	2302.0	
4118.0	1964	0.0		4201.3	2009	0.0	
4123.3+	0	0.0	Yes	4201.6	2010	0.0	
4126.0	1983	0.0		4210.0	2011	0.0	
4129.0	1970	0.0		4212.0	2012	0.0	
4133.0	1972	0.0		4213.5	2014	0.0	
4137.0	1974	2255.5	Yes	4215.0	2015	0.0	
4138.0	1975	0.0		4217.3	0	2311.0	
4143.3	1976	0.0		4230.0	2020	0.0	
4143.5	1977	0.0		4246.0	2023	2320.3	Yes
4143.8	1978	0.0		4248.0	2024	0.0	
4148.0	1979	0.0		4253.0	2026	0.0	
4150.0	0	0.0	Yes	4254.5	2028	0.0	
4154.3	1981	0.0		4255.0	1641	0.0	
4155.0	1982	0.0		4257.0	1495	1678.0	
4160.0	1986	0.0		4262.0	2029	0.0	
4162.5	1988	0.0		4263.3	1257	1392.0	
4168.0	1991	0.0		4274.0	2036	0.0	
4174.3	1992	0.0		4281.5	2038	0.0	
4174.5	1993	0.0		4283.5	2041	0.0	
4175.0	1996	0.0		4284.3	2043	0.0	
4176.5	1997	0.0		4284.5	0	2344.0	
4181.0	1998	2292.5	Yes	4285.0	2044	0.0	
4184.0	1999	0.0